HISTORY BENEATH OUR FEET

BRIAN READ
Illustrated by Patrick Read

ANGLIA PUBLISHING

Watts House, Capel St. Mary,
Ipswich, Suffolk, IP9 2JB

First published in Great Britain by Merlin Books Ltd, Braunton Devon, 1988.
This second revised edition published by Anglia Publishing, Ipswich, 1995.
© Brian Read 1995
ISBN 1 897874 07 3 soft covers
ISBN 1 897874 00 6 hardback

This book is available from:
Anglia Publishing, Watts House, Capel St Mary, Ipswich IP9 2JB.
Telephone: 01473 311138, Fax: 01473 311131

All rights reserved. No part of this book may be reproduced, stored in a retrieval system, or transmitted in any form or by any means, electronic, mechanical, photocopying, recording or otherwise without the prior permission of the publishers.

All line drawings have been reduced to 70% of actual size on each axis. Photographs are *not* to scale.

Designed by Max Newport
Pages laid out by Glenys Rowland
Dust jacket designed by Anthony King
Typeset in Stempel Garamond
Printed in Great Britain byHillman Printers (Frome) Ltd, Frome, Somerset, BA11 4RW.

CONTENTS

	Catalogue numbers	Page
ACKNOWLEDGMENTS		iv
FOREWORD		v
BIBLIOGRAPHY		v
PREFACE		vii
INTRODUCTION		vii
NCMD CODE OF CONDUCT		x
CHAPTER 1 - THE BRONZE AGE	1 - 30	1
CHAPTER 2 - THE IRON AGE	31 - 45	11
CHAPTER 3 - THE ROMANO-BRITISH PERIOD	46 - 157	19
CHAPTER 4 - THE DARK AGES	158 - 183	41
CHAPTER 5 - THE MIDDLE AGES	184 - 614	52
CHAPTER 6 - THE TUDOR PERIOD	615 - 821	103
CHAPTER 7 - THE STUART PERIOD	822 - 1096	131
CHAPTER 8 - THE GEORGIAN & VICTORIAN PERIODS	1097 - 1467	165

For Val and my parents.

ACKNOWLEDGMENTS

Many people assisted with the compilation of this new record of small metallic finds from southern Devon. In particular my grateful thanks are extended to all metal detectives, whether they be local club members, independents or visitors - it is their dedication and interest which has furthered our knowledge of Devon's history and archaeology. Undoubtedly the most important group deserving credit are the many private landowners. But for their ready acquiescence most of the coins and artefacts depicted herein would not have come to light.

I am indebted to the following institutions and their staff for valued opinions or assistance: British Museum - Val Rigby, Ruth Nelson, Ralph Jackson, Elizabeth Savage, Dr Roger Bland and Dr Barry Cook; Museum of London - Geoff Egan; British Dental Association - Tim Thorpe, Prakash Narain and Geoff Barnes; Sotheby's - Philippa Hamilton and Helen Cuneo.

Special thanks go to the undermentioned who willingly shared their expertise: Blanche Ellis - spurs; Nick Griffiths - medieval pendants and mounts, general metalwork and heraldry; Mark Corney -Bronze Age metalwork; Norman Shiel - numismatics; Tim Mole - militaria; Professor Norman Biggs, Bente and Paul Withers - metrology; Barry Sherlock - finger rings and metalsmithing, and the late Richard Hattatt - ancient brooches.

For explanation of some artefacts I drew heavily on the works of metal detecting press writers, particularly: John Webb, Gordon Bailey, Chris Marshall and Michael Cuddeford, and similarly, the writings of one of our foremost antiquarians - Brian Spencer, late of the Museum of London. My appreciation is extended to them all for their prolific pens.

Access to illustrate two finger-rings was granted by John Allan, Curator of Antiquities EM, for which I am appreciative. I am obliged to David Lloyd and Devon Archeological Society who kindly allowed the drawing of the Capton brooch to be reproduced.

Replication of the undermentioned plates was approved as follows: the Goodrington Viking bracelet - **By courtesy of the Trustees of The British Museum;** the Ladram Bay Viking finger-ring - **By courtesy of Sotheby's;** the Torre Abbey Pendant Jewel - **By courtesy of the Board of Trustees of the Victoria and Albert Museum;** the Aller Hoard - Ben Redshaw; the Chudleigh Hoard - Val MacRae; the Beesands Beach ducat - David Copp and the Massachusetts Oak Tree twopence - Derek Rowland. Ross Whitehead provided many of the numismatic photographs. All other plates were provided by the author. I am also indebted to Ross Whitehead for arranging for many of the artefacts found by TMDC members to be illustrated.

Maps of southern Devon are based upon the Ordnance Survey Map with the **Permission of the Controller of Her Majesty's Stationery Office, Crown Copyright Reserved.**

The strong point of this revised edition is the large number of high-quality archeological illustrations. Regrettably, and as always, expense and lack of time, prevented all of the previously included artefacts being re-drawn, however, many have, and much that is new has been added. It is my youngest son to whom I am indebted for undertaking this mammoth task - thank you Patrick. To my Val for her encouragement and support throughout the close on twelve months it took to complete the work - my love and gratitude. Lastly, to my publisher, Derek Rowland, for his enthusiasm in accepting the project in a revised form and his patience in waiting for so long for its fruition.

Brian Read, Huish Episcopi, Somerset, October 1995.

CONVENTIONS AND ABBREVIATIONS

Line drawings and plates are provided with sequential catalogue numbers. Italics indicate findspots. Abbreviations are as follows: diameter - D; length - L; height - H; National Council for Metal Detecting - NCMD; Federation of Independent Detectorists - FID; Council For British Archaeology - CBA; Torbay Metal Detectors Club - TMDC; Devon Archaeological Society - DAS; Royal Albert Memorial Museum, Exeter - EM; Exeter Museums Archaeological Field Unit -EMAFU.

DRAWING CONVENTIONS
Enamel colours - unless otherwise stated, the standard code used throughout the book is:

Red   Black   Blue   Purple   Green   Gold or yellow   Silver or white

FOREWORD

For over twenty years the relationship between metal detectorists and the archaeological world has frequently been a stormy one; attitudes are, however, now beginning to change for the better and we are seeing increasing co-operation between the two groups in many parts of the country. The very fact that, as a professional archaeologist, I have been asked to write this Foreword must be a clear indication of a significant change of attitude on both sides.

One of the main bones of contention between archaeologists and detectorists in the past has been the essential matter of recording finds and their location. The importance of accurate recording of discoveries and their precise position cannot be over-estimated, as anyone who has spent many frustrating hours trying to understand inadequate field-records will readily testify.

With this splendid new and enlarged edition of *History Beneath Our Feet* Brian Read provides a clear indication of just what valuable results a dedicated detectorist who is prepared to thoroughly research and report on his finds can achieve. For local archaeologists and historians there is a wealth of material from all periods here, clearly described, illustrated and provenanced. Such material may be used to advance many aspects of local landscape studies. For other detectorists, as well as providing a very valuable catalogue of material for identification purposes, here is a model of what might be done with their own finds. Many hobbyists, of course, will have smaller collections of artefacts, but this need not mean that they are any less interesting. The bulk of historical and archaeological research is concerned not with the spectacular but with the mundane items that were commonly used in every-day life. Metal objects of this type will be particularly familiar to detectorists, yet many of these artefacts are not without importance or interest and there is still much which is worthy of detailed study.

As well as looking at individual items, however, it is perhaps becoming increasingly important to view collections from a given area as a whole. As archaeologists become increasingly familiar with detectorists' finds it is apparent there is still much that is not understood and even more that cannot be accurately identified. For the benefit of the Nation's heritage, our co-operative ventures must continue and expand.

Brian Read is to be warmly congratulated on his achievements in Devon and it is to be hoped that others will be inspired to undertake similar detailed work in different parts of the country.

Keith Parfitt,
Dover,
March 1995

BIBLIOGRAPHY

BOOKS

W, Addison	*The Old Roads of England*, 1980.,
Adkins, L; Adkins, R, A	*Thesaurus of British Archaeology*, 1982.
Andrews, J, Elston, W, & Shiel, N,	*Exeter Coinage*, 1980.
Ayres, J,	*Paupers and Pig Killers, the Diary of William Holland a Somerset Parson 1799-1818*, 1984.
Barker, P,	*Techniques of Archaeological Excavation*, 1982.
Bédoyère, de la, G,	*The Finds of Roman Britain*, 1989.
Berry, G,	*Medieval English Jetons*, 1974.
Biggs, N,	*English Weights*, 1992.
Bowling, A,	*British Infantry Regiments 1660-1914*, 1970
Brears, P,	*Horse Brasses*, 1981.
Campbell, J; John, E; & Wormald, P,	*The Anglo-Saxons*, 1982.
Connor, R,	*The Weights and Measures of England*, 1987.
Dalton, R,	*The Silver Token Coinage 1811-12*, 1968.
Hollis J, Editor,	*Princely Magnificence, Court Jewels of the Renaissance, 1500-1630*, 1980.
Dolly, M,	*Anglo-Saxon Pennies*, 1970.
Egan, G, & Pritchard, F,	*Dress Accessories c1150-1450*, 1991.
Egan, G,	*Lead Cloth Seals and Related items in the British Museum, British Museum Occasional Paper No, 93*, 1994.
Graham, J,	*Weights and Measures*, 1979.
Greene, K,	*Archaeology An Introduction*, 1983.
Griffith, F,	*Devon's Past An Aerial View*, 1988.
Griffiths, G & Griffiths E,	*History of Teignmouth*, 1973.
Griffiths, G,	*The Book of Dawlish*, 1984.
Hattatt, R,	*Ancient and Romano-British Brooches*, 1982.
Hattatt, R,	*Iron Age and Roman Brooches*, 1985.

Hattatt, R,	*Ancient Brooches and Other Artefacts*, 1989.
Holmes, E,	*Thimbles*, 1976.
Holmes, E,	*A History of Thimbles*, 1985.
Hornsby, P; Weinstein, R; Homer, R,	*Pewter, A Celebration of the Craft 1200-1700*, 1989.
Hoskins, W,	*Devon*, 1978.
Hoskins, W,	*Local History in England*, 1984.
Hoskins, W,	*The Making of the English Landscape*, 1988.
Harrison, F,	*The Devon Carys*, 1920.
Hayward Gallery,	*English Romanesque Art 1066-1200*, 1984.
Hilton Price, F,	*Old Base Metal Spoons*, 1908.
Jackson, R,	*English Pewter Touchmarks*, 1970.
Jones, R,	*A Book of Newton Abbot*, 1981.
Kruta, V; Frey, O; Raftery, B; SzabC, M;	*The Celts*, 1991.
Mack, R,	*The Coinage of Ancient Britain*, 1975.
McConnel, B,	*The Letts Guide to Collecting Thimbles*, 1991.
Megaw, R; Megaw, V,	*Celtic Art*, 1989.
Mitchiner, M,	*Jetons, Medalets & Tokens: The Medieval Period and Nuremburg, Vol. I*, 1988.
Mitchiner, M,	*Medieval Pilgrim & Secular Badges*, 1986
Mitchell, S; Reeds, B,	*Coins of England & the United Kingdom*, 1993.
Monk, E,	*Keys Their History & Collection*, 1974.
Muir, R,	*The Lost Villages of Britain*, 1982.
Murdoch, T,	*Treasures & Trinkets*, 1991.
North, J,	*English Hammered Coinage, Vol. I*, 1980.
North, J,	*English Hammered Coinage, Vol. II*, 1991.
Oman, C,	*Victoria and Albert Museum Catalogue of Rings 1930*, 1993.
Pearce, S,	*The Bronze Age Metalwork of South-Western Britain*, 1983.
Pearce, S,	*The Kingdom of Dumnonia*, 1978.
Pike, J,	*Tall Ships in Torbay*, 1986.
Purvey, F,	*Coins & Tokens of Scotland*, 1972.
Read, B,	*History Beneath Our Feet*, 1988.
Richardson, J,	*The Local Historian's Encyclopedia*, 1989.
Saunders, P; Saunders E,	*Salisbury & South Wiltshire Museum Medieval Catalogue*, 1991.
Savory, H,	*National Museum of Wales Guide Catalogue of the Bronze Age Collections*, 1980.
Savory, H,	*National Museum of Wales Guide Catalogue of the Early Iron Age Collections*, 1976.
Seaby, H; Rayner, P,	*The English Silver Coinage From 1649*, 1974.
Seaby, P,	*Coins and Tokens of Ireland*, 1970.
Sear, D,	*Roman Coins and Their Values*, 1981.
Selkirk, R,	*The Piercebridge Formula*, 1983.
Selman, R,	*Aspects of Devon History*, 1985.
Snodin, M,	*English Silver Spoons*, 1982.
Stevenson, M,	*Weight Stamping by the Worshipful Company of Founders and City of London*, 1989.
Strong, D; Brown, D,	*Roman Crafts*, 1976.
Tardy,	*International Hallmarks on Silver*, 1985.
Tonnochy, A,	*Catalogue of British Seal-Dies in the British Museum*, 1952.
Thurlow Leeds, E,	*Early Anglo-Saxon Great Square-Headed Brooches*, 1949.
Ward Perkins, J,	*London Museum Medieval Catalogue*, 1940.
Withers, P & B,	*British Coin-Weights*, 1993.
Wood, M,	*In Search of the Dark Ages*, 1981.
Woodforde, J,	*The Strange Story of False Teeth*, 1968.
Wren, C,	*The Short-Cross Coinage 1180-1247 Henry II to Henry III*, 1992.
Youngs, S,	*The Work of Angels*, 1989.

BOOKLETS

Bailey, G,	*Detector Finds*, 1992.
Bailey, G,	*Detector Finds 2*, 1993.
Barker, D,	*British Naval Officers' Buttons 1714-1975*, (?) date.
Bland, R; Johns, C,	*The Hoxne Treasure*, 1993.
Cuddeford, M,	*Identifying Metallic Small Finds*, 1994.
Houben, G,	*European Coin-Weights for English Coins*, 1978.
Marshall, C,	*Buckles Through the Ages*, 1987. Published privately.
Webb, J,	*Buckles Identified*, 1981, Historic Publications.

MISCELLANEOUS

Brownsword, R,	English Latten Domestic Candlesticks 1400-1700, *Finds Research Group 700-1700, Datasheet 1*.
Goodall, I,	The Medieval Manor of Penhallam, Cornwall, *Medieval Archaeology 18*.
Griffiths, N,	Shield-Shaped Mounts, *Finds Research Group 700-1700, Datasheet 12*.
Lawrence, L,	Coin Weights, *British Numismatic Journal*, 1st Series, Vol. VI.

PREFACE

Since the publication in 1988 of *History Beneath Our Feet* much has happened concerning the metal detecting scene in southern Devon. Hundreds of artefacts and coins, some of which are extremely rare, have been recovered, conserved and recorded. Attitudes and relations between the hobby and various factions of orthodox archaeology have waxed and waned. A new and vigorous club, East Devon Metal Detecting Club, has been formed in the east of the region and existing clubs have strengthened their position. Sadly, several staunch allies of responsible metal detecting from within archaeology and the museum service have moved on - they are a loss to reasoned and unblinkered thinking.

It would have been far easier for this new edition to be a facsimile of the first, however, in the light of these changes a complete update was deemed necessary. Each section reflects current archaeological, antiquarian, numismatic and historical opinion, coupled with the author's personal thoughts.

As before, the section of Devon covered comprises that which is traditionally known as South Devon, but has been increased to include parts of West and East Devon; for convenience it is all described as southern Devon. Reference to place names does not imply that finds in those areas are any more prolific than in others, only that more time has been spent searching them.

INTRODUCTION

Primarily, the intention of this corpus is to illustrate the positive contribution made by responsible metal detecting to Devonshire's history and archaeology. Secondarily, hopefully it will provide a useful comparison for metal detectives, archaeologists, antiquarians and historians in other areas.

Wheras much of the evidence herein is somewhat similar to that from other parts of Britain, some appears to be of a more localised nature which has no recorded parallel. For added interest, a limited number of metal artefacts found by other means are included.

Although every effort was made to provide correct identifications and attributions, regrettably the first edition of HBOF had a number of errors. These have been revised and amended in this edition in the light of current knowledge. Inevitably however, some mistakes may still exist, for which I accept full responsibility.

Apart from persons who have a vested interest in small metalwork, it is hoped that this book will help to prove to all sections of society that metal detecting is a leisure activity which can be enjoyed by anyone who has an interest in the history and archaeology of our country. It offers a unique opportunity for its devotees to escape for short periods into the world of yester-year, devoid of the pressures of modern everyday life. The recovery of ancient coins and artefacts, invariably from areas that have no earthly hope of ever being investigated archaeologically, and their subsequent conservation and recording, surely must be in the best interests of the whole community.

Some objects uncovered by metal detectives contribute little to our knowledge of Devon's archaeology or history, however, it must be said that many do. In particular, the fairly plenteous prehistoric metalwork is providing invaluable information on Bronze Age lowland habitation. Numismatic and artefactual evidence from the Romano-British period has shed new light on the extent of Romanisation. Celtic, Anglo-Saxon and Norman coins have assisted archaeologists and numismatists at national level with coinage distribution patterns and plotting trade routes. Similarly, recording lead tokens has helped with a national survey by Nottingham University. A project by one of Britain's foremost antiquarians and archaeological illustrators, concerning the recording of medieval horse-pendants and associated metalwork, has been underway for many years and Devon's metal detectives have assisted greatly the collator.

Archaeology is defined in the *Oxford Dictionary* as 'the study of human antiquities, especially of the prehistoric period and usually by excavation'. It could be argued therefore, that anyone who locates buried metal objects with the aid of a metal detector and then digs them up, is an archaeologist. This statement is of course nonsense; serious metal detectives understand and accept that modern archaeology covers a wide range of disciplines, indeed so many that no single archaeologist can hope to be proficient in all of them.

Most archaeologists are strictly amateurs with no formal qualifications, and are enthusiastic members of shire archaeological societies guided by a few professionals employed by local authorities, museums, universities and institutions like the Ordnance Survey and National Trust. These part-timers should not be underestimated, for often they have acquired a far greater depth of expertise in their particular field than many of their whole-time counterparts.

The recreational pursuit of metal detecting is akin to field-walking or beachcombing using a sophisticated electronic aid instead of eyes only. Its participants are of all ages and physical ability and come from all walks of life, many hold positions of great responsibility in their everyday station which requires integrity of the highest order. It can be seen, therefore, that the type of person who is a keen metal detective is invariably a highly responsible individual. There are even enthusiastic hobby metal detectives who are qualified archaeologists. It is fact that many metal detectives are extremely knowledgable concerning the history and archaeology of their area, antiquity identification, conservation techniques and recording. It is also true that there are people within the hobby who have a greater understanding and appreciation of the whole spectrum of artefactual and numismatic metalwork than many museum curators and archaeologists. Indeed, this was admitted by the Curator of Antiquities of EM.

Regrettably it must be said that, as with all activities, there is a minority which does not adhere to the hobby's self-imposed strict code of conduct and, as a consequence of its actions, unnecessary problems are created for the genuine enthusiast. Due to these irresponsible few, local authorities, museums and archaeologists in some parts of the country have attempted to ban or impose controls on metal detecting It is fair to say that some of the problems attributed to the misuse of metal detectors are purely and simply due to ignorance on the part of their operators which is why it is important to encourage and support metal detecting clubs where guidance is freely available to all who have an interest in the hobby. Undoubtedly there are poachers who use metal detectors as an aid to plunder richer sites, usually at night, which is why responsible operatives firmly believe that such lawbreakers should be convicted, for they are not metal detectives. However, what has been happening is that in certain sections of the media, orthodox archaeology, the museum service and local authorities, all metal detector users have been branded as criminals as well. This is tantamount to persecution of a minority group.

Because of the unbending attitude of that influential body, the CBA, which for years attempted to eliminate the hobby, much needless animosity was generated between metal detectives and orthodox archaeology. This unfortunate situation forced independent metal detectives throughout the length and breadth of the land to unite and organize themselves to defend their chosen recreation. Many clubs were formed and grouped into regional federations, each club being represented on the regional committee. All regional federations are now represented by two delegates on the Executive Committee of the NCMD the function of which is to promote, protect and encourage responsible metal detecting. The NCMD is comprised of a decision-making committee of hobbyists who have no connection with the commercial side of metal detecting. Manufacturers, importers and the metal detecting press are represented in a non-voting capacity to discuss topics of mutual concern, proffer advice and to learn of the needs and aspirations of member federations.

It is the responsibility of the NCMD to promote the good name of metal detecting at all levels and to lead the fight against any adverse legislation designed to limit the hobby. In fact, the NCMD seeks to encourage a spirit of co-operation between metal detectives and every other interest in the community.

Entirely due to the efforts of the NCMD the hobby is represented on the Outdoor Pursuits Division of The Central Council of Physical Recreation which means that metal detecting is a recognised leisure activity that is entitled to the same considerations as any other sporting or recreational pursuit. As a result of successful negotiations with the Forestry Commission it is now possible for members of clubs affiliated to the NCMD to detect on land under the control of the Commission. The conditions vary and it is necessary to consult the local Head Forester or Warden before commencing to detect.

All members of organisations affiliated to the NCMD must carry their NCMD identification cards with them whilst detecting. This indicates that the holder is a member of a recognized club or FID and as such is covered by Public Liability Insurance whilst detecting which has been accepted, in particular, by the National Farmers Union in relation to detecting on their members' land.

FID is a separate organization formed to represent metal detectives who for whatever reason cannot belong to a club. FID is affiliated to the NCMD in precisely the same way as a regional federation, therefore the lone metal detective who is a FID member is entitled to the same privileges as one who is a member of a club affiliated to the NCMD.

As a direct result of metal detectives banding together in organised clubs, it became possible to offer a free recovery service to the general public, landowners and other organizations such as the police. Many lost items of jewellery or agricultural equipment have been recovered and searches made for murder-weapons or other evidence at the scene of a crime or other incident. Whenever a call for help is received every effort is made to get at least one operative to the scene as quickly as possible. Participation in charity events is a regular occurrence and thousands of pounds have been raised.

It is pleasing to note that due to the efforts of the NCMD, FID and numerous clubs throughout the country, it has become apparent that many archaeologists and museums are not anti-metal detector user and desire a greater degree of cooperation. In Devon there has been an ongoing dialogue for some years which has resulted in metal detectives assisting Torquay Museum with their new archaeological gallery. Much of their illustrating was executed by the illustrator of this book, and nearly 82% of the displayed metal artefacts were donated by hobbyists. The historically important Cockington finger-rings were donated to Torbay District Council's Torre Abbey Museum where they are permanantly exhibited. This goodwill gesture by the finder established a relationship with this museum which resulted in TMDC having their own showcase therein. Liaison with the DAS numismatist continues, and many hundreds of ancient coins and jetons have now been recorded.

Under the guidance of the then archaeological consultant of Torquay Museum, several field-searches were jointly carried out by TMDC and DAS's Tiverton group which although they produced little artefactual or numismatic evidence, were a great success. The consensus from these meetings was that the two disciplines had much in common and should work together whenever or wherever possible.

Introduction

Conversely, it must be said that despite the efforts of responsible metal detectives and individual professionals and amateurs within the archaeological and museum world, there is still an overriding hostile and obstructive attitude from EM, EMAFU, DAS and the County Archaeologist. TMDC has still to receive any acknowledgement from EMAFI for its assistance at the 1985 Totnes or 1986 Colaton Raleigh archaeological digs. In the late 1980s, delaying tactics by the same unit prevented the probable recovery by TMDC of numerous items from a major gas pipeline excavation. A request for volunteers to assist at a major rescue dig in advance of a new reservoir on Dartmoor's western flank was responded to promptly by TMDC - neither an acknowledgment, positive or negative reply was ever received. DAS's publications concerning detector-found coins for a long time persisted in deleting any reference to metal detectors. It is a pity that Devon's archaeological establishment has failed to learn from its colleagues in other parts of the country that they can only benefit from co-operation with metal detecting.

An attempt by Dartmoor National Park to ban metal detecting on all land owned by it failed after representation by TMDC and the NCMD. Detecting is allowed in certain areas by agreement. However, the whole of this archaeologically sensitive area has extremely acid ground and metal objects haven't survived at all well. It has proved a futile exercise to search here, and time is better spent on the lowlands.

Throughout the country there are thousands of acres of land under the custodianship of local authorities; public playing fields, parks, woodlands and other open spaces. On much of it leisure activities such as ball games, mountain bike riding, motorcycling and horse riding take place. These recreational facilities are provided for the use of the general public and are financed wholly or partially from the civic purse. Metal detecting costs the Council Tax payer absolutely nothing; why therefore do some councils go out of their way to create obstacles for people who wish to enjoy this healthy, educational and legitimate pastime? The answer invariably given is that metal detecting causes damage to the ground which is a ridiculous statement when one considers the harm caused by other leisure pursuits. Many undoubtedly cause very serious erosion problems yet rarely is a bad word said against them. Their participants are not required to make good the damage occasioned. Responsible metal detectives, however, always repair the ground after extracting an item and invariably it is virtually impossible to see where a hole has been dug. On grassland the only tools used are small trowels and perhaps long screwdrivers or sharp knives, whilst larger implements may be used on ploughland or beaches. When digging on grassland it is necessary only to cut three sides of a square, two sides of a triangle or part of a circle, flap the turf back and remove the object. On lawned areas the removed soil is placed on a small sheet of plastic which prevents staining the grass.

Teignbridge District Council, more so than other councils in the area, quickly realized the benefits of metal detecting and actually sent officials to witness a field meeting. As a result they opened up many areas under their jurisdiction for the hobby. It is a pity that all local authorities are not so enlightened when dealing with requests to search public land. In today's society, with the ever-increasing problem of unemployment and the extension of leisure time, it is imperative that encouragement is given to all activities which help to fill this void in peoples' lives.

Serious metal detectives spend many hours on research as well as detecting in the field which is a must if consistent success is to be achieved. More often than not the time spent searching, results in a bag full of old rusty iron and other metallic junk. This is disposed of safely rather than being left to be a potential hazard to human and animal life. Most artefactual and numismatic material recovered is rather mundane with little or no monetary value and certainly of no great archaeological or historical significance. Occasionally, however, items of historic and archaeological interest are recovered, some of which prove to be extremely important and it is true that some objects are valuable. This is a bonus and of secondary consideration to genuine metal detectives. The hobby advises all landowners to enter into a simple written legal contract which protects their rights to an agreed percentage of any object(s) of monetary value. This is particularly important in view of the law of Treasure Trove.

Of course, anyone can purchase a metal detector and contrary to popular belief a Home Office licence is not now required to operate one. Many people think that it is an easy way to riches, it being only necessary to switch a metal detector on and coins and artefacts will leap from the ground! How wrong can they be, for once it is realized that to be successful involves much hard work and time, frequently in very unpleasant conditions, the majority fall by the wayside leaving the dedicated few to carry on.

The objects found by metal detectives come from beaches, river foreshores, building sites, farmland, woodlands and other open spaces where they are being continually battered by the elements and subjected to mechanical and chemical damage. In particular, modern farming equipment and agrochemicals are causing untold harm. Even when items are out of the ground they are still liable to further deterioration if the correct conservation techniques are not applied. Museums with conservation laboratories, such as EM, are often willing to proffer advice on which method to be used or may even do it for a fee. Metal detectives have acquired many of these skills and are able to carry out simple cleaning and conservation using laboratory methods.

Most detector finds are made within the top 15cm of the ground. They cannot, therefore, be attributed to a stratified layer. Ploughing, which has gone on for many centuries, churns the top 20 - 50cm of soil; likewise, nature's ploughing, e.g. earthworms and heavy livestock, continually mixes soil to a depth of 30cm or more. This means that even on permanent pasture, the depths of buried objects are constantly being altered. Consequently any metalwork that can be detected is always completely out of archaeological stratified context.

Despite what certain manufacturers and other misinformed people claim, there is not a metal detector made that will detect the average coin sized object at a depth of more than 15cm on every type of ground. Occasionally larger items will be detected up to 25cm - 30cm, however, this is not the norm and even so it is still well within the non-stratified layer.

This anomaly is due to the phenomenon 'ground effect', which masks signals from buried metal objects, and is either positive, negative or neutral or a combination of two of them. Wet salt sand is positive, as is land subjected to centuries of intensive manuring. Negative conditions are caused by natural magnetic ironstone or saturation with minute particles of rust from decomposed iron. Neutral ground has no adverse effect on metal detectors. Combined effect is where rust particles or magnetic ironstone is found on a wet salt beach; this is virtually impossible to eliminate with most types of metal detector. Adverse ground conditions drastically reduce the depth at which metal objects can be detected. Many types of detector will miss a coin lying on the surface. To prove the depth limitation of metal detectors, take any machine and after switching on and tuning it, place the search-head near to a motor car; the nearest that a signal will be received is about 1.20m - 1.50m. If the same car was buried in the ground the detection depth would be considerably reduced.

It is not the intention of this book to describe all of the technical problems associated with operating metal detectors or the operator skills required to overcome them. Potential enthusiasts are advised to read any of the excellent periodicals or books available on the subject or to consult their nearest metal detecting club or competent dealer.

Most of the sites mentioned herein are in private ownership. It has taken many years for responsible metal detectives to establish the excellent relationship which now exists between themselves and these landowners. It is founded on trust - please do nothing to destroy it.

Unless otherwise stated, all items were found with the aid of a metal detector. Plates of numismatics and artefacts are not to scale. Appropriate scales or dimensions of artefacts depicted by photograph or drawing are included in the catalogue, but the drawings have all been scaled down to 70% of their orginal size.

NCMD CODE OF CONDUCT
for responsible metal detector users

1: Do not trespass. Ask permission before venturing on to any private land.

2: Respect the country code. Do not leave gates open when crossing fields, and do not damage crops or frighten animals.

3: Do not leave a mess. It is perfectly simple to extract a coin or other small object buried a few inches under the ground without digging a great hole. Use a sharpened trowel or knife to cut a neat circle or triangle (do not remove the plug of earth entirely from the ground); extract the object; replace the soil and grass carefully and even you will have difficulty finding the spot again.

4: Help to keep Britain tidy - and help yourself. Bottle tops, silver paper and tin cans are the last things you should throw away. You could well be digging them up again next year. Do yourself and the community a favour by taking the rusty iron and other junk you find to the nearest litter bin.

5: If you discover any live ammunition or any lethal object such as an unexploded bomb or mine, do not touch it. Mark the site carefully and report the find to the police and landowner.

6: Report all unusual historical finds to the landowner.

7: Familiarize yourself with the law relating to archaeological sites. Remember it is illegal for anyone to use a metal detector on a scheduled ancient monument unless permission has been obtained from the Historic Buildings and Monuments Commission. Also acquaint yourself with the practice of Treasure Trove.

8: Remember that when you are out with your metal detector, you are an ambassador for our hobby. Do nothing that may give it a bad name.

9: Never miss an opportunity to show and explain your detector to anyone who asks about it. Be friendly, you could pick some useful clues to another site. If you meet another detector user, introduce yourself. You may learn much about the hobby from each other.

The Known Devon Mints
The towns where Anglo-Saxon and/or Norman coins were minted

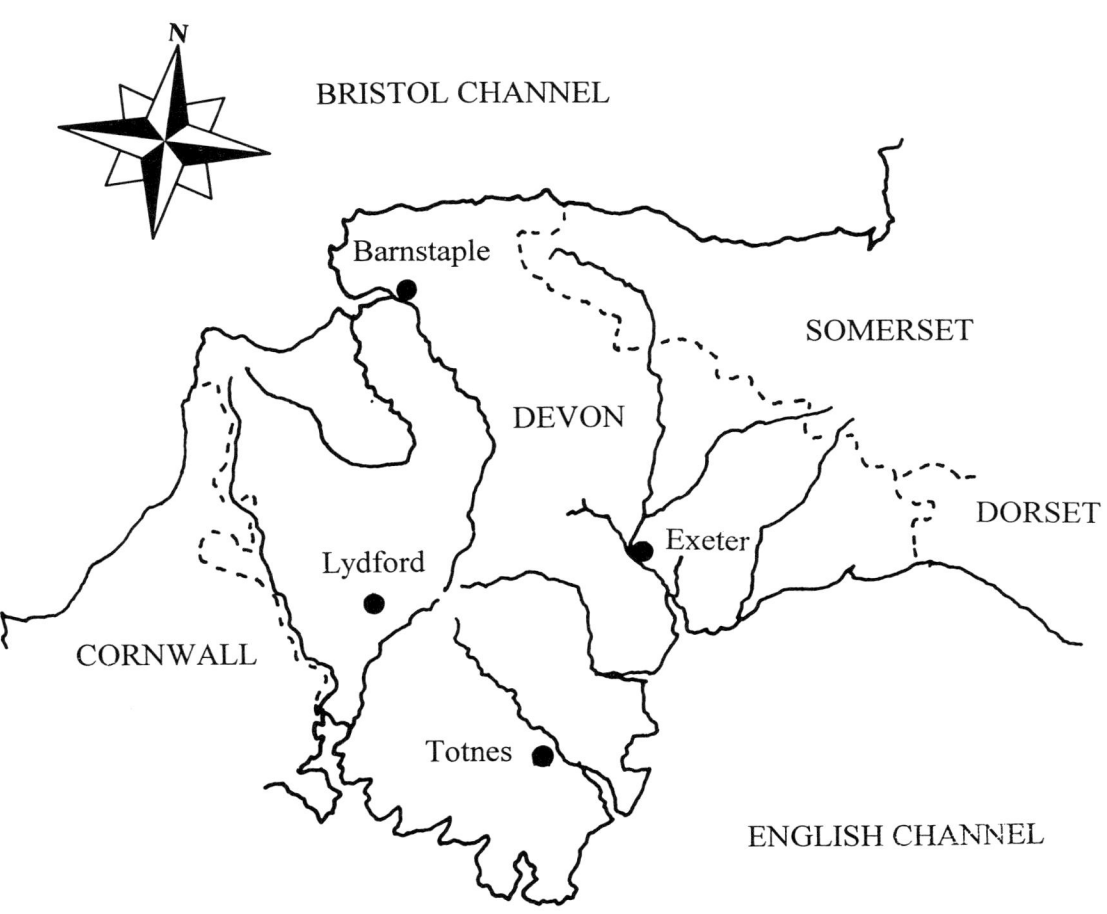

Town	Coins minted
Exeter	Anglo-Saxon and Norman, inclusive of Angevin (to 1249), Edwardian and later (post-1249), Charles I and Civil War.
Totnes	Anglo-Saxon.
Lydford	Anglo-Saxon.
Barnstaple	Anglo-Saxon and Norman.

Based upon Ordnance Survey mapping with the permission of the Controller of Her Majesty's Stationery Office, © Crown copyright.

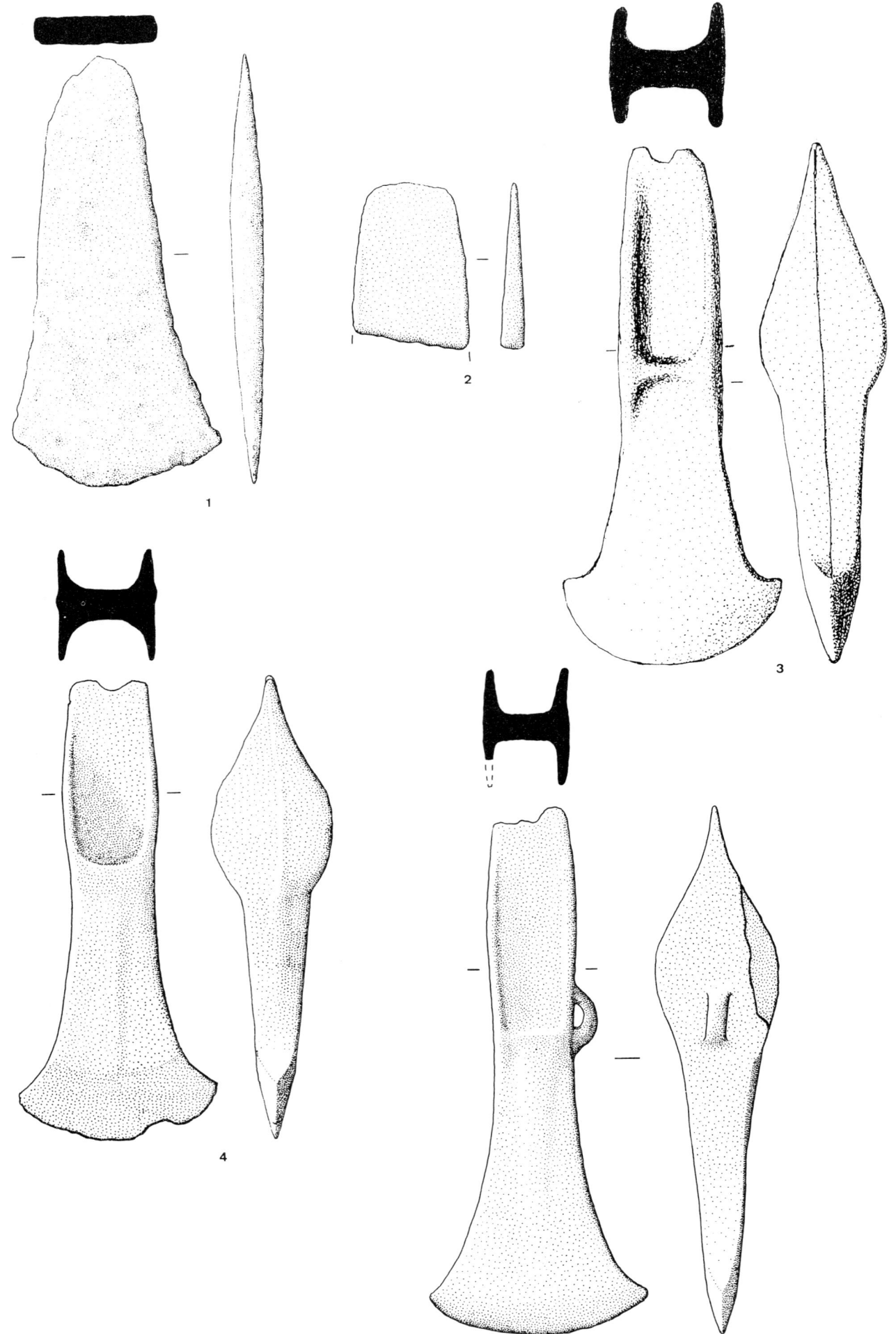

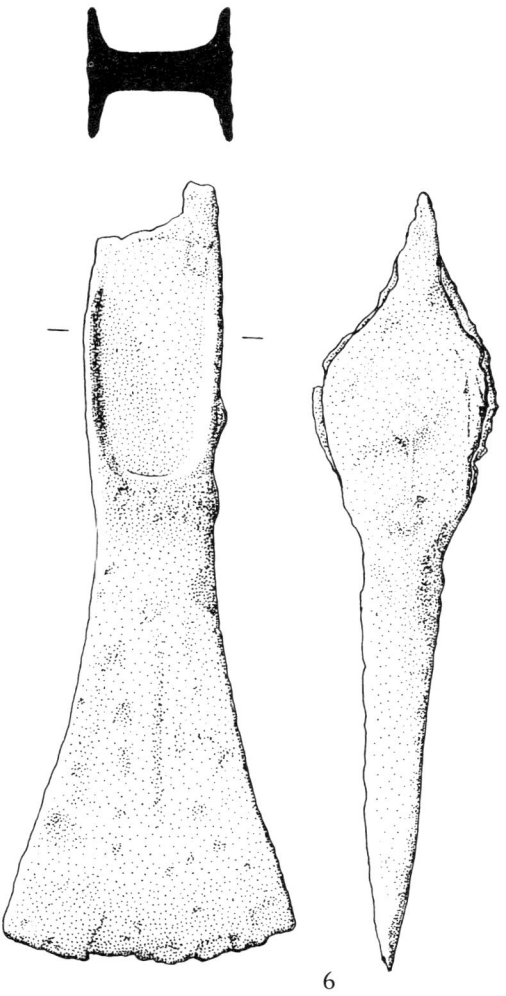

6

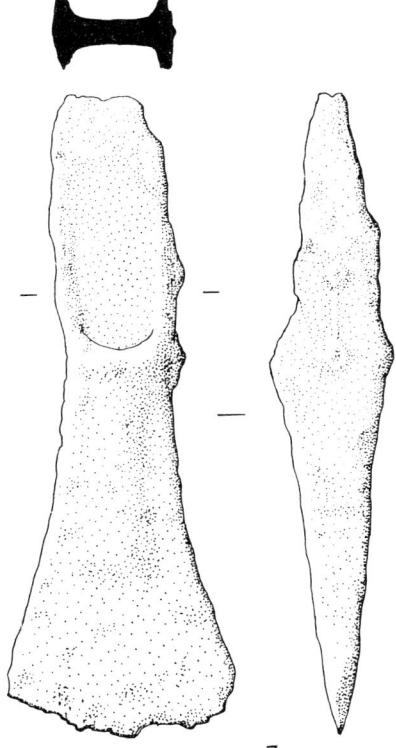

7

Chapter One
The Bronze Age

The story of man's use of metal in the British Isles starts some time during the 26th century BC, although it had already been used for many centuries by the inhabitants of the eastern Mediterranean. This practice slowly spread north and west through Europe and culminated in the crossing of the English Channel by Early Bronze Age people who brought with them their tools, weapons and ornaments of copper, as well as some goldwork. These folk settled throughout the south of England, living mainly in small groups and in some cases quite large communities, engaged in pastoral farming and to a lesser degree, crop cultivation.

It is thought that a noticeable improvement in the climate occurred towards the end of the Neolithic period which continued until about 600 BC. This change allowed the early Bronze Age settlers to occupy Dartmoor's heights as well as the surrounding lowlands and other ranges of hills.

Devon is fortunate in having within its borders much of the best surviving evidence of Bronze Age occupation in the British Isles. By far the majority of these ancient monuments are situated on the hills of western and southern Dartmoor, taking the form of: hut circles, pounds, burial-chambers, standing stones, stone rows and stone circles. In all, some several thousand sites have been identified to date; no doubt many more will be revealed in the fullness of time. The most likely explanation for so many remaining to this day is a climatic deterioration that started at the beginning of the 7th century BC which, coupled with the problem of soil exhaustion caused by over-farming, forced the inhabitants on to lower ground. Later cultures never reoccupied the moors on a sufficient scale which meant that much of the ground wasn't affected by improved ploughing techniques.

In the east, the Woodbury ridge and the greensand plateau between Gittisham Hill and Broad Down reveal considerable Bronze Age settlement, mainly barrows, and at Thorverton and Upton Pyne barrows have been identified. Many hundreds of similar sites must have existed in the lower country which forms the coastal belt and river valleys of southern Devon, but have been obliterated by intensive farming and urban devolopment.

Historical and archaeological consensus differs over the extent of Bronze Age settlement in Devon generally and with Dartmoor in particular. As mentioned earlier, it is thought that Dartmoor was abandoned slowly, starting sometime during the 7th century BC, continuing well into the Iron Age. Later, in the Iron Age chapter, it is mentioned that some historians are of the opinion that the great hillforts were constructed to give protection from a hostile people who lived on the moors. This implies that South Devon's lowlands were not inhabited by

Bronze Age folk, or if they were, the people were friendly or had been subdued by force. Available documentation on this period of Devon's history fails to present a clear picture of the relationship and chronology between the Bronze Age and Iron Age.

Undoubtedly the best documentary evidence which supports the argument for an extensive Bronze Age habitation of southern Devon's lowlands is Suzan Pearce's tome *The Bronze Age Metalwork of South Western Britain*. This outstanding collation of metallic finds, in many cases from unassociated locations, certainly contributes much to the debate.

METAL AXE HEADS

The evolution of Bronze Age metal weapons and tools can only be expressed in general terms, for there was no precise cut-off point for any particular type. Inevitably there was considerable overlapping between the Early (2600-1400 BC), Middle (1400-900 BC), and Late (900-600 BC) Bronze Age periods. Typology varies according to the manufactory, which, coupled with metal analysis, assists with determining the place of origin. Broze Age metal weapons or tools were either cast in stone, clay or copper-alloy moulds, according to geographical location and precise phase, although certain features were occasionally forged. The later Middle Bronze Age saw the first attempts at making sheet metal weapons.

Early Bronze Age flat axe-heads are copper with straight sides and broad butts which were followed by the trapezoid-shaped broad-butted type, and then a form with fairly broad but considerably thinner butts. Punched or engraved ornamentation was frequently applied to both sides. The first hafts were nothing more than a stick split at the top into which the axe-head was fitted before being bound laterally and criss-cross fashion with leather thongs. This developed into the haft with a purpose-made slot in which the axe-head was similarly lashed. Copper is relatively soft, an inconvenience which around 2300 BC. prompted the development of copper alloy.

Copper-alloy flat axe-heads are similar to their copper counterparts but are somewhat thinner and narrower at the butt. This form of flat axe-head was affixed to a slotted wooden haft which also was prone to splitting. An attempt was made to resolve this problem by designing axe-heads with a narrow, forged, longitudinal flange on all four edges which facilitated the use of angled hafts. This was improved further by incorporating a transverse ridge, called a bar-stop, each side of the axe-head between the butt and the blade, widening the flanges, which were now cast, and restricting their length from the butt to just below the ridge. These are known as the flanged axe and haft-flange axe respectively.

Sometime before 1400 BC the palstave evolved, characterised by considerably deepened flanges which descend to or just below the waist, and wide ledges in place of the bar-stop. This development allowed the use of a lateral-headed haft, which had a wedge-shaped aperture, without fear of splitting. The earliest palstaves are wide-bladed, and to improve lashing, the flanges frequently have integral cast knobs on the outer face. A feature of some early palstaves is a moulded decorated blade just below the waist. As time progressed palstaves retained their wide blades but became lighter and c1450 were provided with an integral cast

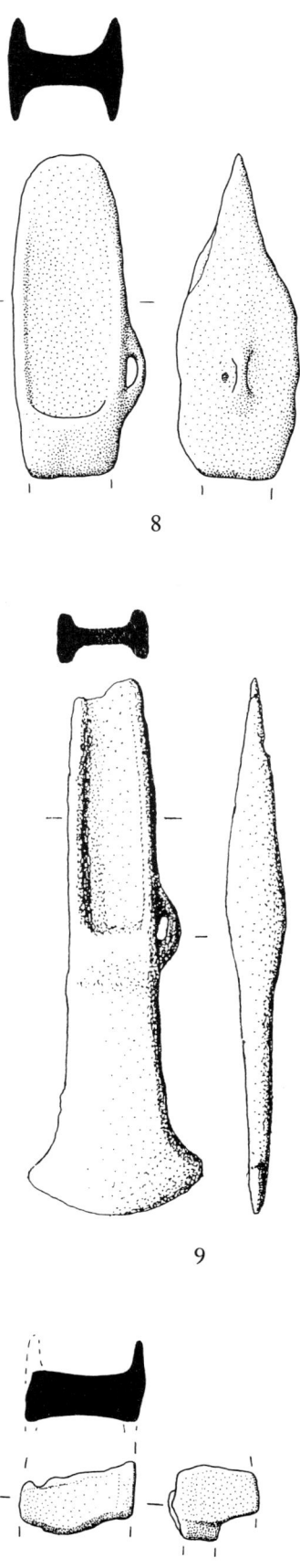

The Bronze Age

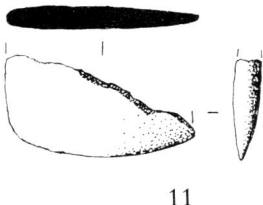

11

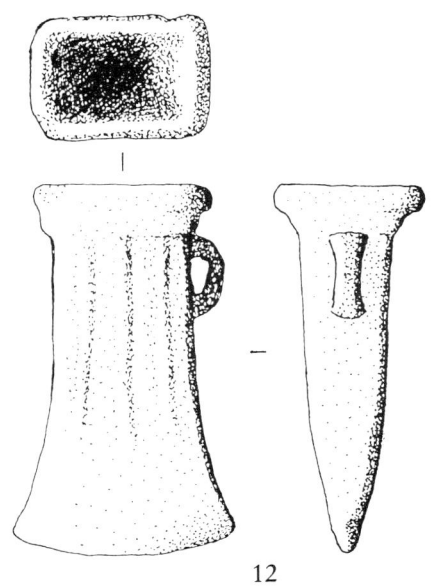

12

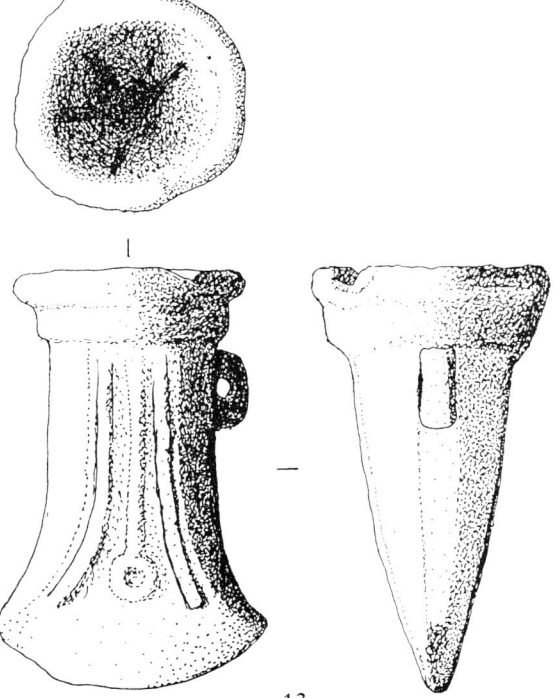

13

side-loop which aided securing to the haft. More rarely found is the double-looped palstave. Around 1200 BC palstave blades started to become narrower and this type remained current until c750 BC.

Much rarer types of axe-head occasionally found in Britain are the intrusive median-winged or terminally-winged attributed to c750-600 BC. The former is unlooped and narrow with a pair of central inturned flanges on both sides, whilst the latter is side-looped and has a widely-splayed blade with similar flanges at the top.

Bronze Age axe-head evolution finalised with the socketed side-looped type, the earliest of which appeared c1050-900 BC. This form is known as the intrusive which is narrow-bladed with a rectangular mouth. Typology of socketed axe-heads is diverse, therefore it will suffice to say here, that they remained current until 600 BC and are known in various sizes, either with rectangular or circular mouths which facilitated lateral-headed hafts. Frequently they exhibit moulded decoration.

Cast copper-alloy flat axe-head, c2500 BC
1: abraded butt and blade edge, 122mm x 57mm - *Tavistock*.

Cast copper-alloy flanged axe-head, c2300 BC
2: fragment, 47mm x 32mm - *Denbury*.

Cast copper-alloy unlooped palstaves, c1450-1250 BC
3: widely-splayed blade, 149mm x 59mm - *Elberry Cove, Torbay*.
4: widely-splayed blade, 131mm x 54mm - *Denbury*.

Cast copper-alloy side-looped palstaves, c1400-1050 BC
5: c1350 BC, widely-splayed blade, 149mm x 59mm - *Colaton Raleigh*.
6: c1350 BC, widely-splayed blade, abraded haft, loop lost, 154mm x 55mm - *Hennock*.
7: c1350 BC, abraded widely-splayed blade, loop lost, 125.5mm x 43mm - *Hennock*.
8: c1350 BC, fragment, probable widely-splayed blade type, 70.5mm x 27.5mm - *Broadhembury*.
9: c1200 BC, narrow, widely-splayed blade, 116mm x 36mm - *Stokeinteignhead*.

Cast copper-alloy unlooped, side- or double-looped palstave, c1450-1050 BC
10: fragment, 16.5mm x 25mm - *Denbury*.

Cast copper-alloy possible winged axe-head or intrusive socketed axe-head, c1050-600 BC
11: fragment, 20mm x 36mm - *Teigngrace*.

Cast copper-alloy side-looped socketed axe-heads, c900-600 BC
12: rectangular mouth with moulded double bands around rim, three moulded vertical ribs each side, 72mm x 42mm - *Stokeinteignhead*.
13: circular mouth with moulded double bands around rim, two moulded splayed ribs and a vertical rib with a circular terminal on each side, 83mm x 51mm - *River Teign, Hackney Marsh*.
14: circular mouth with moulded double bands around rim, blade edge bent, 82mm x 42mm - *Denbury*.
15: fragment, 33mm x 46mm - *Bishopsteignton*.
16: fragment, 28mm x 62mm - *Newton Abbot*.
17: fragment, 21mm x 39mm - *Coffinswell*.
18: fragment, 33mm x 45mm - *Exeter*.

19: fragment, narrow socketed-axe, 58mm x 32mm - *Wilmington*.

METAL SPEARHEADS

The ealiest copper-alloy form of spearhead in Britain, the long-tanged, originated c1600-1400 BC and simply slotted into the end of a wooden shaft. Frequently the tang has a rivet hole which aided securing by means of a rivet. The same phase saw the development of two further types of spearhead: the short-tanged (invariably with a rivet hole), which has a waisted collar and is dagger-like, and the cast integral socketed with side loops. As with axe-heads, thongs were secured to the loops. Characteristic of all three forms of spearhead, on both sides, is a central, raised, tapered, longitudinal rib which resulted in a lozenge-shaped cross-section blade. Blades of some have additional longitudinal ribs either side of the central rib.

Socketed side-looped spearheads, which have leaf or kite-shaped blades, remained current throughout the Middle Bronze Age. Before 1200 BC socketed leaf-shaped basal-looped spearheads appeared which by 1000 BC were superseded by similar spearheads but with triangular blades. A variation of the latter type of spearhead is the peg-hole, named after a pair of rivet holes in the ferrule whereby the head was riveted to the shaft. It was during this phase that the first attempts were made at making spearheads from sheet copper alloy. Sometime between 1000-900 BC the lunate-opening spearhead evolved which has an aperture in the blade each side of the ferrule. Some of the latter type have hollow-cast or stepped blades and occasionally both they and peg-hole forms have bands of engraved ornamentation around the ferrule rim. Another type of spearhead of this phase has a shorter triangular blade with a small protected hole in the blade each side of the ferrule

Hollow-bladed barbed spearheads possibly evolved soon after 1000 BC. Some have rivet holes through the ferrule through which passed a rather long peg-rivet. As these rivets extend to, or past, the barbs, it implies these spearheads were not functional but intended for ritualistic purposes. This type of spearhead has a short ferrule and a long leaf-shaped blade which sometimes has lunate apertures. Regular types of triangular-bladed, pegged and lunate-opening spearheads remained current throughout the Late Bronze Age.

Cast copper-alloy spearheads
20: 1400-1200 BC, side-looped, kite-shaped blade, oblique rib either side of triangular-shaped central rib, 140mm x 33mm - *Stokeinteignhead*.
21: 1400-1200 BC, fragmented, side-looped, leaf-shaped blade, 57mm x 17mm - *Stokeinteignhead*.
22: 1200-1000 BC, fragmented, basal-looped, leaf-shaped blade, 138mm x 33mm - *Kingsland, Torquay*.
23: c1000-700 BC, fragmented, peg-hole, probable triangular blade, 49.5mm x 27mm - *New Barn*.

N.B. It is very evident that the blade of No.23 is recently broken, almost certainly by the plough. It was recovered along with 37 fragments of bun ingot scattered over several square metres.

DIRKS AND RAPIERS

Although tanged or riveted daggers, firstly of copper and then

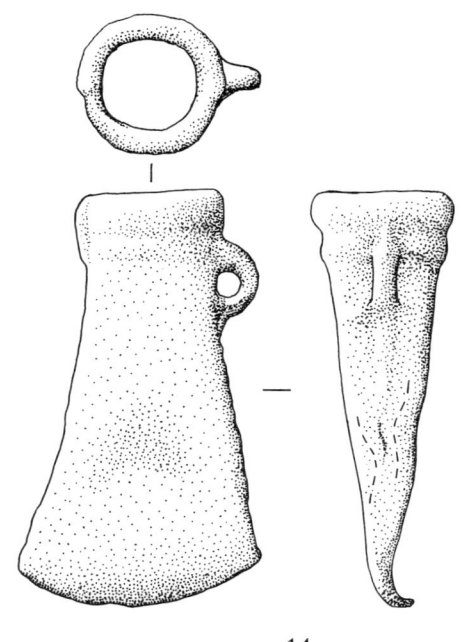

14

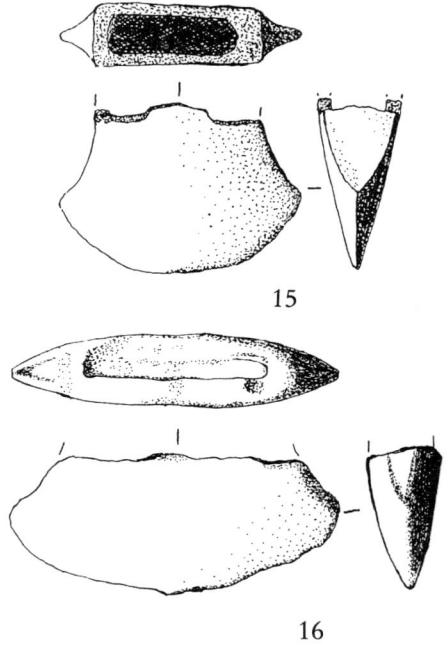

15

16

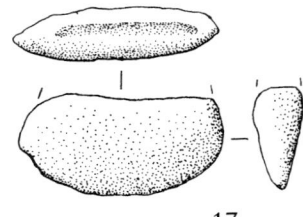

17

The Bronze Age

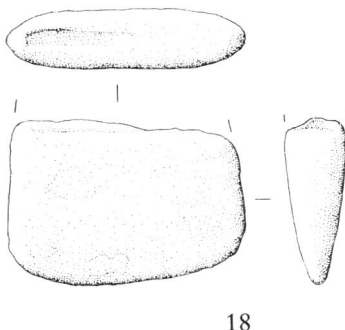

18

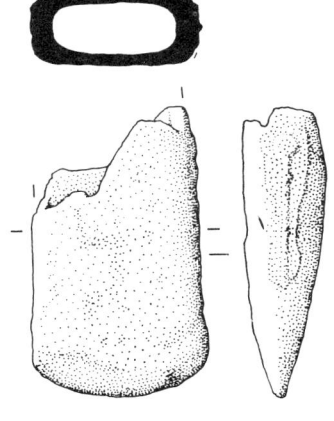

19

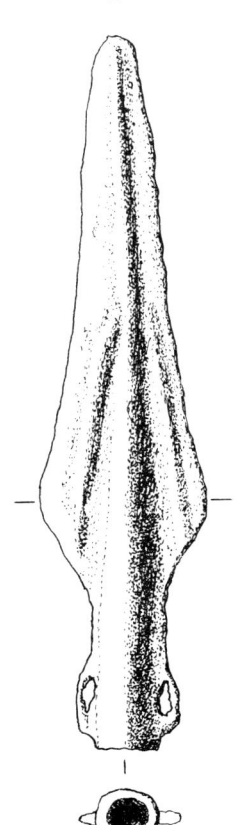

20

copper alloy, had prevailed from soon after the beginning of the Early Bronze Age, dirks and rapiers didn't materialise until c1400 BC. Both evolved from the dagger and are differentiated by their length; rapiers are longer than 355mm, whilst dirks are shorter.

The earliest dirks and daggers have trapezium-shaped flat cross-section hilts with two rivet holes, by which handles were riveted. Blades are straight-sided and fairly narrow with a pronounced longitudinal midrib. The next generation of these weapons have lozenge-shaped cross-section blades, frequently with bevelled edges, which were followed by the triple-ridged, i.e. blades with three longitudinal ribs. The latter type evolved into the flat-rib blade which has bevelled edges and is flat cross-section; the hilt is triangular with two apertures. Lastly, the thicker and wider leaf-bladed rapier appeared, with its flatter midrib, which was transitional with the true sword around 1000 BC.

Cast copper-alloy dirks or rapiers
24: c1400 BC, fragment, lozenge-shaped cross-section, 51mm x 12mm - *Coffinswell*.
25: c1400-1200 BC, fragment, flat-rib blade with bevelled edges, triangular hilt, 72mm x 29mm - *Stokeinteignhead*.

SICKLES

The first Bronze Age sickles are attributed to c1400-1200 BC and are of the tanged knobbed type which are characterised by a triangular cross-section blade at the juncture of the tang. Around 1200 BC ring-socket sickles made an appearance; these have a relatively straight blade and a rivet hole in one side of the socket. Next, c900 BC, came sickles with tangs which have rivet holes. Finally, c700, sickles progressed to a more curved blade with a longer ferrule with one or two rivet holes, a type which remained current into the Iron Age, although copper-alloy sickles with iron sockets were used before 600 BC.

Cast copper-alloy probable tanged and riveted sickle, c900-700 BC
26: ovoid cross-section, traces of probable three rivet holes at junction of tanged haft which is lost, 100mm x 23mm - *Bishopsteignton*

RAZORS

Leaf-shaped short-tanged razors with a rivet hole in the tang first made an appearance sometime between c1750-1450 BC. Around c1400 BC the long-tanged razor was developed. Both types are known with either double- or single-edged blades. Later, c1200-1000 BC, long-tanged oval-bladed razors with bifid ends evolved. Concurrent with this form was the long-tanged circular double-edged blade with triangular openwork. Presumably, tanged types fitted into separate wooden or bone handles, the former being secured by a copper-alloy rivet.

About 900-700 BC elaborate razors with circular blades and long flat handles were current. Both handles and blades of this type frequently have decorative circular openwork. This form was followed c700 BC by the triangular or sub-triangular-bladed razor some of which have a bifid handle comprising a pair of openwork circles, frequently with triangular openwork in the blade.

Cast copper-alloy possible short-tanged with rivet hole or long-tanged razor, c1500-1200 BC
27: fragmented, leaf-shaped double-edged blade, 38.5mm x 20mm - *Stokeinteignhead*.

Cast copper-alloy long-tanged razor, c1500-1200 BC
28: abraded or re-sharpened leaf-shaped double-edged blade, 54.5mm x 15mm - *Denbury*.

DRESS PINS

Since time immemorial man has taken pride in embellishing himself with ornaments which frequently were purely decorative and of a personal nature. However, some had a functional role, e.g. a badge of office, or for fastening garments, as with buttons, dress-pins or brooches.

Cast or forged copper-alloy decorative dress-pins were current throughout the Bronze Age. Attachment was achieved with the aid of a cord. All have long stems, and two types attributed to the Early period are crutch or globular-headed. The former are known with hollow heads and/or spiral stems and engraved heads, whilst the latter frequently have expanded, ribbed stems.

Three types of dress-pin are characteristic of the Middle period: large quoit-headed, the heads of which are circular or flat cross-section; bifid-headed, formed from two conjoined circles; side-looped with lateral disc-heads or expanded stems. Frequently stems or heads carry engraved decoration, whilst heads occasionally have moulded beads and concentric circles. Between 700-600 BC swan-necked dress-pins were fashionable, some of which feature a ribbed knop.

Cast and forged copper-alloy dress-pin, c700-500 BC
29: swan-necked, tapering circular cross-section, engraved transverse ribbed knop, 77mm x 4mm - *Kents Cavern, Torquay*.

N.B. Nos.9,12,20 & 21 were found widely scattered in different parts of the same field. Bronze Age pottery sherds have also been recovered in this area. Patches of oyster and cockle shells are evident after ploughing. This field is on a south facing slope and its highest point is about two-thirds of the way from the summit of the hill. There is a difference in height between this field and the field immediately above of some 1.52m, right on the hedgebank boundary. Therefore there is a possibility that a habitation site did exist which continual ploughing has obliterated. In 1964 an archaeological field-walk was carried out here, and the official report concludes that the shell-scatter represented an Iron Age midden and that sherds of black pottery picked up by the walkers were Iron Age. No.24 was discovered in an adjacent field. No.22 was dug up by the landowner in the 1960s. Apparently, soon afterwards a similar artefact was found at the same place which was subsequently lost. No.29 was recovered during a 19th-century archaeological excavation.

BRACELETS

Early Bronze Age bracelets are known in copper-alloy or gold, although the former is rare and the latter almost unique. Copper-alloy bracelets of this period comprise a simple bangle, whilst a twisted gold composite torc-like spiral bracelet (or thought to be a bracelet), from Wales, has been credited to this period.

Around 1400 BC bracelets of gold became more plenteous, and were crafted torc-like from twisted ribbon, and from circular,

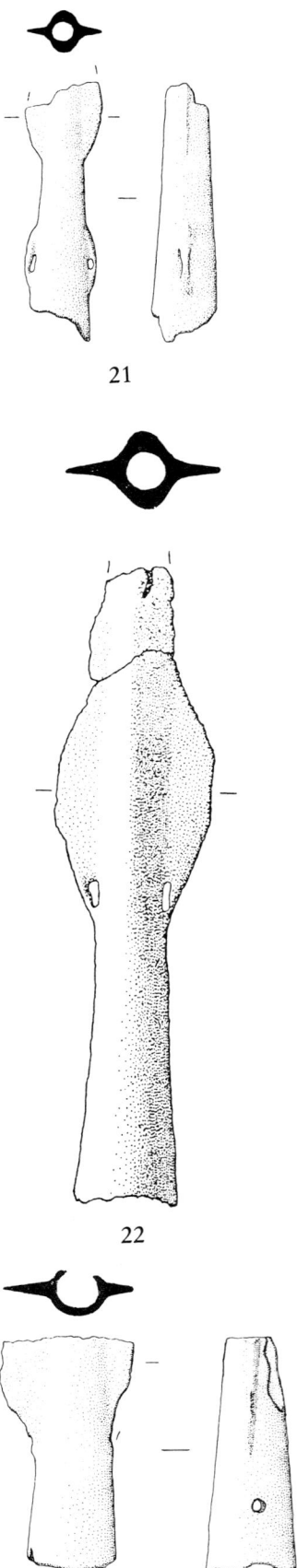

The Bronze Age

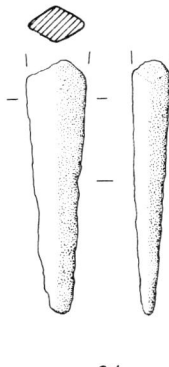

24

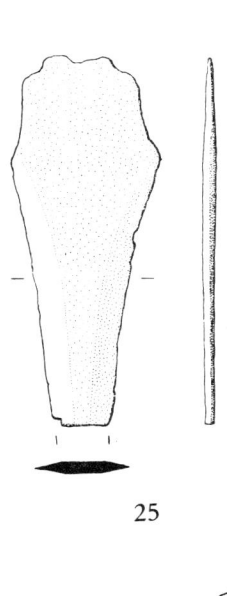

25

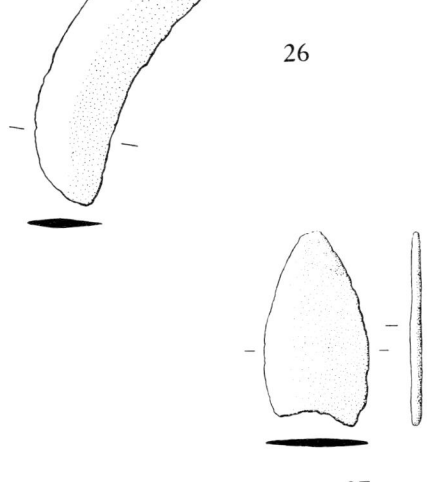

26

27

semi-circular, square or lozenge-shaped cross-section solid rod in both penannular and annular forms. Similar bracelets were also made of copper alloy and frequently have engraved decoration. Repoussé ornamentation features on sheet copper-alloy bracelets of this time, and another solid but wider form is ribbed.

Between 1200-900 BC gold or copper-alloy composite twisted torc-like bracelets with expanded plain cross-section terminals were dominant. Current in the last three centuries of the Bronze Age were solid gold rod penannular armrings of circular or oval cross-section which frequently are quite plain, although some are engraved, but characteristically all have cup-shaped terminals which vary in size. Sheet gold forms were concurrent with the latter type and likewise are either undecorated or are engraved; terminals are simply the sheet backturned. Types of copper-alloy bracelet worn in the Late Bronze Age seem to be much the same as from earlier periods.

The Colaton Raleigh Hoard, 900-600 BC

30: three torc-like sheet gold bracelets, two with simple backturned terminals, one with expanded terminals, and a fragment of scrap sheet gold - *Colaton Raleigh Common, Kingston.*

N.B Undoubtedly this hoard represents the most exciting and spectacular discovery of Bronze Age metalwork from Devon for over a century. It was found in March 1986 on Colaton Raleigh Common near Kingston in the east of the county. Whilst walking along a footpath that had been churned-up by horses hoofs, Nigel Hague noticed something glinting in the mud. Expecting it to be yet another brass cartridge case, for many are found in the area, discarded by Royal Marine Commandos whilst on training exercises, he realised that the object was buried in the ground with one end protruding. Careful digging with a penknife revealed a group of three shiny metal objects enclosed one inside the other. Although he didn't know what they were, Nigel suspected they were possibly very old, therefore he took them to EM.

John Allan, the museum's Curator of Antiquities, realized they probably belonged to the Bronze Age period, therefore transportation to the British Museum was arranged for a second opinion. Eventually the three bracelets, one unfinished, were confirmed as Late Bronze Age, being made of an alloy of gold, silver and copper. The East Devon District Coroner was informed who arranged for a Treasure Trove Inquest to be held on 9 July 1986 which was to be a joint inquest along with a hoard of 17th-century gold coins (see the Stuart chapter).

Meanwhile the County Archaeologist had arranged for archaeologists to excavate a small area of ground surrounding the find spot to determine whether any more artefacts remained - none were found. As the coroner was not satisfied he requested John Allan to arrange for the area to be searched by metal detectors. In particular he asked for Val MacRae, the finder of the aforementioned hoard of 17th-century gold coins, and three other members of TMDC.

A search was duly carried out, using a map supplied by John Allan, however, regrettably nothing was found other

The Bronze Age
Distribution of metal detector finds in Southern Devon

1. Bishopsteignton (**A**)
2. Broadhembury (**MA**)
3. Coffinswell (**MA**)
4. Colaton Raleigh (**A**)
5. Denbury (**MA**)
6. Elbury Cove (**A**)
7. Exeter (**A**)
8. Hennock (**MA**)
9. Newton Abbot (**A**)
10. New Barn (**H**)
11. River Teign, Hackney Marsh (**A**)
12. Stokeinteignhead (**MA**)
13. Tavistock (**A**)
14. Teigngrace (**A**)
15. Wilmington (**A**)

Key: **A** = artefact   **MA** = multiple artefact   **H** = hoard

than dozens of brass cartridge cases. Later it was learned that the four had been searching in the wrong place, due to a misinterpretation of the map. A few weeks later Val, accompanied by one member of TMDC and Nigel Hague, returned to the correct area for another search. Within a few minutes of starting searching, Val recovered a small fragment of worked gold, about 12.5-15cm deep, in the patch of ground dug by the archaeologists. Nothing else of interest was found. This case highlights that the metal detector has a place in the armoury of the modern archaeologist!

Initially archaeologists had thought the hoard represented a votive offering or the belongings of a chieftain: the discovery of the tiny piece of worked gold changed their view. The consensus now, is that the four pieces of the hoard denote a contemporary itinerate goldsmith's wares, who, for some reason, deposited them in the ground and failed to collect them. The British Museum have named these finds the 'Colaton Raleigh Hoard'.

At the Treasure Trove Inquest the hoard was declared Treasure Trove, and afterwards it was put on temporary display at the EM. In December 1986 the hoard was sent to the British Museum for assessment by an 'independent' valuation committee who decided that a monetary value of £5,000.00 was appropriate. Thankfully the British Museum said they didn't wish to acquire this important hoard for the nation, therefore EM purchased it, thereby assuring its final resting place was on public display in Devon.

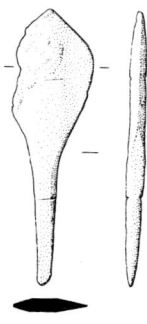

28

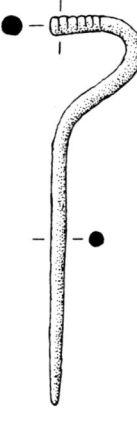

29

30

Chapter Two
The Iron Age

31

32

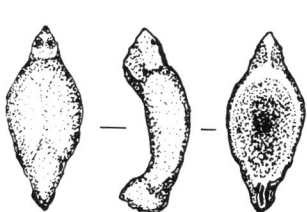

33

Like the rest of Early Iron Age Britain, Devon was populated by a mixture of indigenous Bronze Age folk and Celtic migrants. Precisely when the first Celts arrived isn't certain. However, it is known that over a period of many centuries they had spread across the European mainland and eventually reached the English Channel. Small-scale sporadic migration across the Channel probably occurred many years before and after 600 BC, with perhaps the occasional larger incursion.

It was around the 1st century BC that migration from Brittany escalated which resulted in a rapid rise in Devon's population. These Belgic colonists probably came ashore on Devon's southern beaches, and the majority occupied the land in the south and east, forming part of the Celtic Kingdom of Dumnonia which embraced the whole of what is now Cornwall, Devon and part of Somerset and Dorset. Compared to Celtic tribes in the rest of the country, little is known about the Dumnonii.

Few confirmed Early Iron Age habitation sites have been found in Devon, although traces of occupation have been discovered at Kes Torre on Dartmoor, Dainton, near Newton Abbot, Torquay's Kents Cavern, and Foales Arrishes in the east of the region.

A system of hillforts was built that encompassed Dartmoor. Some historians say these were to provide protection from hostile natives who still occupied the moors, but who these folk were isn't clear, for most of Dartmoor had supposedly been depopulated.

Many of these hillforts are extant, particularly in the south and east of the county. The most notable are Broadhembury's Hembury Fort, which is built on a Neolithic causewayed camp on a spur of the Blackdown Hills, and Milber Down near Newton Abbot, commanding a strategic position overlooking the River Teign and Dartmoor's southern slopes. Others are located at: Slapton, Stanborough, Denbury, Ugbrooke, Holne Chase, Woostan, Prestonbury, Cranbrook, Axemouth, Cadbury, Luppit, Membury, Musbury, Hawkesdown, Woodbury, Sidbury, Southleigh, Belbury, Sidmouth, Stockland, and perhaps Tiverton and Shobrooke.

It is believed by some, that Milber Down is not a true fort but more a series of ramparts that provided protection for livestock as well as its human inhabitants. Lesser camps existed at: Walls Hill (Torquay), Chelston (Torquay), Dawlish, Exminster, Bishopsteignton, Teignharvey, Berry Head, Dartington, Stoke Gabriel, and perhaps Cockington (Torquay) among many others.

COINS

Devon's Iron Age populace did not have their own coinage; it is probable that for the whole of the period they used a system of barter. However, towards the end of the Early Iron Age, iron currency- bars came into use, apparently confined mainly to the south and west of England. Few individual currency-bars have been found, although several hoards have. Undoubtedly they have been uncovered during agricultural or building work but were not recognised, for they resemble many other pieces of rusty iron which litter the ground.

The first recorded discovery of currency-bars in Devon, in the 1920s, was a hoard in Holne Chase Camp - no doubt others are secreted in other hillforts. The most important find of currency-bars from the county, and possibly the whole country, occured in early 1990. Whilst a TMDC member was searching near Daccombe he was informed by the farmer that a pile of rusty iron bars had been pulled up by the plough. These were recognised as being similar to currency bars, therefore the consultant archaeologist at Torquay Museum was informed. A joint investigation of the site was carried out by archaeologists from Exeter University's Archaeological Field Unit and TMDC, and a large encrusted mass of approximately 100 currency-bars was uncovered. At the time of writing, July 1994, these are still undergoing a conservation process at the EM conservation laboratory.

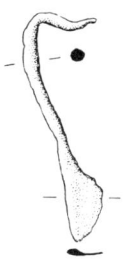

34

In Britain the first true coins, now known as 'staters', were made of gold and were brought into England in the late 2nd century BC by Belgic settlers. Later, around 75 BC, another type of stater, made of base silver, entered the country from the Channel Islands and North-West Gaul. These imported coins were in general circulation along with gold staters which were first struck in Britain c90 BC. Later still, silver and bronze staters, gold 'quarter staters', bronze 'potins', silver 'units' and 'half' and 'quarter-units' came into use.

35

All of the tribes other than the Dumnonii had their own coinage, numerous examples of which have been found, both by orthodox archaeology and casual methods. However, it is the metal detector that has contributed most to numismatic knowledge of this period: many new types and variants of Celtic coins have been discovered in other parts of the country. Why the Dumnonii didn't have their own coinage system isn't known, indeed numismatists suggest they probably didn't even use coins of other tribes. However, they certainly did, for examples have been found in Devon, albeit very few, at: Exeter, Mount Batten, Princetown and Holne Chase Camp. Hoards are scant, one being revealed at Mount Batten, one at Cotley Farm near the Somerset border two miles from Chard, and one from Axminster.

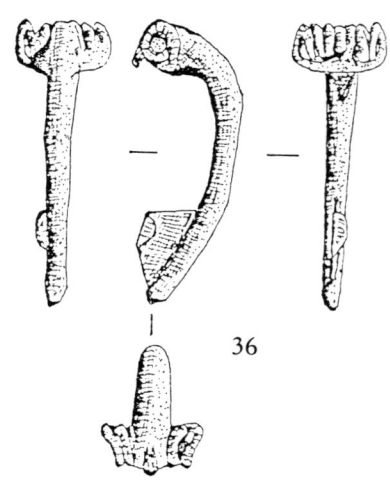

36

It is difficult to accept that the Dumnonii didn't use coinage to a greater degree. Why would Devon have been bypassed, particularly when Cornwall has produced a fair quantity of coins? Surely many more single coins and even hoards must exist in Devonshire's countryside awaiting discovery.

Silver coin
31: Iceni, quarter-unit, c10 BC-AD 60 - *Uffculme*.
   Obv. boar facing right.
   Rev. horse facing right.

The Iron Age

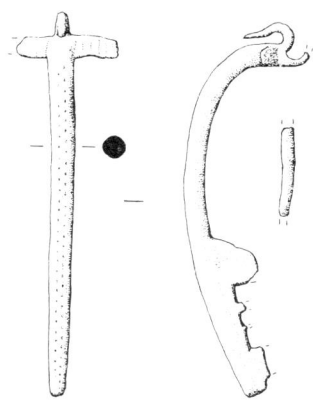

37

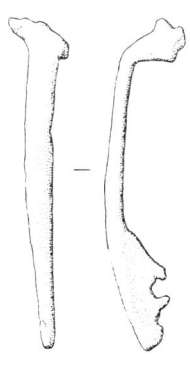

38

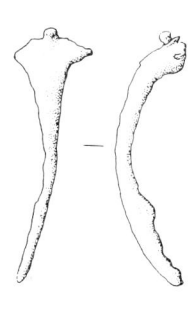

39

Billon coin

32: Armorican, stater, c75-50 BC - *River Teign, Hackney Marsh.* Obv. bust facing right. Rev. horse, boar below.

BROOCHES

Although brooches of the Bronze Age are rare (and unrecorded from southern Devon), Iron Age brooches are fairly ubiquitous nationwide. Copper-alloy brooches of this period were either cast, forged, or cast and forged; whatever, both had to be finished by hand. Iron brooches, however, were forged as the technique for casting in iron had yet to be invented.

The bulk of the earliest Iron Age brooches probably arrived in Britain during the Hallstatt period of the 6th century BC, although some may have filtered through before. Initially such brooches were formed from a single piece of wire bent into a simple bow which operated on the safety-pin principle. Infrequently the bows of brooches of this type have moulded or engraved decoration.

A particularly rare type of Iron Age brooch is the Upavon, which has been attributed to 6th-3rd century BC. Characteristically all have a bow with protruding lugs and hinge pin. Pierced lugs are a feature of some, which invariably held decorative rivets. Most are without any moulded ornamentation.

On the Continent and less so in Britain, the 4th and 3rd centuries BC saw the development of the La Tène I one-piece Bilateral Spring bow brooch which has a pair of wire multi-coils joined by a chord integral with the pin. The catch-plate end of the bow projects forwards and then laterally backwards and is invariably decorated direct or with an applied stud.

The La Tène I brooch probably remained current well into the 2nd century BC, but around 150 BC a new type evolved, the La Tène II, which carried through to the 1st century AD. This brooch, which is rare in Britain, is differentiated from the La Tène I by a further extension of the catch-plate end of the bow which is then clipped to the hump of the bow, and invariably the chord is hidden beneath the head. Lastly, we find the La Tène III Nauheim derivative brooch which came to Britain from Gaul early in the 1st century BC and remained current until c.AD 75. The bow, which may be circular or flat in cross-section, tapers to a narrow foot which has an integral triangular or trapezoid-shaped perforated or solid catch-plate. From the foot the bow slopes gently upwards and then drops sharply to the start of the four-coiled spring.

Concurrent with the La Tène III Nauheim derivative brooch was the Colchester Bow brooch brought to Britain from Gaul by the Belgics. The life of this type extended well into the 1st century AD's third quarter. It also has an integral sprung pin, although some later examples have hinge pins. Characteristically, chords are secured beneath a hook on top of the head. A similar brooch, but rarely found in Britain, and current until c.AD 50, is the Eye brooch which was conceived in what is now Germany.

Cast copper-alloy possible Upavon three-dimensional, brooch, 6th-3rd century BC

33: zoomorphic, perhaps a shrew or a mole, hinge pin lost, 37mm x 14mm - *Coffinwsell.*

The Iron Age
Distribution of metal detector finds in Southern Devon

1. Coffinswell (**A**)
2. Combeinteignhead (**A**)
3. Exeter (**MA**)
4. Haccombe (**A**)
5. Ipplepen (**MA**)
6. River Teign, Hackney Marsh (**C, MA**)
7. Stokeinteignhead (**MA**)
8. Uffculme (**C**)

Key: **C** = single coin   **A** = artefact   **MA** = multiple artefact

Forged copper-alloy La Tène III Nauheim derivative brooches, early 1st century BC - c.AD 75

34: fragmented, circular cross-section, abraded catch-plate, 47mm x 15mm - *Combeinteignhead.*

35: fragmented, tapered oval cross-section, abraded catch-plate, two coils of integral four-coil spring; remains of iron corrosion trapped between coils, perhaps from a contemporary attempt at replacing a lost pin, 41mm x 10mm - *Stokeinteignhead.*

Forged copper-alloy Bow brooch of indeterminate type, c50 BC-AD 75

36: an oddity which is midway between the La Tène III and the Colchester, integral seven-coil spring and chord, fragmented integral pin, 56mm x 18mm - *River Teign, Hackney Marsh.*

Forged copper-alloy Colchester brooches, c25 BC-AD 75

37: forward facing hook on head, remains of integral spring and pin, fragmented openwork catch-plate, two longitudinal bands of punched dots on bow, transverse bands of punched dots on wings, 75mm x 19mm - *Exeter.*

38: remains of forward facing hook on head, fragmented openwork catch-plate, 60.5mm x 12.5mm - *Exeter.*

39: remains of forward facing hook on head, 50mm x 15mm - *Stokeinteignhead.*

N.B. Nos.33 & 36 have no recorded parallel.

KNIFE OR RAZOR TERMINAL

Celtic iron triangular-bladed knives or razors with cast copper-alloy three-dimensional griffin, bird or lion-shaped terminals are relatively ubiquitous discoveries on Continental Roman sites. The nearest Celtic settlement to Britain where such artefactual evidence has been found is Wijster, Holland. From Britain, however, non-associated examples are extremely rare, although grave-goods in Late Iron Age burials have revealed several, e.g. Welwyn Garden City, Snailwell and Walmer. Their precise function is uncertain; culinary purposes or for shaving animal skins are the most probable. Examples have been recovered with remains of a wooden sheath attached to the blade.

Cast copper-alloy probable triangular-bladed knife or razor three-dimensional terminal, c50 BC-AD 250

40: zoomorphic, bird head, deep sunken eyes and gaping mouth, two transverse moulded grooves around the neck which comprise two integral flanges with iron corrosion trapped between, 29mm x 25mm- *Haccombe.*

40a: how No.38 may have looked when complete.

FIGURINES

Solid or hollow-cast three-dimensional zoomorphic or hominoid representations are a feature of some Celtic metalwork, e.g. figurines, utensil mounts, or terminals of torcs and bracelets. The precise function of the former isn't known; possibly they were purely ornaments or perhaps even deities.

Hollow-cast copper-alloy three-dimensional figurine, c50 BC - AD 50

41: zoomorphic, swimming duck holding a disc-shaped object in its beak - *Newton Abbot.*

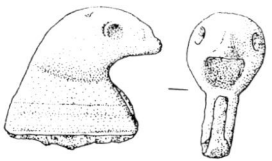

40

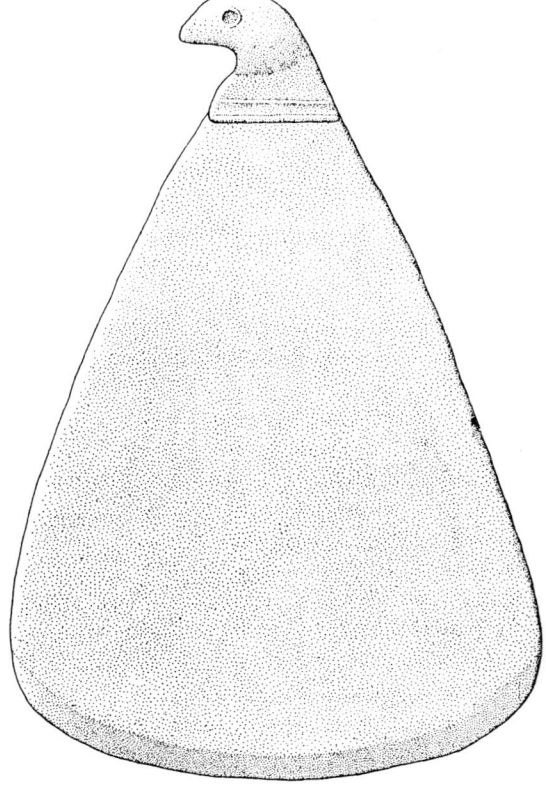

40a

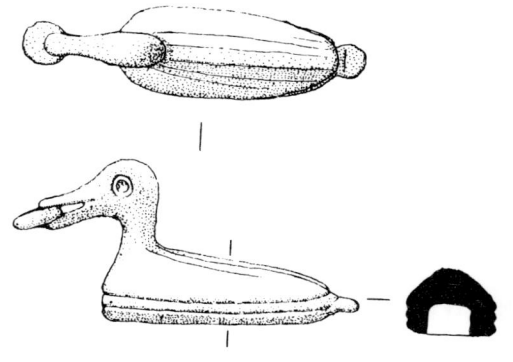

41

The Iron Age

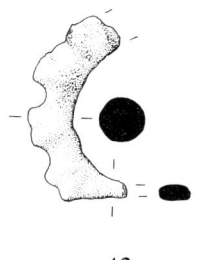

42

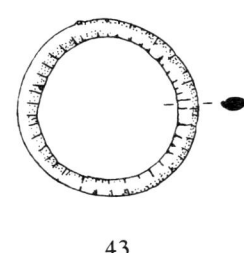

43

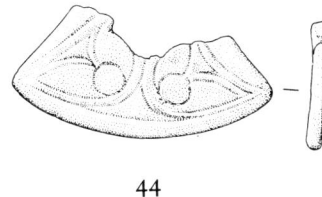

44

N.B. No.41 forms part of a small group of three-dimensional copper-alloy zoomorphic figurines from Milber Down hillfort excavated by archaeologists.

HORSE-HARNESS TRAPPINGS

Although metal horse-trappings were current in southern Britain during much of the late Iron Age it is the Belgic settlers of the 1st century BC - 1st century AD to whom most known examples are attributed. Such objects were either cast and/or forged from copper alloy, iron or combinations of both metals, and include: circular harness-rings, annular terret-rings, linchpins, bridle-bits, pendants and mounts. Characteristic of some terret-rings and mounts is ornate engraving or enamelling.

Cast copper-alloy probable terret ring, c1st century BC - 1st century AD

42 fragment, circular and oval cross-section, moulded bifid knops and transverse grooves, 35mm x 8.5mm - *Ipplepen*.

Cast copper-alloy possible harness-ring, c1st century BC - 1st century AD

43: annular, ovoid cross-section, moulded transverse grooves, D. 35mm - *River Teign, Hackney Marsh*.

Cast copper-alloy possible mount, c1st century BC - 1st century AD

44: fragmented, sub-triangular, engraved circles and curvilinear, 25.5mm x 49mm - *Ipplepen*.

Cast copper-alloy and forged iron possible horse-harness fitting, linchpin from a horse-drawn vehicle or a decorative mount from an iron receptacle such as a bucket, c100 BC-AD 50

45: annular, oval, moulded quatrefoil lateral knop with transverse grooves, iron corrosion sandwiched between both sides, four bands of engraved oblique lines and a wedge of cross-hatching on one side, 49mm x 44mm - *Stokeinteignhead*.

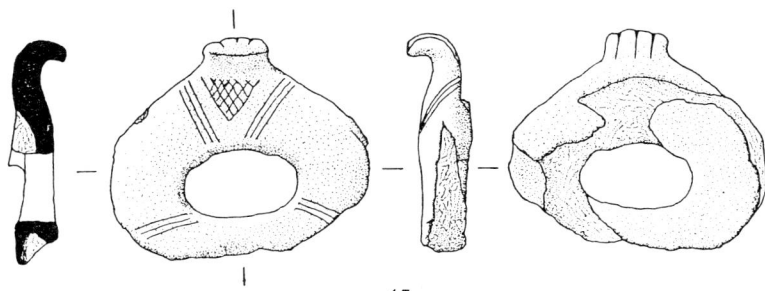

45

18　　　　　　　　　　　　　　　　　　　　　　　　　　　　　　　　　　*History Beneath Our Feet*

Chapter Three
The Romano-British Period

58

59

60

61

62

63

We know that Devon at the time of the Roman conquest of Britain was occupied by people of the Celtic Dumnonii tribe. History alludes that these inhabitants were not hostile to the Roman advance and indeed may have entered into an alliance with them. It is reasonable to accept that if the natives were friendly and offered no resistance it wouldn't have been neccessary to have large numbers of troops based throughout the region. The Second Augustan Legion established a fortress at Exeter around AD 50, this military occupation is thought to have ended c.AD 75, therefore Roman troops remained in Devon for approximately 25 years.

Traditional archaeology has proved that Exeter was a Roman garrison town and it is generally accepted that this was the most westerly of their military outposts in the south-west peninsula. Until the advent of the metal detector, archaeological and historical consensus was that the Romans had little influence on the inhabitants of the land that lay west of the River Exe. In the east four Roman villa sites have been discovered in the River Axe valley: Membury, Uplyme and two at Seaton; to date, no others have come to light in the county.

Archaeologists have also confirmed that the small riverside town of Topsham, some four kilometres downstream from Exeter, was a Roman settlement; sufficient building remains have been excavated to indicate that it may have been a small port or even a naval base. A Roman farmstead and foundations of a possible combined corn mill and bakehouse were found on the north-west outskirts of the present-day town.

Throughout Devon a small number of other occupation sites of this period have been located, including farmsteads and permanent forts, where various items of Roman material have been recovered, and a fair number of random non-associated objects, mainly coins, have turned up.

The existence of an engineered Roman road system connecting Exeter to Somerset and Dorset in the east, and to the coast at Axmouth, which was the southern terminus of the Fosse Way, is well proven. Topsham was linked by a Roman road to nearby Exeter, whilst to the north-west of Exeter, sections of Roman road have been discovered which probably ran on into Cornwall near Launceston. At North Tawton a Roman marching camp and a permanent fort have been revealed, both on the line of this road. Another Roman road is suspected of running from Exeter to North Devon.

It is has been established that a Roman road ran from Exeter to just north-west of Newton Abbot where possibly it forked near Whitehills, one branch turned east towards Newton Abbot, whilst the other may have continued south-west towards

Highweek. Some historians have said that at Teign Bridge another fork turned north-west towards Teigngrace. There is no conclusive evidence to prove whether or not these roads existed and if they did, whether or not they continued any further, where they led to and where they terminated. However, it is believed by some historians that from Highweek the south-westerly road ran on to Bridgetown (Totnes) on the River Dart, which was probably the lowest place this river could be safely forded. Local legend at Totnes still calls Harpers Hill, an ancient trackway that continues from the town's western boundary up Broomborough Hill's steep scarp, the Roman road. This implies that a Roman road continued from the ford and through Totnes in a westerly direction, perhaps to Mount Batten situated on the shore of Plymouth Sound.

Stonework purported to be Roman was found at Bowden House, which is known to date from Anglo-Saxon times, just outside Totnes on the Ashprington Road. It is possible that beneath the present house, or located nearby, are the remains of a substantial Roman building - perhaps a villa!

If the easterly Roman road terminated in the vicinity of Whitehills, surely there must be buried here, the remains of Roman buildings; however, no such archaelogical evidence has been found (although rumour has it a Roman building once stood near Teign Bridge) which implies that the road continued onwards to the coast at Torbay. Perhaps it went by way of the old turnpike road from Newton Abbot to Torquay via: Decoy, Kingskerswell, Whilborough, Kingsland Hill and then down Cockington valley to the sea at Livermead.

A more likely route would have been across Forde Marsh, through Milber Wood in line with Pinewalk to Milber Down hillfort and an adjacent Romano-British farmstead, and along the St Marychurch Road ridge to: Barton, Hele, Torre, and Torre Abbey Sands. Allegedly a Roman building was revealed (and hastily covered over again) during building excavations at the Centrax factory near St Marychurch Road. This story does match with confirmed archaeological Romano-British evidence at Milber Down, Teignharvey and Roccombe. Again it is interesting to note that local legend at Barton calls Barton Hill Road, the Roman road!

Undoubtedly both of the aforementioned routes from Whitehills to Torbay, and the one to Totnes, were ancient British trackways that must have been used by the Romans and may have been improved by them, however, there is no evidence to suggest major engineering work was ever carried out. Other Romano-British habitation sites have been archaeologically proven at: Dartington, Stoke Gabriel, Walls Hill and Kents Cavern, Torquay. Likewise, it is probable that existing British trackways were used to serve them.

Where the Roman road crossed the River Teign at Teign Bridge there originally must have been a ford, nowadays it is spanned by a stone-built bridge. When this was in the course of construction it became apparent that a number of bridges had crossed the river at this point. Ancient timbers were discovered at a very low level and these were thought to be of Roman origin. It appears that no artefactual or numismatic evidence has ever been found to support the view that originally a Roman bridge stood here, or indeed that the road was Roman, that is until the coming of the metal detector!

The Romano-British Period

69
70
71
72

Regarding the possible route from Teign Bridge to Teigngrace, perusal of modern and old Ordnance Survey maps suggests a Roman road may have been built as far as, at the very least, Bovey Tracey. This route is logical for such a road and the intention may have been to join the Exeter/North Tawton Roman road which lay to the north.

An ancient British trackway from Haldon, which connected with the St Marychurch Road ridge, crossed the River Teign between Hackney on the northern shore and Buckland on the southern shore, however, due to dredging over the years and the construction of Hackney Canal, the ford's precise location is lost. Detector users have spent many hundreds of hours wallowing in the deep sticky mud of Hackney Marsh searching for evidence of Romano-British use, which they have found. Allegedly, large dressed flag-stones were once visible, evidently laid by the Romans to facilitate crossing.

After invading the Kentish coast it is probable that the Romans later sailed along the southern coast and established strategic bases. Eventually they would have discovered the: Axe, Otter, Exe, Teign, Dart and Tamar rivers (they may have already known of them) where contact would have been made with the local Dumnonii. After their initial reconnaissance forays, trade may have started which would have led to permanent bases being set up in the river valleys. This is of course conjecture, but nonetheless a possibility in the absence of hostilities with the local inhabitants. If correct, the Romans would have soon found that the land was extremely fertile and therefore ideal for farming. Likewise, it wouldn't have taken them very long to learn of the area's substantial clay deposits, suitable for tile- and pottery-making. Various types of stone were available particularly: slate, granite, sandstone and limestone. Beer, in the east of the county, is famous for its quarries which are Roman in origin, no doubt they worked others. Copper and tin were present on Dartmoor, and although unproven, it is a possibility that this was mined.

The accepted theory on the Roman conquest of Britain is they achieved it by constructing roads. However, an exciting alternative is suggested by Raymond Selkirk in his book *The Piercebridge Formula*, in which he states that he has proved it was achieved by the use of water transport, utilising pound-locks and dams, and not by road! Roads were built much later, after an area had been conquered. This point of view fits in with the South Devon enigma.

Devon is well blessed with rivers, more than any other English county - many of them would probably have been navigable for much greater distances in Roman times, particularly if the pound-lock and dam system was utilised. Some of these rivers and their tributaries would have provided convenient routes for Roman craft to penetrate deep into the hinterland - a careful search of their banks may reveal evidence of former pound-locks and dams.

Sufficient Romano-British metalwork has been retrieved by metal detectives in the Stokeinteignhead/Roccombe district to suggest the existence of at least four habitation sites, one of which has since been confirmed by an aerial crop-mark. This area has good access to the River Teign and the sea which presumably were then prolific fishing grounds. Evidence of oyster and cockle shell scatters are common, an indication of early human occupation, frequently representing the exsistence of a midden.

The terrain in this locality is best described as tortuous, making the building of an access road very difficult. Why bother when an easier route was close to hand, i.e. Arch Brook that flows into the River Teign.

To the north, lying between the Teign and Exe rivers, runs a band of very fertile land forming the slopes of the Haldon and Little Haldon Hills, stretching from Exminster in the north-east to Chudleigh in the west. Very little positive evidence of Romano-British occupation has been revealed in this region, with the exception of the Exeter/Whitehills Roman road in the west and a possible farmstead at Exminster. The drought of 1984 revealed an Iron Age/Romano-British crop-mark between Teignmouth and Bishopsteignton. This site had been searched by metal detectives on several occasions prior to the discovery of the crop-mark and nothing was found that could be confirmed as Iron Age or Romano-British. The drought showed up similar Iron Age/Romano-British crop-marks near Dawlish. Rumour has it that fragments of tiles thought to be Roman were found at Hackney during building construction work on the Passage House Inn, and a number of allegedly Roman objects were found in recent years at Sandygate near Kingsteignton. Land in the vicinity of Cockwood on the Exe estuary is slowly surrendering evidence of Romano-British occupation.

Much of the Romano-British metalwork found in the Hackney Marsh mud is attributed to the 1st century AD. Some of the coins are in excellent condition with very little wear which suggests they may have been deposited without being in circulation for any great length of time. The two brooches are also in superb condition which implies a short life in use. One of the Teign Bridge coins is 2nd century AD and two are 4th century AD and all three are fairly abraded, an indication that they had been in circulation for a long time. This suggests that the Hackney Marsh crossing-place was used by the native population long before the Romans built their bridge, and probably the road, at Teign Bridge. The Teign Bridge brooch, which is late 1st century AD, does appear to disprove this hypothesis but is not conclusive as brooches were sometimes handed down from generation to generation. If the Romans had been using the Hackney ford satisfactorily for many years to cross the River Teign why did they go to the trouble of building a road and a bridge at Teign Bridge? There must be a good reason which, as yet, is not understood, but it implies that there must have been something of extreme importance in the Newton Abbot area or beyond.

All of the Coffinswell Romano-British metalwork finds, as well as those from Haccombe, could well be associated with the Romano-British farmstead on nearby Milber Down. However, it is probable there was a Romano-British settlement in the immediate vicinity of Coffinswell.

It can be quite rightly argued that the finding of a relatively small number of Roman coins and Romano-British metal artefacts over such an area is not conclusive proof of a great number of habitation sites existing. However, the use of metal detectors by responsible people has proved beyond doubt that, in particular, the land between the River Dart and River Exe in Roman times supported a much higher population than previously thought.

73

74

75

The Romano-British Period

COINS

Roman coins were not struck in Britain before the very last few years of the 3rd century AD when Carausius the usurper established a mint at London and another at an unknown place, until then all coins were Imperial issues, mainly from Rome. London became an official Roman mint after Carausius' rebellion was defeated and remained in use until AD 325. Unofficial coins were struck in Britain on several occasions throughout the occupation.

Roman coin denominations are as follows - 'Gold: aureus, originally 1/60 lb, discontinued AD 324; solidus, 1/72 lb from AD 312, the 's' of the S.S.D. Silver: antoninianus, originally 1? denarii in AD 214 (later debased to bronze); argenteus, a revived denarius; denarius, originally 10 then 16 asses (25 to the aureus), later debased, the 'd' in S.S.D.; quinarius, ? denarius or 8 asses, later debased; siliqua, 1/24 solidus. Copper alloy: As, early currency unit, reduced in size and equal to 1/16 denarius in Imperial times; sestertius, four asses or Y denarius; centenionalis, replaced the depleted follis in AD 346; dupondius, 2 asses or X denarius; follis, silver-washed, 1/5 argenteus, c.AD 290; quadrans, Y As or 1/64 denarius; semis, ? As or 1/32 denarius'.

Little evidence has been found to endorse the hypothesis that the old turnpike road from Newton Abbot to Torquay was a route used by the Romans, other than a large hoard of Roman copper-alloy coins from Kingskerswell Down in 1838 (the fate of which isn't recorded), a single Roman copper-alloy coin found in Kingkerswells' Fore Street before the advent of the metal detector, and in 1985 two Roman copper-alloy coins found near the village. Further on towards the sea Roman copper-alloy coins have turned up at Whilborough, whilst Cockington produced a single Roman copper-alloy coin and two of base silver.

Random finds of Roman copper-alloy coins have been made over the years along the St Marychurch Road route from Whitehills to the coast at Torbay, and discoveries of Roman coins by members of TMDC have added more evidence of considerable Romano-British use. Nestling in the valleys to the north-east and lying between the St Marychurch Road ridge and the River Teign are the villages of: Combeinteignhead, Stokeinteignhead, Ringmore and Shaldon, the shrunken village of Haccombe and the hamlets of Roccombe and Netherton. A small band of metal detectives have been engaged in research and fieldwalking in these areas for some years, and their patience has been rewarded with the discovery of a fair number of Roman copper-alloy coins and a few of silver. To the south-west of the St Marychurch Road ridge lies Coffinswell Village which has produced one Roman silver coin and several of copper-alloy.

Roman coins have been picked up in fields bordering Harpers Hill at Totnes and at other locations around the town over the years, and some years ago a small hoard of Roman copper-alloy coins was found by a walker near Kings Ash, Paignton. They were fused together and were probably a casual loss from a purse or similar container rather than a deliberately concealed hoard. Apparently, hoards of Roman copper-alloy coins were found many years ago at Haldon Belvedere, Hennock and Ashburton. Many Roman copper-alloy coins have been found by visitors in the vicinity of Brixham's Berry Head, where there is evidence of Romano-British occupation, over a period of some two centuries - occasionally they still turn up here.

The Romano-British Period
Distribution of metal detector finds in Southern Devon

1. Abbotskerswell (**A**)
2. Alphington (**C, A**)
3. Axminster (**MC, MA**)
4. Bicton (**MC, MA**)
5. Bishopsteignton (**C**)
6. Cockington (**MC**)
7. Cockwood (**MC**)
8. Colaton Raleigh (**MC, MA**)
9. Coffinswell (**MC, MA**)
10. Combeinteignhead (**C, A**)
11. Dainton (**C**)
12. Denbury (**MC, MA**)
13. Exeter (**A**)
14. Exwick (**MC**)
15. Goodrington Beach, Paignton (**MC, A**)
16. Haccombe (**MC, MA**)
17. Halwell (**A**)
18. Honiton (**MC**)
19. Ide (**A**)
20. Ipplepen (**MA**)
21. Kingskerswell (**C, MA**)
22. Lympstone (**C**)
23. Mamhead (**C**)
24. Musbury (**MC**)
25. Newton Abbot (**MC**)
26. Newton Poppleford (**C**)
27. Offwell (**A**)
28. Otterton (**C, A**)
29. Paignton (**C**)
30. Paignton Beach (**MC**)
31. Plymouth (**MC, MA**)
32. Ringmore (**MC, MA**)
33. River Teign, Teign Bridge (**MC A**)
34. River Teign, Hackney Marsh (**MC, MA**)
35. River Teign, Salcombe Dip (**MC**)
36. Shaldon Beach (**HC, MC**)
37. Stokeinteignhead (**MC, MA**)
38. Stoneycombe (**C,A**)
39. Teignmouth (**C**)
40. Thorverton (**C**)
41. Uffculme (**C, MA**)
42. Whilborough (**C**)
43. Wolborough, Newton Abbot (**A**)

Key: **C** = single coin **MC** = multiple coin **HC** = hoard of coins
       A = artefact **MA** = multiple artefact

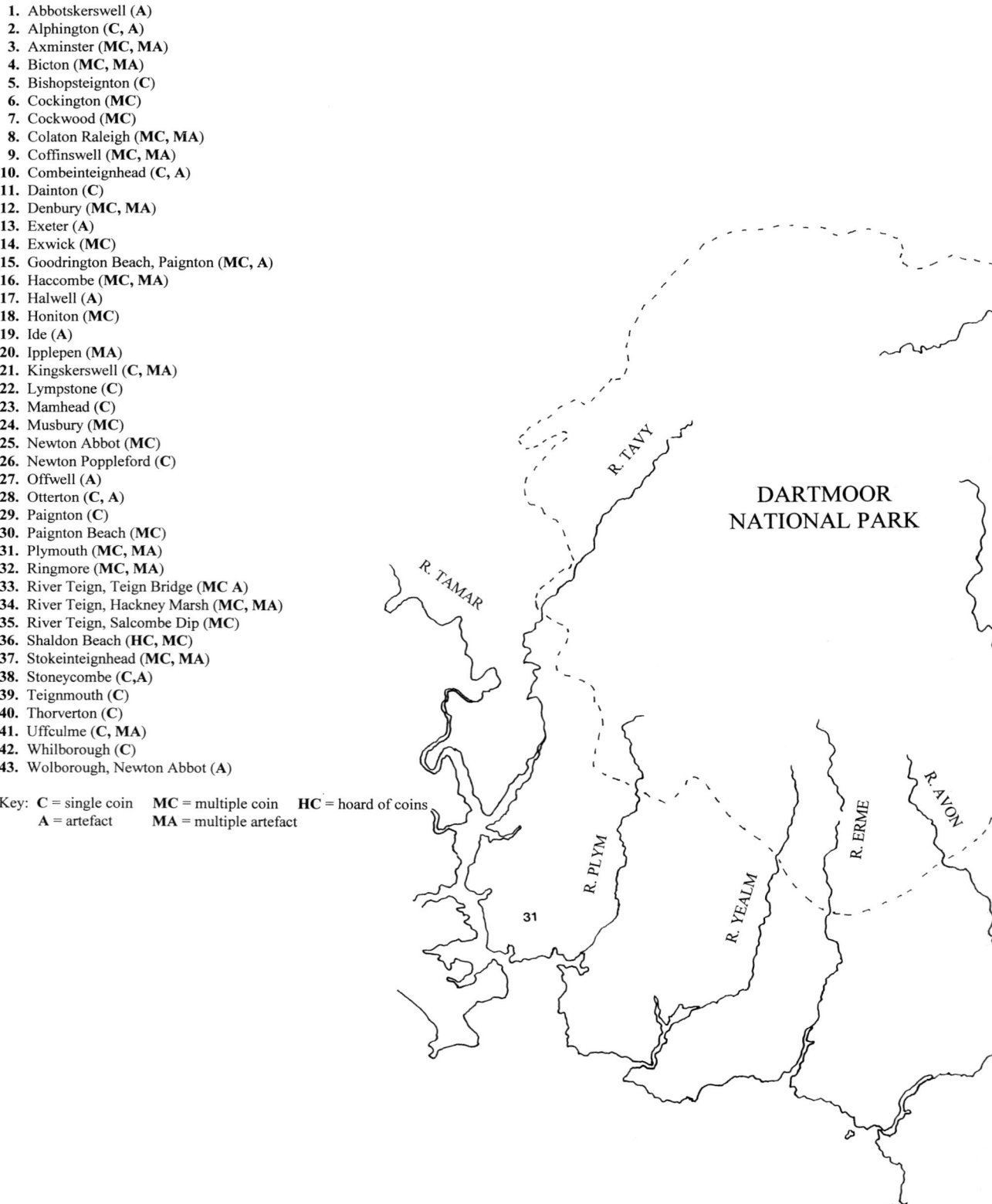

R. EXE
R. CULM
R. CLYST
R. OTTER
R. AXE
R. TEIGN
R. DART

41
40
14 13
19 2
26
18 27
3
24
22
4 8
28
23
7
33 5 35 39
34 32 36
25 10
16 37
43
12 1
21 9
20 11 38
42
6
29 30
15
17

N

Scale = 1:316,000 (approx.)

5 miles
8 kilometres

Based upon Ordnance Survey mapping with the permission of the
Controller of Her Majesty's Stationery Office, © Crown copyright.

Two copper-alloy coins and one silver Roman coins were recovered from the River Teign at Teign Bridge which were probably deposited as votive offerings before crossing the river, a common practice that continued long after conversion to Christianity. This superstitious rite of yesteryear is a bonus for both archaeologists and metal detectives, for it often provides primary or secondary evidence of past cultures. A fair number of Roman copper-alloy coins have been extricated from the mud at Hackney Marsh; it is reasonable to assume that some of these can also be attributed to votive offerings.

Evidence that ancient saltings existed on the River Teign's eastern bank at Salcombe Dip has been substantiated by the finding of Roman copper-alloy coins on the foreshore. Diligent searching has revealed that another salting may have existed further upstream from Salcombe Dip, on the same side of the river, where a number of Roman copper-alloy coins have been found.

In the mid 1970s a hoard of 114 Roman copper-alloy coins was recovered from Shaldon Beach at the mouth of the River Teign, no container was found. It is estimated that the number of coins would have been about 600, regrettably the majority of which were a totally unrecognizable heap of green sludge. Whether these were deliberately concealed is doubtful, for they could represent a loss from a ship wrecked whilst trying to negotiate the treacherous current, but could be a votive offering distributed by a landfall. Tidal currents may have deposited them all in one spot where they became trapped.

For centuries Torbay has been considered by seafarers to be one of the safest anchorages on England's southern coast, protected from all but the strongest easterly and south-easterly winds, with its gently sloping sands ideal for beaching ships. There is no reason to suspect it was any different in Roman times. Evidence found on these beaches supports the hypothesis that the Romans almost certainly came ashore at Paignton and Goodrington, or their ships were wrecked here, for copper-alloy coins of this period have turned up in fair numbers. There are reports of Roman copper-alloy coins from Livermead Beach and Torre Abbey Sands, found by eyes only.

Other locations which have produced Roman silver or copper-alloy coins for metal detectives are: Newton Abbot, Dainton, Ipplepen, Denbury, Uffculme, Axminster, Musbury, Exwick, Mamhead, Thorverton, Bicton, Colaton Raleigh, Exmouth, Lympstone, Honiton, and Newton Poppleford.

What is noticeable about the finds of Roman coins in the southern part of Devon, which are few compared to other parts of the country, is the high proportion of silver. It will be interesting to see if this distribution pattern continues, and if it does, what conclusions can be drawn. A larger military presence than previously thought would have injected a high proportion of silver coins into the local economy. This, coupled with ground acidity possibly accounting for the scarcity of copper-alloy coins, is perhaps the reason. It is also noteworthy that Byzantine copper-alloy coins are appearing, so far coming from Paignton Beach and Cockwood. Whether these are contemporary losses is at present unknown, however, there is a strong possibility they are.

The Romano-British Period 27

Silver coins

46: C. Scribonius, c154 BC, denarius - *Coffinswell*.
    Obv. Roma right.
    Rev. Dioscuri horsemen galloping right.
47: M. Porcius Cato, 93-1 BC, quinarius *Honiton*
    Obv. bust right, ROMA behind, M . CATO.
    Rev. Victory seated right, VICTRIX.
48: Augustas, 8 BC, denarius - *Cockwood*.
    Obv. laureate bust right.
    Rev. Caius Caesar galloping right; legionary eagle between two standards in background, AVGUST.
49: Nero, AD 64-5, denarius - *Newton Abbot*.
    Obv. bust right, NERO CAESAR AUGUSTUS.
    Rev. Concord seated left with Patera, CONCORDIA AUGUSTA.
50: Nerva, AD 96-8, denarius - *Stokeinteignhead*.
    Obv. laureate head right, IMP . NERVA CAES AVG . P . M . TR . POT.
    Rev. sacrificial implements, COS . III . PATER PATRIAE.
51: Trajan, AD 98-117, denarius - *Denbury*.
    Obv. laureate and draped bust right, IMP . TRAIANO AVG . GER . DAC . P . M . TR . P . COS . VI . P . P.
    Rev. Pax enthroned left, holding a branch in right hand and transverse sceptre in left hand, kneeling Dacian in front, S . P . Q . R . OPTIMO PRINCIPI.
52: Trajan, AD 98-117, denarius - *Dainton*.
    Obv. laureate and draped bust right, IMP . CAES . NER . TRAIANO OPTIMO AVG . GER . DAC.
    Rev. Mars advancing right, P . M . TR . P . COS . VI . P . P . S . Q . R.
53: Hadrian, AD 117-38, denarius - *Denbury*.
    Obv. laureate head right, HADRIANVS AVGVOTVS P . P.
    Rev. seated figure, COS III.
54: Hadrian, AD 128-38, denarius - *Musbury*.
    Obv. laureate head right, HADRIANVS AVG . COS . III . P . P.
    Rev. Tellus standing left holding plough handle and rake: in ground right two corn ears, TELLVS STABIL.
55: Sabina, wife of Hadrian, denarius - *Denbury*.
    Obv. diademed and draped bust right, SABINA AVGUSTA HADRIANI AVG . P . P.
    Rev. Pudicitia standing, PVDICITIA.
56: Antoninus, Pius, AD 138-61, denarius - *Denbury*.
    Obv. laureate head right, ANTONINVS AVG . PIVS P . P . IMP . II.
    Rev. Fortuna standing right, TR . POT . XIX . COS . IIII.
57: Faustina, wife of Antoninus Pius, denarius - *Combeinteignhead*.
    Obv. draped bust right, DIVA FAVSTINA.
    Rev. Juno standing left with sceptre, AETERNITAS.
58: Marcus Aurelius, AD 161-80, denarius - *Denbury*.
    Obv. laureate bust right, M . ANTONINVS AVG . ARM . PARTH . MAX.
    Rev. Pax with branch and cornucopiae, TR . P . XX . IMP . IIII . COS III.
59: Faustina Junior, wife of Marcus Aurelius, denarius - *River Teign, Teign Bridge*.
    Obv. draped bust right, AVG . PII . AVG . FIL.

Rev. Spes standing right holding flower and raising skirt, AVGVSTI PII FIL.
60: Lucius Verus, AD 161-9, denarius - *Stokeinteignhead*.
Obv. bare bust right, IMPI . VERVS AVG.
Rev. Providence standing left, holding globe and cornucopiae, PROV . DEOR . TR . P . II . COS . II.
61: Commodus, AD 177-92, denarius - *Stokeinteignhead*.
Obv. laureate and draped bust right, IMP . CAES . L . AVREL . COMMODVS GERM . SARM.
Rev. Salus standing left, feeding serpent arising from altar, TR . POT . II . COS.

62: Gordian III, AD 238—44, antoninianus - Thorverton.
Obv. radiate and draped bust right, IMP . CAES . M . ANT . GORDIANVS AVG.
Rev. Pax standing left, PM TRP II COS PP.
63: Gordian III, AD 238-44, antoninianus - *Cockwood*.
Obv. radiate and draped bust right, IMP GORDIANVS PIVS FEL AVG.
Rev. Jupiter standing left, IOVI STATORI.
64: Gordian III, AD 238-44, antoninianus - *Honiton*.
Obv. radiate and draped bust right, IMP. CAES. M. ANT. GORDIANVS AVG.
Rev. Jupiter standing left, holding thunderbolt and sceptre; at feet left, small figure of Gordian. IOVI CONSERVATORI.

Copper-alloy coins
65: Claudius, AD 41-54, dupondius - River Teign, Hackney Marsh.
Obv. bare head left, TI . CLAVDIVS CAESAR AVG . P . IMP.
Rev. Ceres seated left, holding ear of corn, CERES AVGVSTA
66: Claudian copy, AD 41-54, dupondius - River Teign, Hackney Marsh.
Obv. bare head left
Rev. standing figure left.
67: Claudian copy, AD 41-54, dupondius - River Teign, Hackney Marsh.
Obv. bare head left.
Rev. abraded.
68: Nero, AD 54-68, dupondius, River Teign, Hackney Marsh.
Obv. laureate head right, IMP . NERO CAESAR AUG . P MAX . TR . P . P. P.
Rev. (?) Security seated right.
69: Trajan, AD 98-117, dupondius - *Stokeinteignhead*.
Obv. laureate and curiasse bust right.
Rev. standing figure left.
70: Hadrian, AD 117-38, as - *Stokeinteignhead*.
Obv. laureate head right, HADRIANVS[...] .
Rev. Emporer & Felicitas clasping hands.
71: Hadrian, AD 117-38, sestertius - *Axminster*.
Obv. laureate bust right.
Rev. Hadrian galloping right, raising right hand.
72: Antoninus Pius, AD 138-61, sestertius - *Denbury*.
Obv. laureate bust right, ANTONINVS AVG . PIVS P .P.
Rev. Emperor standing sacrificing at tripod altar, VOTASVSCEP DECENN III.
73: Marcus Aurelius, AD 161-80, dupondius - *Denbury.*

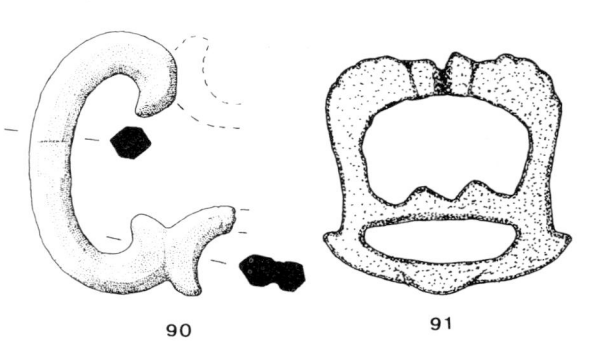

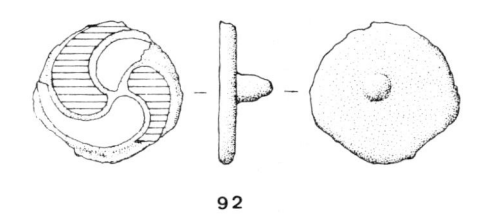

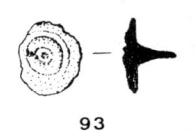

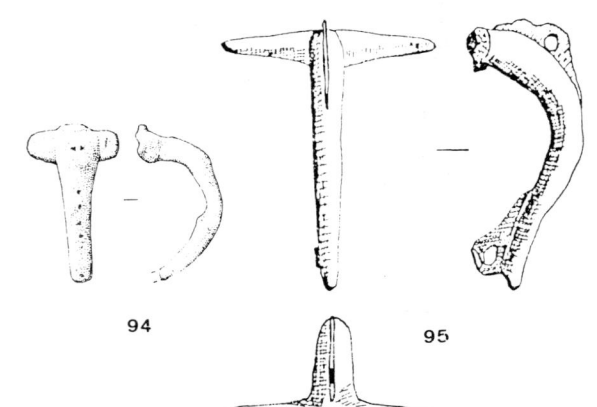

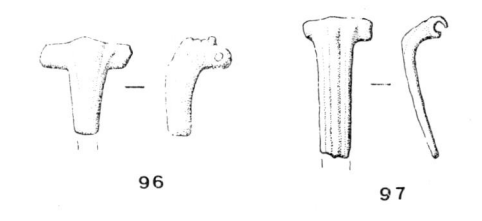

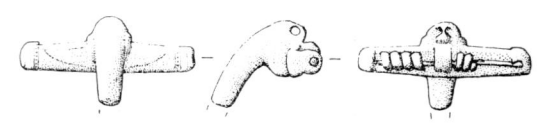

The Romano-British Period

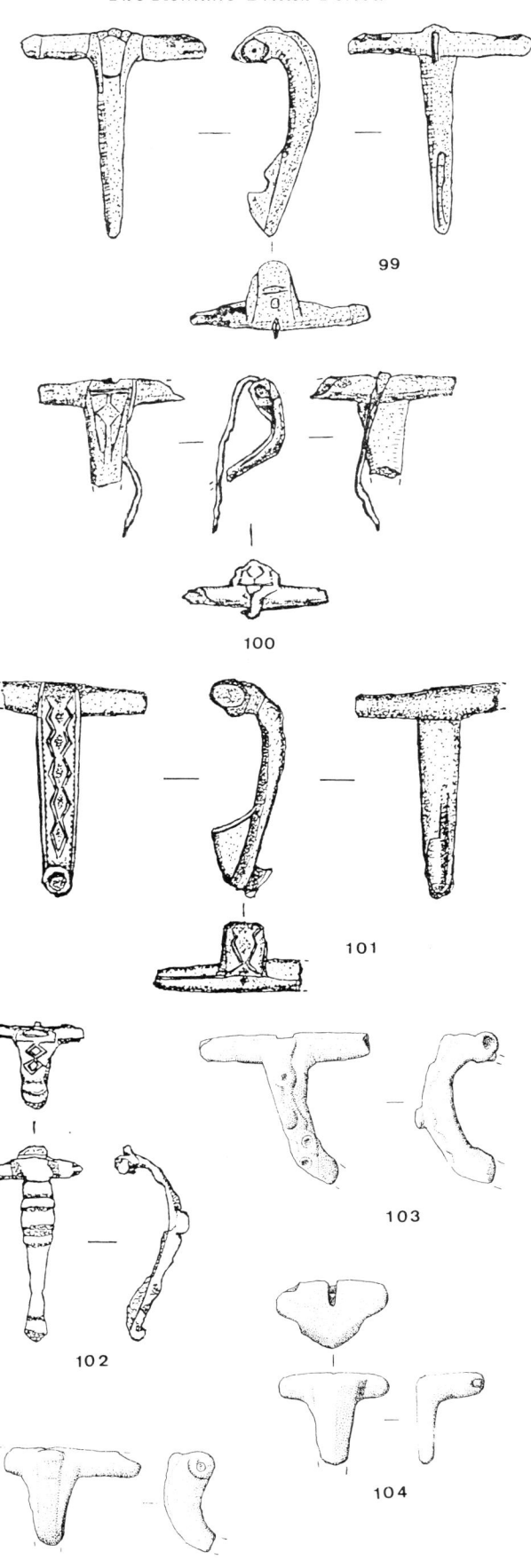

Obv. radiate bust right, M ANTONINVS AVG TRP[...] .
Rev. Roma seated left on cuirass, IMP . VI . COS . III . S.

74: Lucilla, wife of Lucius Verus, sestertius - *Denbury*.
Obv. draped bust right, LUCILLAE AVG. ANTONINI AVG . F.
Rev. Vesta standing left, holding simpulum and palladium, altar at feet, VESTA S . C.

75: Commodus, AD 180-92, sestertius - *Denbury*.
Obv. laureate bust right, M . COMMODVS ANTONINVS AVG . PIVS.
Rev. Felicity standing left, III . TR . P . VIII . IMP . VI . COS . IIII . P . P . S . C.

76: Philip II, AD 247-9, sestertius - *Newton Poppleford*
Obv. bare-headed and draped bust right, M. IVL. PHILIPPVS CAES.
Rev. Philip II standing left, holding spear and globe, PRINCIPI IVVENT.

77: Gallienus, AD 253-68, antoninianus - *Mamhead*.
Obv. radiate cuirasse bust right, GALLIENVS AVG.
Rev. Peace standing left, PAX AVG.

78: Victorinus, AD 268-70, antoninianus - *Shaldon Beach*.
Obv. laureate and draped bust right, IMP . C . VICTORINVS P . F . AVG.
Rev. Pax standing left, PAX AVG.

79: Victorinus, AD 268-70, antoninianus - *Shaldon Beach*.
Obv. radiate bust right, IMP . C . VICTORINVS P . F . AVG.
Rev. Salus standing left, feeding from patera, a serpent rising from an altar, SALVS AUG.

80: Galerius, AD 305-11, follis - *Musbury*.
Obv. laureate head right, MAXIMIANVS NOB . CAES.
Rev. Sol standing left, GENIO POPVLI ROMANI.

81: Constantine I, the Great, AD 307-37, reduced follis - Cockington.
Obv. laureate and cuirasse bust right, IMP . CONSTANTINVS P . F . AVG.
Rev. Sol standing with right arm outstretched and holding globe in left hand, SOLI INVICTO COMITI.

82: Constantine I, the Great, AD 307-37, Ae3 - *Exwick*.
Obv. laureate and draped bust right, CONSTANTINVS MAX . AVG.
Rev. two soldiers standing, one vexillum, GLORIA EXERCITVS SMNB.

83: Constantine I, the Great, AD 307-37, Ae3/4 - *Exwick*.
Obv. laureate head right, CONSTANTINVS AVG.
Rev. camp-gate surmounted by two turrets, PROVIDENTTIAE AVGG.

84: Crispus, Caesar, AD 317-26, Ae3 - *Haccombe*.
Obv. laureate and cuirasse bust right, CRISPVS NOB .CAES.
Rev. Altar, VOTIS XX . BEATA . TRANVILLITAS.

85: Constantius II, AD 337-61, Ae3/4 - *River Teign, Hackney Marsh*.
Obv. lauriate and cuirassed bust right, FL . IVL . CONSTANTIVS NOB . C.
Rev. two soldiers standing either side of two standards, **GLORIA EXERCITVS.**

86: **Constans, AD 346-50, Ae centenionalis - River Teign,** *Hackney Marsh.*
   Obv. diademed, draped and cuirassed bust left, D . N . CONSTANS P . F . AVG.
   Rev. soldier advancing right, dragging young barbarian from hut beneath tree, FEL . TEMP . REPARATIO.
87: Valens, AD 364-78, Ae3 - *River Teign, Teign Bridge.*
   Obv. diademed, draped and cuirassed bust right, D . N . VALENS P . F . AVG.
   Rev. Victory advancing left, SECVRITAS REIPVBLICAE.
88: Valens, AD 364-78, Ae3 - Shaldon Beach.
   Obv. diademed, draped and cuirassed bust right, D . N . VALENS P . F . AVG.
   Rev. Victory advancing left, SECVRITAS REIPVBLICAE.
89: **Part of a hoard of 114 Roman copper-alloy coins -** *Shaldon Beach.*

BUCKLES

It is generally accepted that buckles were brought to Britain by the Romans, whose troops wore them as functional parts of their uniform. Undoubtedly buckles formed part of their horse-harness accoutrements as well. Later, buckles became more widespread among the civilian populace, on horse-harness and personal-costume girdles and other straps. Most buckles of this period are made of cast copper alloy or forged iron, some of which have gilt, silver or tin applied-surface decoration.

Types current range from simple plain D-shaped loops, ornate moulded D-shaped loops and rectangular or sub-rectangular loops. Rectangular or sub-rectangular buckles invariably have knops on two or even four of the corners. A feature of later Roman buckles is zoomorphic representation, particularly dolphins or horses as part of the frame or knops on the front edge. Tongues in many cases are somewhat similar to those of much later periods though often they are very robust and ornate. Buckle-plates invariably are decorated with engraving, punchwork, embossing or openwork and are either integral or separate, whilst some buckles are attached direct to the strap.

Cast copper-alloy buckles, possibly military
90: **1st-4th century AD, fragmented, sub-D-shaped, hexagonal cross-section, involute terminals, 40mm x 52mm -** *Combeinteignhead.*
91: **4th-5th century AD, much abraded, involuted terminals, conjoined zoomorphic heads, two hinge-bars integral with the loop, 48mm x 47mm -** *Stokeinteignhead.*

MOUNTS

Decorative mounts of the Romano-British period are classified into four groups according to the method of attaching to the primary object, viz: soldered flat back, integral rivet/s, projecting pointed stud or studs, and integral shank with a lateral plate. Some mounts were functional as well as ornamental. Heads are found in a variety of shapes, e.g: circular, rectangular, elliptical, hexagonal or representational, and may be flat, umbonate or three-dimensional. Enamel applied-surface decoration is commonplace. The main metal of manufacture seems to be cast copper alloy, though it is reasonable to assume that gold or silver was current. Likewise, sheet fabrication was

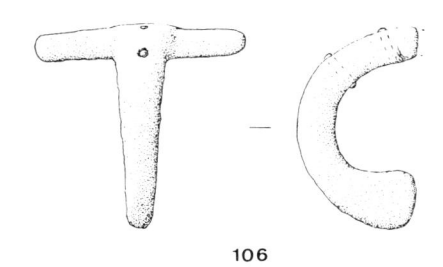

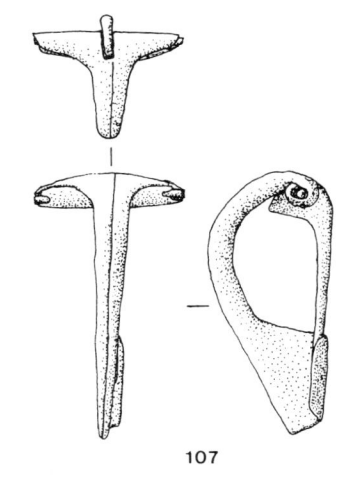

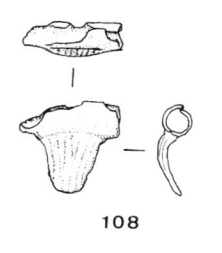

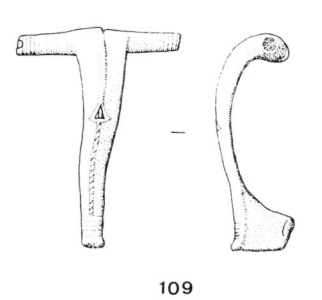

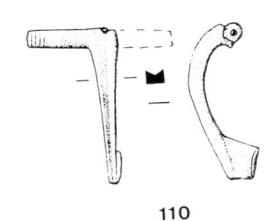

The Romano-British Period 31

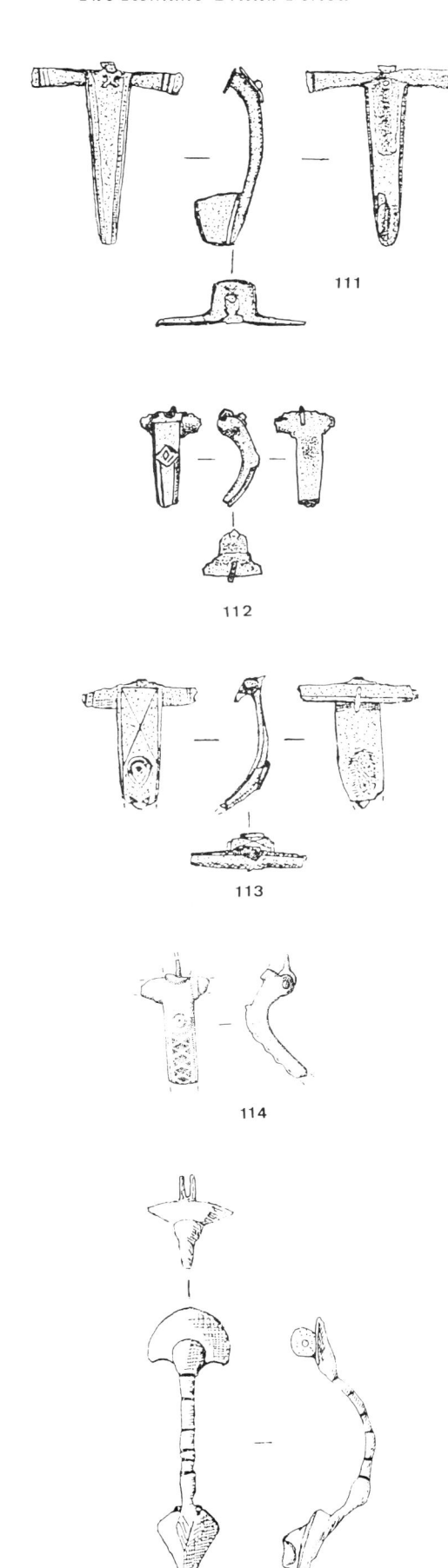

probably used also. Known applications for mounts were: personal costume leatherwork, wheeled vehicle metalwork and woodwork, metal or leather utensils and receptacles or walls of buildings.

Cast copper-alloy stud-like mounts, c1st-4th century AD
92: circular, slightly abraded perimeter, integral projecting (?) abraded pointed stud on rear, blue and white enamelled triskele, 10mm x 29mm - *Halwell*.
93: circular, abraded perimeter, pointed stud, moulded concentric circles, 10mm x 14mm - *Stokeinteignhead*.

BROOCHES

Types of brooch current in Roman Britain fall into three main categories: Bow, Penannular and Plate - with many sub-divisions. Some were imported from the Continent whilst others were produced by native British craftsmen. Copper alloy was the chief metal employed, followed by iron and silver and occasionally gold, however, examples of the latter are rare. Likewise, ferrous specimens are nowadays uncommon due to their poor survival rate.

Iron brooches and early one-piece types were forged, whilst all other copper-alloy forms were cast or cast and then forged or cut from sheet metal, all of which were finished by hand. Elaborate moulded, engraved, carved or punched ornamentation is commonplace as is gilding, silvering, tinning or enamelling. Other rich applied-surface decoration current was: niello, millefiori, insets of glass mosaic, glass boss or gemstone boss, though these have rarely survived intact. Repoussé work is found on some Plate brooches. Attachment to clothing was achieved by means of either a hinge or sprung pin.

Following the native British Colchester brooch came its derivatives, distinctive by their separate sprung or hinge pin, which were the first true Romano-British Bow brooches, and are classified under four types: Dolphin, Polden Hill, T-shaped or Tapering Bow, and Headstud. The Dolphin and Polden Hill types remained current until around AD 100, whilst the T-shaped survived to c.AD 150 and the Headstud to AD 200. A feature of some Colchester derivatives is a small integral suspension loop on the head, to which a chain was attached (notwithstanding, other types of Romano-British brooch also have suspension loops). Not infrequently such brooches were used in pairs, a practice which is thought to have been purely a British custom.

On their arrival from the Continent in AD 43 the Roman invaders of Britain brought with them seven types of brooch, viz: Langton Down, Aucissa, Hod Hill and its variants, Bagendon, Thistle, Bow-and-Fantail and the Trumpet-head and variants. Of these only the latter two continued into the 2nd century AD, the Bow-and-Fantail until AD 150 and the Trumpet-head until AD 200. A rare form of brooch, which is a cross between the Trumpet-head and the Plate, is the Plate-and-Leg. This type seems to date between AD 150 - AD 200 (precisely which type of pin was utilised isn't clear). Two further types of Bow brooch, both of which used either hinge or sprung pins, came over from the Continent - in the mid second century AD the Knee brooch, and early in the 3rd century AD the Crossbow brooch. The former survived until c.AD 250 and the latter remained current throughout the 4th century AD.

The Penannular brooch is an ancient form, probably native British, which dates from c.3rd century BC and remained current until the Viking incursions. The cross-section of the ring is usually circular, although twisted rectangular or flat examples are known. Pins, which vary in length, have pierced heads and normally taper to a sharp point. The ring has no constriction, therefore the pin is free to move around the circumference. Although onamentation is normally restricted to terminals, some rings have transverse grooves, wholly or partially, or punchwork. Terminals, the styles of which are diverse, are always expanded in order to prevent the pin from slipping off. Some terminals are enamelled. Attribution is difficult unless found in a datable context.

Plate brooches are thought to have originated on the Continent and first appeared in Britain in the last half of the 1st century AD. Provided with either a hinge or sprung pin, they are of disc or other form and are found in a multitude of types, some extremely ornate. A rare type in Britain is the Continental 2nd century AD Bridge brooch which has a hinged pin, a pronounced bow of wide form and a terminal on each end for the catch-plate and lugs. Native British variants with sprung pins are known, though on these the terminals are generally absent or rudimentary. With the exception of the Glass Centre-boss type of Plate brooch, which didn't materialize until the latter half of the 3rd century AD and remained current well into the 4th century AD, Plate brooches had succumbed by c.AD 200.

Cast and forged copper-alloy Bow brooches

94: AD 40-65, abraded, possible Dolphin, traces of moulded circles and blue enamel, 31mm x 17mm - *Denbury*.

95: AD 50-150, Colchester derivative, Dolphin, longitudinal wavy ridge with circular hole, circular openwork in catchplate, 52mm x 40mm - River Teign, *Teign Bridge*.

96: AD 50-150, Colchester derivative, Dolphin, fragmented, moulded longitudinal tapering semi-circular ridge with transverse grooved head, copper-alloy axis bar, 21mm x 18mm - *Stokeinteignhead*.

97: AD 50-150, Colchester derivative, Dolphin, fragmented, longitudinal moulded grooves with slight projection on head, 28mm x 13.5mm - *Stokeinteignhead*.

98: AD 40-100, Colchester derivative, Polden Hill, fragmented, slightly expanded wing terminals, moulded curvilinear on each wing, copper-alloy axis bar, fragmented copper-alloy spring, 17mm x 32mm - *Uffculme*.

99: AD 50-150, Colchester derivative, T-shaped, moulded longitudinal and transverse grooves on head and wings, formally probable circular openwork in catchplate, 47mm x 40mm - *Stokeinteignhead*.

100: AD 50-150, Colchester derivative, T-shaped, fragmented, engraved lozenge and transverse and oblique grooves, copper-alloy axis bar, copper-alloy sprung pin, 24mm x 32mm - *Stokeinteignhead*.

101: AD 50-150, Colchester derivative, T-shaped, unusual circular projection on foot, longitudinal band of engraved zigzags, 50mm x 31mm - *Alphington*.

102: AD 50-150, Colchester derivative, T-shaped, pronounced moulded transverse ribs, two engraved lozenges on head, copper-alloy axis bar, fragmented copper-alloy sprung pin,

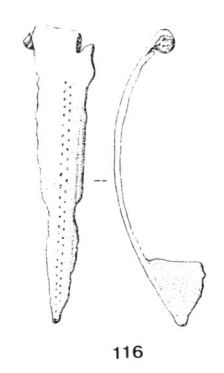

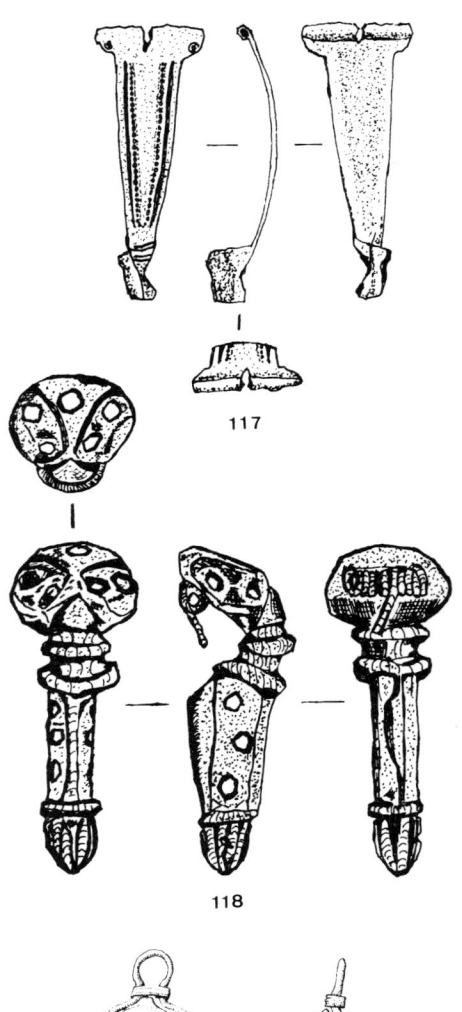

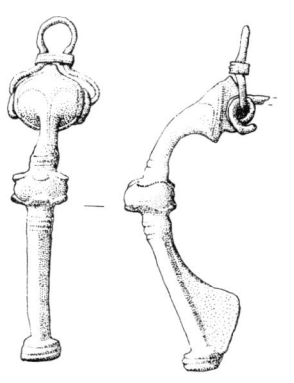

The Romano-British Period

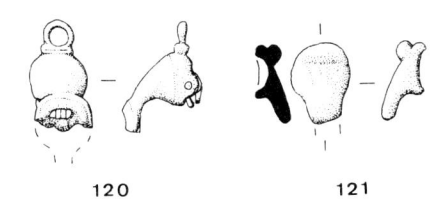

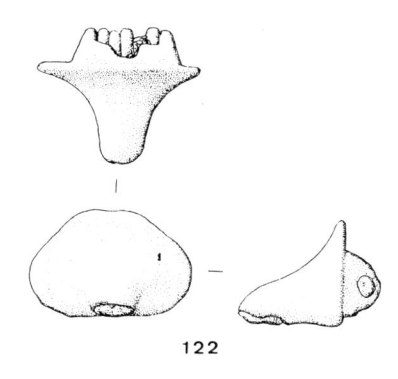

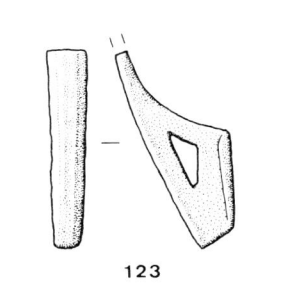

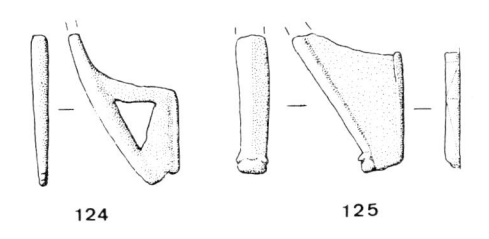

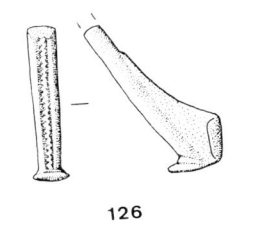

43mm x 20mm - *Stokeinteignhead.*

103: AD 50-150, Colchester derivative, T-shaped, fragmented; moulded longitudinal irregular band of circles, blind holes and a knob on bow, remains of iron axis bar, 33mm x 36mm - *Otterton.*

104: AD 50-150, Colchester derivative, probable T-shaped, fragmented, 20mm x 24mm - *Uffculme.*

105: AD 50-150, Colchester derivative, T-shaped, fragmented, moulded longitudinal semi-circular ridge with two transverse grooves and lobed end, 22mm x 29mm - *Kingskerswell.*

106: AD 50-150, Colchester derivative, T-shaped, two rivet holes through head, two copper-alloy rivets, 40mm x 40mm - *Kingskerswell.*

107: AD 50-150, Colchester derivative, T-shaped, longitudinal groove along bow, copper-alloy axis bar, hinge pin, 52mm x 29mm - *Tavistock.*

108: AD 50-150, Colchester derivative, possible T-shaped, fragmented, longitudinal grooves on head, 18.5mm x 19mm - *Stokeinteignhead.*

109: AD 50-150, Colchester derivative, T-shaped, moulded sub-triangle with red enamel, longitudinal groove above triangle and ropework below, transverse grooves on ends of wings and foot, copper-alloy axis bar, 42.5mm x 31.5mm - *Stokeinteignhead.*

110: AD 50-150, Colchester derivative, T-shaped, fragmented, chevron longitudinal groove along bow, transverse grooves on end of wing, copper-alloy axis bar, 31mm x 17.5mm - *Combeinteignhead.*

111: AD 50-200, Colchester derivative, Headstud, asymmetrical headstud riveted to head, copper-alloy rivet, engraved transverse grooves on wings and longitudinal grooves on bow, 41mm x 33mm - *Coffinswell.*

112: AD 50-200, Colchester derivative, Headstud, fragmented, lozenge-shaped headstud, longitudinal moulded semi-circular rib, copper-alloy axis bar, fragmented copper-alloy sprung pin, 22mm x 13mm - *Stokeinteignhead.*

113: AD 50-200, Colchester derivative, Headstud, fragmented, ovoid headstud, engraved cross, 30mm x 25mm - *Stokeinteignhead.*

114: c.AD 50-200, Colchester derivative, Headstud, fragmented, fragment of integral chain-loop, longitudinal band of moulded lozenges and triangles, concentric circles headstud, copper-alloy axis bar, fragment of copper-alloy hinge pin, 25mm x 15mm - *Abbotskerswell.*

115: c2nd century AD, a Hinge pin oddity which doesn't fit in with any known type, lunular flat head, lozenge-shaped flat foot, transverse moulded ribs, 61mm x 18mm - *River Teign, Hackney Marsh.*

116: AD 43-70, Hod Hill variant, abraded edges to bow, two longitudinal bands of punched dots and dashes, remains of iron axis bar, 59mm x 12mm - *Bicton.*

117: AD 43-70, Hod Hill variant, two engraved longitudinal lines and two longitudinal rows of punched circles, punched concentric circles on each wing, 54mm x 21mm- *Coffinswell.*

118: c50 BC-AD 50, Trumpet, traces of red enamel, copper-alloy axis bar, fragment of copper-alloy chord, fragmented copper-alloy sprung pin, 65mm x 25mm - *River Teign,*

Hackney Marsh.

119: c50 BC-AD 50, Trumpet, moulded curved transverse grooves on head, oval mid-bow flange in the round with moulded 'petals' and moulded transverse grooves either side, moulded transverse grooves around foot knob, copper-alloy chain loop, copper-alloy axis bar, fragmented copper-alloy sprung pin, 67mm x 18mm - *Offwell.*

120: **c.AD 150, Trumpet Head, probable Disc type, fragmented, integral chain-loop, trace of red enamel in disc, copper-alloy axis bar, remains of copper-alloy spring and pin, 22mm x 10.5mm -** *Denbury.*

121: c50 BC-AD 175, Trumpet or Trumpet Head brooch, fragment, abraded moulded longitudinal grooves and transverse lobed projection on head, 16mm x 11mm - *Stokeinteignhead.*

122: c50 BC-AD 175, Trumpet or Trumpet Head, fragment, iron core, copper-alloy axis bar, copper-alloy spring, 20.5mm x 30.5mm - *Ringmore.*

123: c.AD 50-150, fragment, probable Colchester derivative, moulded longitudinal flat ridge, triangular openwork in catch-plate, 39mm x 15mm - *Ipplepen.*

124: c.AD 50-150, fragment, probable Colchester derivative, triangular openwork in catch-plate, 30mm x 15mm - *Ipplepen.*

125: c.AD 40-65, fragment, probable Colchester derivative Dolphin, lobed foot knop with trefoil collar, incised transverse and oblique lines on return of catch-plate, 27mm x 21mm - *Stokeinteignhead.*

126: c.AD 40-65, fragment, probable Colchester derivative Dolphin, lobed foot knop, moulded longitudinal band of zigzags, 30.5mm x 10.5mm - *Ipplepen.*

Cast and forged Bow-and-fantail brooches, 1st-2nd century AD

127: fragment, blue and white enamel quadrents around a central pellet, 33mm x 15mm - *Stokeinteignhead.*

128: moulded concentric circles on central disc, moulded projection and oblique grooves on head, fragmented copper-alloy hinge pin, 36mm x 23mm - *Denbury.*

129: late 1st century AD, Maxey type, moulded longitudinal grooves on head and upper half of bow, bands of punched dots on fantail, moulded concave oval at centre of bow with convex roundel at top end, remains of copper-alloy spring and cord, 28mm x 17mm - *Denbury.*

Cast Disc brooches, c2nd century AD

130: umbonate, scalloped perimeter, punched dot-and-circle, D. 40mm - *Stokeinteignhead.*

131: umbonate, abraded perimeter, sunburst design, 20mm x 13mm - *Ringmore.*

132: umbonate, fragmented, traces of blue, red and yellow or white enamelling, fragmented copper-alloy hinge-pin, 26mm x 21.5mm - *Stokeinteignhead.*

133: umbonate centre, six peripheral knobs (two lost), traces of orange and blue enamel in the form of a cinquefoil and peripheral sunburst, fragmented copper-alloy hinge pin, 38mm x 33mm - *Bicton.*

134: umbonate variant, blue and white enamelled quatrefoil, 25mm x 20mm - *Haccombe.*

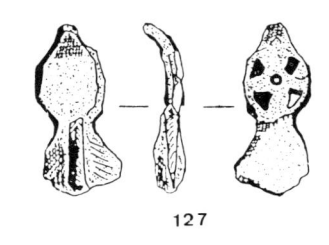

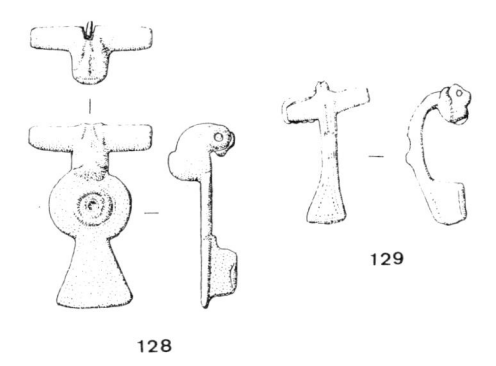

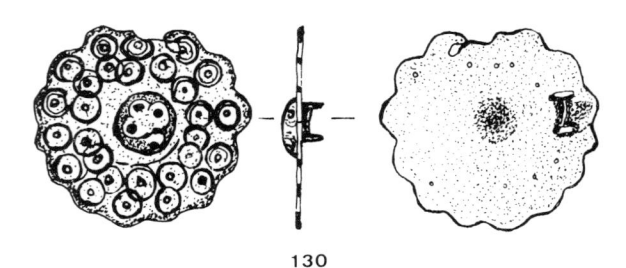

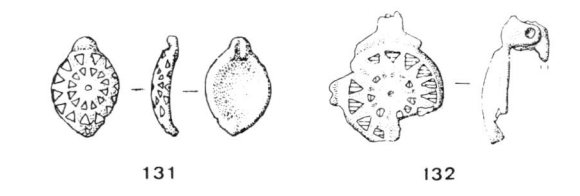

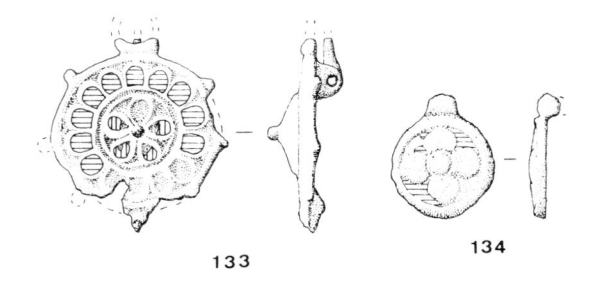

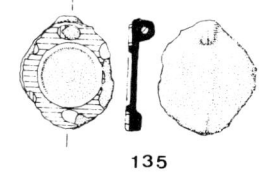

The Romano-British Period

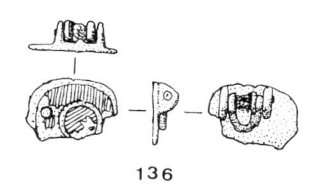

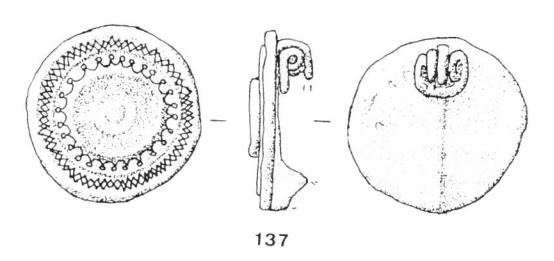

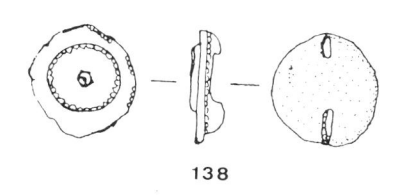

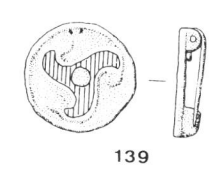

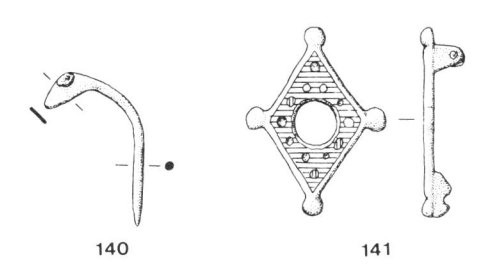

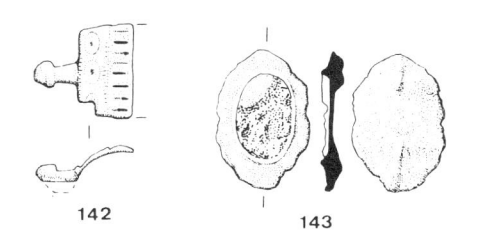

135: flat, abraded perimeter, traces of red and orange enamel in the form of small circles around a central circle, 22mm x 19mm - *Bicton*.
136: flat, fragmented and abraded, copper-alloy axis bar, traces of red enamelled concentric circles, fragmented copper-alloy sprung pin, D. 13mm x 18mm - Bantham.
137: raised centre of moulded concentric circles, traces of gilding, copper-alloy axis bar, copper-alloy chord, fragmented copper-alloy sprung pin, circular bands of engraved zigzags and scrollwork and small punched circles, 36mm x 32mm - *Haccombe*.
138: raised central circle, abraded perimeter; engraved circle, scrollwork and border of circles, D. 22.5mm - *Haccombe*.
139: flat, triskele of red enamel with traces of blue enamel field, central and terminal roundels, copper-alloy hinge-pin, D. 22mm - *Wolborough, Newton Abbot*.
140: Disc or Plate brooch copper-alloy hinge-pin, bent, L. 33mm - *Stokeinteignhead*.

Cast copper-alloy Plate brooch, 2nd century AD
141: flat, lozenge-shaped, lobed knops on angles, central circular openwork, enamelled blue field with red and yellow circles, copper-alloy axis bar, 37mm x 27mm - *Denbury*.

Cast copper-alloy Continental Bridge brooch, 2nd century AD
142: fragmented, wide bow with moulded transverse ridges, engraved horizontal lines and punched dots forming ovals with punched dot centres, lobed and waisted terminal, 18mm x 18.5mm - *Denbury*.

Cast glass Centre-boss brooches, c.AD 250 - 5th century AD
143: oval, abraded perimeter, boss lost, 27mm x 18mm - Bicton.
N.B. Nos 107 and 136 were archaeologically excavated. No.130 has no recorded parallel. No.131 is the smallest recorded example of this type from Britain or the Continent. No.134 is only the third recorded with this style of decoration.

BRACELETS & ARMLETS

In Roman Britain the wearing of bracelets or armlets was commonplace. Gold or silver examples were confined to the wealthy, whilst the less well off were restricted to iron, copper alloy, bone, shale, jet or glass. Craftsmen utilised both sheet or rod metal for making this type of jewellery, either in bangle form which slipped over the hand, or torc-like, i.e. with open ends that were prized apart and passed over the arm. Cross-sections of solid bracelets or armlets are invariably circular or oval, although some combine flat beaten sections.

Other than simple flat faces, serrated edges, transverse and oblique grooves or punchwork, base metal bracelets and armlets are usually scantly decorated. Rectangular or circular cross-section wire rods were twisted together to form a particular type and are known in precious or base metal. Gold or silver examples may incorporate any of the former ornamentation and were also made from sheet metal beaten into grooves, corrugations, repoussé, or pierced by intricate openwork. Casting produced many ornate types, particularly with zoomorphic terminals - snakes heads were a favourite. Applied-surface decoration was also popular, i.e. niello or gilt. Gold or silver wire or gemstone appliqués are found on both gold and silver jewellery of this type.

Forged copper-alloy bracelets, c1st-4th century AD.
144: semi-circular cross-section at the centre tapering to slightly expanded flat terminals, punched dots and engraved transverse and oblique grooves, 63mm x 16mm, uncoiled 16.9cm - *Roccombe*.
145: fragmented, three sub-rectangular tapered wire rods twisted together, circular cross-section, D. 54mm - *Ipplepen*.

N.B. No.144 was found by William Pengelly in 1865 whilst excavating a Romano-British midden.

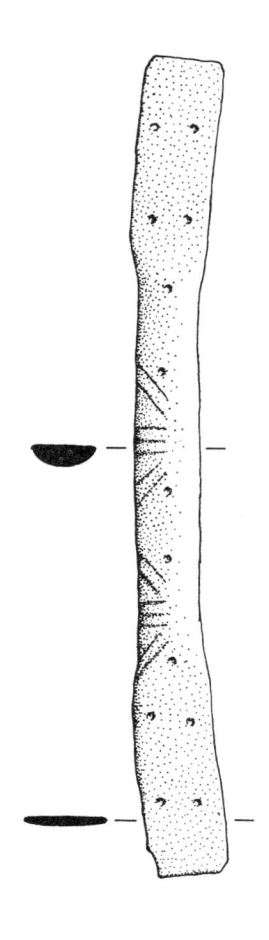

FINGER RINGS

Perhaps the most personal of all jewellery is the finger ring which has been worn by man since civilisation's dawn. Finger rings from the Roman period are known made from: gold, silver, iron, copper, copper alloy, lead, lead/tin alloy, bone, shale, jet or glass and are either annular or penannular. The latter type frequently have zoomorphic terminals, whilst a version of the former is made of coiled wire. Styles of this period are numerous, ranging from simple plain hoops, gemstone insets, through to extremely ornate bezel-types. Hoops are uniform in thickness or have expanded shoulders, whilst bezels, which are usually oval, circular, rectangular or asymmetrical, may be integral or separate. An especially rich form of box-bezel is crafted from delicate openwork.

Undoubtedly many Romano-British finger-rings had a particular significance which is now impossible to define. One type is the signet which invariably is plain-hooped with directly engraved or intaglio-set bezel. Devices range from: a portrait, inscription, monogram, initials, mythological, religious, personal or other motif. Base metal and some silver finger-rings are frequently set with glass, paste or semi-precious gemstones, some of which have their appearance enhanced by a foil-back.

Cast copper-alloy or silver bezel finger-rings, c1st - 4th century AD.
146: silver, fragment, tapering oval cross-section hoop, oval bezel set with a dark red gemstone, perhaps glass or garnet, with traces of engraving, external D. 17.5mm - *Stoneycombe*.
147: semi-circular cross-section hoop, expanded shoulders with oblique grooves on edges, oval flat bezel with four punched semi-circles, external D. 20mm, internal D. 17mm - *Uffculme*.

NECKLACES

Necklaces were worn by women at all levels of Romano-British society. The wearing of gold was restricted to the aristocracy until just before the close of the 1st century AD, thereafter it was in general use. Rich necklaces fashioned from gold or silver were concurrent with copper-alloy. Chain-link types were popular for both precious or base metal forms which frequently were set with precious or semi-precious gemstones. Coloured glass beads or amulets were strung on fine cord. Some necklaces were a continuous band which was passed over the head, whilst others had a simple hooked catch.

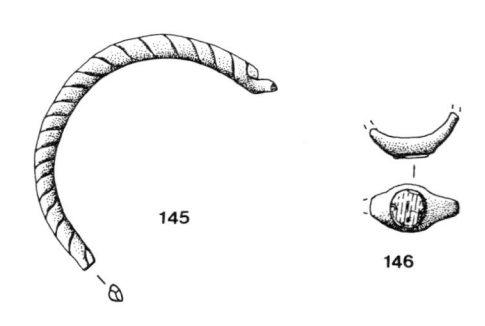

Forged copper-alloy necklace catch, c4th century AD
148: each part triangular; rectangular cross-section with flattened

The Romano-British Period

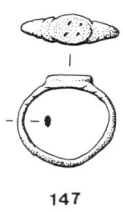

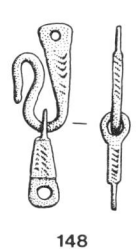

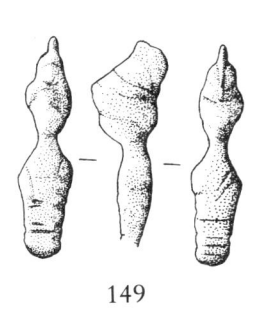

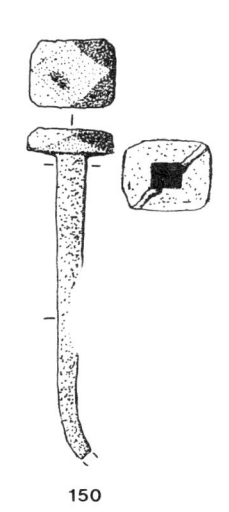

ends pierced with a circular hole; one part with a circular cross-section swan-neck hook, the other with a lateral flattened circular eyelet; engraved chevrons and oblique lines, 38mm x 11.5mm - *Denbury.*

FIGURINES

Three-dimensional representations of popular gods, other hominoids or animals were a feature of Romano-British society and would be found in temples, dwellings, public buildings or gardens. They vary in size from colossal statues down to miniature figurines and are sculptured in stone or cast in metal. Household implements, e.g. mirrors, knives and utensils, frequently have figurative representations for handles.

Cast copper-alloy figurine, c1st-4th century AD
149: Minerva, abraded, possibly a knife or mirror handle, 46mm x 13mm - *Ide.*

NAILS

Forged iron nails of varying sizes were used by the Romano-British for protecting the soles of leather footwear, and in the construction of buildings, furniture and vehicles. Consequently, habitation sites of this period invariably are littered with their remains, frequently as rust particles. Nonetheless, complete nails have survived, but unless found in a proven Roman context they are difficult to identify as such.

Very large copper-alloy nails were used in furniture-making and ship and boatbuilding. Again, attribution is difficult unless from a datable context, for they are similar to modern nails. For good luck, occasionally they were marked with a talismanic inscription and driven into a wooden doorpost.

Forged copper-alloy nail, 1st-4th century AD
150: rectangular tapered cross-section, rectangular head with champhered corners forming a lozenge, oblique groove on lower side of head, point lost, 70mm x 17mm - *Stokeinteignhead.*

SPOONS

Apart from the knife, the spoon is the oldest of man's purpose-made eating-implements, dating back for thousands of years. In Britain the earliest are attributed to the Iron Age and are made of copper alloy with quite large circular bowls and wide, flat, circular stems.

Bowl shapes have changed with the passing years and provide one of the most reliable guides of a spoon's age. Similarly, the stem changed in length and style which provides another accurate method of attribution. Various materials have been used for making spoons, including: horn, bone, ivory, wood, gold, silver, and base metal.

Spoons current in Roman Britain are found in: bone, cast lead/tin alloy, and cast and forged gold, silver or copper alloy. The latter metal is the most ubiquitous, followed by silver (frequently gilded), although gold is extremely rare. The use of lead/tin-alloy spoons would have been widespread, but few have survived the extremes of the British climate.

Early Romano-British spoons, 1st - 2nd century AD, have long, narrow, circular cross-section spiked-stems and relatively small circular bowls. Concurrent with circular bowls, but used throughout the period, are similar sized bowls of pear or purse shape, however, the latter two types are characterised by a distinctive elbow where the stem joins the bowl. Pointed stems, which were used for extracting molluscs from their shells, are frequently plain, although some have exquisite forged decoration. A larger type of spoon has an oval bowl and a short, coiled or curved handle with a zoomorphic terminal - either a duck or swan head. A rediscovered variety of spoon formed part of the Hoxne hoard of Roman metalwork. The bowl is of similar size and shape to the coiled or curved handle form, but is perforated with small holes. A straight but ornate stem joins the bowl transversely.

Romano-British ladles, although not strictly spoons, generally are circular-bowled, with long, wide, straight stems. At the juncture with the bowl, the stem increases in width and is frequently elaborate. Similar in appearance to the ladle, but smaller, is the perforated wine-strainer.

Many Romano-British spoons are engraved inside the bowl with personal names and other inscriptions which occasionally are nielloed. Similarly, bowls and stems of ladles and wine-strainers are frequently engraved with mythological representations, dolphins, Chi-Rho monogram or abstract decoration.

Cast copper-alloy spoon, 1st-4th century AD
151: pear-shaped bowl, fragmented stem, 42mm x 24mm - *Axminster*.

RECEPTACLES

Complete and undamaged Romano-British metal receptacles, such as: jugs, flagons, bowls and dishes, are extremely rare finds in this country. However, large spectacular hoards have been found which included beautiful pieces made of precious metals as well as base metal. Random finds of damaged or fragmented receptacles do occasionally turn up on Roman or non associated sites, but from Devon anything is extremely rare.

Cast and forged lead/tin-alloy flagon, 4th century AD
152: squashed, H. c225mm - *Goodrington Beach, Paignton*.

Cast copper alloy, possibly part of a jug handle, c1st-4th century AD
153: T-shaped, slightly convex, moulded vertically grooved rectangular projection, moulded oblique lines on both arms, 37mm x 25mm - *Coffinswell*.

N.B. Two flagons similar to No. 152 were found on the same beach in 1883. These receptacles are noteworthy, for the British Museum, who examined one of them, reported that the tin in the alloy is from South-West England.

TOILET OR WRITING INSTRUMENTS

Copper-alloy or iron toilet-instruments are not uncommon finds on Romano-British sites, although examples of the latter metal are rare due to corrosion. A tool associated with the custom of bathing is the strigil, a curved-bladed tool used for scraping the skin after induced sweating and for the removal of massage oil. Tweezers, ear-scoops and nail-picks, often quite small, were part of personal toilet equipment. Larger forms of all three were kept in the bathroom or bedroom, whilst smaller types were mobile, and suspended from a ring about the person - chatelaine-style.

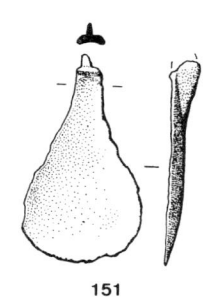

The Romano-British Period

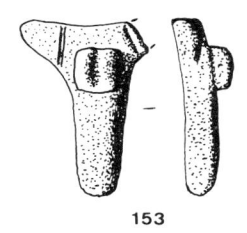

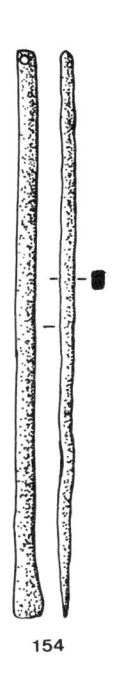

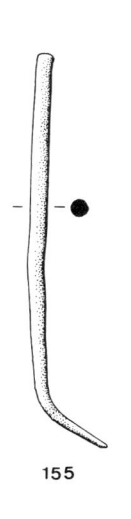

Tweezers are made from a narrow sheet of copper alloy folded equidistant to form a loop at the top and with inturned square-edged ends. Nail-picks are similarly made from sheet metal, with the business-end notched. The ear-scoop is a thin rod provided with a small circular dished probe. The smaller type of toilet instrument used in sets, always have a suspension loop. Many metal toilet-instruments are quite plain, however some are decorated with engraving or punched concentric circles.

For scribing on wax-covered tablets a stylus was used. Made of either copper alloy, iron, bone or wood, several type are known, but all are characterised by a sharp point on one end. Frequently the other end exhibits a flattened wedge-shaped terminal which served as an eraser. Concurrent with the composite wax-tablet writing instrument was a separate eraser which frequently had a suspension loop at the opposite end.

Forged copper-alloy possible wax-tablet eraser, c1st-4th century AD

154: rectangular cross-section, circular suspension loop, 120mm x 6mm - *Coffinswell.*

N.B. The cross-section of No.154 is unusual for a toilet instrument or stylus of the Romano-British period. Quite possibly it is Anglo-Saxon.

Forged copper-alloy cochleare spoon handle or part of a surgical instrument, dress-pin or needle, c1st - 4th century AD.

155: fragmented, point bent, tapered, circular cross-section, 80mm x 3.5mm - *Denbury.*

WEIGHTS

A host of different types of cast copper-alloy, lead or iron weights have appeared from farmland, tidal river foreshores, building sites and beaches. One wonders why they are found in such locations as so many are a long way from known habitation. Probably many were accidently thrown out with nightsoil; however, it is likely that others were lost whilst actually being used.

Rather crude and irregular-shaped lead weights up to 8oz are the most pervading, the majority of which are impossible to date as they were rarely officialy stamped; however, some do have obscure marks. Usually the only method available is by comparison with the age of other datable coins and artefacts from the same site. Flat-circular or free-standing: conical, square, lozenge, bell, hexagonal, cylindrical and globular, amongst others, have been recovered. Many of the conical or globular lead weights feature a pierced hole and some have an integral or separate metal suspension loop. Presumably looped types were also used as plumb-bobs and loom-weights. No doubt some of these weights are Romano-British.

Roman period steelyard weights are cast copper-alloy, sometimes with a lead infill for weight adjustment, or cast lead and are the type with a separate metal suspension loop. The simplest are undecorated but frequently they are three-dimensional busts, acorns or zoomorphic.

Cast lead steelyard-weight, probably 1st-4th century AD

156: 4 ounce, cylindrical, corroded iron suspension-loop, 36mm x 25mm - *Axminster.*

Cast copper-alloy flat circular trade- or coin-weight, possibly Romano-British, c1st - 4th century AD.
157: 3.36 grammes, punched dot-and-circle, D. 6mm - *Exeter*.

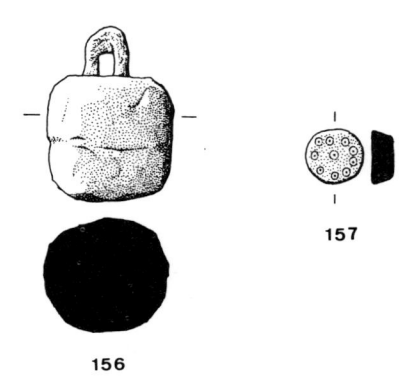

Chapter Four
The Dark Ages

158

159a

The period between the beginning of the 5th century AD when the Romans left Britain and the arrival of the Saxons in the last quarter of the same century, is virtually a blank page as far as the history of Devon is concerned. Little evidence is available to provide an insight into the lives of the native Romano-British who were left behind in Celtic Dumnonia. Presumably they continued their Romanised lifestyle for some time, but without the presence of Roman discipline slowly reverted to a more fragmented and disorganized existence. Styles of dress of the Romano-British had largely been influenced by Roman fashion, although a Celtic flavour had remained to a considerable degree throughout the occupation which probably remained current for some time. This was noticeable with their metalwork, particularly jewellery.

Early Saxon occupation east of Wiltshire is fairly well documented in the Anglo-Saxon Chronicle, however, knowledge of happenings in the west is scant. The Saxon advance on Dumnonia was marked by a mighty battle at Penselwood, on the borders of Somerset and Wiltshire, in AD 668. Devon succumbed in stages and by AD 712 the southern part, the last, had been assimilated into Anglo-Saxon Wessex

It is probable that the majority of Devonshire's farms and villages are of Anglo-Saxon origin and in many cases were established even earlier. Axmouth, Axminster, Bampton, Colyton, Ottery St Mary, Silverton, Tiverton, Sidbury, Woodbury, Kenton, Dawlish, Paignton and Brixham are among the earliest; the coastal villages were probably settled direct from the sea. Axminster and Exminster were monastic communities from soon after AD 705, whilst Exeter may have been even earlier. The latter, however, may be a Celtic foundation. A monasterium or minster was founded at Crediton in AD 739. At the time of the Saxon westward thrust, Exeter, vacated by the Romans and now occupied by native Dumnonii, was still the main provincial town. It is probable that a Saxon settlement was established at Totnes before AD 959.

One of the most attractive features of Devonshire's pastoral landscape are the massive hedgebanks that enclose the fields and bound the sunken lanes. The county is credited with retaining more miles of hedgebank than any other English county and, coupled with Kent, has some of the oldest in the country. It is now thought that the predominance of the smaller enclosures are Celtic in origin, however, the Saxons undoubtedly constructed many boundaries, particularly those surrounding their estates and open-field system of farming. Devon's only surviving example of open field is the Great Field at Braunton in North Devon. Saxon society used a variety of metal objects in their everyday life, many of which were made of iron, a material that usually fails to survive great lengths of time when buried in the ground. However, their jewellery of copper alloy, gold and silver, and a host of other creations in copper alloy, lead and lead/tin- alloy, are more durable and better able to withstand the ravages of chemical and mechanical damage. Such artefacts include: brooches, buckles, strap-ends, dress pins, garter hooks, finger rings, bracelets and weights.

Burials are the most productive source of artefacts, though from time to time random non-associated pieces do turn up. Until metal detectives started searching Devon's fields, finds of Anglo-Saxon jewellery, or indeed any Anglo-Saxon metalwork, were almost unheard of from the county; however, several confirmed pieces are now credited to the hobby.

The first record of the Danes attacking Devon is in the year AD 851; a great battle was fought at a place not far from the shores of Torbay, thought to be Weekaborough. On this occasion Devon's fighting men were victorious. Between AD 851 and AD 1016, when Wessex passed into Danish rule under Cnut, many places in the south of Devon suffered harassment by marauding Danes. They captured Exeter in AD 876 but lost it to King Alfred in AD 877, and the villages of Paignton, Teignmouth and Kingsteignton were, in turn, all torched. In AD 1001 the Danes again struck Exeter but were beaten off, then, near Pinhoe, just outside the city, a battle was fought which the Danes won. In revenge for not taking Exeter they burned Pinhoe and Broadclyst. Exeter, however, didn't escape, for in AD 1003 King Swein of Denmark plunderd and incinerated the city.

As the purpose of the Danish hit and run raids was to pillage, it is reasonable to assume that they would't have remained in any one place for too long. Even if they occupied a site for only a short period, inevitably they would have lost or discarded personal effects such as jewellery and even weapons. There is, however, no record of any Danish artefacts being found away from Devon's coastline.

COINS

After the collapse of the Empire, Roman coins remained in circulation for some time. Probably the first coins of the Germanic settlers were Merovingian gold 'tremisses', however, these did not appear until the late 6th century AD. The first true Anglo-Saxon coins, gold 'thrymsas', were struck around AD 630s, but by c.AD 650 they were being debased with silver. The very first English silver 'pennies', 'sceattas', finally replaced the gold and debased thrymsas c.AD 675. From early in the 8th century AD debased thrymsas were struck, these remained current in Northumbria along with copper/copper-alloy issues until c867 AD.

Broad-flan silver pennies were probably first struck in England by King Offa of Mercia c775-80. Similar pennies were also issued about the same time by the Kentish kings, Ecgberht and Heaberht. Five of the seven Heptarchy kingdoms also minted their own pennies and it is possible that the other two did likewise. Additionally, pennies were struck by a Bishop of London, the Archbishops of Canterbury, the Hiberno-Norse kings of York and the Danes in the Danelaw. Other than halfpennies, struck by most kings between AD 871-973, and Offa's gold dinars and pennies, for close on 500 years the silver penny was the only denomination of English coin.

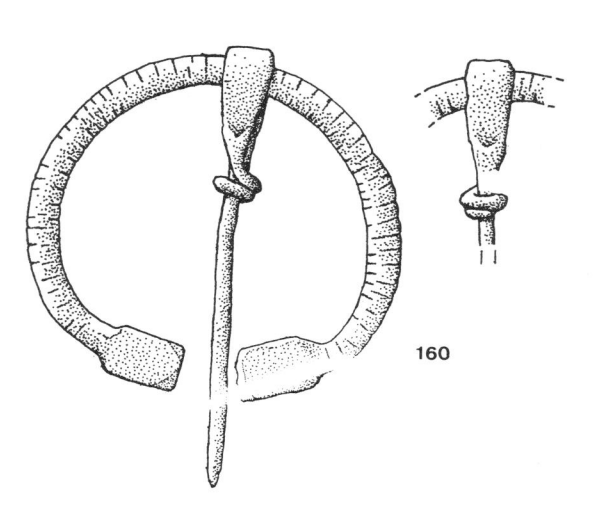

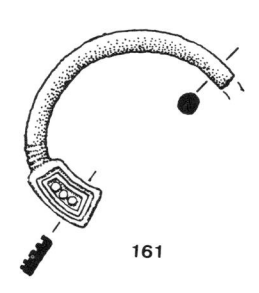

The Dark Ages 43

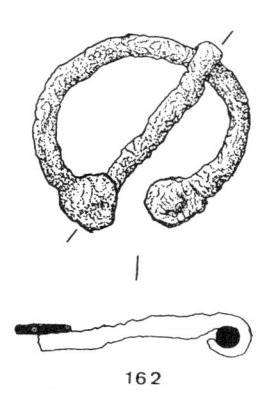

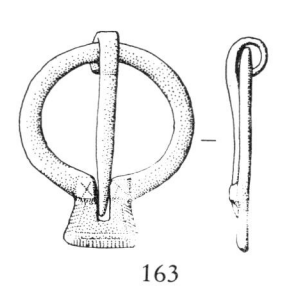

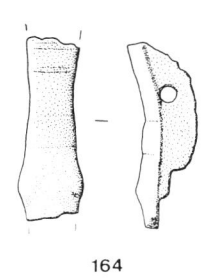

Coins were made from small disc-shaped pieces of sheet metal called flans. The moneyer placed a blank flan between two dies which were then struck with a heavy hammer, one die would impress the obverse and the other die the reverse. It is obvious from this basic description of the minting process how the phrase 'hammered coin' was derived.

Most Anglo-Saxon coin finds in this country are single examples, very few hoards are recorded, probably due to the practice of withdrawing from circulation and melting down old coins each time a new issue was struck, or the payment of Danegeld, a tax levied by King Ethelred which he used to pay off the Danes. However, many hoards of Anglo-Saxon coins have turned up on the Continent, not unexpectedly, most of them in Scandinavia.

It is known that there were four Anglo-Saxon mints in Devon, viz: Exeter, Barnstaple, Lydford and Totnes. Accepting the fact that much of the currency wasn't in circulation for a great length of time, it doesn't explain the almost complete absence of Anglo-Saxon coins from the county. The advent of the metal detector has verified that a high proportion of coinage of other periods was lost whilst in general circulation - it is reasonable to assume the same could be said for Anglo-Saxon. Allegedly, in recent years late Anglo-Saxon pennies were found by a walker on Berry Head, Brixham. If true, their present whereabouts are unrecorded.

Silver coins
158: Edward the Elder, 899-924, penny, minster on central line, Wulfgar, north-western mint - *Exmouth*.
159: Edward the Confessor, 1042-66, penny, expanding cross type, SPRACELINE of London - *Stokeinteignhead*.
159a: enlarged illustration of a complete example of No.158.

BROOCHES

Penannula brooches attributed to the Sub-Roman Anglo-Saxon period, generally are cast copper alloy, however, silver was current but only two examples are recorded from Britain. Cast copper-alloy Sub-penannular brooches are attributed to the 3rd-7th centuries. They have circular or sub-circular cross-section annular rings with a lateral chevron protrusion, the sides of which may be flat or circular cross-section. The flat type of protrusion is also known in trapezoidal shape or with apertures forming zoomorphic knops. It is uncommon for the ring itself to be decorated, although the protrusion may have dot-and-circle punchwork or engraving. The pin is free to move around either side of the chevron protrusion.

Similar to the former type of brooch, because it has a chevron aperture, is the 3rd-7th-century cast copper-alloy or silver Quoit brooch, but thereafter is somewhat different. Additional to the annular ring is an outer, wide, flat cross-section ring, the two of which are integrally attached by several narrow transverse strips. The pin is trapped in one of the apertures so formed. Invariably openwork decoration is found in the outer ring. The Quoit brooch has a variant: both rings are joined together to make a solid ring and a small aperture is provided to take the pin, thereby restricting movement. Both Sub-penannular and Quoit brooches are rare in Britain

The early Saxon incursions, between c.AD 450-650, brought into Britain several new types of brooch, viz: Saucer, Annular and

Long, as well as variants of the Disc. Primary materials of construction are gold, silver or copper alloy, which may be cast or forged or both. Elaborate ornamentation is characteristic of all types, and engraving or puchwork, as well as: gilt, silver, tin, glass, gemstone, enamel, or metal appliqué applied-surface decoration is commonplace on some.

Saucer brooches are similar to the Disc form of the Roman period, but differ by having upturned rims. A feature of many is chip-carving, repoussé appliqué or glass, enamel or garnet central boss decoration. Probably the most well known design on chip-carved types is the stylistic hominoid face. Invariably pins are hinged.

Although some Anglo-Saxon Disc brooches are attributed to the 8th-10th centuries, most are a product of the 7th. Good quality brooches of this type, which are known in gold or silver, are invariably richly decorated with glass or garnet insets and twisted gold, silver or gilt or silvered-copper-alloy wire appliques. Lesser Disc brooches are either copper alloy or lead/tin alloy. The former frequently have engraved or punched decoration and are usually tinned, silvered or gilded, whilst the latter often have moulded designs. Pins are hinged.

Hattatt classifies several buckle-like circular artefacts as Anglo-Saxon Annular brooches; however, this is refuted by other scholars (see medieval chapter). Nonetheless, he lists a number of c.7th-century copper-alloy small Annular brooches with zoomorphic representations either side of a constriction in the ring.

Of all Anglo-Saxon brooches the Long brooch, attributed to between the 5th-7th centuries, is perhaps the most evocative. Of two main types, Cruciform and Square-headed, they are further sub-divided into many varieties. Copper alloy is the dominant metal, although silver examples of the Square-headed are known. Pins of both types are usually sprung, although some are hinged.

The Cruciform brooch evolved from the Gothic and Roman Crossbow brooches and retains a distinctive bow. Characteristic of many is a zoomorphic foot, flattened arms and globular knops. Decoration is invariably engraved or punched.

Similar to the Cruciform brooch the Square-headed has its bow, but the rectangular head is much larger, and often with lateral protrusions on the body and foot. Decoration can be very rich chip-carving, sometimes enamelled or punched and engraved. Tinning is commonplace.

Lastly, the Equal-armed sprung-pin brooch of the 7th-9th centuries is considered. As the name implies, this type has a pair of identical inline terminals with a central bow. Several shapes are known, and some are decorated with embossing, chip-carving or dot-and-circle punchwork.

Cast and forged Penannular brooches

160: c400-600AD, silver, circular cross-section, transverse grooves, cuboid terminals with faceted corners, silver pin, D. 36mm - *Capton*.

161: c5th century AD, copper alloy, fragment, circular cross-section, band of transverse grooves above terminal, sub-rectangular flattened terminal decorated with three moulded or engraved sub-rectangles and three pellets, D. c43mm - *Bantham*.

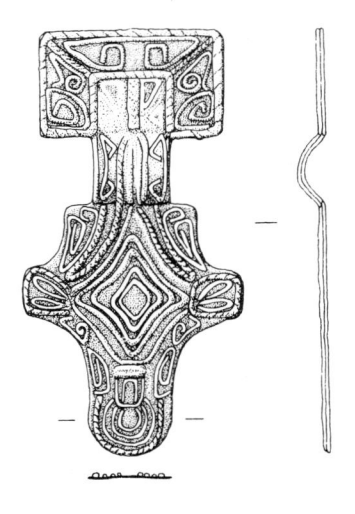

165

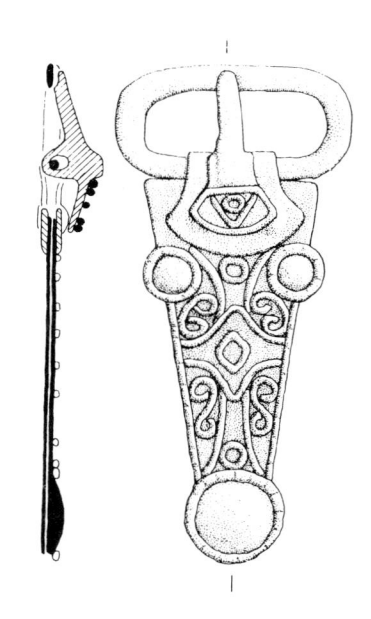

166

The Dark Ages 45

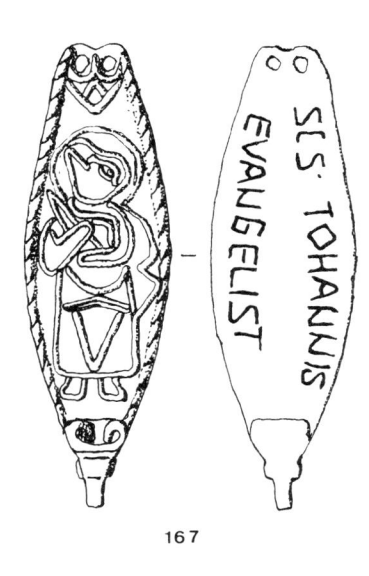

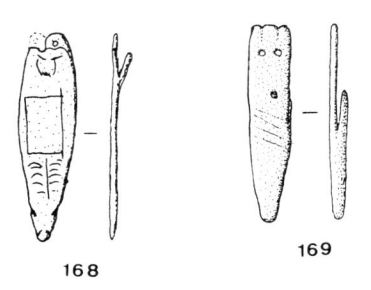

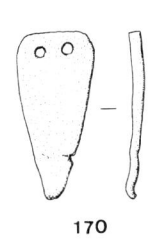

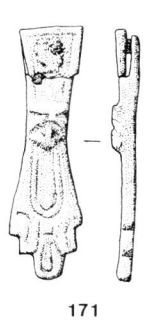

Forged iron Penannular brooch, c4th-5th century AD
162: very corroded, circular cross-section, spherical terminals, iron pin, D. 41mm - *Bantham*.

Cast and forged Sub-penannular brooch, c.AD 400-597
163: sub-circular cross-section ring, subrectangular flat cross-section protrusion with rectangular slot, copper-alloy pin, border of oblique engraved grooves around protrusion, moulded raised square engraved with a St Andrews cross at each junction of ring and protrusion, 41mm x 33mm - *Denbury.*:

Cast and forged Cruciform Long, Crossbow or Trefoil-head brooch, c.AD 500-25
164: fragment, moulded transverse ribs, integral single lug with circular hole, 36mm x 12.5mm - *Denbury*.

Cast copper-alloy fake Anglo-Saxon brooch, 18th-19th century
165: square-headed, tinned, tooled decoration, 85mm x 42mm - *River Teign, Hackney Marsh*.

N.B. No.160 was found in 1982 by farmer David Lloyd. Nos.161 & 162 were archaeologically excavated. No.163 is only the sixth recorded from Britain.

BUCKLES

Anglo-Saxon buckles are often very elaborate and frequently carry zoomorphic representations, a practice carried over from the Romans. Sizes range from the quite small to the very large. The simple plain D-shape is perhaps the commonest, though some of this type have one or two knops on the front edge of the loop. Some of the very large buckles have oval frames. Square or kidney-shaped frames seem to be less common.

Buckle-plates are either integral or separate and are found on all sizes of buckle, however, some buckles were riveted direct to the strap. A feature of many Anglo-Saxon buckle-plates is their high degree of ornamentation; applied-surface decoration of: gilt, silver, niello or enamel was frequently employed, whilst: chip carving, punchwork, openwork and appliqués of gemstones were also current. A particular type of buckle-plate found on large buckles is triangular with three large dome-headed rivets. Other shapes of buckle-plate current were rectangular, sub-triangular, semi-circular and cordate. Perhaps the most distinguishing feature of some of the large buckles is their fiddle-shaped tongues which frequently have ornamented hominoid heads.

Copper alloy and iron were the normal metals of manufacture, though examples of gold or silver are known. Finds of Anglo-Saxon precious metal and jewelled buckles are usually associated with grave-goods, but less grand types are more widely scattered and usually represent casual losses. Nonetheless, Anglo-Saxon buckles are rare finds anywhere and, as yet, have eluded Devon's metal detectives and there is no record of any found by other means.

Cast tinned-copper-alloy fake Anglo-Saxon buckle, 18th-19th century
166: separate triangular buckle-plate, three large dome-headed rivets, tooled decoration, copper-alloy tongue, 99mm x 45mm - *River Teign, Hackney Marsh*.

The Dark Ages
Distribution of metal detector finds in Southern Devon

1. Clyst St Mary (**MA**)
2. Cockington (**A**)
3. Denbury (**MA**)
4. Exeter (**MA**)
5. Exmouth (**C**)
6. Haccombe (**MA**)
7. Kingsteignton (**A**)
8. Ladram Bay Beach (**A**)
9. Stokeinteignhead (**C, A**)
10. Wolborough, Newton Abbot (**A**)

Key: **C** = single coin   **A** = artefact   **MA** = multiple artefact

R. EXE
R. CULM
R. CLYST
R. OTTER
R. AXE
R. TEIGN
R. DART

Scale = 1:316,000 (approx.)

5 miles
8 kilometres

Based upon Ordnance Survey mapping with the permission of the Controller of Her Majesty's Stationery Office, © Crown copyright.

STRAP-ENDS

Strap-ends, which had already been used for centuries before the Germanic arrivals in Britain, are decorative terminal fittings affixed to straps, e.g. girdles, on the opposite end to the buckle. Generally they are made of cast or sheet metal, viz: gold, silver, lead/tin alloy, copper alloy or iron, though other materials such as ivory were utilized. Niello, enamel, gilt, silver or tin applied-surface decoration was frequently employed.

Cast tinned-copper-alloy fake Anglo-Saxon strap-end, 18th-19th century

167: one-piece, zoomorphic, moulded St John the Evangelist motif on front, moulded inscription STS IOHANNIS EVANGELIST on reverse, two rivet holes, 91mm x 28mm - *River Teign, Hackney Marsh*.

Cast copper-alloy strap-ends, 9th century

168: one-piece, zoomorphic, engraved crescents, rectangular panel for applied-surface decoration, two rivet holes (one lost), 41mm x 11mm - *Cockington*.

169: one-piece, rear flange fragmented, trefoil top, engraved oblique lines, three rivet holes, 39mm x 8mm - *Haccombe*.

Cast lead strap-end, c9th century

170: one-piece, two rivet holes, 32.5mm x 15mm - *Kingsteignton*.

Cast copper-alloy Anglo-Saxon/Romanesque strap-end, 10th-11th century

171: one-piece, trefoil terminal, front flange cracked, moulded eye-like protrusion; grooved border on top half and engraved curlicues, teardrops and transverse line on bottom section, two rivet holes, two copper-alloy rivets, 49mm x 14mm - *Wolborough, Newton Abbot*.

N.B. All three of these fake Anglo-Saxon artefacts were found in the vicinity of the ancient ford but on different occasions. Initial research indicated that they were indeed Anglo-Saxon and therefore represented discoveries of extreme historical and archaeological importance for the county. However, lengthy examination at the British Museum and the Museum of London revealed that they were not contemporary but 18th-19th-century reproductions.

It seems that perhaps they are similar to 'Billies' and 'Charlies', fake artefacts made by two unscrupulous Victorian Londoners, William Smith and Charles Eaton, and sold to unsuspecting collectors as genuine articles. They first appeared on the antiquity market in 1857-8 during the rebuilding of Shadwell Dock where many genuine antiquities were found. Billies and Charlies are now collectors items in their own right and are much sought after.

DRESS PINS

Anglo-Saxon dress-pins come in a variety of sizes and invariably have ornate knops. Some were cast one-piece and others in two or more and then soldered. Frequently stems were forged. Copper alloy examples are the most ubiquitous, although due to the advent of the metal detector the once scarce silver-gilt solid or hollow spherical-headed type is now relatively common. Gold specimens are rare.

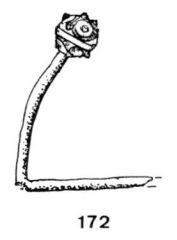

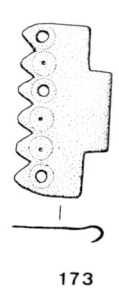

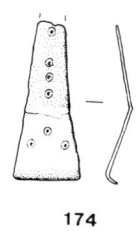

172

173

174

175 see end of chapter

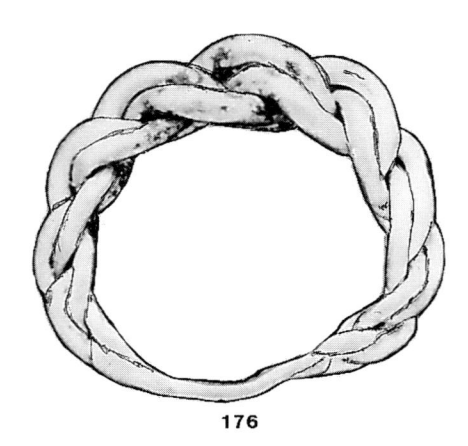

176

The Dark Ages

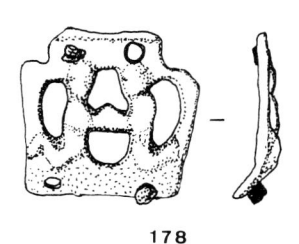

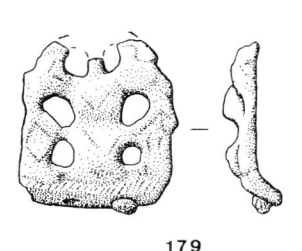

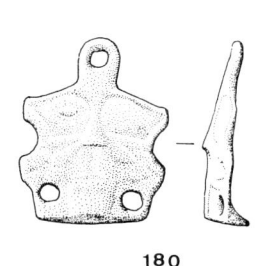

Cast and forged Anglo-Saxon Dress-pin, c9th-10th century

172: two-piece, silver, gilded solid spherical-head decorated with moulded circles and rosettes which imitate appliqués, greenstick fracture and lost point, L. 75mm - *Stokeinteignhead.*

WRIST CLASPS

A type of clothing-fastener current in the Middle and Late Anglo-Saxon period is the two-piece Wrist-clasp which secured two sides of a slit in a costume sleeve. They are made from sheet, cast or wire copper alloy. Several styles of sheet or cast are known, though all have an integral hook on one section and an integral eyelet on the other. Both sections have two or more circular sewing-holes. Many are quite plain, though moulded, chip carved, punched or engraved decoration is commonplace. Inside longitudinal edges are frequently serrated, or lobed in which are drilled the sewing holes. Some wire forms of Wrist-clasp comprise a simple hook and eye with loops for sewing, whilst others have elaborate coils.

Sheet copper-alloy Wrist-clasp, c6th-7th centuries

173: hooked section, serrated inside edge, three circular sewing-holes, punched dot-and-circle and circles, 34mm x 17mm - *Denbury.*

TWEEZERS

Tweezers current in Anglo-Saxon Britain are similar to those of the Romano-British period, a simple folded strip of sheet copper alloy with a suspension loop and inturned terminals. They are known in several sizes and frequently have engraved or punched decoration, of which dot-and-circle is perhaps the most ubiquitous.

Sheet copper-alloy tweezers, c6th-10th century

174: fragment, bent and cracked, punched dot-and-circle, 32mm x 13mm - *Denbury.*

BRACELETS AND FINGER RINGS

Viking metalwork is extremely rare. Most known British-found examples have come from graves or major archaeological excavations, such as York's Coppergate. However, metal detectives and others have made random finds of unassociated material, e.g. coins, jewellery and weapons. Characteristic of this period is twisted or plaited gold, silver or copper-alloy wire construction for bracelets and finger rings.

Drawn and forged gold wire bracelet, Viking, 8th-10th century AD

175: three twisted tapering strands, terminals enclosed by a polyhedral capsule decorated with punched circles, 114.675 grammes, max D. 95mm - *Goodrington Beach, Paignton.*

Drawn and forged gold wire finger-ring, Viking, 10th-11th century AD

176: four twisted tapering strands, plain terminals, 14.38 grammes, D. 19mm - *Sandy Cove Beach, Ladram Bay.*

N.B. No.175 was found in 1979 by holidaymaker Kay Creasey. At a Treasure Trove inquest the bracelet was declared not Treasure Trove and returned to the finder who later sold it at a Sotheby's auction to the British Museum for £7,150.00. No.176 was found in 1987 by Stanley French. On 10 July 1990, after a Treasure Trove inquest where it was declared not Treasure Trove, it was sold at a Sotheby's auction to a private bidder for £3,200.00.

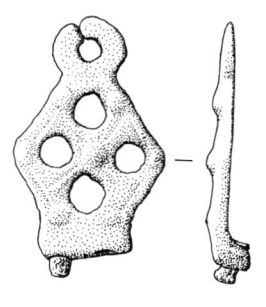

BEADS

Viking craftsmen were adept at making fine necklaces of: glass, crystal, amber, cornelian or silver beads. Some of their glass was manufactured by themselves but much they imported from other Western European locations. Beautiful multicoloured glass beads are characteristic of this period. Silver beads are hollow globular, made from two hemispheres soldered together, decorated with appliqués of twisted silver wire and tiny silver granules. Other than necklaces, beads were also strung between pairs of brooches.

Cast and sheet silver bead, possibly Viking, c8th-10th century AD.

177: globular, two bands of silver granule appliqués; single twisted silver wire appliqués around all granules and both holes, double band of silver wire appliqués around centre, 26mm x 24mm - *Goodrington Beach, Paignton.*

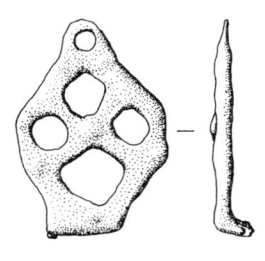

STIRRUPS AND STIRRUP-MOUNTS

Whether the stirrup came to Britain prior to the Viking incursions isn't certain. It seems the earliest known type comprised a simple wire loop with an integral twisted suspension loop through which the stirrup leather was riveted. Later, the lower half was flattened to provide a better foot-rest. Although several early progressions from the aforementioned are known from Scandinavia, the next form in Britain has a long body with a wide, flattened, foot-rest and lateral rectangular suspension loop. The last half of the 10th century perhaps saw the introduction of a much shorter and rounded form with similar flattened foot-rest and sub-rectangular suspension loop.

The earliest discoveries from the county and associated with stirrups are Late Anglo-Saxon Early Norman stirrup-mounts which until recently were described variously as: 'bucket-mounts', 'book-mounts', 'strap-ends', 'clasps', or 'decorative mounts for wooden chests'. Variable in shape from asymmetrical, rectangular, lozenge, sub-lozenge, pentagonal, triangular or sub-triangular, they are cast copper alloy, convex or flat, with the bottom edge having a backturned flange, and have two, three, or four rivet holes. Ornamentation is a feature of all, and ranges from openwork, moulded, or engraved hominoid, mystical beast or zoomorphic representations. Rivets were either iron or copper alloy.

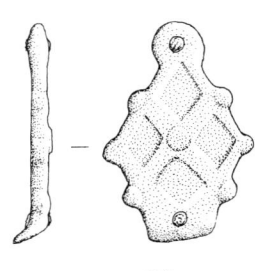

Cast copper-alloy Anglo-Saxon/Romanesque stirrup-mounts, c11th century

178: sub-rectangular, semi-circular and asymmetrical openwork, two moulded confronted kneeling hominoid figures, four rivet holes, two iron rivets, 33mm x 34mm - *Haccombe.*
179: sub-rectangular, fragmented, asymmetrical openwork, abraded moulded design, two rivet holes, one copper-alloy rivet, 32.5mm x 30mm - *Exeter.*
180: asymmetrical, grotesque of a hominoid face which may represent the woodland sprite Jack-o'-the-Green, three rivet

holes, 36mm x 28mm - *Clyst St Mary*.

181: sub-lozenge-shaped, abraded moulded sub-lozenge-shape and possible St Andrews cross, central moulded roundel, three rivet holes, one copper-alloy rivet, 51mm x 29mm - *Exeter*.

182: sub-lozenge-shaped, circular and asymmetrical openwork forming a St Andrew's cross, central moulded roundel, one rivet hole, 42mm x 29mm - *Clyst St Mary*.

183: sub-lozenge-shaped, moulded lozenge-shape and St Andrews cross with central roundel, six lobed-knops, two rivet holes, two copper-alloy rivets, 43mm x 29mm - *Exeter*.

N.B. No.178 has no recorded parallel.

175

Chapter Five
The Middle Ages

By the 8th century AD the area now known as Devon had been embodied into the political organisation of Wessex and was first recognised as a shire sometime during the third quarter of the same century, although the exact boundary line separating it from Cornwall is unclear.

In the reign of Edmund, AD 939-46, shires in the south of England were subdivided into hundreds, the function of which was purely administrative, e.g. law and order and taxation. Some hundreds were themselves subdivided, each section being in a different geographical location, e.g. Wonford and Carsuelle. Each hundred held court which usually met monthly at a prominent place, e.g: crossroads, hill, boundary stone, tree or barrow, and was presided over, on behalf of the king, by a Hundred Reeve.

At the time of William I's Domesday survey, Devon's population was probably no more than between 60,000 and 80,000 souls, most of whom lived in small villages, hamlets and farmsteads scattered throughout the landscape. Exeter was the largest town with about 1,500 residents, followed by Totnes and Lydford each with between 300 and 400 people. Outside of these towns, the areas of greatest settlement were the Torbay district and the vale of Exeter, each with about 32 folk to the square mile. The rest of the county averaged about 27 to the square mile.

Other than cottage-type activities, such as cloth-making and pottery, little industry existed. Most people would have been engaged in the back-breaking work of eking a frugal existence from their own small plot of land. The 12th century saw the beginning of a remarkable transformation. Immigration commenced on a grand scale, many new villages and towns were established, and hundreds of new farms were created, usually taking the name of the first family to work them. Many of these place-names can be traced to this day. Charters for boroughs were granted, governed by an elected Mayor and Municipal Corporation, each having the right to hold a weekly market and in some cases regular fairs. Totnes is the oldest borough in the south of the county, dating from the middle of the 10th century, followed by Ashburton in the 12th century. Devon has the greatest number of recorded medieval boroughs of any English county and boasts the two oldest, Barnstaple followed by Totnes. This injection of new blood continued until c1350, being halted only by the advance of the dreaded pestilence or Black Death.

Many other villages and towns were granted charters, in the 13th and 14th centuries, to hold a weekly market and an annual fair, viz: Newton Bushel, Wolborough, Kingskerswell, Cockington, Kingsteignton, Morleigh, Holne, Ideford, South Brent, Buckfastleigh, Bovey Tracey, Clifton-Upon-Dartmouth,

The Middle Ages

186

187

188

189

Denbury, Kenton, Axminster, Bradninch, East Budleigh, Colyton, Colyford, Ottery St Mary, Plympton St Maurice, Silverton, Sampford Peverell and Sidmouth. Of these fairs Axminster's, to whom King John grantered its charter in 1215, was the largest and most important, being held for eight days.

The first record of tin mining on Dartmoor is dated about the middle of the 12th century, and for a time was the largest producer in Europe. Ashburton, Chagford, Tavistock and Plympton were stannary towns, where tin ingots were weighed and stamped. Woollen textile production increased throughout the county during the later medieval period; Exeter, Ottery St Mary, Tiverton, Totnes and Chudleigh became focal points for this industry. Much of the yarn was spun in peasants' cottages and transported to the cloth-towns for dyeing and weaving. Dartmouth, due to its strategic position and safe anchorage, experienced a rapid growth in sea trade at the end of the 12th century, and, along with Exeter, was one of Devon's most important 14th-century seaports.

Many of the churches in the south of the county were built between 1100-1300, but sadly, because of rebuilding in later centuries, they retain little of their Romanesque architecture. Likewise, during the same period, numerous fine manor-houses sprung up and rivers were bridged in stone. Devon's oldest extant bridge is at Clyst St Mary and dates to at least 1238; it's causeway is 183m long.

There is little recorded evidence of deserted medieval villages or hamlets in the region, the only one of note is Hound Tor near Manaton on Dartmoor. Haccombe is more accurately described as a shrunken village which as late as the 19th century was a sizeable community. Nowadays just the church, which retains some interesting medieval interior features, a late Georgian house and the parsonage are all that remain. The bulk of the village was probably cleared when the estate was emparked in the 19th century. An undated estate-map, which is probably 17th-18th century, shows in great detail the layout of the village; many of the roads and other topographical features can be traced to this day.

Much research remains to be done in locating and recording medieval deserted or shrunken village and hamlet sites in southern Devon. There must be more awaiting discovery, and perhaps the most likely group of people to do so is metal detectives, for probably they do more fieldwalking than any other section of historical or archaeological society.

An infinite variety of medieval metalwork has been found and is continuing to be found by metal detectives, most of which is attributed between 1200-1484 which verifies this was southern Devon's most populated period during the Middle Ages.

COINS

Although from the Norman kings some coins had a form of cross on the reverse, it wasn't until Henry II's issue of 1180-9 that all pennies had such a cross - these are known as 'Short Cross' coins. An attempt to stop clipping and filing was made by Henry III, 1216-72, who in 1247 issued pennies, including some of gold, with crosses which extended to the edge of the flan. Unfortunately it proved unsuccessful against tampering but the 'Long Cross' remained current on some denominations of coinage until the end of Elizabeth I's reign.

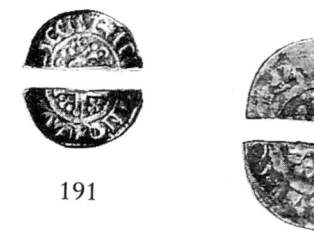

King John's, 1199-1216, Irish issues included round 'halfpennies' and 'forthlings' ('farthings'), however, it wasn't until Henry III's reign that these denominations became widespread in England. Edward I's re-coinage of 1279 introduced the 'groat', whilst 'halfgroats' were first issued by Edward III in 1351. In 1344 he also issued the first regular gold coins since the thrymsa, i.e. 'florins' ('double leopards'), 'half-florins' ('leopards') and 'quarter-florins' ('helms'). This issue was replaced in the same year with gold 'nobles' and 'quarter-nobles', and in 1346 'half-nobles'. Edward IV issued new gold coins in 1465, the 'ryal' ('rose noble'), 'half-ryal', 'quarter-ryal' and 'angel'. During Henry VI's restoration period 'half-angels' were struck.

Prior to the appearance of round halfpennies and farthings, in order to overcome the problem of small change, it was the practice to cut pennies into halves and quarters ('cut-halfpennies' and 'cut-farthings') by snipping along the lines of the cross on the reverse.

Gold coins
184: Edward III, quarter-noble, 1356-61, mm cross 3 (4), London - *Haccombe*.
185: Edward III, quarter-noble, cut half, 1361-9, mm cross potent, London - *Stokeinteignhead*.
186: Henry V, quarter-noble, 1413-22, mm probably pierced cross with pellet centre, London - *Coffinswell*.
187: Edward IV, quarter-ryal, 1468-9, mm rose, London - *Cockington*.

Silver coins
188: William II, penny, 1087-110, London, fragment - *Bishopsteignton*.
189: Stephen, penny, 1135-54, Cross moline (Watford) type - *Cockington*.
190: Henry II, Tealby penny, 1161-5, Carlisle or Canterbury - *Haccombe*.
191: Henry II, cut-halfpenny, 1180-9, Winchester - *Kingsteignton*.
192: Henry II or Richard II, cut-halfpenny, 1180-99, York - *Bishopsteignton*.
193: William I, Scotland, penny, 1205-30, Roxburgh - *Cockington*.
194: William I Scotland, cut-halfpenny, 1205-30, (?) mint - *Cockington*.
195: John, penny, 1210-15, London - *River Teign, Coombe Cellars*.
196: unidentified, Short Cross cut-farthing, R0 DEN[...], probably London - *Haccombe*.
197: unidentified, Short Cross cut-farthing, R) SIM(ON[...], possibly Canterbury or Chichester - *Cockington*.
198: Henry III, penny, 1216-47, London - *Cockington*.
199: Henry III, penny, 1247-72, London - *Whilborough*.
200: Henry III, cut-halfpenny, 1247-72, (?) Oxford - *Newton Abbot*.
201: Edward I, penny, 1279-1307, London - *Coffinswell*.
202: Edward I, penny, 1279-1307, Canterbury - *Bishopsteignton*.
203: Edward I Ireland, penny, 1279-1302, Dublin - *River Teign, Ringmore*.
204: Edward I Ireland, halfpenny, 1279-1302, Dublin - *Exmouth*.
205: Continental sterling, late 13th century - early 14th century - *Whilborough*.

The Middle Ages

206: Edward II, penny, 1307-27, Canterbury - *River Teign, Hackney Marsh.*
207: Edward III, penny, 1327-77, (?) mm, London - *Stokeinteignhead.*
208: Edward III, groat, 1334-51, mm cross pattée, London - *Haccombe.*
209: Edward III, half-groat, 1354-5, mm cross 2, London - *Cockington.*
210: David II Scotland, groat, 1357-67, mm cross pattée, Edinburgh - *Stokeinteignhead.*
211: Henry V, halfpenny, 1413-22, (?) mm, London - *Stokeinteignhead.*
212: Henry VI, groat, 1422-7, mm pierced cross, London - *Bishopsteignton.*
213: Henry VI, halfpenny, 1422-7, mm pierced cross, Calais - *Stokeinteignhead.*
214: Edward IV, groat, 1464-5, mm rose, London - *Cockwood.*
215: Edward IV, half-groat, 1465-6, mm sun, Canterbury - *Cockington.*

N.B. A Henry III, 1247-72, Exeter penny found at Cockington, unfortunately broken in four pieces whilst in police hands, is the only coin of that monarch and minted in Exeter remaining in the county (Torre Abbey Museum). The William I Scotland penny and cut-halfpenny are noteworthy because a survey on the distribution of Norman coinage (including Scottish kings) has revealed that few complete Scottish pennies have been found in England, though cut-halfpennies are known. This pair of Scottish coins of this king are the most distant from their mint so far recorded.

JETONS

Throughout Europe prior to c1250 manual accountancy was performed by manipulating coins on a delineated counting board or cloth. Coins for reckoning were discontinued after the introduction of jetons, which are coin-like with a hammered design on the obverse and reverse.

The first jetons (or jettons) (from the French jeter - to throw)) used in England were early French and made of copper alloy. These were issued between c1250-1325 by Queens who were responsible for the financial administration of their own royal households. By c1350 and up until 1521, French copper-alloy jetons struck mainly in Tournai and Paris were dominant in England.

Copper-alloy reckoning counters, also known as jetons, of English manufacture, probable Tower Mint, were struck between 1280-1400. There is evidence to suggest that some English jetons were minted in the provinces.

In England the Royal Exchequer Table was located at either Westminster or Winchester, where sheriffs were required to present their accounts in person - they also used counter reckoning in their own shires. From c1350 the same system was widely used by merchants.

Italian copper-alloy jetons struck by the Lombard bankers between c1280s - 1340s were current in their country of origin and France, however, there is no evidence of an extensive contemporary circulation in England. Between 1305-84 the Low Countries produced copper-alloy jetons which were current in

History Beneath Our Feet

202

203

204

205

206

207

208

209

210

211

212

213

214

The Middle Ages

England.

A number of English lead/tin-alloy jeton issues were struck between c1350-1425 and similarly, French betwixt 1425-1500, and the Low Countries in the 15th century. Finds of such jetons are now rare. From c1330 until 1450 Anglo-Gallic copper-alloy and lead/tin-alloy jetons were struck by Edward III, Henry V and Henry VI for use in their French provinces; however, these are also now rare finds. German copper-alloy jetons, which were manufactured in Nuremberg, appeared towards the end of the 15th century and were dominant into the Stuart era.

English copper-alloy jeton, 1327-99

216: Edward III - Richard II
 Obv. King under canopy, REX left, GRA right.
 Rev. Three-stranded cross with rampant lion in each spandrel -*Stokeinteignhead.*

French copper-alloy jetons, 14th century

217: Obv. A bear secured to a tree on which a large flower grows, similar trees to the left and right; enclosed in a double inner circle, the outer one is granulated.
 Rev. Three-stranded cross fleur-de-lisée and fleuronnée with a quatrefoil in the centre; enclosed in a tressure of four arches, fleuronnée at each angle.
 (In the 14th century the inhabitants of Toulouse believed that a terrible animal called a 'Malle Beste' or 'Bugbear' roamed the streets at night. An amulet was struck at the Hotel de Ville for the protection of those who wore it) - *Kingskerswell.*

218: Obv. Three circles arranged in a triangle, enclosing a flower of four petals.
 Rev. Cross pattée within a double inner circle the outer one plain and cusped; from each cusp issues a flower of petals and three stamens which fill the cantons of the cross - *Newton Abbot.*

219: Obv. Heater shield, charged with a lion rampant, within a tressure of six arches, in each spandrel a pellet.
 Rev. Long bowed cross of two strands of fleurdelisée, its voided centre enclosing a lys, cantoned by four rampant lions and cutting an inner circle - *Newton Abbot.*

French copper-alloy jeton, 1380-1422

220: Obv. Shield of France modern, bearing three fleur-de-lys, six pellets above shield, seven pellets each side + AVE rosette MARIA rosette GRACIA.
 Rev. Triple stranded straight cross fleuretty within quadruple-arched tressure: trefoil - rosette - trefoil x 4 - *Ottery St Mary.*

Duchy of Burgundy, copper-alloy shield of France - Burgundy variant jeton (? Nuremberg imitation), c1384

221: Obv. shield quarters: 1,4 - lis, France; 2,3 - bends, Burgundy ancient, AVE MARIA [....].
 Rev. triple-stranded straight cross fleuretty, four-arched tressure with alternate stars and (?) pellet in external angles - *Exeter*

BUCKLES

After the Norman Conquest of England the use of buckles became widespread on personal costume, horse-harness and in other contexts. Some medieval buckles are iron or cast lead/tin alloy, consequently few are found, however, those of cast copper alloy, which are frequently gilded, silvered or tinned, are not uncommon. Royalty and nobility did use precious metal buckles but such examples are extremely rare.

Medieval double-loop buckles and some single-loop buckles were riveted directly to leather or fabric straps, however, buckles which have integral or separate plates were either riveted to straps or metalwork, e.g. armour. Size isn't a reliable method of differentiating personal costume buckles from those used, for example, on horse harness. For many buckles one can only speculate at their function. Some styles remained fashionable for centuries; this overlapping makes attribution extremely difficult unless from a datable deposit.

Cast copper-alloy single-loop ornate oval buckles, with or without folded sheet copper-alloy plates, 1200-1380

222: four lobed-knops on front, lobed knops on ends of offset and narrowed strap-bar, 18mm x 23mm - *West Ogwell*.

223: two lobed-knops and transverse grooves, offset and narrowed strap-bar, 22mm x 29mm - *Cockington*.

224: seven irregular lobed-knops, offset and narrowed strap-bar, 25mm x 19.5mm - *Haccombe*.

225: three lobed-knops, oblique and transverse engraved grooves, offset and narrowed strap-bar, fragmented copper-alloy tongue, plate with two rivet holes and engraved zigzags, 18mm x 49.5mm - *Newton Abbot*.

226: notched lip with lobed knop each side, offset and narrowed strap-bar, copper-alloy tongue, fragmented plate with two rivet holes, 23mm x 39.5mm - *Haccombe*.

Cast copper-alloy single-loop rectangular or subrectangular buckles with or without folded sheet copper-alloy plates, 1350-1400

227: wide front with slight bifid knop and three engraved transverse grooves, two tiny protrusions on each side, recessed strap-bar with concave centre, 20mm x 16mm - *Exeter*.

228: extremely wide front, slightly convex sides, offset and narrowed strap-bar, copper-alloy tongue, 13mm x 19mm - *Cockington*.

229: slightly narrowed front bar, narrowed strap-bar, plate with two rivet holes, 13mm x 31mm - *Alphington*.

230: convex sides. slightly concave front, offset and narrowed strap-bar, fragmented copper-alloy tongue, plate with two rivet holes, 20.5mm x 42mm - *Cockington*.

231: notched front, plate with one rivet hole, 25.5mm x 40mm *Cockington*.

232: very crude, 22mm x 13.5mm - *Cockington*.

233: narrowed strap-bar, 20mm x 14mm - *Haccombe*.

Cast copper-alloy single-loop oval or subrectangular buckles with sheet copper-alloy roller, with or without folded sheet copper-alloy plates, 1200-1400

234: knops on angles, convex sides, offset and narrowed strap-bar, transverse engraved lines on roller, 21mm x 21mm - *Ringmore*.

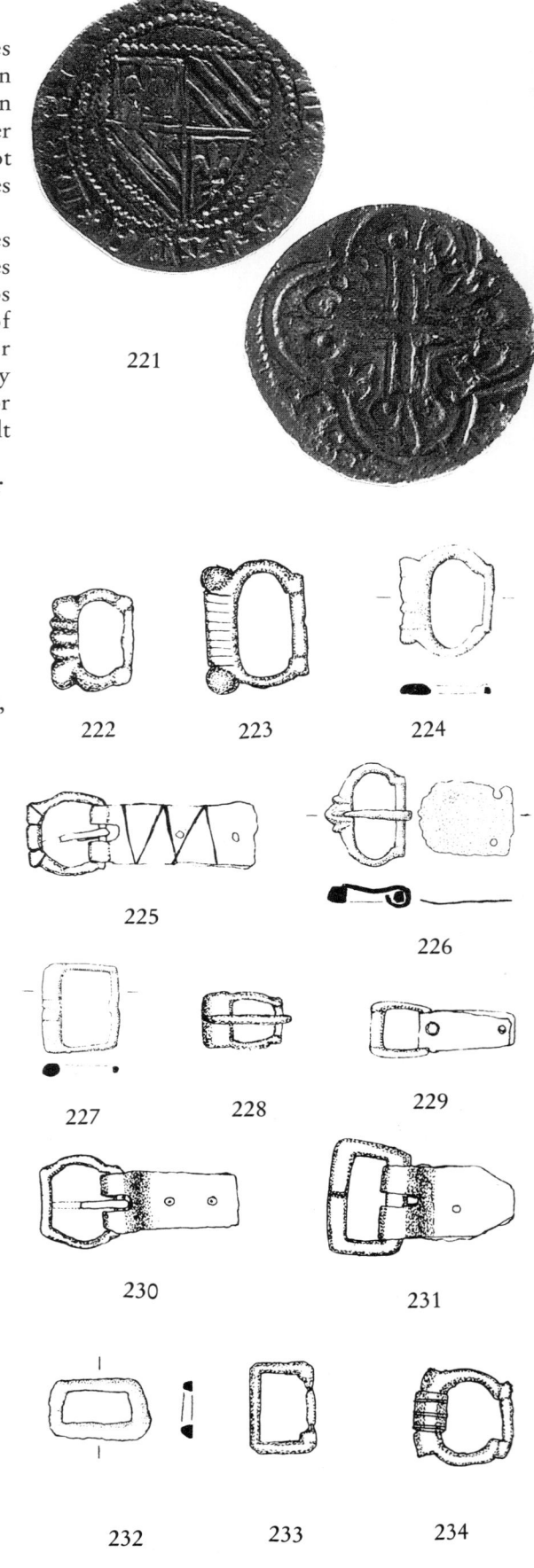

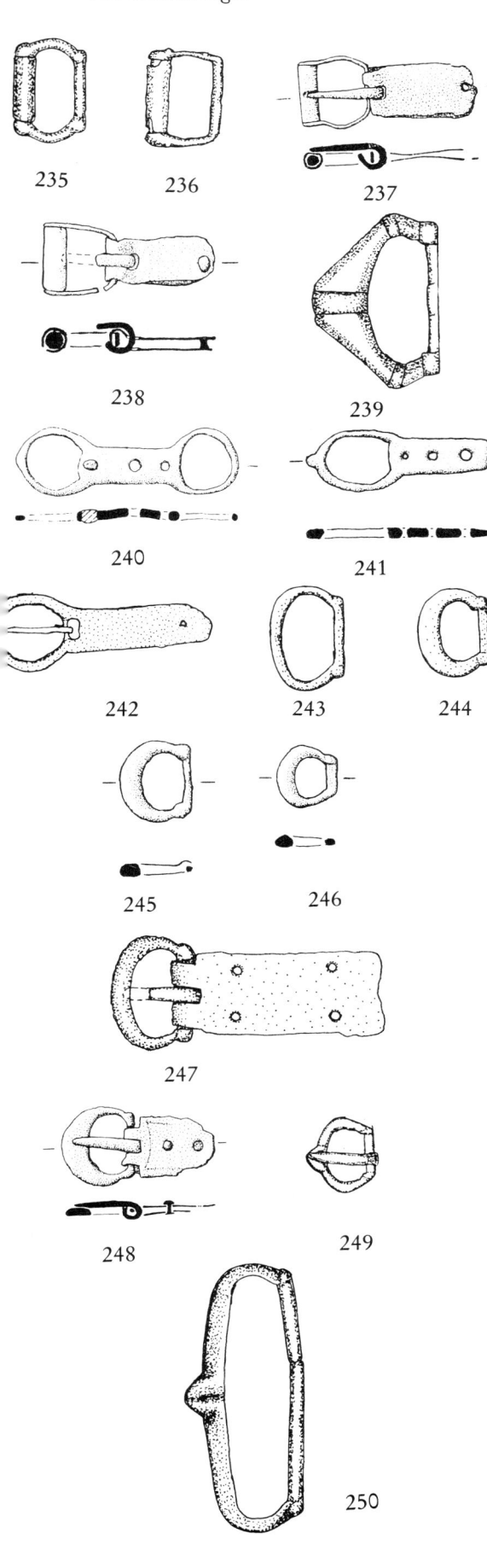

235: knops on angles, convex sides, 24mm x 16mm - *Stokeinteignhead*.
236: slightly convex sides, two slight protrusions on each side, 23mm x 17mm - *Combeinteignhead*.
237: convex sides, copper-alloy tongue, plate with one rivet hole, 17mm x 39mm - *Cockington*.
238: one side broken, fragmented copper-alloy tongue, plate with one rivet hole, copper-alloy rivet, 17mm x 38.5mm - *Haccombe*.

Cast copper-alloy single-loop sub-triangular buckle, 1250-1350

239: slightly trefoil and notched front, moulded ribs on angles, offset and narrowed strap-bar, evidence of abrasion on strap-bar caused by plate, 40mm x 28mm - *Cockington*.

Cast copper-alloy double-loop buckle separated by integral plate, late 13th-14th century

240: two circular loops one with pointed front, frament of iron tongue in tongue hole, two rivet holes, 49.5mm x 15.5mm - *Musbury*.

Cast copper-alloy single-loop buckles with integral plates, 1250-1400

241: gilded, lobed lip, tongue hole, two rivet holes, 14mm x 42mm - *Cockington*.
242: tongue hole, one rivet hole, copper-alloy tongue, 18mm x 50mm - *Alphington*.

Cast copper-alloy single-loop D-shaped buckles with offset, narrowed strap-bars, with or without folded sheet copper-alloy plates, 1350-1450

243: 24mm x 16mm - *Cockington*.
244: 20.5mm x 15.5mm - *Alphington*.
245: 19mm x 16mm - *Haccombe*.
246: 14mm x 13.5mm - *Haccombe*.
247: fragmented copper-alloy tongue, plate with four rivet holes, 27mm x 61mm - *Cockington*.
248: abraded plate with engraved linear border, two rivet holes, one copper-alloy rivet, copper-alloy tongue, 34mm x 18mm - *Cockwood*.

Cast copper-alloy lipped, D-shaped buckles, with or without folded sheet copper-alloy plates, 1250-1500+

249: notched lip, narrowed strap-bar, copper-alloy tongue, 17mm x 15mm - *Cockington*.
250: notched lip; offset, narrowed strap-bar, 61mm x 26.5mm - *Stokeinteignhead*.
251: strap-bar abraded by tongue, plate with bifed terminal and two rivet holes, 20mm x 47mm - *Cockington*.
252: notched lip, narrowed strap-bar, plate with tongue hole and rivet hole, 23.5mm x 35mm - *Exeter*.
253: engraved oblique grooves, 24.5mm x 24mm - *Cockington*.
254: rectangular notch, narrowed strap-bar with rectangular notch, 47mm x 31.5mm - *Stokeinteignhead*.
255: copper-alloy tongue with moulded transverse ridge, 24mm x 38mm - *Teignmouth*.

Cast copper-alloy probable single-loop D-shaped buckle, c1250-1500

256: fragmented; curvilinear, transverse and oblique lines, lozenge and fleurets formed from punched dots, 70mm x 19mm -

The Middle Ages
Distribution of metal detector finds in Southern Devon

1. Alphington (**MC, MA**)
2. Axminster (**MC, MA**)
3. Berry Pomeroy (**A**)
4. Bicton (**MA**)
5. Bishopsteignton (**MC, MA**)
6. Bovey Tracey (**A**)
7. Broadhempston (**A**)
8. Broadsands Beach, Paignton (**A**)
9. Chudleigh (**MA**)
10. Clyst St Mary (**A**)
11. Clyst Honiton (**A**)
12. Cockington (**MC, MA**)
13. Cockwood (**MC, MA**)
14. Coffinswell (**MC, MA**)
15. Combeinteignhead (**MC, MA**)
16. Combefishacre (**MA**)
17. Colaton Raleigh (**A**)
18. Cullompton (**A**)
19. Denbury (**A**)
20. Exeter (**C, MA**)
21. Exmouth (**MC**)
22. Gappah (**MA**)
23. Haccombe (**MC, MA**)
24. Ipplepen (**A**)
25. Kenn (**A**)
26. Kenton (**A**)
27. Kingskerswell (**MC, MA**)
28. Kingsteignton (**MC, MA**)
29. Kilmington (**A**)
30. Kingsbridge (**MC, MA**)
31. Littlehempston (**MA**)
32. Lympstone (**A**)
33. Maidencombe (**MA**)
34. Mamhead (**A**)
35. Musbury (**A**)
36. Netherton (**A**)
37. Newton Abbot (**MC, MA**)
38. Otterton (**A**)
39. Ottery St Mary (**MA**)
40. Paignton (**A**)
41. Pinhoe (**A**)
42. Poltimore (**MA**)
43. Ringmore (**MC, MA**)
44. River Exe, Starcross (**A**)
45. River Teign, Coombe Cellars (**MC**)
46. River Teign, Ringmore (**MC, MA**)
47. River Teign, Hackney Marsh (**MC**)
48. Starcross (**A**)
49. Shaldon (**A**)
50. Stokeinteignhead (**MC, MA**)
51. Stokenham (**A**)
52. Stoke Gabriel (**A**)
53. Stoke Canon (**A**)
54. Teignmouth (**A**)
55. Teigngrace (**MA**)
56. Torquay (**A**)
57. Uffculme (**MA**)
58. Watcombe (**A**)
59. Whilborough (**MC**)
60. West Ogwell (**MA**)
61. Woodbury (**A**)
62. Wolborough, Newton Abbot (**MC, MA**)

Key: **C** = single coin   **MC** = multiple coin   **HC** = hoard of coins
      A = artefact   **MA** = multiple artefact

Stokeinteignhead.

Cast copper-alloy circular or oval single-loop armour-buckles, with folded sheet copper-alloy plates, c1400-c1600

257: one rivet hole, copper-alloy tongue, 19mm x 36mm - *Chudleigh.*
258: one rivet hole, copper-alloy tongue, 18mm x 30mm - *Cockington.*

Cast copper-alloy circular or oval single-loop armour slides, with folded sheet copper-alloy plates, c1400-c1600

259: one rivet hole, 20.5mm x 38mm - *Cockington.*
260: one rivet hole, 15mm x 32mm - *Cockington.*
261: one rivet hole, 20mm x 38mm - *Cockington.*

Cast copper-alloy buckles with single pointed-loop, forked spacers and double sheet copper-alloy plates, 1350-1450

262: plate lost, 38mm x 24mm - *Cockington.*
263: one rivet hole, remains of fabric trapped between plates, copper-alloy tongue, 41mm x 16mm - *Cockington.*

Cast copper-alloy trapezium-shaped single-loop buckle, 1350-1500+

264: concave front, engraved oblique lines, 21.5mm x 24mm - *Stokeinteignhead*

Cast copper-alloy lyre-shaped one-piece buckles, 1390-1420

265: box-plate only, two rivet holes, two copper-alloy rivets, inlaid tin or silver black letter IHC on front, 27mm x 29m - *Alphington.*
266: box-plate and fragment of frame, two rivet holes, two copper-alloy rivets, black letter N on front, 33mm x 23mm - *Exeter.*

Cast copper-alloy kidney-shaped single-loop buckles, 1450-1500+

267: concave front with bifid knop, engraved oblique lines, 38mm x 21mm - *Exeter.*
268: slightly concave front, engraved oblique lines on front and one side, copper-alloy tongue, 39mm x 22.5mm - *Bicton.*
269: concave front, engraved transverse lines in hollow, fragmented copper-alloy tongue, 38mm x 20mm - *Combefishacre.*
270: slightly concave front, engraved zigzags and oblique lines, 37.5mm x 20mm - *Chudleigh.*

Cast copper-alloy rectangular or subrectangular buckles with drilled frames for separate spindles, c1350 - c1400

271: notched front with two transverse grooves, copper-alloy tongue, copper-alloy spindle with fragmented locking arm, 32mm x 29mm - *Stokeinteignhead.*
272: offset front, copper-alloy integral spindle and tongue, 13mm x 19.5mm - *Kingskerswell.*

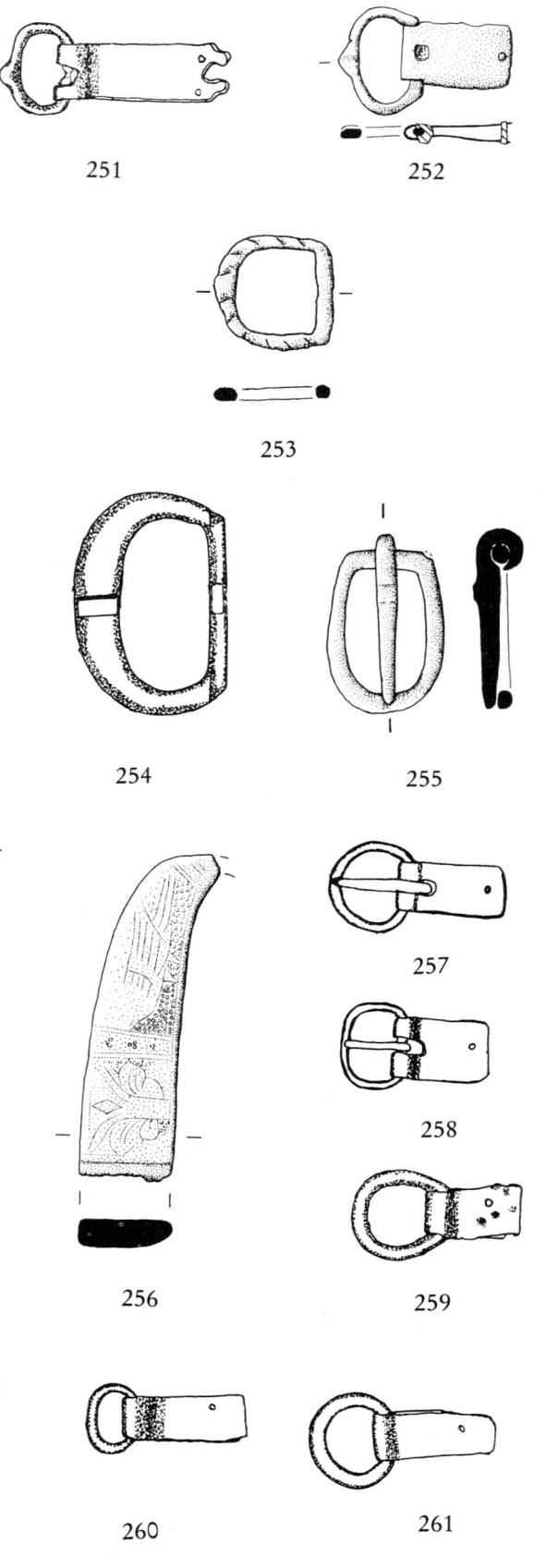

Cast lead/tin-alloy subrectangular buckle with drilled frame for separate spindle, c1350 - c1500

273: pointed front with moulded cabling, pellets triangles and trefoil; moulded transverse lines on end bar, traces of iron around spindle holes, 18.5mm x 35.5mm - *River Teign, Ringmore.*

The Middle Ages

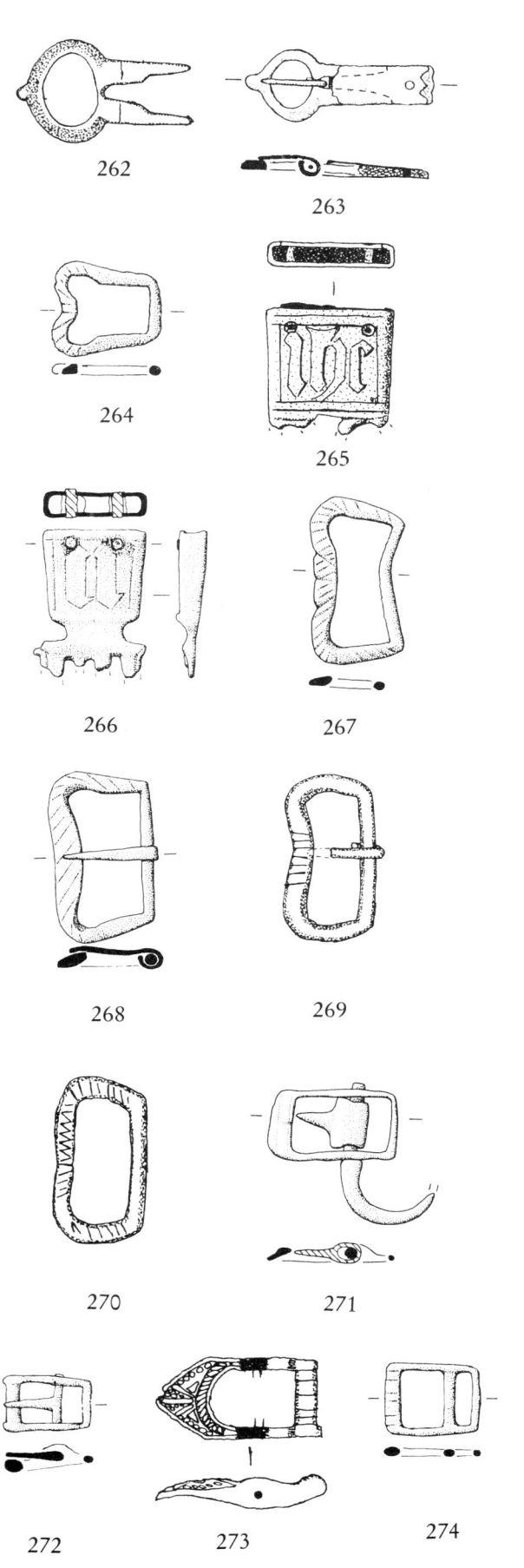

Cast copper-alloy subrectangular buckle with offcentred bar, c1350 - c1400

274: engraved transverse lines on front, 16.5mm x 21mm *Exeter*.

Cast copper-alloy double-loop buckles, c1400-50

275: oval main loop with notch, rectangular strap-loop, copper-alloy flanged tongue, 32.5mm x 27.5mm - Exeter.
276: fragment, subrectangular, fleuret knops on angles, 55mm x 36mm - *Haccombe*.

Cast copper-alloy circular shoe-buckle, 1300-1435

277: copper-alloy tongue, D. 15mm - River Teign, *Ringmore*.

Forged iron circular possible shoe-buckle, 1300-1435

278: frame and tongue welded together by corrosion, D. 17mm - Wolborough, *Newton Abbot*.

Cast copper-alloy circular buckles with central bar, 1370-1500

279: fragmented copper-alloy tongue, D. 23mm - *Cockington*.
280: notched frame, copper-alloy tongue, D. 31mm - *Cockington*.
281: fragmented copper-alloy tongue, D. 27mm - *Coffinswell*.
282: copper-alloy tongue, D. 37mm - *Ringmore*.
283: D. 31mm - *Stokeinteignhead*.
284: D. 37mm - *Kingskerswell*.
285: copper-alloy tongue, D. 42.5mm - *Kingskerswell*.
286: copper-alloy tongue with transverse ridge, D. 44mm - *Cockington*.
287: copper-alloy tongue, D. 39mm - *Stokeinteignhead*.
288: fleuret, border of engraved oblique lines, copper-alloy tongue, D. 41mm - *Cockington*.
289: fleuret, border of engraved oblique lines, D. 28mm - *Alphington*.
290: abraded moulded fleurets, engraved oblique lines and chevrons, fragmented copper-alloy tongue, D. 53mm - *Kingsteignton*.
291: moulded transverse grooves on one loop, four lobed knops on other loop, D. 33mm - *Coffinswell*.
292: two oblique projections each with three engraved transverse grooves, 39mm x 30mm - *Cockington*.

Forged copper-alloy tongue for probable circular buckle, c1370-1500

293: slight rectangular ridge with five punched circles, L. 54mm - *Denbury*.

Cast copper-alloy oval double-loop buckles with or without folded sheet copper-alloy plates, 1350-1500+

294: acorn knops on front of each loop and at each end of narrowed central bar, engraved cross-hatching, copper-alloy tongue, 69mm x 56mm - *Bovey Tracey*.
295: traces of gilt, narrowed central bar, punched dot scrollwork, 43mm x 40mm - *Cockington*.
296: engraved oblique and transverse lines on each each loop, 35mm x 39mm - *Cockington*.
297: slight protrusion at ends of narrowed central bar, engraved oblique and transverse lines on each loop, 33mm x 39mm - *Cockington*.
298: engraved oblique lines on each loop, 30mm x 34mm - *Haccombe*.
299: protrusions on ends of narrowed central bar, engraved oblique and transverse lines on each loop and protrusions, 27.5mm x 36mm - *Stokeinteignhead*.

300: 33.5mm x 42mm - *Ringmore*.
301: slightly narrowed central bar, 21mm x 24.5mm - *Cockington*.
302: 24mm x 34.5mm - *Cockington*.
303: 21mm x 28.5mm - *Coffinswell*.
304: 19mm x 23.5mm - *Cockington*.
305: copper-alloy tongue, 16.5mm x 25mm - *Haccombe*.
306: 15mm x 26mm - *Haccombe*.
307: 14mm x 21mm - *Cockington*.
308: 9.5mm x 16.5mm - *Cockington*.
309: narrowed central bar, 13mm x 15mm - *Stokeinteignhead*.
310: protrusions on ends of central bar, copper-alloy tongue, plate with one rivet hole 11mm x 26.5mm - *Cockington*.
311: plate with two rivet holes, 21mm x 33mm - *Cockington*.
312: abraded curvilinear on each loop, plate with abraded engraved linear and transvere decoration and two rivet holes, remains of iron rivet, 27mm x 47mm - *Uffculme*.
313: fragmented, narrowed central bar; lobed knops around perimeter, each with a blind hole, notched frame, engraved curvilinear and oblique lines, 48mm x 32.5mm - *Netherton*.
314: bifid knops on each loop, narrowed central bar, 30mm x 23mm - *Stokeinteignhead*.
315: tripartite loops, slight protrusion at each end of central bar, 28mm x 31.5mm - *Haccombe*.
316: moulded trefoils and lobed knops on each loop, lobed protrusions on ends of central bar, 25mm x 44mm - *Cockington*.
317: six lobed-knops on each loop, 22mm x 32mm - *Stokeinteignhead*.
318: bifid knops on each loop, copper-alloy tongue, 26mm x 41mm - *Cockington*.
319: chevron grooves on each loop, 15mm x 23mm - *Stokeinteignhead*.

Cast copper-alloy rectangular folding strap-clasps with separate bar-mounts, with or without folded sheet copper-alloy plates, 1270-1450

320: convex sides with two moulded transverse ribs each side, plate with one rivet hole, 18mm x 26.5mm - Wolborough, *Newton Abbot*.
321: slightly convex sides with two moulded transverse ribs each side, folding end abraded on front, 18mm x 20mm - *Cockington*.
322: slightly convex sides with two moulded transverse ribs each side, 18mm x 16.5mm - *Haccombe*.
323: convex sides with two moulded transverse ribs each side, bar mount at an angle, plate with one rivet hole, copper-alloy rivet, 13.5mm x 33.5mm - *Cockington*.

Folded sheet copper-alloy rectangular buckle-plate, 14th century

324: traces of gilt, five copper-alloy dome-headed rivets, 17mm x 28mm - *Stokeinteignhead*.

Cast silver asymmetrical buckle-plate, 14th-15th century

325: heavily gilded, circular openwork inset with a moulded fleur-de-lis, moulded foliate and acorn knop, one rivet hole, 11mm x 26mm - *Berry Pomeroy*.

N.B. Nos. 259-61 were used as tensioners in tandem with armour buckles. Regarding No.265, 'IHC' or 'IHS' are the

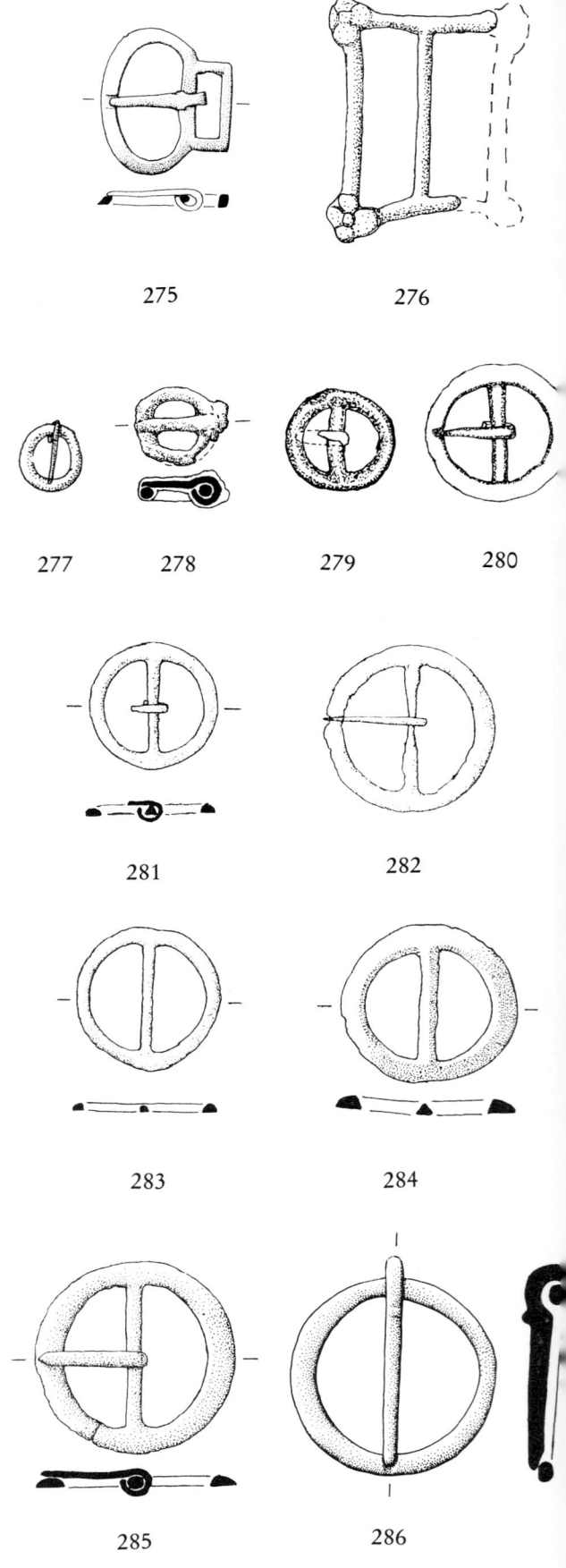

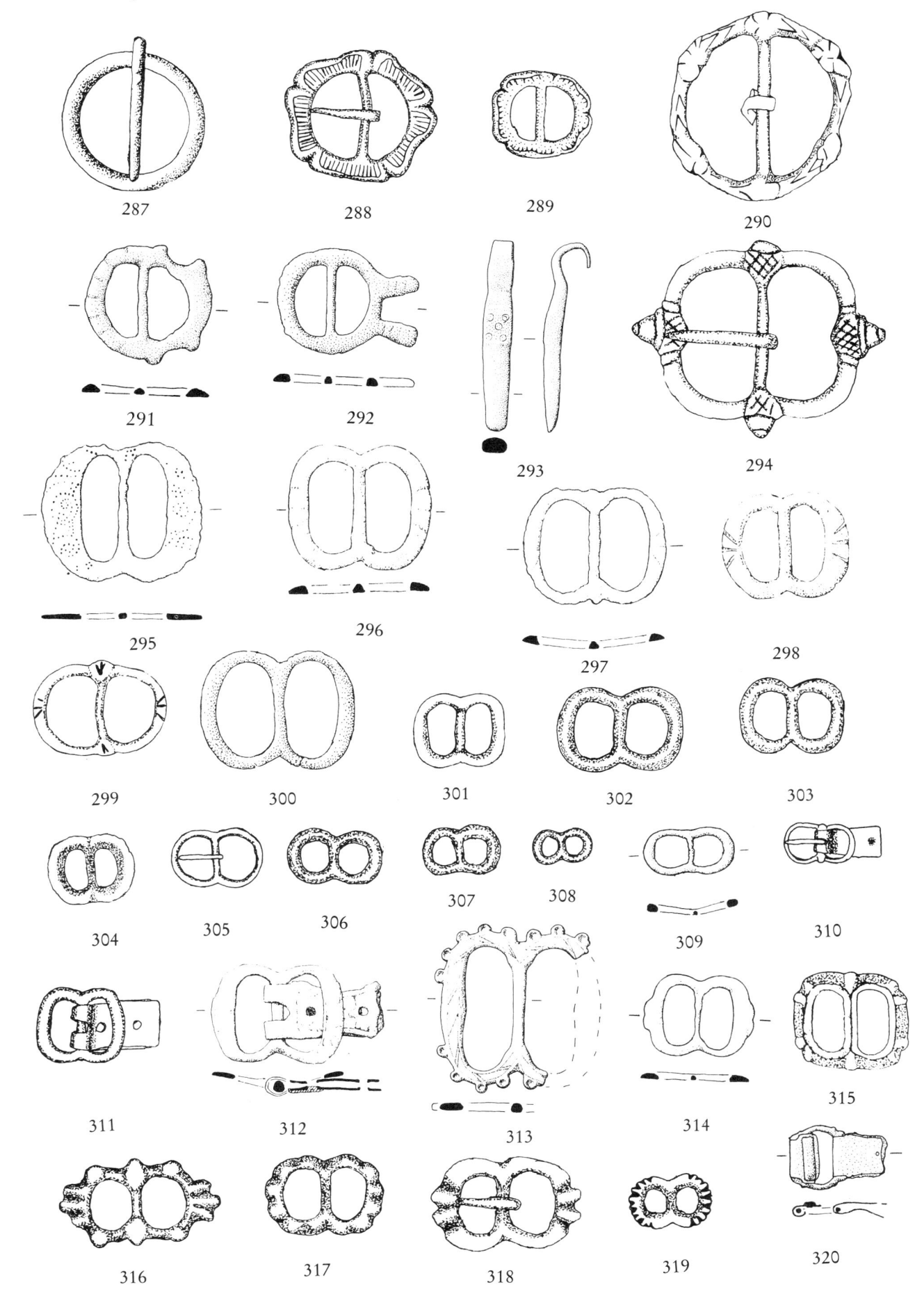

The Middle Ages

287 288 289 290
291 292 293 294
295 296 297 298
299 300 301 302 303
304 305 306 307 308 309 310
311 312 313 314 315
316 317 318 319 320

first three letters of the Greek form of the name Jesus - 'I(esus) H(ominum) S(alvator)', meaning 'Jesus Saviour of Mankind'. The foliate on No.325 may represent a lilly, emblem of the Virgin Mary.

STRAP-ENDS

For wealthy people in the Middle Ages strap-ends were frequently made of precious metal or ivory, sometimes set with gemstones; however, copper alloy, lead/tin alloy or iron were the metals normally used, which were not uncommonly gilded, silvered, tinned or nielloed. Different metals, or their alloys, were frequently employed in the fabrication of individual strap-ends. According to fashion, girdle lengths varied. At times long tails were popular which meant the strap-end hung in the vertical, whilst sometimes shorter tails were prefered, therefore strap-ends remained horizontal.

Medieval metal strap-ends come in a multitude of designs and sizes. There are four basic types which were all riveted to the strap, viz: folded single sheet, double sheet, double sheet separated by a spacer, and cast. These four types can be subdivided into, viz: those with soldered side strips, partially soldered double sheet, hinged-plate and hinged, and those incorporating bar-mounts, loops, or hooks.

Folded single sheet copper-alloy strap-ends, c1350 - c1400

326: bifid terminal, abraded engraved linear, one rivet hole, copper-alloy rivet, 42.5mm x 11mm - *Ringmore.*

327: cinquefoil separate terminal formed from intertwined wire, circular knop, one rivet hole, copper-alloy rivet, 62mm x 22mm -*Cockington.*

328: trefoil knop, front plate with fragmented bifid top and engraved linear border, back plate has quatrefoil top, body with bifid sides outlined with semi-circular cross-section wire applique forming two cordates, two rivet holes, two copper-alloy rivets, 45mm x 20.5mm - Wolborough, *Newton Abbot.*

329: expanded end at the fold, border of two rows of punched triangles, five rivet holes, five copper-alloy dome-headed rivets, 46mm x 21mm - *Cockington.*

330: subrectangular, opened up, abraded engraved rectangular panel of curvilinear and a triangle, four rivet holes, remains of one iron rivet, 18mm x 25mm - *Cockwood.*

Soldered and riveted double-sheet copper-alloy strap-ends, 14th century

331: trefoil terminal, one rivet hole, copper-alloy rivet, 51mm x 14mm - *Cockington.*

332: two rivet holes (one lost), remains of one iron rivet, 50mm x 17mm - *Haccombe.*

333: abraded edges, two rivet holes, 40mm x 11mm - *Haccombe.*

334: septfoil terminal, two bands of engraved zigzags, one rivet hole, copper-alloy rivet, 52mm x 14mm - *Haccombe.*

335: front plate, semi-circular apertures in sides near top; engraved transverse, vertical, curviliniar and oblique lines, longitudinal band of punched circles, two rivet holes, one copper-alloy rivet, 69.5mm x 15mm - *Gappah.*

Riveted double-sheet copper-alloy strap-ends, 14th century

336: elaborate trefoil terminal, front plate fragmented at top,

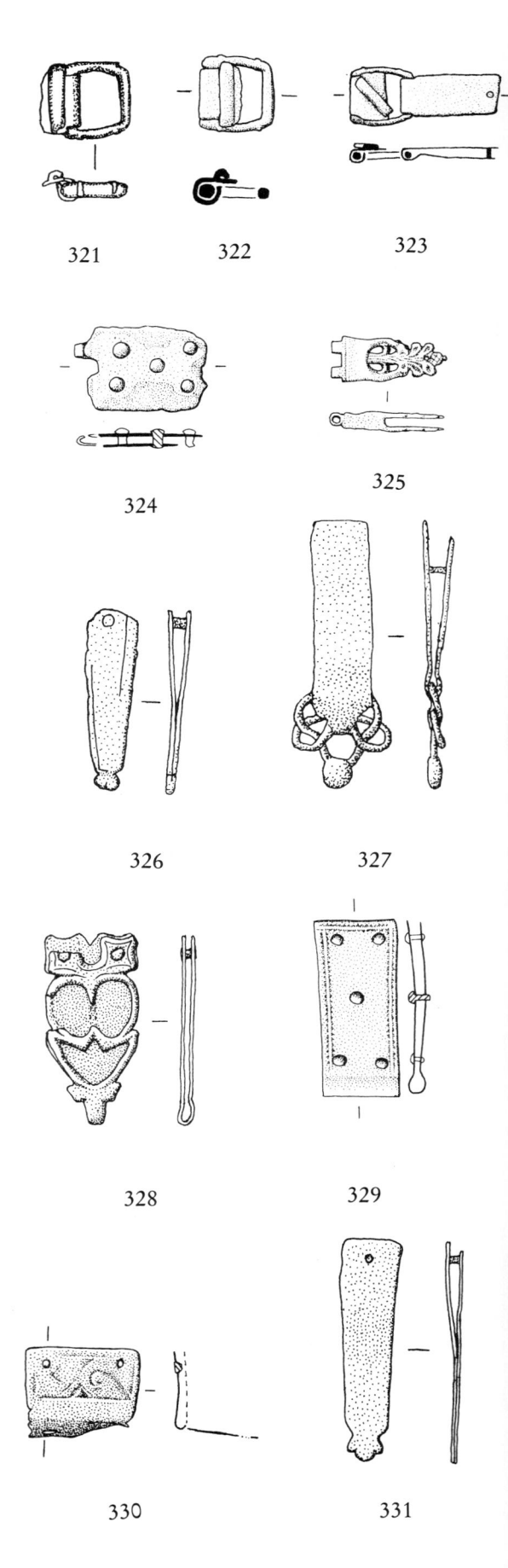

The Middle Ages

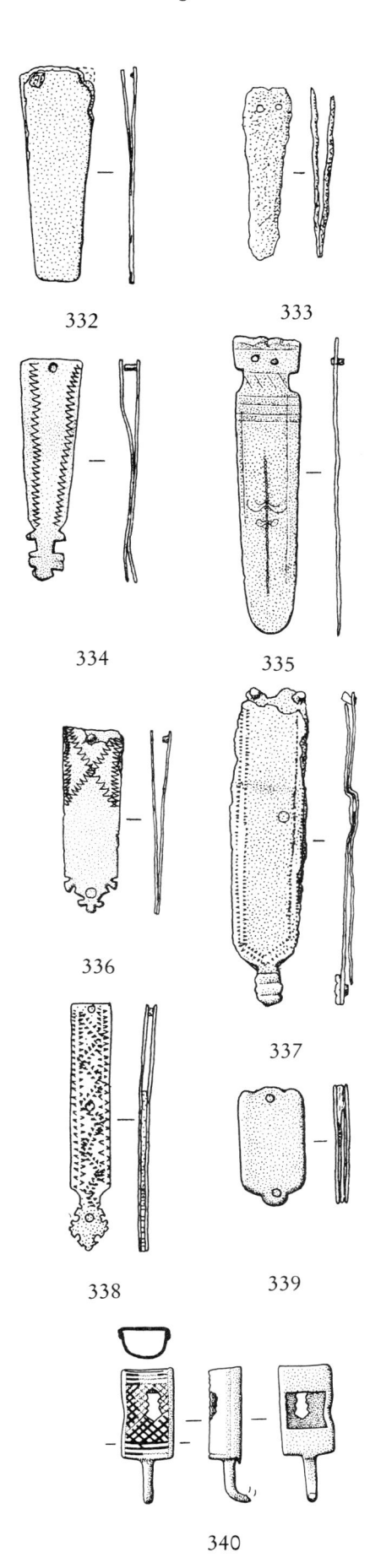

engraved zigzags forming a cross, two rivet holes, two copper-alloy rivets, 42.5mm x 14mm - *Newton Abbot.*

337: separate copper-alloy applique with transverse grooves on knop, top of front plate fragmented, border of two bands of punched triangles, four rivet holes, four copper-alloy rivets, 73.5mm x 17.5mm - *Haccombe.*

Double sheet copper-alloy strap-end with side strip, 14th century

338: elaborate quatrefoil terminal, bands and zigzags of punched chevrons, three rivet holes, three copper-alloy rivets, 57mm x 9mm - *Stokeinteignhead.*

339: shield-shaped, two rivet holes, two copper-alloy rivets, remains of leather strap between sheets, 27mm x 15mm - *Teigngrace.*

Double sheet copper-alloy strap-end with bent sides and hook, 15th century

340: convex front plate, damaged, nielloed cross-hatching and transverse lines, square openwork in back plate, fragmented hook, 31mm x 12mm - *Cockington.*

Cast copper-alloy lozenge-shaped strap-end with lateral circular eyelet, c14th-15th century.

341: one rivet hole, remains of iron rivet, moulded transverse lines, engraved vertical lines, fragment of leather strap between plates, 40mm x 17.5mm - *Broadhempston.*

Double sheet copper-alloy strap-ends with bent sides, c15th-16th century

342: shield-shaped; tinned or silvered front with nielloed intertwined IHS, lobed knop, four rivet holes, four copper-alloy rivets, keyhole-shaped openwork in backplate, 35mm x 27mm - *Cockington.*

343: shield-shaped, tinned front, two rivet holes, two copper-alloy rivets, keyhole-shaped openwork in backplate, leather fragment sandwiched between the plates completely blocks the orifice, 29mm x 23mm - *Stokeinteignhead.*

344: shield-shaped, two rivet holes, two copper-alloy rivets, keyhole-shaped openwork in backplate, 27mm x 21mm - *Stokeinteignhead.*

345: oval frontplate with six lobed-knops and acorn knop, bottom hook is probably a damaged acorn knop, shield-shaped backplate with keyhole-shaped openwork and six rivet holes, two copper-alloy rivets, 36mm x 29mm - *Poltimore.*

346: shield-shaped with trefoil top, bottom and sides; four rivet holes, two copper-alloy rivets, 25mm x 20.5mm - *Stoke Gabriel.*

Fragmented sheet copper-alloy strap-ends of indeterminate type, 14th century

347: abraded edges, single rivet hole, copper-alloy rivet, 46.5mm x 12mm - *Haccombe.*

348: abraded edges; engraved linear, zigzags and vertical lines, 53mm x 11.5mm - *Haccombe.*

349: shield-shaped, border and chevron of two bands of engraved zigzags, two rivet holes (one lost), 41mm x 32mm - *Ringmore.*

Cast and sheet copper-alloy composite strap-ends with forked spacers, c1270 - c1350

350: fragmented fork, abraded (?) acorn knop, 46mm x 15mm - *Stokeinteignhead.*
351: fragmented fork, abraded acorn knop, 33mm x 14mm - *Stokeinteignhead.*
352: circular, acorn knop, two rivet holes, two copper-alloy rivets, 33mm x 25mm - *Axminster.*
353: possibly the lower part, acorn knop, small circular openwork, 32mm x 11mm - *Coffinswell.*

Cast and sheet copper-alloy two-piece strap-end with hinged loop and plate, c1350-1400

354: loop only, central circular hole, lateral circular knop with a circular hole, fragment of plate attached to hinge, 20.5mm x 10.5mm - *Axminster.*

Cast copper-alloy single piece strap-ends, 14th century

355: longitudinal central moulded groove, bifid protrusion each side, two rivet holes, 70mm x 25mm - *Cockington.*
356: lozenge-shaped terminal with an moulded lozenge and a zoomorphic gaping jaws beast knop, fragmented box-section plate engraved with a panel of cross-hatching and black letter inscription D V, four rivet holes, one copper-alloy rivet, 76.5mm x 23mm - *Maidencombe*

Sheet copper-alloy strap-end with separate bar-mount, c1350-1400

357: shield-shaped, engraved transverse grooves, rectangular bar-mount, four rivet holes, twp copper-alloy rivets, 21mm x 22mm - *Cockington.*

Cast and sheet copper-alloy possible composite strap-end with pendant loop, c14th-15th century

358: fragmented loop, forked spacer, shield-shaped plates, six rivet holes, six copper-alloy rivets, 66mm x 28.5mm - *Exeter.*

N.B. The keyhole orifice strap-ends are enigmatic. It has been suggested (British Museum) that No.342 is made from an old lock. Another opinion is that the keyhole-shaped openwork accepted a male member fitted to the opposite end of the strap, therefore it was one half of a clasp. This doesn't square for a short-tailed girdle as the initials would lie side view.

Possibly they are not girdle strap-ends but rather strap-ends forming one half of catch-plates attached to straps of, or even direct to, something similar to leather carrying-bags. If correct, No.342s knop would be uppermost and initials the correct way up. The male member, which must have had an enlarged terminal, would fit into the circular part of the openwork and then slide down the slot, thereby securing it closed. This hypothesis seemed logical until No.343 was found, seemingly precluding such a use!

The discovery of three additional artefacts all with similar keyhole openwork and from differnt geographical locations of the county discredits the discarded lock theory. In the absence of positive evidence, here, they are attributed as strap-ends.

MOUNTS

Medieval personal costume, e.g. waistcoats, archer's wrist-guards or straps, as well as horse harness (including mouthpiece ends of curb-bits), were invariably embellished with cast or sheet:

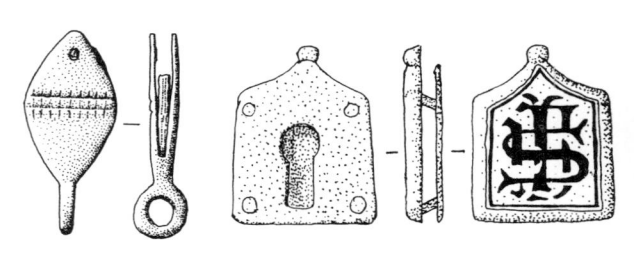

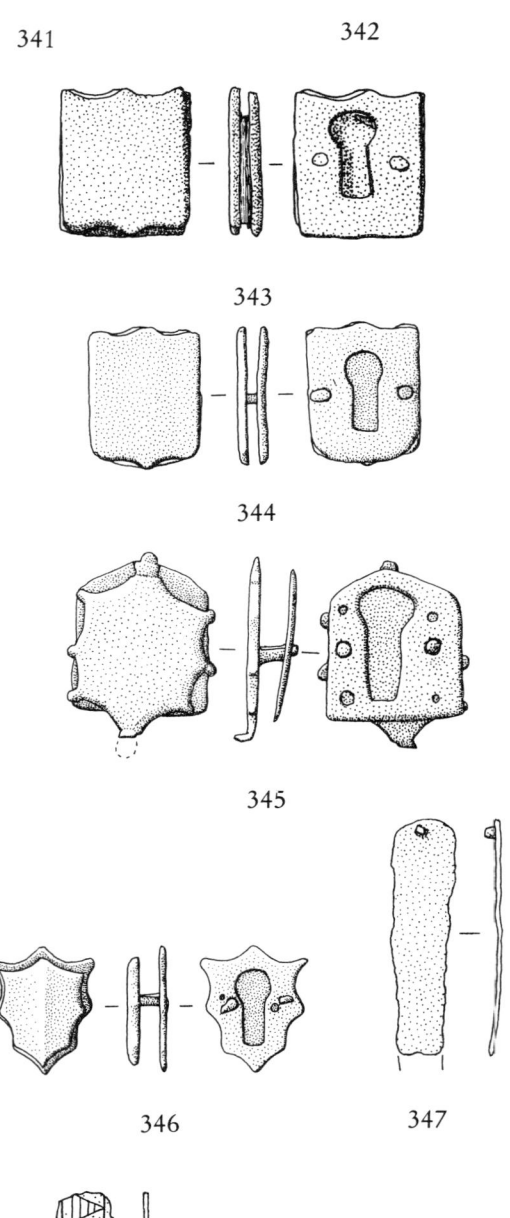

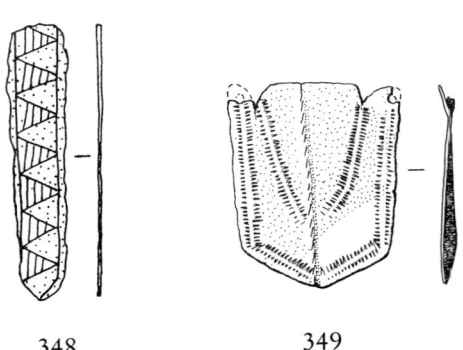

The Middle Ages

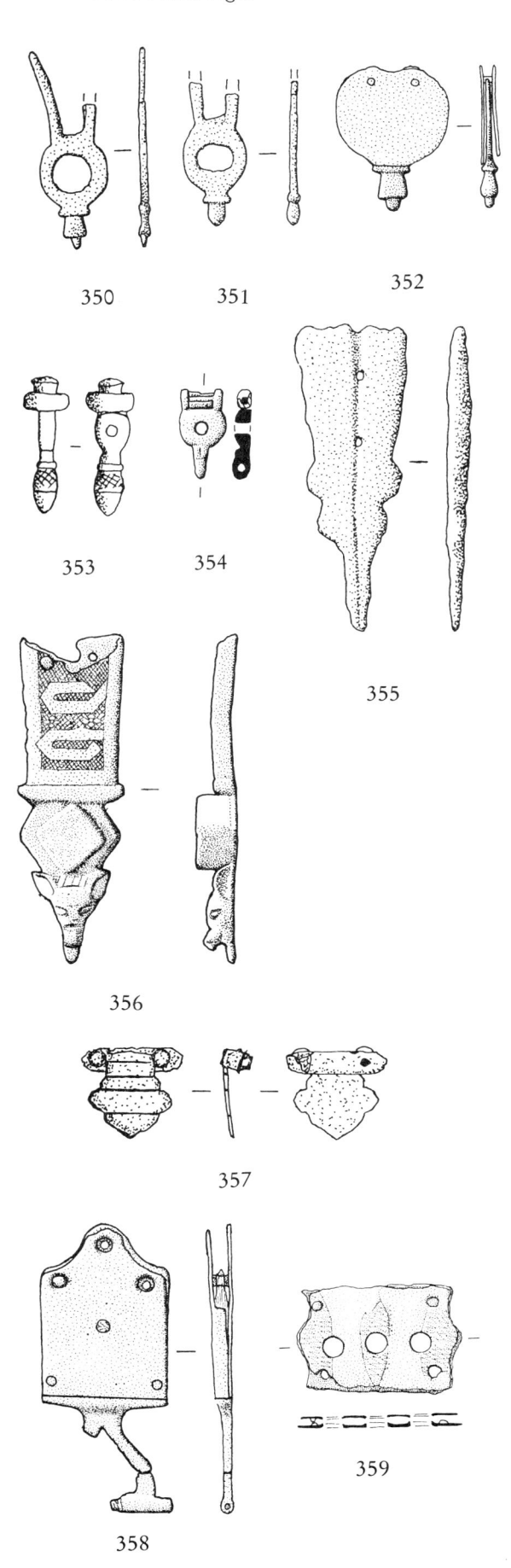

copper-alloy, lead/tin-alloy, iron, silver or gold appliques (some were both decorative and functional). Base metal was frequently gilded, silvered or tinned. Similarly, other everyday objects, e.g: book covers, costrals, purses, caskets, chests or furniture were frequently so ornamented.

The sheer diversity of mounts coupled with lack of research data, in many cases precludes correct attribution. In the absence of conclusive evidence all that can be said is that smaller types are likely to be from personal costume and larger more robust examples from elswhere. Attachment methods vary, which can assist classification, viz: integral rivets, separate rivets, integral nail-like spikes, integral blunt or pointed lugs, soldered, glued or inset. For some pieces it is difficult to ascribe precisely which way up they were affixed, therefore it is likely that some mounts depicted herein are incorrectly illustrated.

Double sheet copper-alloy rectangular strap-plates, 1300-1430

359: engraved fish-scale decoration in three panels on front sheet with abraded edge, equidistant circular openwork down longitudinal centre, four rivet holes, two copper-alloy rivets, 25mm x 36.5mm - *Cockington*.

360: fragmented front sheet, central circular openwork, engraved border of vertical and transverse lines, four rivet holes, four copper-alloy rivets, 29mm x 46mm - *Bishopsteignton*.

Single sheet copper-alloy rectangular strap-plates, 1300-1430

361: central countersunk circular openwork, engraved rectangle with two panels each containing an engraved quatrefoil, a St Andrew's cross and transverse lines, two rivet holes, remains of two iron rivets, 33mm x 16mm - *Kingskerswell*.

Cast copper-alloy hook-mounts without rivets

362: c13th-14th century, three-dimensional, circular cross-section zoomorphic knop, circular cross-section hook much abraded, L. 63mm - *Coffinswell*.

363: c13th-14th century, three-dimensional, square cross-section zoomorphic knop, circular and part semi-circular cross-section hook, L. 54mm - *Haccombe*.

364: c15th century, acorn, abraded edges, fragmented hook, two rivet holes, 27.5mm x 20mm - *Cockington*

Cast copper-alloy stud-like mounts, c14th - early 16th century

365: vesica-shaped, circular cross-section stud, moulded pellets, 24mm x 15mm - *Kingskerswell*.

366: circular, tinned, square cross-section stud; moulded concentric circles, pellets and beaded border, 22mm x 12mm - *Exeter*.

367: sexfoil, square cross-section stud, moulded pellets and concentric circles, 15mm x 7mm - *Exeter*.

368: lozenge-shaped, circular cross-section stud, moulded fleuret and border of pellets, 18.5mm x 25mm - *Exeter*.

369: shield-shaped, circular cross-section stud, remnants of three roundels in red enamel on a gold field, trace of blue enamelled label of three points. Without the label, this is the coat of arms of the French family Courtenay, one son of whom possibly came to England with William I. Descendants of the Courtenays used the same arms but differenced with a label of three points, viz blazoned: 'Or three torteaux a label of three points azure'. Sir Hugh de Courtenay bore these arms at the battle of Falkirk in 1298 and the siege of Caeslaverock 1300. He became Earl of Devon in 1335 which is probably the attribution for the mount. 35.5mm x 28mm - *Poltimore*..

Cast copper-alloy lozenge-shaped, mounts with integral rivets, c15th century
370: moulded lozenge-shape, single rivet, 24mm x 19mm - *Haccombe*.
371: angled edges, lozenge-shaped openwork, two rivets 29mm x 20mm - *Cockington*.

Cast lead/tin-alloy circular mount with integral rivets, c15th century
372: incuse six-point star each arm terminating in a moulded roundel, two moulded pellets in each segment, remains of two rivets, D. 27mm - *Axminster*.

Sheet copper-alloy circular mount with integral rivet, c1365-1435
373: stamped concentric circles with an engraved multi-point star and small circles, remains of one rivet, D. 19mm - *Axminster*.

Cast copper-alloy bar-mounts with separate rivets, 1175-1425
374: lobed terminals, central lobe, circular openwork, two rivet holes, two copper-alloy rivets, 24mm x 8.5mm - *Stokeinteignhead*.
375: embossed ribbed central lobe, two rivet holes, 23mm x 11mm - *Cockington*.
376: lobed terminals, central lobe, circular openwork, two rivet holes, remains of two iron rivets, 20mm x 7mm - *Cockington*.

Cast copper-alloy possible bar-mount with separate rivet, perhaps c1175-1425
377: similar to a medieval bar-mount but circular cross-section and with a central (?) rivet hole, L. 42.5 - *Cockwood*.

Cast copper-alloy bar-mount with pendent loop and separate rivets, c1350 - c1400
378: bar-mount lost, circular, circular cross-section, moulded collared globular knop, 18mm x 12mm - *Stokeinteignhead*.

Cast copper-alloy circular mount with separate rivet, c1365-1435
379: moulded eight-point star with pellet in each segment, central rivet hole, D. 21mm - *Axminster*.

Sheet copper-alloy mounts with separate rivets, 14th century
380: shield-shaped, possibly 'barry of six, overall a bend ? ermine', one rivet hole, 46mm x 36mm - *Haccombe*.
381: book-mount, lozenge-shaped, circular openwork with abraded convex sides probably held a gemstone, four rivet holes, four copper-alloy rivets, engraved zigzag border and concentric circles in angles, border of punched shield-shapes each enclosing a trefoil of punched dots around openwork, 69mm x 61mm - *Kingskerswell*.
382: octofoil, embossed concentric circles and curvilinear with

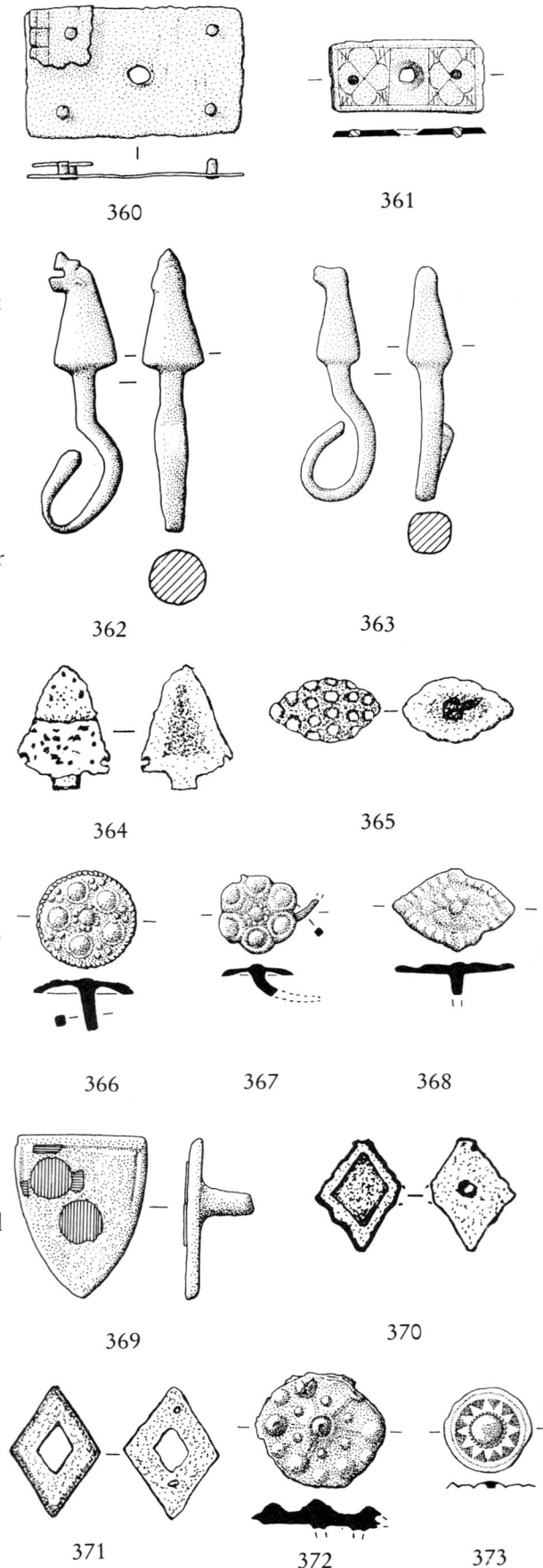

The Middle Ages

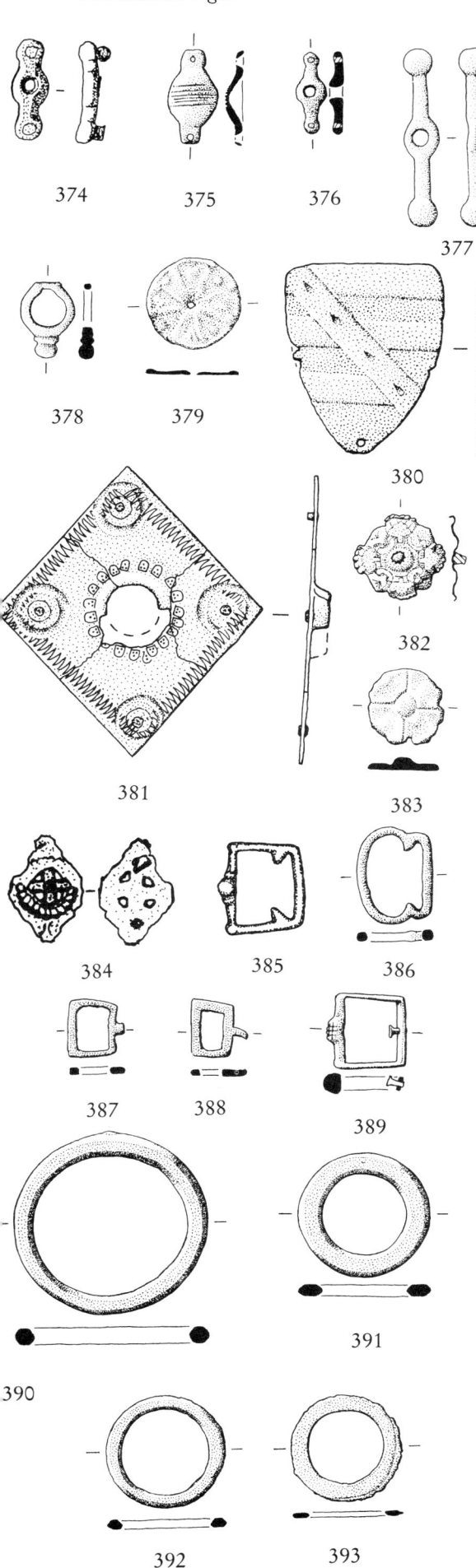

four escallop knops, central rivet hole, copper-alloy rivet, D. 20.5mm - *Axminster.*

Cast copper-alloy quatrefoil mount without rivets, c1270-c1350
383: moulded cross and domed roundel, D. 16.5mm - *Axminster.*

Cast copper-alloy lozenge-shaped mount with integral pointed lugs, c.late 15th century
384: tinned, abraded edges, moulded cross and central circle with openwork spandrels, abraded beaded border, two lugs, 26mm x 17mm - *Alphington.*

Cast copper-alloy strap-loops with integral internal projections, 1160-1390
385: subrectangular, lobed knop between oblique ridges, lobed knops on front corners, 22mm x 20mm - *Stokeinteignhead.*
386: oval, 23mm x 18mm - *Haccombe.*

Cast copper-alloy strap-loops with external integral rivets, c1300-c1385
387: subrectangular, 14mm x 12mm - *Cockington.*
388: subrectangular, 14mm x 13mm - *Cockington.*

Cast copper alloy strap-loop with separate internal rivet, 1300-1400
389: subrectangular, moulded quatrefoil cross-hatched knop, one rivet hole, copper-alloy rivet, 18mm x 18mm - *Bicton.*

ANNULAR RINGS

It is reasonable to believe that the widely found copper-alloy so-called 'horse harness-rings' were mass-produced multi-function items current from the late medieval period through to the 17th century or later. These enigmatic, cast, irregular, annular rings, of varying sizes, most of which have a flattened cross-section, are frequently unfettled and exhibit file marks and a casting sprue.

Small examples used as pendant loops of bar-mounts still attached to leather straps have been excavated in London. In Somerset a tiny example complete with a separate copper-alloy folded sheet bar-mount with a single rivet hole was found by a metal detector. A similar but much larger ring, complete with copper-alloy folded sheet bar-mount, was recovered in Dorset by another metal detector. Utilisation on horse harness seems unlikely as most are quite lightweight, although strap-junctions of indeterminate type is a distinct possibility. Many rings have a transverse groove which implies use as Ring brooches or Circular-frame buckles.

Cast copper-alloy annular rings, c13th - c17th century
390: slightly flattened sexfoil cross-section, D. 45mm - *Cockington.*
391: flattened sexfoil cross-section, D. 30.5mm - *Haccombe.*
392: flattened sexfoil cross-section, D. 27.5mm - *Stokeinteignhead.*
393: very flat oval cross-section, unfettled, D. 25.5mm - *Bishopsteignton.*

LACE CHAPES

Other than buttons, during the 13th-14th century period, certain items of personal costume, such as male and female upper garments, were fastened by means of a leather or plaited-textile lace. To prevent fraying of the lace-ends and to facilitate threading through eyelets, metal chapes, or tags, were affixed. Lace-chapes were current into the 16th century and even later (today's shoe laces still have them). Archaeologically dated examples indicate that manufacture from sheet copper alloy was the norm, though one found in Devon is sheet silver.

Lace-chapes are tapered, pointed or blunt, tubes with either butt jointed or overlapped seams. Attachment was achieved by a single rivet or by crimping. Most recorded lace-chapes are quite plain, although examples with engraved decoration are known. Some artefacts classified as lace-chapes almost certainly performed another function, which is unknown. Unless the remains of a lace are in situ, caution is advised regarding attribution.

Sheet silver lace-chape, c13th-16th century
394: pointed, slightly abraded around socket, no evidence of a rivet hole or crimping, no joint is visible which may indicate a well-soldered seam, 40mm x 5mm- *Coffinswell*.

Sheet copper-alloy lace-chapes, c13th-14th century
395: pointed, butt-jointed seam, socket end closed by (?) crimping, 57mm x 8mm - *Axminster*.
396: pointed, overlapped seam, 43mm x 6mm - *Axminster*.
397: pointed, overlapped seam, 30mm x 5mm - *Axminster*.

N.B. A suggestion has been made that No.395 is perhaps a crude home-made copper-alloy nail, or a lace-chape which has been reused for that purpose.

BROOCHES

During the Middle Ages, particularly the Plantagenet period (Henry II - Richard II), brooches were commonly worn by all classes of society. Some types, especially those in the form of a ring and pin, i.e. annular, were worn at the neck as functional objects used to fasten clothing. Annular brooches were made in cast, sheet or twisted wire forms. Copper alloy or lead/tin alloy was the norm with lower classes, though similarly produced gold or silver examples were readily available to the wealthy. Elaborate and rich decoration, including: inscriptions, gemstones, paste stones, glass, gilding, silvering or tinning was commonplace. Apart from circular, other shapes of Annular brooch are known, e.g: hexagonal, pentagonal, lozenge, rectangular, quatrefoil, oval or lobed.

There has been much confusion over the identification of plain Circular-frame buckles and plain Annular brooches, for they are very similar. The best aid for differentiating the two is that true Annular brooches have either a constriction or hole in the frame which prevents the pin moving around the frame; plain Circular-frame buckles generally have no such in-built restriction. Invariably Annular brooches have sharper pins. However, caution is advised, for some such artefacts share the characteristics of both plain Annular brooches and plain Circular-frame buckles.

It seems that this muddle is due to an error when transcribing archaeological working notes of stratified Annular buckles from Visby on the island of Gotland, Sweden (where a body had such a buckle at each thigh). A published report comparing similar finds from London with those from Visby clearly states that the body had 'a brooch on either thigh'. See Ward-Perkins 1940, 275 and pl LXXVII, nos. 1 & 2 (Reference Museum of London, Dress

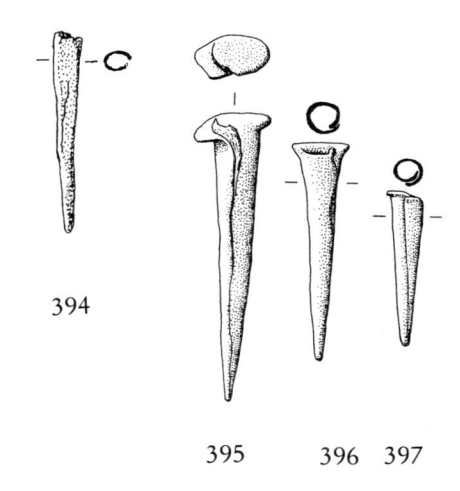

The Middle Ages

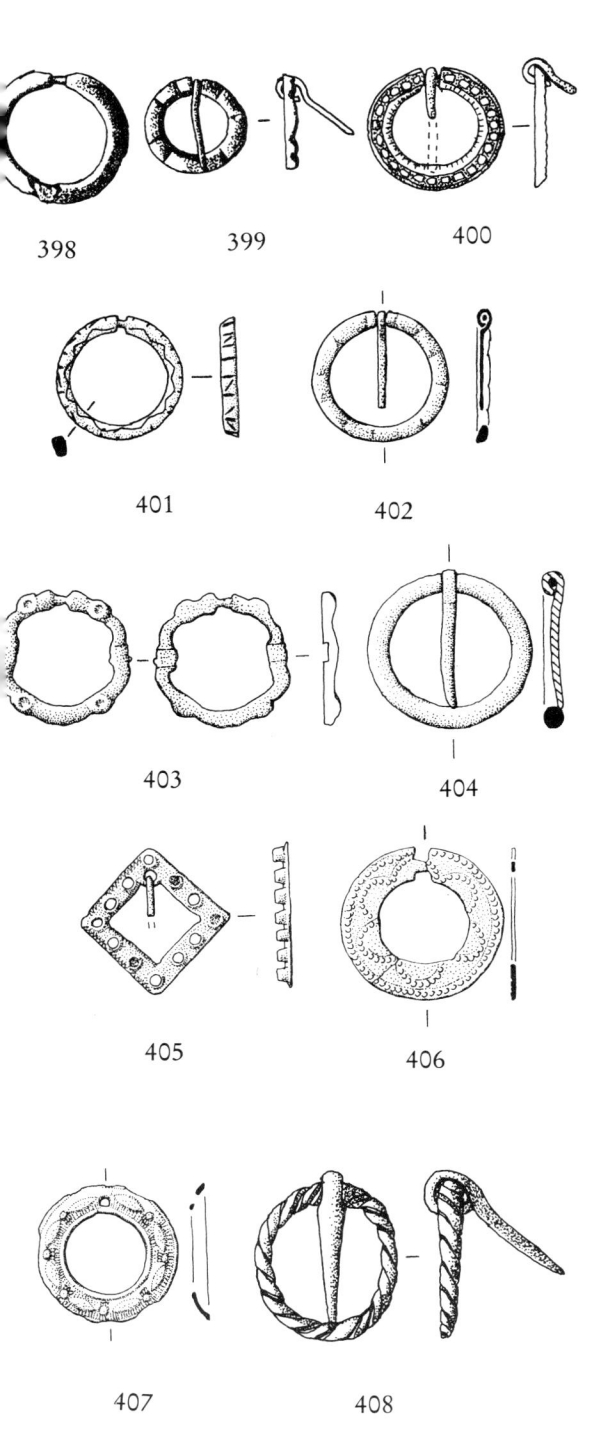

Accessories pp 64 & 65). However, despite this evidence, Hattatt, ARBB. pp 176, 213 & ABOA. pp 382, describes such artefacts as Ring (Annular) brooches, some of which are classified as Anglo-Saxon.

Another form of medieval brooch, which was probably purely decorative, is the cast lead/tin-alloy or cast copper-alloy Plate or Disc type with integral pins. Undoubtedly some are pilgrim or secular badges which is difficult to confirm unless the design can be attributed to a known shrine or family.

Cast copper-alloy Annular brooches, c13th century

398: circular, semi-circular cross-section, with constriction, D. 26mm - *Cockington*.

399: circular, semi-circular cross-section, with constriction, moulded transverse grooves, copper-alloy pin, D. 20mm - *Haccombe*.

400: circular, semi-circular cross-section, with constriction, moulded beading, fragmented copper-alloy pin, D. 25.5mm - *Newton Abbot*.

401: circular, semi-circular cross-section, with constriction; engraved zigzags, oblique and transverse lines, D. 24mm - *Ringmore*.

402: circular, semi-circular cross-section, with constriction, moulded transverse grooves, fragmented copper-alloy pin, D. 26mm - *Haccombe*.

403: circular, semi-circular cross-section, with constriction, four moulded turrets which probably held past stones, two moulded rectangular grooves on underside, D. 26mm - *Cockington*.

404: circular, circular cross-section, with constriction, slight collar on copper-alloy pin, D. 31mm - *Kenn*.

405: lozenge-shaped, moulded turrets with remains of white paste stones, traces of engraved zigzags border, fragmented copper-alloy pin, 29mm x 28mm - *Woodbury*.

Sheet copper-alloy Annular brooches, c13th century

406 circular, flat, with constriction, sexfoil formed from engraved semi-circles and punched crescents, border of punched crescents and dots, D. 30mm - *Haccombe*.

407: circular, convex, abraded perimeter, circular pin-hole; punched dot border, circles and vesica shapes (oval with pointed ends), engraved transverse lines, D. 27mm - *Combeinteignhead*.

Twisted copper-alloy wire Annular brooch, 13th century

408: circular, three strands of tapered wire, with slight constriction, copper-alloy pin, D. 28mm - *Exeter*.

FINGER RINGS

A finger-ring which enjoyed great popularity with medieval merchants and ecclesiastics, among others, was the signet. They are found in either base-metal, silver (frequently gilded) or gold, and invariably are engraved on the bezel with the owner's mark which is either a: representational portrait, simple initial or initials, monogram, arms or crest, inscription; religous, heraldic or miscellaneous device or rebus. More sophisticated signet finger-rings of gold occasionally were set with engraved gemstones or classical-style intaglios.

Other types of finger-ring which were worn for a specific purpose were current, e.g: iconographic religous, ecclesiastical, symbols of love (including betrothal and wedding), magical, mourning, commemorative and serjeants. Highly decorative finger-rings worn primarily for personal adornment were also in vogue. Cabochon cut gemstones were the norm in finger-rings until the 15th century, although sliced garnets were current in the earlier Middle Ages, whilst from before the 12th century longitudinal facet or pyramid cut gemstones were used. Cheaply produced peasant-type finger-rings frequently had semi-precious gemstones, glass, or glass-paste stones enhanced by a coloured foil backing.

Bezels of 12th-13th-century finger-rings set with cabochon cut gemstones are normally irregular-shaped, however, contemporaneous bezels holding cut gemstones, glass, or glass paste-stones are usually rectangular. From the 15th century many finger-rings were elaborately enamelled around the hoop and on the shoulders, although rarely has this decoration survived. Silver finger-rings of this period manufactured in Italy were often nielloed, a treatment which has a higher survival rate than the former.

Other than on the first finger joint, rings were worn on the middle or third joint, and between the 14th and 16th centuries, men even wore them on the thumb. Very large finger-rings, particularly the 'Papal' variety, were worn over gloves by ecclesiastics. Apart from digital adornment, a 15th-century practice was for finger rings to be suspended from rosaries.

Cast and forged gold finger-rings

409: 12th-13th century, lozenge-shaped cross-section hoop, sexfoil-shaped bezel set with a cobachon probably a garnet, external D. 20mm, internal D. 18mm - *Exeter*.

410: c1450-1500, oval cross-section hoop, black letter inscription interspaced by tay crosses sideways NUL SY BEN (NUL SI BIEN) meaning, none so good (a charm against illness), external D. 19mm, internal D. 16mm - *Kingsbridge*.

Cast and forged silver finger-rings

411: c.late 15th - early 16th century, gilt, semi-circular cross-section hoop inscribed inside in blundered Roman capitals, possibly - . SI . GEMELL . SEM . PER. (?) IF [WE] TWO ARE TOGETHER ALWAYS [...]), external D. 24mm, internal D. 19mm - *Kingsbridge*.

412: late 15th century, gilt, iconographic (?) St Barbara, semi-circular cross-section wreathed hoop, rectangular bezel, external D. 22.5mm, internal D. 19mm - *Alphington*.

413: late 15th century, iconographic, semi-circular cross-section hoop, engraved cross-hatching on hoop and shoulders, rectangular bezel with engraved saint, external D. 23mm, internal D. 20mm - *Cockington*.

414: possibly late 15th - early 16th century, rectangular cross-section hoop, engraved oblique lines on shoulders; subrectangular bezel engraved with a rectangle, a cross and transverse lines, external D. 24.5mm, internal D. 20mm - *Axminster*.

415: 15th century, rectangular cross-section hoop, chevrons and crosses formed from punched dots, separate quatrefoil bezel with punched fleurets, external D. 20mm, internal D. 18mm - *Ottery St Mary*.

416: 15th century, rectangular cross-section hoop, oblique and transverse lines of punched dots, separate cinquefoil bezel

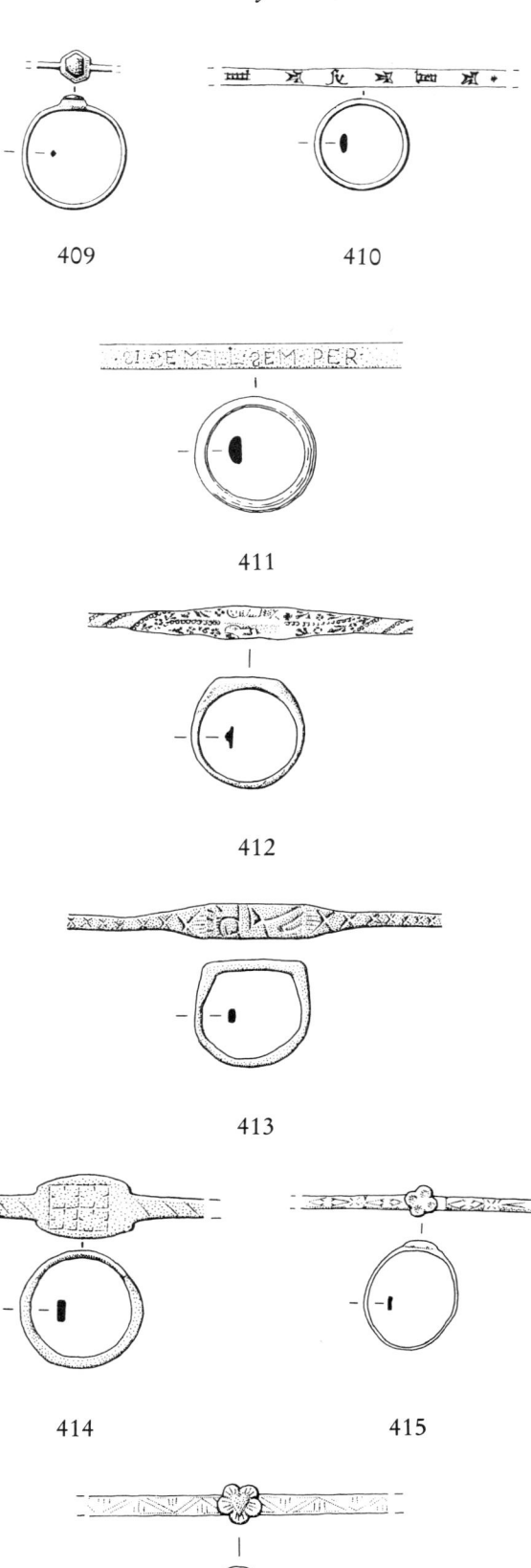

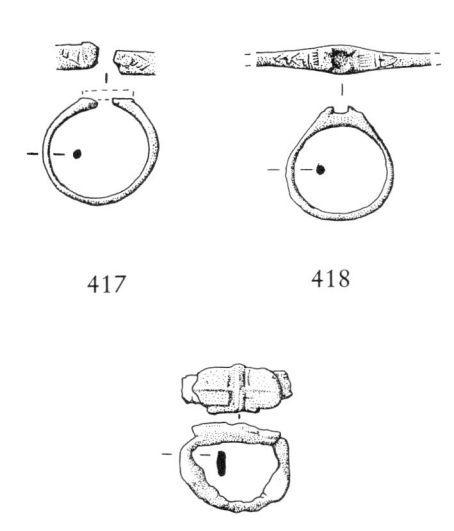

The Middle Ages

with cordate centre and oblique lines, external D. 21mm, internal D. 19mm - *Cockwood.*

417: c15th century, semi-circular cross-section hoop, separate bezel lost, abraded engraved oblique and transverse lines on shoulders, external D. 22mm, internal D. 18mm - *Axminster.*

Cast and forged copper-alloy finger-ring, 13th century

418: stirrup-shaped, oval cross-section hoop, subrectangular bezel with four claws, gemstone lost, external D. 20mm, internal D. 17mm - *Stokenham.*

Cast lead finger-ring, possibly a pilgrim souvenir, 13th-14th century

419: very crude, rectangular cross-section hoop, oval bezel with a moulded cross, external D. 20mm, internal D. 17mm - *Kilmington.*

NB. No.409 was found on an excavation spoil-heap by a member of an archaeological team using a metal detector. No.411 may have had a companion finger-ring inscribed with the remainder of the verse

SEAL MATRICES

One meaning of the word 'seal' is the impression made on wax, clay, lead or glass by a die called a matrix (plural matrices). Seal matrices have been in use for over two millennium; the Romans employed several types, including seal finger-rings, the forerunner of the signet finger-ring. Although other materials are known, e.g. ivory, wood or stone, most medieval seal matrices were made of cast metal, including copper alloy, lead, lead/tin alloy, silver or gold.

Matrices used by the monarchy, Boroughs, towns and cities, guilds and the church, are frequently very large, but generally personal types are relatively small. Blank seal matrices were hawked around fairs and markets by itinerant traders, as well being sold direct by manufacturers or in shops, thereby allowing customers to choose their own die device which was engraved.

Most personal seal matrices of the 12th century and the first half of the 13th are lead; however, silver examples are known but are very rare. Usually they are vesica-shaped, though circular or oval forms were current. Between c1250 - c1350 copper-alloy personal matrices were dominant, either circular, oval, shield or lozenge-shaped, although lead, and to a lesser degree silver, continued in use. Handle shapes also differed. Early lead and copper-alloy matrices have either a small unpierced projection, a pierced longitudinal flange or a single or double loop. From the late 13th century until the latter part of the 15th, typical personal seal matrices were circular or eliptical-shaped, with tapering hexagonal cross-section handles terminating in trefoil, circular or lozenge-shaped suspension loops. Copper alloy, lead or silver were used during this period. Pendant seal matrices were suspended about the person by means of a chain.

Dies of the aforementioned types of personal seal matrice are usually engraved direct, although some early silver examples have a separate inset Roman intaglio. Seal finger-rings of gold, silver, and base metal remained current during the Middle Ages, the bezel-dies of which are engraved direct with either: initials surmounted by a crown, merchant's mark, religious motto, or the sacred cipher IHS or IHC. And, as with pendant seals, Roman intaglios are occasionally seen. To facilitate using a seal correctly, a small x or transverse line was sometimes engraved on the back of the die which denotes the top of the impression.

Attributing medieval seal matrices can be fraught with difficulty. Apart from the die shape, the lettering of the legend and handle shape are helpful. Old French, Middle English and Latin were languages current, using lettering of either Roman capitals, Lombardic capitals, or black letter. Until c1350 personal names on seals were in vogue; these gave way to standard mottoes and phrases. The iconography of dies is sometimes a good guide to the age. Heraldic devices were prevalent; on early types confined to simple representations which became more ornate by the end of the 14th century. Likewise, designs of a religous or secular nature were very popular. Hunting scenes made an appearance in the 12th century and often they have the word 'Sohou', a hunting cry, included in the legend.

Tudor pendant seal matrices are similar to those of the Middle Ages. Mostly they are copper alloy, though lead/tin alloy or silver examples were current. Circular or elliptical dies were the norm which at the beginning of the period had tapering hexagonal handles and trefoil, circular or lozenge-shaped suspension loops. These gave way to quatrefoil loops. Catergories of device and legend are comparable to the medieval period, though later in the 16th century the use of legends decreased. Script is either Lombardic capitals or black letter.

Cast lead seal matrix, 13th century
420: vesica-shaped, Lombardic legend S' ROGERI L' BARERE (SEAL OF ROGER BARERE), St Andrew's cross and cruciform with petal-shaped arms, single-loop handle with moulded longitudinal arrow-shaped flange and curlicues, 31mm x 22mm - *Combefishacre*.

Cast copper-alloy seal matrices, 14th century
421: circular, cross each side of (?) staff within circle, Lombardic legend [...]AL:., hexagonal cross-section handle, lozenge-shaped suspension loop, 27mm x 20mm - *Cockington*.
422: circular, slightly abraded perimeter, squirrel, Lombardic legend PRIVE SUI (I AM PRIVATE), hexagonal cross-section handle, circular suspension loop, 20mm x 14mm - *Axminster*.
423: circular, stag's head, Lombardic legend LATVHSVX (? personal name), hexagonal cross-section handle, circular suspension loop, remains of iron chain in loop, 18mm x 16mm - *Exeter*.
424: circular; arrow piercing a heart, sprig of foliate each side, surmounted by a crown, Lombardic legend SIGLIN . IANVIER (SEAL OF JANVIER), circular cross-section handle with collar at junction of trefoil suspension loop which has three circular and keyhole-shaped openwork, x mark, 25mm x 20mm - *Ringmore*.
425: oval, figure under canopy, hexagonal cross-section handle, fragmented suspension loop, 18mm x 21mm - *Stokeinteignhead*.
426: circular, probably stylised G; abraded Lombardic legend, perhaps PRIVE SVOIS (PRIVE SUI) (I AM PRIVATE), hexagonal cross-section handle, fragmented trefoil suspension loop, 23.5mm x 19mm - *Exeter*.

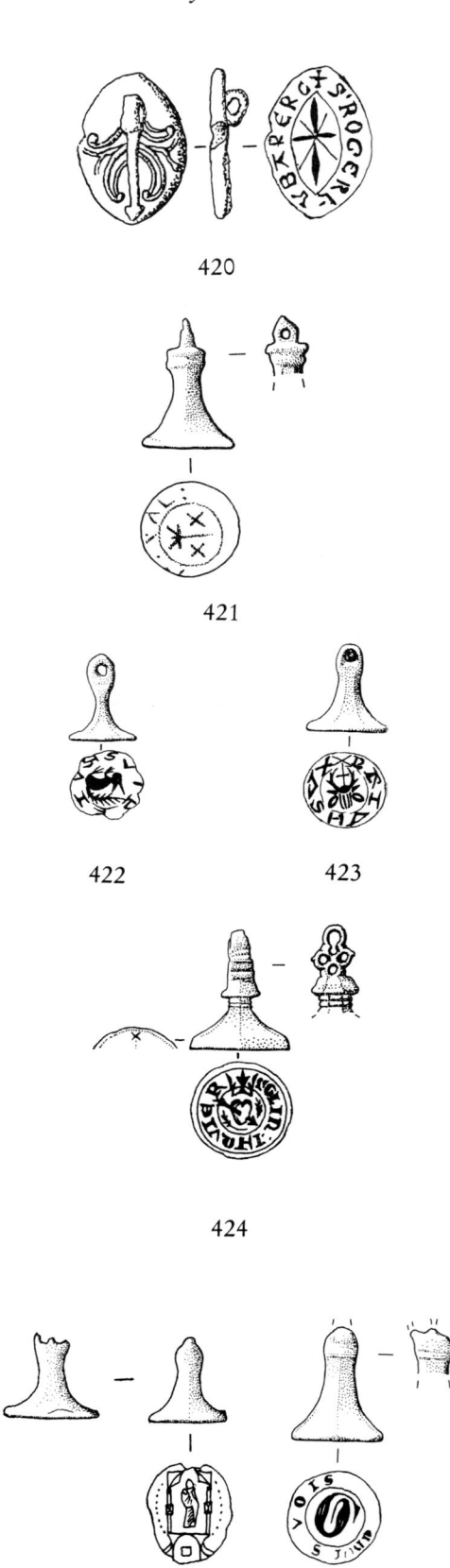

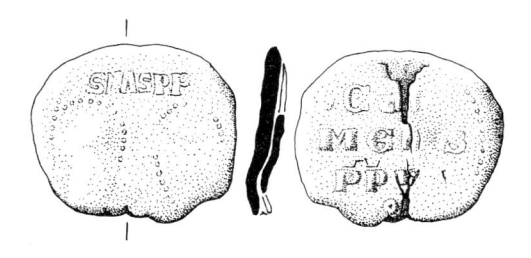

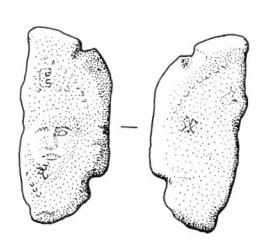

PAPAL BULLAE

From c.AD 590 Papal remissions, indulgences and edicts were sealed with large cast, circular lead seals, known as bullae (singular - bulla) which have moulded ornamentation and Latin inscriptions on both sides. Some very early bullae are quite plain, having the name of the respective Pope on the obverse and the word PAPAE (Pope) on the reverse.

One early example has on the obverse a beaded border and a central beaded circle enclosing an eight-point fleuret with IOHANNIS (John V AD685-6) around it. The reverse depicts PAPAE and a Greek cross. A 7th-century specimen shows on the obverse a central monogram within a beaded circle surrounded by SERGII (Sergius I AD 687-701), whilst the reverse has PAPAE and the Chi-Rho monogram. The obverse of the commonest type, John VIII AD 872-82, depicts SPASPE (St Peter and St Paul) surmounting a cross with on the left an effigy representing St Peter and on the right St Paul (the size of the busts and cross differs). A beaded border surrounds the flan and similar beadwork encloses each portrait. The reverse bears the name, PP, and number of the respective Pope within a beaded border. Although variations in the ornamentation of this type of bulla are numerous, the basic design remained current until the 20th century.

Another bulla depicts on one side St Peter and St Paul enthroned, with a cross between, and PAU PET (Peter Paul) within a beaded border. The other side depicts the Pope enthroned flanked by Cardinals, with kneeling figures and the Pope's name within a beaded border.

Cast lead Papal bullae, 1305-14
427: Pope Clement V, much abraded, D. 39mm - *Axminster*.
428: fragment, much abraded, unidentified, D. 39.5mm - *Stokeinteignhead*

THIMBLES

Though they have been in use for over two millenium it isn't known who invented the humble thimble. Examples in bone, ivory, leather, wood, glass, china and metal have been found throughout the world. Before the 17th century, despite a limited home-based manufacturing capability, most raw copper alloy was imported into Britain from the Continent. Copper-alloy objects, such as thimbles, were made here from the 14th century onwards. Strangely, there is no archaeological proof of the Romans using thimbles in Britain; nonetheless, copper-alloy thimbles are not uncommon finds for metal detectors when searching known Roman sites (however, Hattatt, ABOA. pp 495, 497 describes a bronze thimble as Roman period).

Fourteenth-century copper-alloy thimbles, known as 'acorn tops' or 'skeps' (which take their name from the medieval straw or wicker skep beehive), were made by casting or hammering sheet metal into a mould. The latter method sometimes created pleats in the sides of the thimble due to the metal being too cool. Hand-punched indentations, which may be circular, D-shaped or triangular, commence at the open base, often in vertical or horizontal lines up to the start of the inward curve of the crown, and then concentric circles to just short of the crown. Other patterns of indentations, spiral or random, are common. This distinctive bald spot or tonsure on the crown and one or two engraved lines or bands of tiny punched dots around the base are characteristics of many 14th-century thimbles but not all. Cast thimbles have a small hole in the centre of the tonsure which allowed hot air to escape during manufacture.

Some 15th-century copper-alloy thimbles are similar to their antecedents. The manufacturing processes were the same, indeed up until the 16th century, and indentation patterns continued in the same vein. However, frequently they are taller with a more rounded crown. Similarly they may have one or two engraved lines or bands of punched dots around the base and perhaps another just below the crown. Occasionally lines or dots are absent, particularly from open-top sewing rings which appeared at this time.

Hammered copper-alloy skep thimbles, 14th century
429: vertical, concentric and random small circular indentations, two bands of tiny punched dots around base, tonsure crown, 17mm x 16.5mm - *Kenton*.
430: vertical and concentric small circular indentations, two bands of tiny punched dots around base, tonsure crown, 16.5 x 16mm - *Stokeinteignhead*.

Cast copper-alloy thimbles, 15th century
431: horizontal and concentric large circular indentations, slightly pointed crown with tonsure, 24mm x 21mm - *Haccombe*.
432: rounded crown, spiral of small circular indentations, two bands of tiny punched dots around base, two engraved short oblique lines running upwards from base, 20mm x 20mm - *Cockington*.
433: rounded crown, spiral of small circular indentations, band of tiny punched dots around base, 18mm x 18mm - *Stokeinteignhead*.

Cast open-top sewing rings, 15th century
434: horizontal triangular indentations, 13.5mm x 19.5mm - *Hacombe*.
435: horizontal circular indentations, 10mm x 17mm - *Cockington*.
436: horizontal circular indentations, 7mm x 19mm - *Stokeinteignhead*.

PURSES

Early medieval purses were simple cloth or leather bags which were secured at the neck by strings or a metal ring, and were suspended from the girdle by means of a cord or thong. Towards the end of the 15th century and remaining current until the early 16th, a different form of purse became fashionable, a similar fabric or leather bag hanging on a metal bar or pendant frame which in turn dangled from the girdle by means of a separate suspension loop. The purse itself either passed over the top of a horizontal metal bar or hung from integral pierced longitudinal flanges on the underside of the bar. Alternatively, some bars have separate ferrule-type flanges which swivel.

A variety of types and sizes of bar and pendant frame are known, either cast and forged from copper alloy or forged from iron. Some are made from a combination of metals. Frequently the frames have become detached from the bar which can make it difficult to establish whether a horizontal bar originally had a pendant frame. Gilt or niello applied-surface decoration is commonplace, as is engraving or inscriptions. Zoomorphic

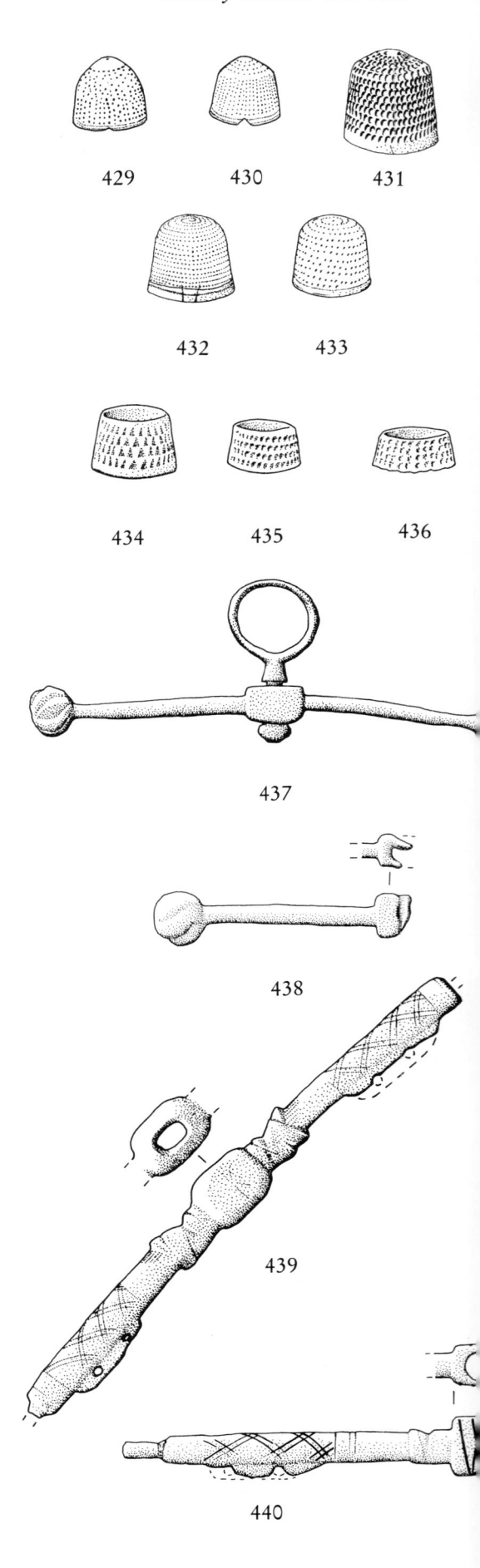

The Middle Ages   77

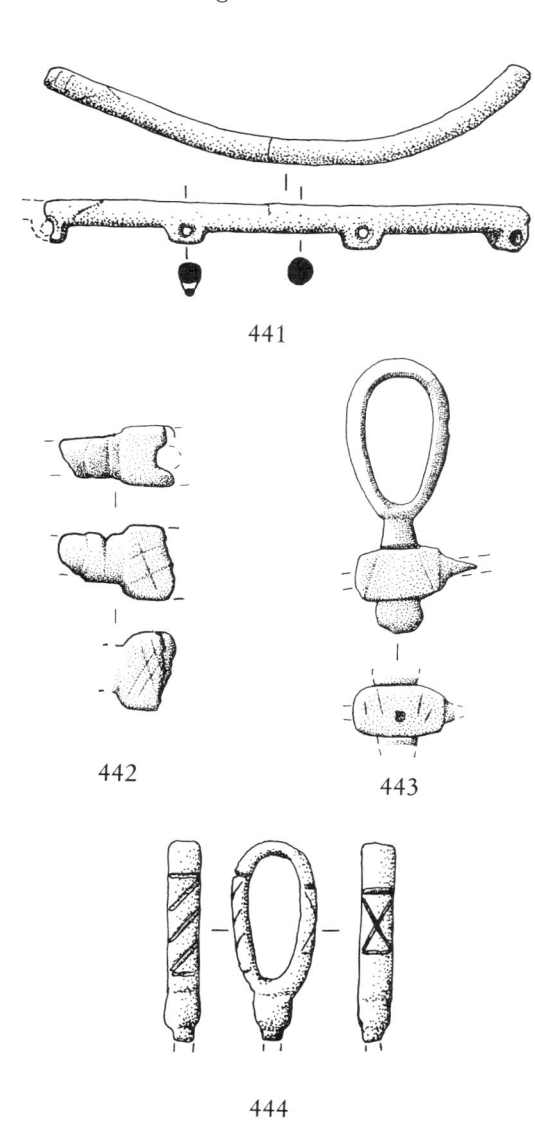

terminals at the juncture with the central boss is a feature of some.

Cast and forged copper-alloy horizontal purse-bars or pendant frames, c1475-1550

437: circular cross-section, moulded spherical wrythen knops and shield-shaped boss; separate circular, circular cross-section suspension-loop, 110mm x 39mm - *Maidencombe*.

438: fragment, circular cross-section, moulded spherical wrythen knop and shield-shaped boss, L. 58mm - *Combeinteignhead*.

439: circular cross-section, engraved cross-hatching, traces of niello, moulded zoomorphic heads gripping rectangular boss which has champhered edges; two integral moulded flanges, one with two holes the other fragmented, L. 137mm - *Coffinswell*.

440: fragment, circular cross-section, moulded zoomorphic head gripping subrectangular boss, broken integral flange with two holes; nielloed cross-hatching and transverse lines on bar and oblique lines and cross-hatching on boss, L. 83mm - *Mamhead*.

441: fragment, circular cross-section, four integral flanges (one fragmented) each with one hole, traces of engraved oblique and transverse lines, L. 92mm - *Chudleigh*.

442: fragment, circular cross-section bar with moulded collar at juncture of rectangular boss with engraved cross-hatching, 14.5mm x 22mm - *Kingskerswell*.

443: fragment, oval suspension loop, oval cross-section, moulded subrectangular boss with engraved oblique grooves each side, 54mm x 19mm - *Paignton*.

444: fragment, oval suspension loop, oval cross-section, transverse and oblique lines engraved on one side and a cross within two transverse lines on the other, 40mm x 16mm - *Cockington*

BOOK CLASPS

Most people in the later Middle Ages through to the 17th century were illiterate. Until latterly, books are thought to have been confined to a very small proportion of the populace who could read, e.g. the nobility, ecclesiastics and merchants. Frequently a bible or other book was suspended from the girdle by means of a chain, and to prevent the book from opening, a clasp was fitted to the cover. Notwithstanding, book-clasps were current on many books, irrespective of whether they were static or mobile. The regularity of book-clasps recovered from agricultural land by metal detectives implies that perhaps the use of books was even more widespread, and feasibly farm account books are a likely source for many of them.

Book-clasps are usually sheet copper alloy, though some may have been cast. Silver examples are known. Most attributed to the medieval and Tudor periods are subrectangular with an integral hooked appendage at the front end. Characteristic of many are pronounced flared sides and a serrated back-edge. Another frequent feature is longitudinal edges with apertures, often of simple waisted form. Some book-clasps, which may be later in date, are oval

Attribution of book clasps is extremely difficult as styles were similar throughout. Some are quite plain, though usually ornate engraving or punched artwork has been employed. Tiny circular openwork is a feature of many book-clasps; though some of these are undoubtedly rivet holes, it is by no means certain that all of them are, for many retain no evidence of ever having held a rivet. However, herein they are described as rivet holes. Applied-surface decoration such as gilt or silver was commonplace.

Book clasps comprise three separate sections, usually two small pieces of much the same size and one larger, and are of two types. One is where the largest section is riveted to the end of a short leather or fabric strap, the opposite end of which is itself concealed with a small appliqué and riveted securely to the rear book-cover. The strap has sufficient length to span the thickness of the book which allows the hooked end of the main clasp to clip into a hasp appliqué riveted to the front cover. The clasp is held shut by tension. The main book-clasp comprises a front-plate and a back-plate, between which the strap is sandwiched or, alternatively, a front plate which is riveted directly to the strap. On the former type the front and back plate are usually riveted together, however, frequently the back plate is soldered at the front-end to the front plate and riveted at the other. Either copper-alloy or iron rivets were used.

The second type of book-clasp functions without the aid of a strap; the clasp and back-cover appliqué are hinged together, and, as with the former, the main clasp clips into a hasp appliqué fitted to the front cover. On both kinds of book-clasp, frequently the hasp appliqué is omitted from the rear cover, and, instead, a metal edging around the cover incorporates a hasp.

Sheet copper-alloy rectangular and subrectangular book-clasps, 13th-17th century

445: flared front plate, serrated back edge, hook lost, six rivet holes, remains of one iron rivet, engraved concentric circles and oblique lines, 91mm x 28mm - *Cockington*.

446: front plate, back edge abraded, six rivet holes, remains of two iron rivets, engraved concentric circles and oblique lines, 84.5mm x 18.5mm - *Kingskerswell*.

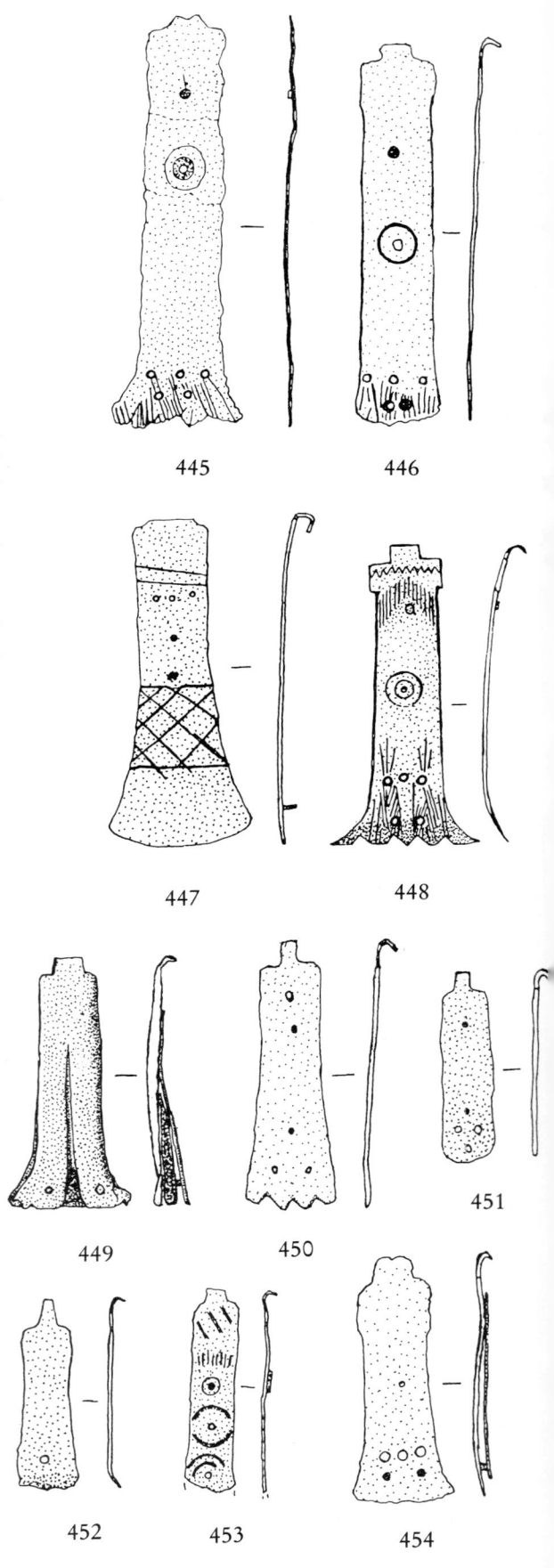

447: flared front plate, six rivet holes, one copper-alloy rivet, remains of two iron rivets, band of engraved cross-hatching and two oblique lines, 72mm x 30.5mm - *Stokeinteignhead*.

448: flared front plate, serrated back edge, six rivet holes, remains of one copper-alloy rivet; engraved zigzag, vertical and oblique lines and concentric circles, 65mm x 32mm - *Haccombe*.

449: flared front and back plate soldered at front end, remains of leather strap, two rivet holes, two copper-alloy rivets, triangular aperture and longitudinal tapering groove on front plate, 55mm x 26.5mm - *Haccombe*.

450: flared front plate, serrated back edge, five rivet holes, remains of two iron rivets, 59mm x 19mm - *Cockington*.

451: front plate, abraded back edge, five rivet holes, remains of two iron rivets, 42mm x 11.5mm - *Haccombe*.

452: flared front plate, abraded back edge, one rivet hole, 41.5mm x 13mm - *Stokeinteignhead*.

453: flared front plate, two rivet holes, remains of iron rivet, engraved concentric circles and oblique and vertical lines, 44.5mm x 14mm - *Stokeinteignhead*.

454: flared front and back plate soldered at front end, six rivet holes, two copper-alloy rivets, 53mm x 21.5mm - *Cockington*.

The Middle Ages

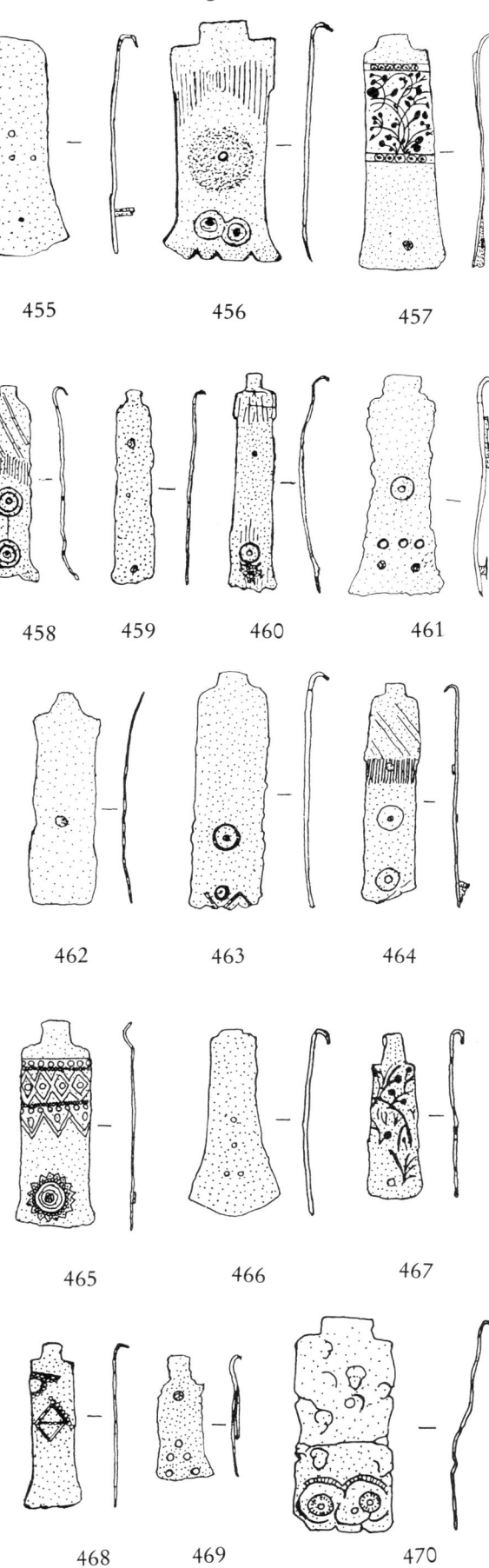

455
456
457
458
459
460
461
462
463
464
465
466
467
468
469
470

455: flared front plate, six rivet holes, two copper-alloy rivets, 50mm x 23.5mm - *Cockington*.
456: flared front plate, serrated back edge, three rivet holes, remains of two iron rivets, engraved vertical lines and concentric circles, 54mm x 26mm - *Coffinswell*.
457: flared front plate, one rivet hole, remains of iron rivet, engraved foliate between two bands of circles and crosses, 53mm x 19mm - *Cockington*.
458: front plate, back edge abraded, three rivet holes, remains of iron rivet, engraved concentric circles and oblique and vertical lines, 44mm x 11mm - *Stokeinteignhead*.
459: front plate, back edge abraded, three rivet holes, remains of two iron rivets, 44m x 9.5mm - *Haccombe*.
460: front plate, serrated back edge abraded; engraved circle, oblique, vertical and transverse lines, two rivet holes, remains of iron rivet, 50mm x 11mm - *Haccombe*.
461: flared front plate, remains of back plate, engraved circle, six rivet holes, two copper-alloy rivets, 50mm x 21mm - *Cockington*.
462: front plate, one rivet hole, remains of iron rivet, 48mm x 15mm - *Stokeinteignhead*.
463: front plate, back edge abraded, one rivet hole, remains of iron rivet, engraved concentric circles and zigzag, 54mm x 16mm - *Cockington*.
464: front plate, back edge abraded, remains of two copper-alloy rivets, two rivet holes, engraved concentric circles and oblique and vertical lines, 50mm x 12mm - *Ringmore*.
465: flared front plate, one rivet hole, remains of iron rivet; engraved transverse lines, zigzags, circles and concentric circles, 46mm x 17.5mm - *Ringmore*.
466: flared front plate, four rivet holes, 42mm x 20mm - *Cockington*.
467: front plate, one rivet hole, engraved foliate, 37mm x 12mm - *Stokeinteignhead*.
468: flared front plate, engraved lozenge and circles, 37mm x 13mm - *Coffinswell*.
469: flared front plate, remains of back plate, six rivet holes, copper-alloy rivet, 28.5mm x 12.5mm - Cockington.
470: front plate, serrated back edge, two rivet holes; engraved acorns, concentric circles and oblique lines, 48.5mm x 22mm - *Teigngrace*.
471: front plate, fragmented back edge, three rivet holes, engraved concentric circles, 88mm x 24mm - *Haccombe*.
472: flared front and back plate soldered at top end, serrated back-edge, six rivet holes, one copper-alloy rivet, engraved concentric circles, transverse and vertical lines, 58mm x 37mm - *Exeter*.
473: flared front plate, abraded back edge, two rivet holes, one copper-alloy rivet, engraved fleuret around a convex roundel; engraved zigzag, punched circles and crescents forming two horizontal lines and fleurets, sunburst circle formed from punched crescents, 73mm x 29mm - Wolborough, *Newton Abbot*.
474: flared front plate, serrated back edge, four rivet holes, one copper-alloy rivet; three engraved slightly oblique bands of zigzags and transverse lines, concentric circles and oblique lines, 63mm x 30mm - *Exeter*.

475: flared front plate, serrated back edge, four rivet holes, four copper-alloy rivets, four engraved slightly oblique zigzags, two bands of engraved vertical zigzags and three circles, 41mm x 14mm - *Stokeinteignhead*.

476: front plate with semi-circular aperture each side, serrated back edge, two rivet holes; engraved zigzag, concentric circles and fleurets, 46mm x 26mm - *Stokeinteignhead*.

477: front plate with trefoil aperture each side, four rivet holes, abraded engraved fleurets and oblique lines, 61mm x 23mm - *Stokeinteignhead*.

478: flared front and back plate soldered at top, semi-circular aperture each side, chevron aperture on back-edge, five rivet holes, three copper-alloy rivets, engraved concentric circles, 46mm x 22mm - *Stokeinteignhead*

479: flared front plate, two rivet holes, engraved circle and oblique and vertical lines, 51mm x 16mm - *Stokeinteignhead*,

480: flared front plate, bifid protrusion on sides, chevron aperture in back-edge, two large circular holes with convex perimeters, six rivet holes, two copper-alloy rivets, engraved concentric circles, circle and oblique lines, 58mm x 20mm - *Ringmore*.

481: flared front plate, fragmented serrated back-edge, semi-circular aperture each side, four rivet holes, one copper-alloy rivet, remains of iron rivet, two circles formed from punched dots and punched fleurettes, 50mm x 25mm - *Haccombe*.

482: flared front plate, five rivet holes, two copper-alloy rivets; engraved zigzags, oblique and vertical lines and concentric circles, 74mm x 20mm - *Haccombe*.

483: front plate, trefoil sides and back-edge, one rivet hole; engraved curvilinear, oblique lines and CB, 28mm x 20mm - *Newton Abbot*.

484: oval plate, one rivet hole, copper-alloy rivet, small rectangular openwork, engraved curlicues, 27mm x 28mm - *Haccombe*.

485: front plate, trefoil sides, one rivet hole, embossed and engraved floriate and fleurets, iron hinge-pin piercing two integral projections on back edge, 41mm x 30mm - *Torquay*.

486: front plate, two subrectangular protrusions on each side, one rivet hole, copper-alloy rivet, 10.5mm x 42mm - *Haccombe*.

CASED MIRRORS

Until recently, small circular metal hinged-mirror-cases of the medieval period were relatively uncommon and invariably erroneously classified as Roman seal-boxes. However, metal detecting has proved their distribution is widespread. To find a complete example is rare, and even rarer with the glass mirror intact, although sometimes glass fragments and traces of calcium carbonate adhesive are present. Occasionally the lead-foil backing of the glass, which contributed to the reflective capability, is in situ. Larger mirrors of a grander nature were current at this time, e.g. those with ivory cases, but the norm was copper alloy or lead/tin alloy which was either cast or sheet form. Decoration of one or both sides of the case is frequently elaborate - either: pierced, punched, drilled, repoussé or enamelled. Iconographic representations were also popular.

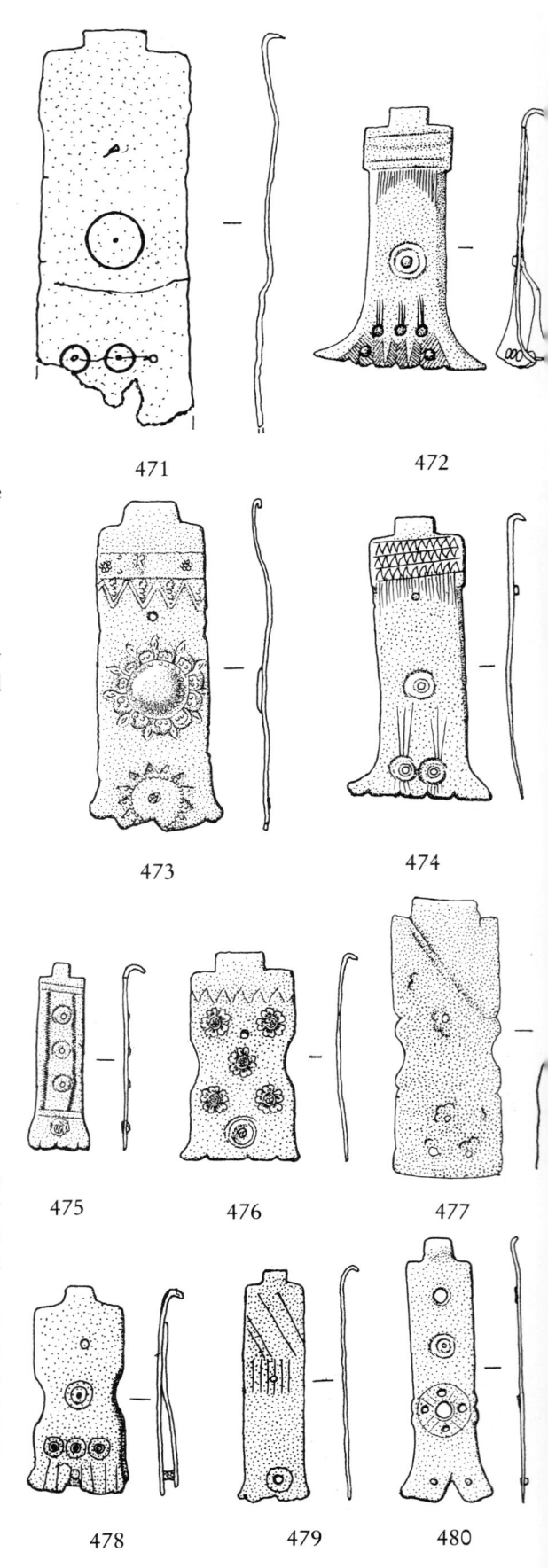

The Middle Ages

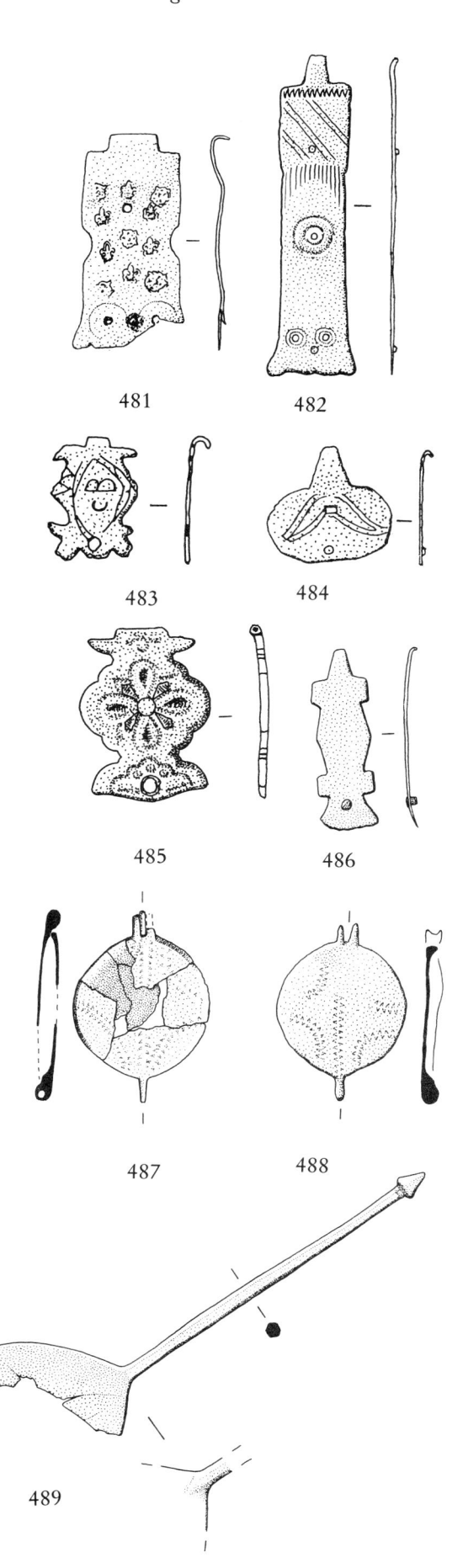

Cast copper-alloy mirror case, c14th century

487: fragmented front disc with single lug catch and one of two pierced hinge lugs, fragmented back disc with pierced hinge lug, voided cross formed from double lines of punched triangles and a diametric double line of punched triangles, 44mm x 30.5mm - *Littlehempston*.

488: front disc with single lug catch and two pierced hinge lugs, voided cross formed from double lines of punched triangles and a diametric double line of punched triangles, 40mm x 29mm - *Stokeinteignhead*.

SPOONS

Early medieval spoons, i.e. Anglo-Saxon or Viking, are extremely rare. It seems that the widespread use of spoons started in England around the 12th century; these have small leaf-shaped bowls, whilst those conceived between the 13th-15th centuries tend to have circular bowls. Later bowls are fig, oval, or pear-shaped.

The majority of spoons anteceding the 13th century were probably made of either wood, bone or horn; there is no evidence to suggest that metal spoons were in general use at this time. However, non-metalic spoons probably remained current throughout the Middle Ages. From the 13th century gold spoons were used only by royalty and the nobility, whereas silver spoons were widely available to folk of somewhat lesser means. As copper-alloy or lead/tin-alloy spoons were relatively cheap to purchase, they would be found in even the humblest of dwellings. Of these, copper alloy was more durable. Spoons of the latter metal are usually tinned, whilst gilding of silver spoons and knops of lead/tin-alloy spoons is not uncommon.

Stems, which are either: rectangular, cylindrical, twisted, hexagonal or lozenge-shaped cross-section, of early and middle medieval spoons are quite short, but from the 15th century onwards they increased in length. Some stems are extremely slender, and lead/tin-alloy stems are known with an iron core.

Regarding knops, the earliest form seems to be the acorn which is first chronicled in a will dated 1351, whilst the strawberry knop occurs in a will of 1440. The maidenhead knop (thought to represent a bust of the Virgin Mary in a variety of contemporary medieval head-dresses) receives its first mention in a Durham Priory inventory of 1446. Robert Morton's inventory of 1487 is the first published account of the writhen knop. Diamond-point knops are said to be 15th-century in origin. Other knops are known, viz: jester, the wild-man 'Woodwose', horned head-dress, ball, alderman, acorn derivative, and finial. The origin of the Apostle spoon and lion sejant spoon is attributed to the last quarter of the 15th century. There is an example of lead/tin-alloy ball-knopped spoon which has a ball on the stem between the knop and the bowl.

Apart from bowl and stem shapes as a guide to attribution, silver spoons frequently carry an official mark or marks. In England hallmarking started in 1180. Medieval silver spoons are usually hallmarked inside and at the top end of the bowl. Base metal spoons are sometimes stamped with the makers touchmark on the inside of the bowl at the top end where it joins the stem. Alternatively, the touch mark may be found on the underside of the bowl or on the lower part of the stem. Regrettably, there is no extant record of London pewterer's marks prior to 1666, for their touchplates were destroyed in the Great Fire.

Cast and forged silver spoons, 15th century

489: tapered hexagonal cross-section stem, diamond-point knop, fragmented fig-shaped bowl, L. 111.5mm - *Ringmore*.

490: tapered cylindrical stem, (?) diamond-point knop, fragmented fig-shaped bowl, L. 97mm - *Ottery St Mary*.

Cast copper-alloy spoon, 15th century

491: fragment of cylindrical stem, fig-shaped bowl, L. 74mm - *Combeinteignhead*.

Cast lead/tin-alloy spoon, late 14th - 15th century

492: cylidrical stem, acorn knop, fragmented fig-shaped bowl with (?) fleuret maker's touchmark, L. 141.5mm - Bishopsteignton.

N.B. No.492 was found buried in a cob wall of an old farmhouse. The rarest spoon from Devon was found by Malcolm Laws at Bridford, lodged in the roof timbers whilst stripping thatch from an old farmhouse. This Richard II silver spoon of 1380 has a rectangular cross-section stem, diamond-point knop and fig-shaped bowl, L. 150mm, inside top end of of bowl hallmarked with the crowned Syrian Leopard's Head. Subsequently, on 22 January 1982, this spoon was auctioned at Phillips' London saleroom where it realised £13,000.00. On 11 November 1993 it was sold at Sotheby's London saleroom for £27,600.00.

KNIVES AND DAGGERS

From the early Middle Ages it was normal for men to carry about their person a knife which served as both a weapon and for culinary use. Similar knives were kept within dwellings for general purposes. True daggers, i.e. the quillon or rondel types, were widely used later in the medieval period but were confined mainly to the military. Knife-daggers were carried by civilians and include kidney-daggers, baselards and scramasax. Notwithstanding, knives and daggers were occasionaly used out of the above contexts which can cause confusion regarding attribution.

Somewhat similar in appearance to contemporaneous swords, late medieval military daggers are attributed from the 12th century of which the earliest is the quillon-dagger that remained current until the end of the period. Characteristic of this type is a 'quillon' guard which has a central rectangular hole through which passes the tang. Quillons are frequently quite plain but may be moulded or have curled ends.

Rondel-daggers were current from c1350 until well into the 16th century. They usually feature a circular guard and pommel both set laterally to the tang, though pommels are occasionally globular. Kidney-daggers date from the mid-14th century and remained popular into the Tudor period, and are either single or double-edged, although the former was dominant. They have transverse metal guards seated on the tang with kidney-shaped, normally wooden, guards affixed to metal pins, one each side of the metal guard. The baselard-dagger is probably attributable to the c1360s - c1450s period. Frequently they have quillons and pommels of equal proportions, both lateral to the hilt and blade.

From Anglo-Saxon times through to the mid-12th century the basic type of knife was the scramasax, a triangular-bladed

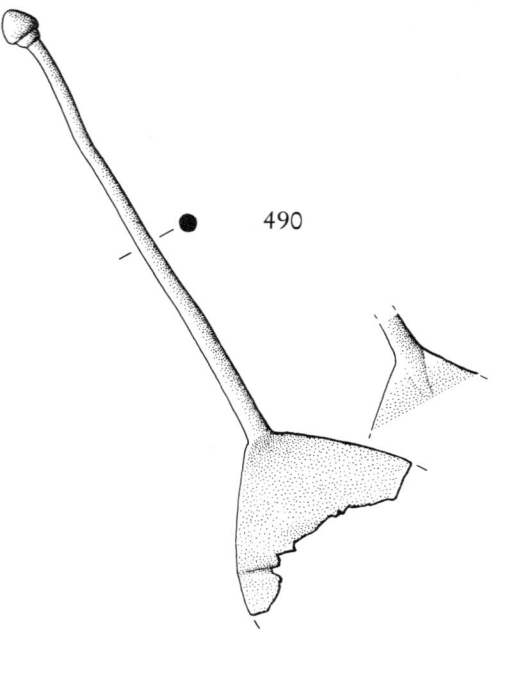

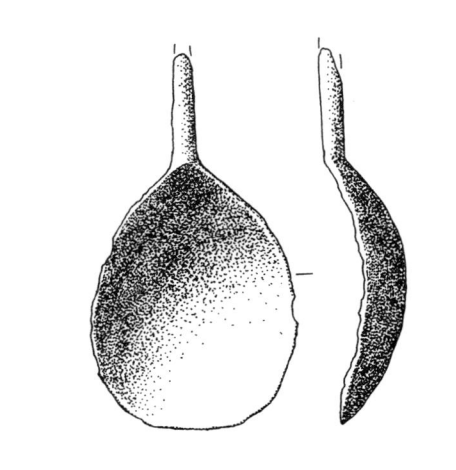

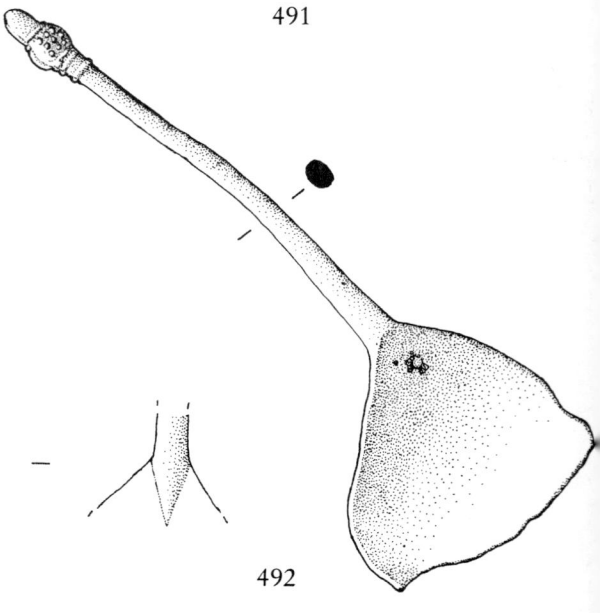

The Middle Ages

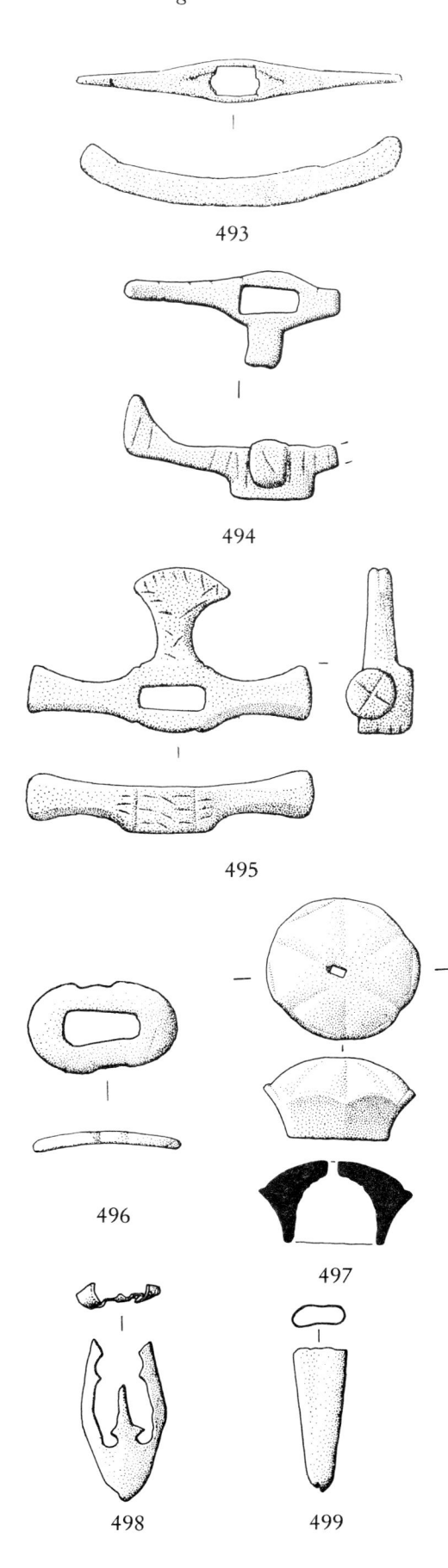

triangular cross-section single-edged knife. Midway down the back of the blade of earlier examples there is frequently a pronounced angle. Blades of this form of knife may be quite short or conversely, long, but both have long triangular whittle tangs to which a solid handle was afixed by hammering. Whittle-tanged knives remained the basic type until c1300, though they remained current to a much lesser degree for the remainder of the medieval period. However, whittle tangs were revived in the late 16th century and continued into the 17th.

In the 14th century there evolved a somewhat longer-bladed knife with a wide scale tang to which a composite plate handle was riveted. This form was dominant beyond the Tudor period. Knife-daggers are differentiated from knives or daggers proper, mainly by their increased length. Blades are usually triangular cross-section and single-edged with scale tangs to which handles were riveted. Handles for all of the aforementioned knives are made from either: wood, bone, metal or leather. Composite plate handles have metal end and plate caps and are frequently decorated with either: rivets, pins, wire, engraving or punchwork.

Cast and forged copper-alloy quillon dagger guards, c15th-16th century

493: crescent-shaped, tapered rectangular cross-section, subrectangular tang-hole with moulded chevron either side, 72mm x 7mm - *South Devon*.

494: fragmented, downturned end, tapered rectangular cross-section, lateral projection, subrectangular tang-hole, engraved oblique and transverse grooves, 48mm x 22mm - *Stokeinteignhead*.

495: tapered circular cross-section, lateral flattened crescent-shaped projection with moulded groove around end, subrectangular tang-hole, engraved St Andrews crosses on ends of quillons, moulded transverse grooves on sides with engraved or stamped oblique and transverse lines, 37.5mm x 63mm - *Exeter*.

Cast and forged rondel dagger guard, c1350 - 16th century

496: oval, slightly curved, subrectangular tang-hole, bifid apertures in sides, 21mm x 23mm - *Poltimore*.

Cast quillon dagger pommel, c15th-16th century

497: hexagonal, moulded sexfoil top with rectangular tang-hole, 18.5mm x 33.5mm - *Haccombe*.

DAGGER-CHAPES AND SWORD-CHAPES

Daggers or swords were stowed in leather sheaths kept about the person, often hanging from or simply tucked behind the girdle. Some sheaths, particularly the military types, had a metal terminal called a chape, either silver, copper alloy or iron, at the bottom end. Dagger-chapes and sword-chapes are often ornate, especially openwork, moulded ropework and applied-surface decoration such as gilt, silver, tin or bituminous paint.

Four basic types of dagger-chape and sword-chape were current, one of which is simply a piece of cast flat or convex metal with turned over edges glued to the sheath. It's function was mainly decorative but it did tend to provide rigidity to the sheath.

Another type, similar to the former, has a separate flat plate soldered to the back, and was glued or riveted in place. The third type consists of a tubular sheet metal terminal that was glued or riveted. Lastly is the cast tubular type which was glued or riveted to the sheath. Better-quality chapes of the latter variety sometimes had a soldered seam, however, many are very crude with no apparent attempt at marrying the join. Due to their similar appearance, it can be difficult to differentiate sword-chapes from dagger-chapes, the main aid being size.

Cast copper-alloy flat dagger-chape with turned over edges, c13th century

498: fleur-de-lis projection within aperture, 37mm x 19mm - *Coffinswell*.

Sheet tubular copper-alloy dagger-chapes, 14th-15th century

499: soldered seam, 33mm x 12mm - *Haccombe*.
500: soldered seam, globular knop, punched dots forming a band of zigzags and vertical lines between transverse lines, 72mm x 14mm - *Broadsands Beach, Paignton*.
501: fragmented, butt-jointed seam; one side with engraved transverse and vertical lines and a cordate infilled with punched circles and crescents; other side with a chevron formed from punched circles and crescents with crescents in the angle, 41mm x 19m - *Newton Abbot*.
502: fragmented, trefoil of blind holes, 32mm x 20mm - *Kingskerswell*.
503: fragmented bottom, butt-jointed seam, 33.5mm x 25mm - *Haccombe*.

Cast copper-alloy tubular sword chapes, 15th-16th century

504 fragmented, globular knop, moulded spiral both sides, two rivet holes, 42mm x 24mm - *Exeter*.
505: fragmented, globular knop, originally had apertures or openwork, 33mm x 35mm - *Exeter*.

Cast copper-alloy convex sword-chape with soldered separate flat back, 15th-16th century

506: lobed knop, semi-circular aperture with engraved linear border, cordate openwork, 35.5mm x 25.5mm - *Haccombe*

Cast copper-alloy convex or flat sword-chapes with turned over edges, late 15th-16th century

507: tinned, slightly convex, lobed knop, circles and teardrop-shaped openwork, blind holes, transverse and vertical bands of moulded ropework, serrated top edge damaged, 47mm x 30mm - *Chudleigh*.
508: convex, lobed teardrop knop, quatrefoil openwork, transverse bands of punched dots, 36mm x 23mm - *Stokeinteignhead*.
509: tinned, slightly convex, transverse moulded band, abraded (?) trefoil top, abraded sides, 42mm x 24mm - *Cockington*.
510: bituminous paint coated, cruciform-shaped openwork, 25mm x 27mm - *Haccombe*.
511: lobed knop, rectangles and trefoil openwork, trefoil aperture in top edge, 42mm x 35mm - *Newton Abbot*.
512: lobed knop; circles, teardrop and trefoil openwork, transverse moulded band of ropework, serrated top edge, 50mm x 33mm - *Newton Abbot*.

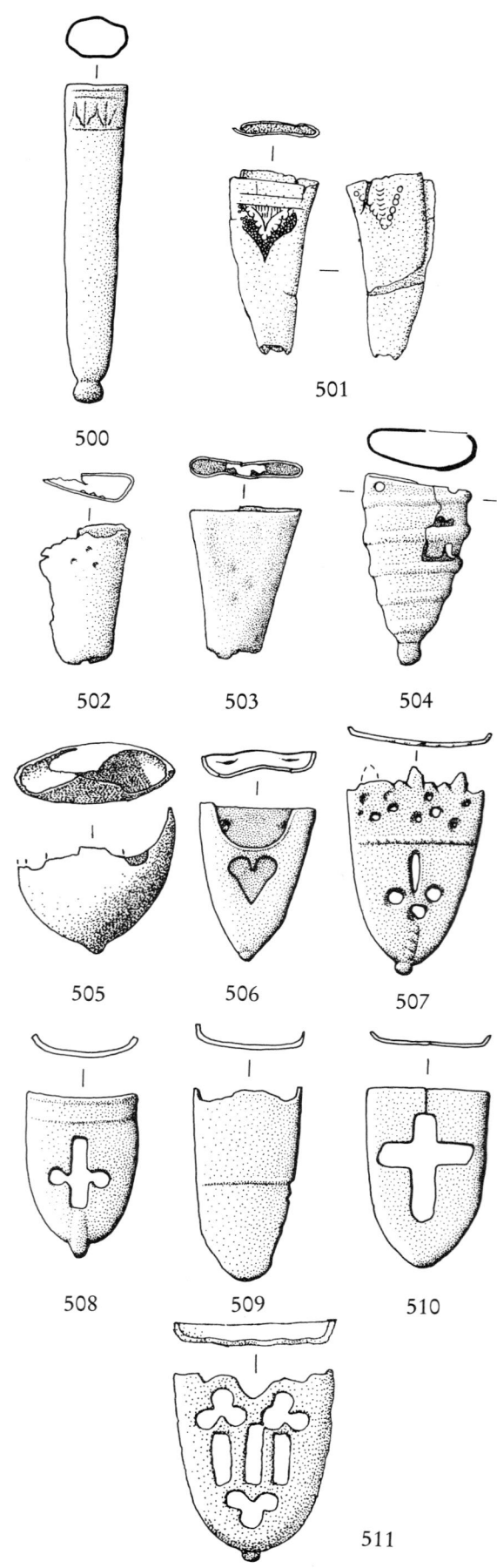

The Middle Ages

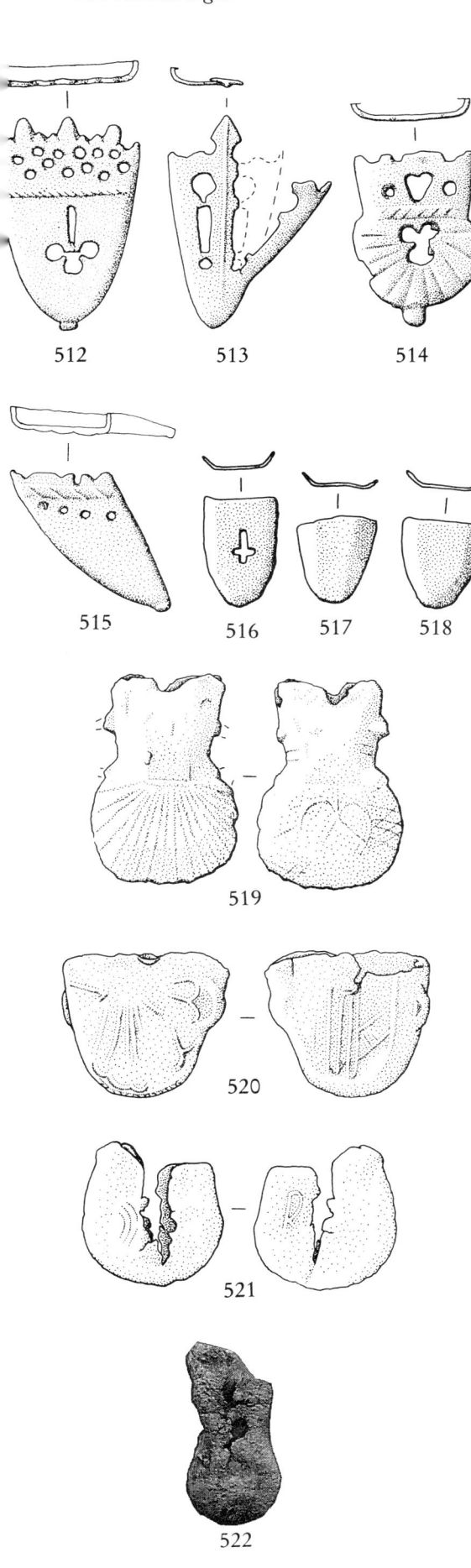

513: damaged, serrated top edge with pointed protrusion; circular, rectangular and asymmetrical openwork, 50mm x 26mm - *Pinhoe*.

514: lobed knop, serrated top edge, moulded transverse band of ropework and oblique grooves; cordate, circular and trefoil openwork, 41mm x 39mm - *Newton Abbot*.

Cast copper-alloy curved knife-dagger-chape, 14th-15th century

515: traces of bituminous paint coating, lobed knop, serrated top edge, moulded transverse band of ropework, four circular holes, 32mm x 23mm - *Chudleigh*.

Cast copper-alloy convex or flat dagger-chapes with turned over edges, 15th-16th century

516: bituminous paint coated, cruciform-shaped openwork, 25.5mm x 17mm - *Cockington*.

517: abraded top edge, bituminous paint coated, 21mm x 18mm - *Cockington*.

518: bituminous paint coated, 20.5mm x 18.5mm - *Cockington*.

PILGRIM SOUVENIRS

In medieval England, from around the 12th century's last quarter until the 15th, many folk from all levels of society undertook at least one pilgrimage in their lifetime. England's most important shrine was St Thomas' at Canterbury, Kent; next was probably Our Lady's miracle-working statue at Walsingham Priory, Norfolk. There were many others of lesser importance such as that of St Kenelm at Winchcombe, Gloucestershire, or the Rood of Grace at Boxley, Kent. Apart from English shrines there were many others on the Continent, particularly St James the Great at Compostella, Spain, and in the Middle East, which the more adventurous and pious could visit.

Enterprising monks and licensed secular craftsmen made cast lead, cast lead/tin-alloy, sheet copper-alloy, sheet silver or jet souvenirs to sell to pilgrims, either directly or indirectly, as proof that a pilgrimage had been accomplished. This practice of tourist souvenirs is still commonplace today at any of the main shrines or holy places. Medieval stone moulds for casting some forms of pilgrim-souvenirs have been found at the sites of several English shrines.

Numerous patterns of pilgrim-souvenir exist, each of which invariably relates to a particular shrine. Ampullae, are small flasks, with an annulet or handle either side, which were filled with holy water and then sealed by squeezing the lips together. Badges, often represent a saint or an animal as well as a miscellany of other shapes. Pendants are sometimes quite crude but elaborate examples are known; the cross features regularly on both types. Bells are either of the crotal or open-ended form (see later). A host of other trinkets were available, with finger-rings being especially popular, though these were not functional.

Moulded ornamentation is a feature on one or both sides of many pilgrim souvenirs. Ampullae were normally sold at the site of the well or shrine or official church-shop, whereas it was permissable for licensed craftsmen or secular shops to sell other types of souvenir. Although ampullae remained current for the whole of the pilgrimage period, from the early 14th century they were outnumbered in particular by badges and pendants. Souvenirs were hung around the neck or pinned to hats or collars.

Attribution can be extremely difficult due to the sheer number of dedications. New types turn up regularly and one can only speculate on their provenance.

Travel in medieval times was fraught with hazard; journeys were usually long and arduous, across rugged and wild country, often without any sort of road. Considering that pilgrim-souvenirs are extremely delicate, it is no wonder that thousands were lost on the way home. However, allegedly most pilgrim souvenirs travelled for only two or three kilometers from the shrine! For good luck, after arriving home, pilgrims would unseal their ampulla and sprinkle the contents on the land. Ampullae were then discarded or perhaps buried..

Cast lead ampulla, 1175 - 15th century
519: possibly St James of Compostella, annulets lost, moulded cockle shell radiating ribs and abraded (?) rectangle, abraded cross-hatching and possible concentric circles enclosing a chevron, horizontal band at juncture of neck and throat, 50mm x 33mm - *Cockwood.*
520: fragmented, unidentified; moulded (?) escallop, vertical and oblique lines, 33mm x 38mm - *Starcross.*
521: fragmented, unidentified, moulded curvilinear and (?) R, 33mm x 32.5mm - *Stokeinteignhead.*
522: fragmented, unidentified, 53mm x 26mm - *Ringmore.*
523: probably Our Lady of Walsingham, traces of moulded crowned W, 63mm x 33mm - *Ringmore.*

Cast lead possible pilgrims pendant, 13th-15th century
524: circular, moulded St Andrew's cross within a circular border, circular suspension loop, 35mm x 27mm - *River Exe, Starcross.*

Cast lead pilgrims-badge, c13th century
525: possibly Winsor, moulded (?) Henry VI holding sceptre, integral pin, H. 32mm - *Newton Abbot.*
525a: No.525 enlarged to show detail.

KEYS

Who invented the lock and key isn't known, but they were in use at least as far back as the ancient Egyptians. The Romans are credited with introducing the lock, including the barb-spring padlock, and key into Britain. Most of their keys are cast copper alloy. Doorlocks are forged iron, whilst chest and casket locks are either cast copper alloy or silver, and padlocks forged iron or cast copper alloy. It was the Romans who designed the ward-lock to prevent the use of inexact keys.

A characteristic of many Roman keys is a circular bow which conveniently fitted over a finger, hence 'finger-ring key'. Another type of Roman-key has a copper-alloy openwork trefoil-shaped bow with an iron bit. Barb-spring padlock keys consist of a long rectangular cross-section stem, an annular bow and a lateral disc bit with subrectangular openwork clefts. Some key-bits current during this period were rather crude with large clefts. Roman period keys were often carried about the person, suspended from a chain or on a wire ring.

Little is known about the use of locks and keys between the 5th-7th centuries AD, moreover whether they were even used. Although there is no conclusive proof, it is suggested that towards the end of the latter century churchbuilders from France may have introduced Romanesque locks and keys into England.

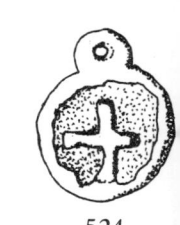

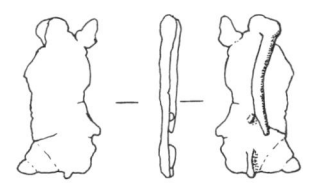

523

524

525

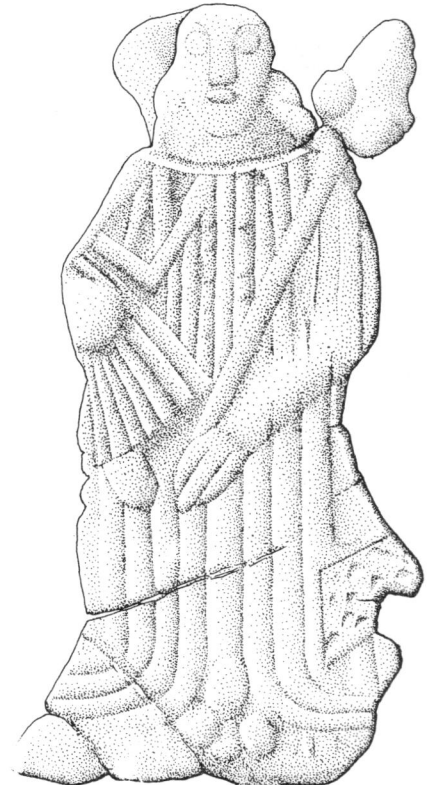

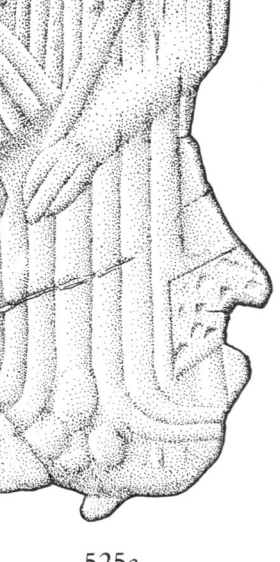

525a

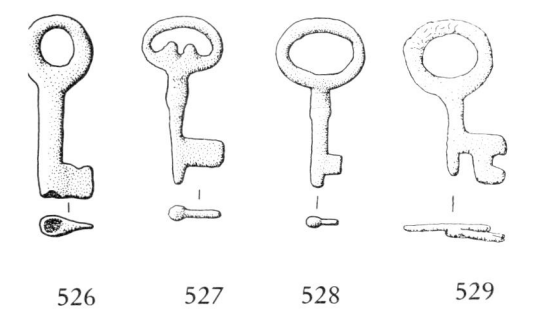

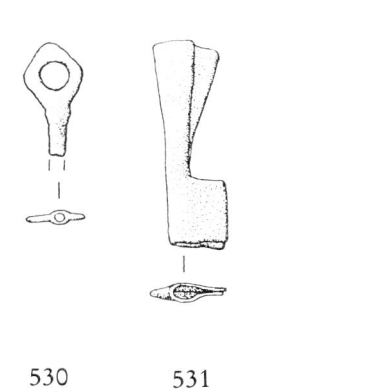

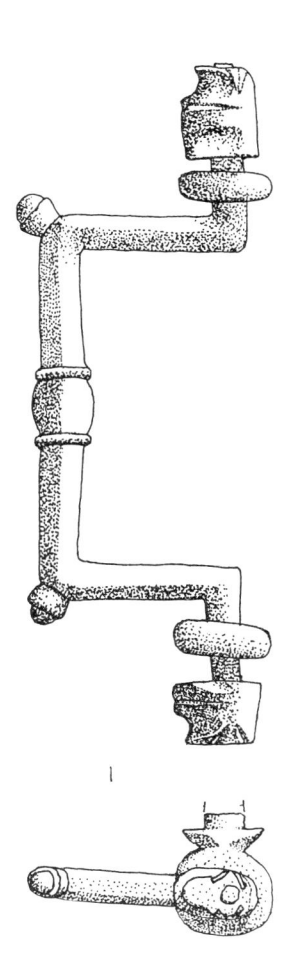

The Middle Ages

Whatever, after the conquest of 1066, Norman keys, which are cast copper alloy or forged iron, were dominant until the 12th century. A feature of some keys of the Norman period is their large ovoid-looped bows, although circular and oval were also current, which extend down to or just above the juncture with the bit. The bits of such keys are frequently large with wide clefts and some have bits with lateral bends. An additional safeguard incorporated into some locks was a pin, over which a key with a hollow, or pipe, stem fitted. This type was usually used on chests and caskets which, unlike a door or gate in a structure, could only be operated from one side.

By the 13th century keys with Romanesque large bows had been largely superseded by a type with a straight stem and an oval or circular bow. Some 11th-century keys have a slightly projecting pin, a feature used sporadically well into the 12th century, however, it seemed to disappear in the last half of the same century and re-emerged in the 14th. Bows of lozenge-shape with knops on the external angles appeared in the 13th century and remained current, particularly on casket keys, throughout the 14th, whilst plain lozenge-shaped bows with quatrefoil-shaped openwork were in vogue until the end of the 15th century. Sheet copper alloy for key-making seems to have started around the 13th century.

The projecting-pin keys of the 14th century are characterised by narrow long pins which terminate around the upper third of the bit; the stem has a greater diameter thereby creating a distinct waist or step. This type of key has either a circular, oval or kidney-shaped bow. The latter shape continued through the 15th century into the post medieval period. Tiny copper-alloy casket-keys current in the later Middle Ages are invariably facsimiles of larger keys and can be attributed accordingly; however, a form of 14th-15th-century casket-key, also current in Roman and Viking Britain, has a circular bow and a subrectangular annular bit with openwork clefts. The end of the bit has a definite point.

Forged iron or cast copper-alloy padlocks of the barrel type only became widely used in England between Viking times and the 13th century. Characteristics of barrel padlock-keys attributed to the later Middle Ages are a long, wide stem which terminates at the top with a simple circular or hooked bow, whilst a bit, found in a variety of shapes, set with either external or internal clefts, sits laterally at the business end. Latch-lifters seem to date to around the 12th century, and are a simple device of either iron or copper alloy with a circular bow at one end and a large-diameter open-hook at the other.

Cast copper-alloy casket-keys, 13th-14th century
526: circular bow, cylindrical stem with pipe end, plain bit, L. 35mm - *Haccombe*.
527: oval bow with two lobed-protrusions inside at juncture of stem, cylindrical projecting tapered pin stem, plain bit, L. 33mm - *Clyst Honiton*.
528: oval bow, cylindrical projecting pin stem, plain bit, L. 33mm - *Lympstone*.
529: circular bow, flat cross-section, bit with two clefts and two bullets, 32.5mm - *Stokeinteignhead*.
530: fragmented, lozenge-shaped bow, cylindrical stem with pipe end, L. 22mm - *Stokeinteignhead*.

Folded sheet copper-alloy casket-key, c14th century

531: triangular bow, cylindrical stem, plain bit, probably homemade, 40.5mm - *Kingskersell*.

CHESTS AND CASKETS

Throughout the Middle Ages wooden or metal chests and caskets of varying sizes were utilized for storing important records and valuables. Frequently such containers were clad in leather or fabric and ornamented with cast copper-alloy or forged iron mounts as well as both functional and decorative metal components, e.g. handles, clasps, hinges and locks. Although uncommon, this form of copper-alloy metalwork has been found in non-associated contexts.

Cast copper-alloy chest or casket-handle, 14th-15th century

532: circular cross-section, moulded acorn knops on angles, moulded zoomorphic terminals, expanded centre flanked by transverse moulded ribs, two separate copper-alloy securing eyelets, 117mm x 47mm - *Combeinteignhead*.

Sheet copper-alloy casket-clasps, 14th-15th century

533: rectangular, two hinge-like folded sheet sections joined by a copper-alloy pin with a looped head, six rivet holes, four copper-alloy rivets (two of which form part of a pivoted locking-catch and projecting stud), fragment of woven fabric trapped beneath one rivet head, two trefoil apertures on each edge, engraved chevrons and transverse bands of zigzags, 57mm x 38mm - *Stokeinteignhead*.

534: similar to No.533 but undecorated and fragmented, L. 53.5mm - *Stokeinteignhead*.

N.B. Almost identical handles to No.532 have been found at Salisbury and in Cornwall. London has produced fragmented examples similar to Nos.533 & 534.

CROTAL BELLS

Although they have been used in various parts of the world for over three millenium no one knows the origin of the bell. In medieval England two types were current: open-ended with a suspended clapper, and enclosed, with a tin, iron, or clay pea. Open-ended bells are found in various forms of the familiar bell-shape, whilst enclosed bells (the crotal) are spherical, straight-sided with hemispherical ends or pear-shaped.

Sheet tin or copper was used for crotal bell manufacture before the 13th century but lost favour by the 14th to more durable sheet copper alloy and cast tin or lead/tin alloy. Until the end of the 15th century the design of copper-alloy crotal bells remained constant, however, tin or lead/tin alloy crotals were made in various forms.

Copper-alloy crotal bells comprise four sections: an upper and lower half of the spherical body made from hammered sheet which was soldered together, a narrow strip of sheet for the suspension loop, and the pea. Very early tin or copper crotals were similarly made but had a copper wire suspension loop. This latter type of bell had two small circular sound-holes in the top half whilst the former was provided with two circular sound-holes conjoined by a slit in the lower half. Although examples are known, it was uncommon for these types of crotal bell to be decorated, however, tinning was current.

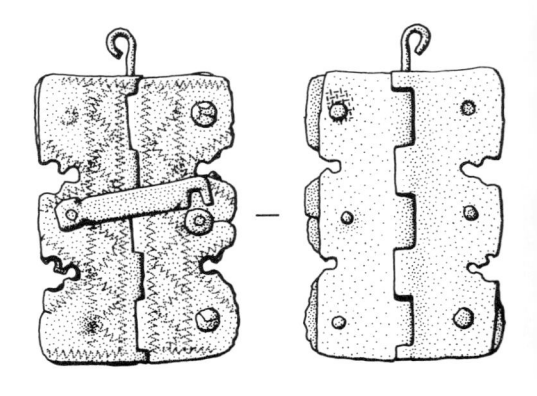

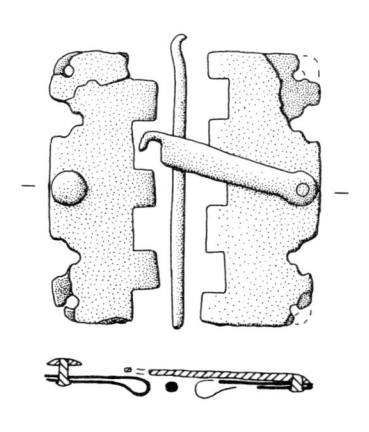

The Middle Ages

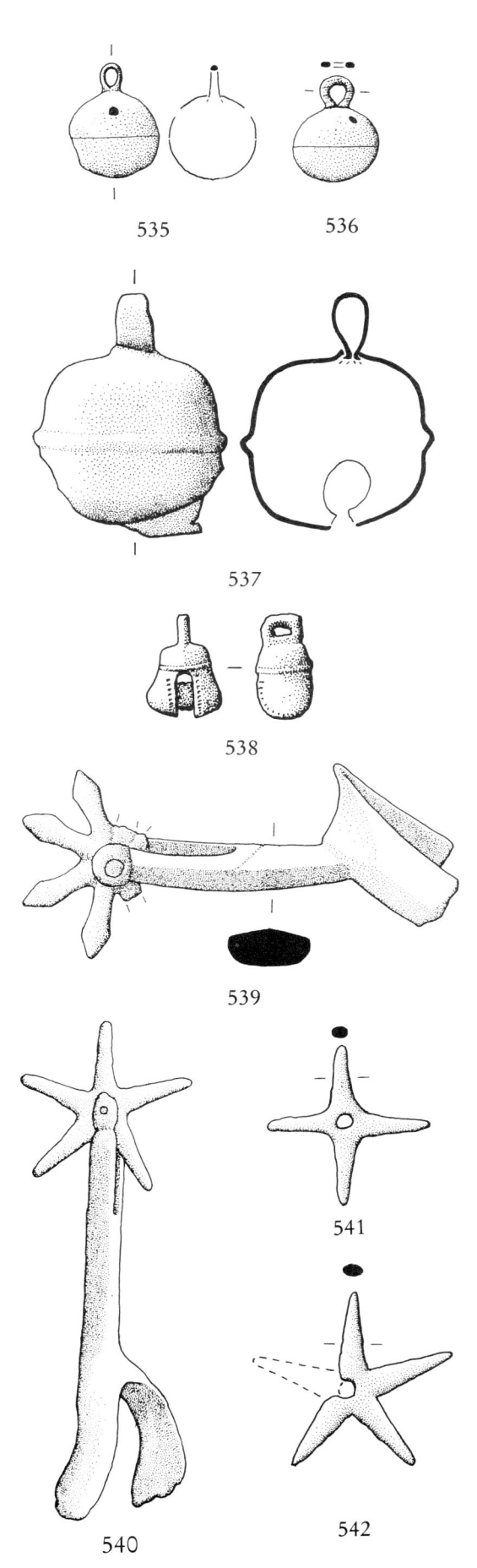

Several methods of casting later tin or lead/tin-alloy crotal bells were current, viz:

A: one-piece, including integral suspension loop, the end being left open for the insertion of the pea, the two sides were then squeezed together.

B: two-piece, including integral suspension loop, with a soldered girth seam, the pea being inserted before soldering.

C: one-piece (the same as A), with an integral stem which was bent over to form a suspension loop.

D: one-piece, including integral suspension loop, the lower half having four petal-shaped tabs which after the pea had been inserted were squeezed together.

These casting techniques resulted in crotal bells of differing shapes which frequently have moulded decoration. Contemporaneus representations from the Middle Ages and later periods imply that crotal bells were made of either silver or gold - no such piece seems to be extant. Crotal bells embellished: girdles, hats, sashes, collars and necklaces of folk of both sexes, including: priests, pilgrims, acrobats and jesters. They also adorned horse harness, dog collars and hawk jesses.

Clapper type bells range in size from huge church-bells down to tiny examples sold as pilgrim souvenirs or for personal costume beautification. However, the scope of this book is confined to the latter smaller forms. Again, it is likely that small clapper-bells antecede the late 13th century, which is the beginning of the period covered here. They remained in popular use certainly well into the 15th century, and probably considerably later. Manufacturing was by one-piece casting, with integral circular suspension-loops, although trefoil- or quatrefoil-shaped are known. Clappers seem to have been either iron or lead/tin alloy. Two shapes of small clapper-bell have been identified, though there may be others - the typical bell-shape or cylindrical, both of which usually have a small circular sound-hole in the top.

Sheet copper-alloy crotal bells, early 13th century

535: four-piece, separate copper-alloy wire suspension loop, two small circular sound-holes in top half, pea lost, 27mm x 20.5mm - *Cockington*.

536: four-piece, traces of tinning, separate copper-alloy wire suspension loop, two small circular sound-holes in top half, with probable iron pea, 25mm x 19mm - *Exeter*.

Sheet copper-alloy crotal bells, late 13th-14th century

537: four-piece, separate copper-alloy sheet suspension loop, two circular sound-holes conjoined by a slot in lower half, pea lost, 56mm x 44mm - *Newton Abbot*.

Cast tin or lead/tin-alloy crotal bell, late 13th-14th century

538: two-piece, integral suspension loop, rectangular sound-slot in lower half, iron pea, 24.5mm x 16.5mm - *Ringmore*.

SPURS

Spurs have been worn by horseriders for centuries, certainly as far back as the Romans, however, again it was the Vikings who probably introduced them nto Britain. The earliest Scandinavian spurs are forged iron with a conical goad which gave rise to the name 'prick-spur'. As time progressed, other designs of goad were introduced which eventually resulted in about eleven by the 11th century. Likewise, styles of terminal and sides changed. Viking spurs invariably are straight-sided with flat plate terminals, but curved sides and single or double circle terminals were current by the 13th century. Copper-alloy-clad iron prick-spurs seem to be attributed to the 12th century and later.

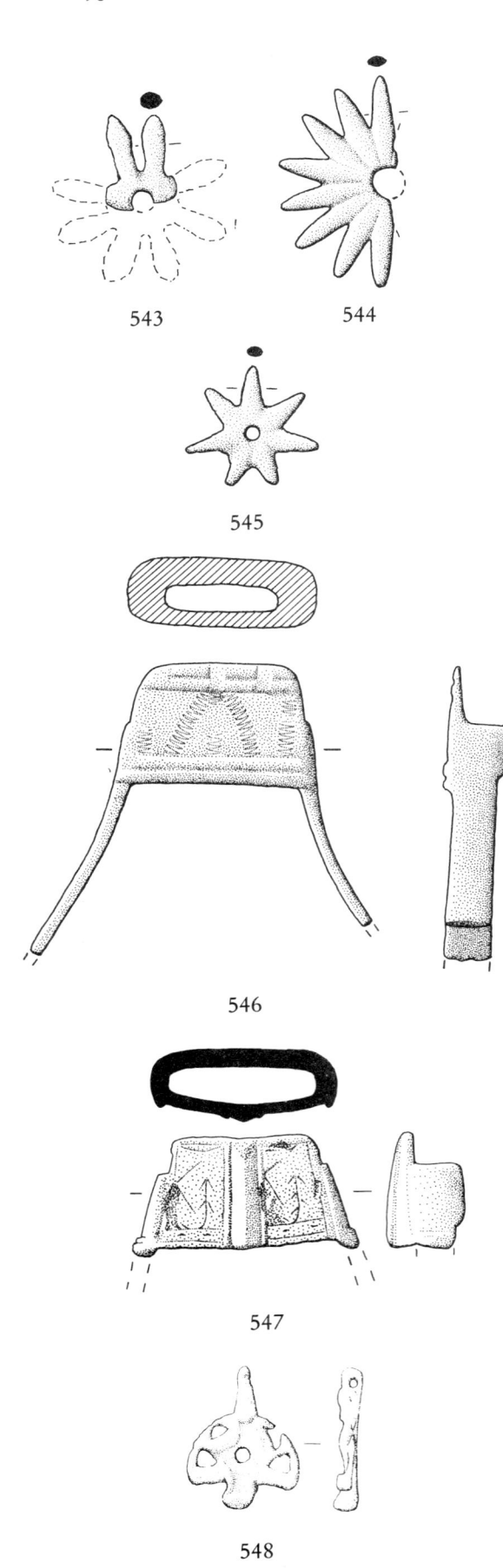

Precisely when the rowel-spur first appeared in Britain is debatable, possibly it was the late 13th century by which time spurriers were making cast and forged copper-alloy spurs in addition to forged iron. Both prick-spurs and rowel-spurs were current until about the middle of the 14th century when prick-spurs lost favour (albeit prick-spurs were revived for a while in the 17th century). Early rowel-spurs have very short necks and small six or seven-point rowels; after c1350 the multi-point rowel became in vogue, however, the former type of rowel continued to be used, including four-point cruciform rowels. Sides of spurs attributable to this time are either pronouncedly bent or have a slight curve, and at the juncture of the sides there is invariably a high crest point. Until c1350 a multiplicity of terminals were popular, after which it was confined to figure-8 or plain circle. The rapid development of armour in the 15th century caused necks of rowel-spurs to be considerably increased in length, a style which continued until the start of the 16th century.

Cast and forged copper-alloy rowel-spurs
539: mid to late 14th century, remains of both downward curved sides, high crest point at juncture of sides, slightly curved neck, large eight-point rowel, four points lost, L. 98`m - *Cockington*.
540: probable mid to late 15th century, remains of both downward curved sides, long neck, six-point rowel, L. 115`m - *Cockington*.

Cast copper-alloy rowels
541: mid-14th century, four-point (cruciform), D. 37`m - *Cockington*.
542: 14th-17th century, five-point rowel, one point lost, D. 43`m - *Cockington*.
543: mid to late 14th century or perhaps 15th century, multi-point, fragmented, R. 20`m - *Stokeinteignhead*.
544: mid to late 14th century or perhaps 15th century, multi-point, fragmented, D. 48`m - *Gappah*.
545: 13th-19th century, seven-point, D. 28`m - *Cockington*.

STIRRUPS
By the 13th century a stirrup had evolved which had an expanded foot-rest decorated with openwork but lacking a suspension loop. Come the 14th century development achieved asymmetrical and symmetrical types, some of which have an integral expanded plate, often decorated, covering the suspension loop. Although it was used before, in the 15th century applied ornamentation was common, e.g. copper-alloy or silver bosses, inlaid silver and copper-alloy plate. Decorative, bosses were sometimes functional, for they held together stirrups made in two parts, i.e. sides and foot-rest. Other than variations in the width of the sides and the foot-rest, and the addition of a projecting tongue on the front of the foot-rest, stirrups underwent little further change.

Cast and forged copper-alloy stirrup, 14th century
546: fragment, trapezium-shaped, integral expanded front plate

The Middle Ages

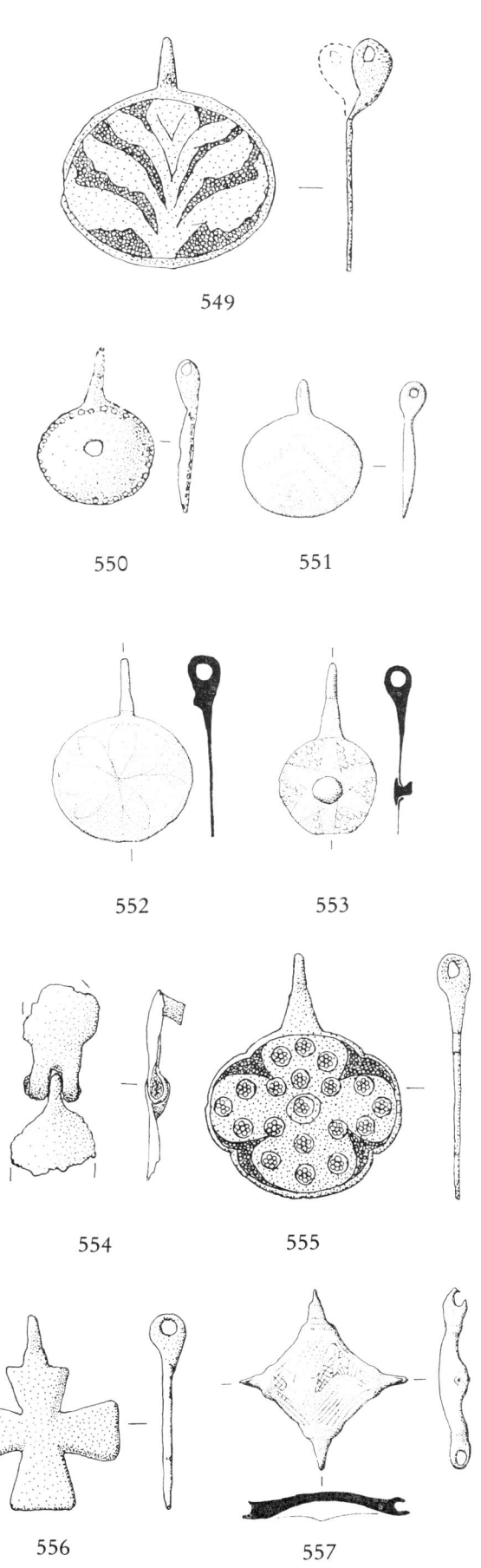

549

550 551

552 553

554 555

556 557

moulded with transverse ridges and vertical grooves forming a rectangular panel engraved with zigzags, 67mm x 74mm - *Shaldon*.

547: fragment, trapezium-shaped; integral expanded front plate moulded with transverse and vertical ridges forming two trapezoidal panels each with a border, chevron, curvilinear and oblique lines of punched dots, vertical and transverse lines of punched dots on sides, 27mm x 49.5mm - *Exeter*.

PENDANTS

From around the 11th century until the 14th horse-harness was frequently embellished with elaborate cast or sheet metal pendants. Copper alloy was the normal metal employed, though at least one example of lead is known. It is reasonable to assume that silver or gold may have also been current with extremely wealthy persons. Early pendants are rare but examples from the 13th-14th centuries are relatively common. Shapes include: shield, circular, semi-circular, oval, rectangular, square, lozenge, cruciform or quatrefoil. Pendants either rotated or swung in sometimes equally stylish metal-mounts which were riveted to the leatherwork. From the 11th century gilding was usually applied but by the 14th enamelling was increasingly popular. Openwork or separate decorative rivets are a feature of some. Two types of pendant are known, heraldic, which represents the coat of arms or badge of the owner, and non-heraldic, which is some form of artistic design. Many have pseudo-heraldic artwork, probably to satisfy the vanity of lesser mortals.

Until the advent of metal detecting, medieval pendants were uncommon and the archaeological consensus of opinion was that they only adorned the personal saddle-horses or coaches of important people. However, due to the large number that have come to light, and their widespread distribution, it seems certain they were used by a greater proportion of the populace. Logically, the saddle-horses of retainers would have carried pendants to identify their owner. There is strong evidence which indicates that pendants were also associated with dog collars and personal costume, however, invariably the distinction is difficult to define.

Cast copper-alloy pendant, probably Romanesque, c12th century

548: semi-circular, lobed knop at bottom, two moulded perched birds and typical Romanesque openwork, 32mm x 25mm - *Uffculme*.

Cast copper-alloy pendant, perhaps late Romanesque, therefore late 12th-13th century

549: oval, traces of gilt, engraved foliate or plume within engraved linear border, punched circles field, 52mm x 47mm - *Haccombe*.

Cast or sheet copper-alloy pendants, c13th-14th century

550: oval, traces of gilt, convex, border of punched circles, central circular hole probably held a decorative rivet, 36mm x 25mm - *Haccombe*.

551: oval, traces of gilt, convex, punched dots forming chevrons, 31mm x 26.5mm - *Stokeinteignhead*.

552: oval, protrusion on suspension loop, punched dots forming an octofoil within a linear border, 42mm x 31mm - *Exeter*.

553: circular, punched dots forming a six-point star, field of punched crescents, central rivet hole holding a copper-alloy decorative rivet, 39mm x 21mm - *Exeter*.
554: circular, fragment, convex, with fragmented convex circular mount, copper-alloy pin, 32mm x 13mm - *Stokeinteignhead*.
555: quatrefoil, traces of gilt; punched fleurets, circles and concentric circles within a quatrefoil, punched circles field, 55mm x 43mm - *Kingskerswell*.
556: quatrefoil, 44mm x 33mm - *Haccombe*.
557: quatrefoil, convex, an oddity with upper and lower suspension loops, one abraded, abraded punched dots, 41mm x 37mm - *Littlehempston*.
558: sexfoil, central rivet hole with a separate copper-alloy decorative rivet, sexfoil swinging frame with lobed protrusions in the angles, 50mm x 33.5mm - *Haccombe*.
559: fragmented pendant swinging frame for a probable sexfoil pendant, bifid protrusions in the angles, 46mm x 38mm - *Axminster*.
560: indeterminate shape, fragmented, traces of moulded design, 35mm x 11mm - *Exeter*.

Cast copper-alloy pendant, possibly c13th century
561: quatrefoil, an oddity which is large for a medieval pendant, quatrefoil openwork, fragmented suspension loop, 59.5mm x 44.5mm - *Stokeinteignhead*.

Cast copper-alloy pendants, 14th century
562: quatrefoil, fragmented suspension loop, traces of red enamelled shield-quarters with a metal cross and surround on blue field, elongated beasts as space fillers. Possibly the cross and edging were originally gilded or silvered, therefore blason is probably 'gules, a cross argent (or 'or' if gold)'. If 'argent', perhaps these are the arms of Sir Steven de Cobham who bore them at the Battle of Boroughbridge in 1332 or Stephen Pencestre who used them in Henry III's reign, 36mm x 30mm - *Kingskerswell*.
563: quatrefoil, pointed protrusions in the angles, metal lion passant guardant on red enamelled field and fleurs on a blue enamelled field. Probably post 1340 when Edward III incorporated the French arms into the English royal arms; perhaps pseudo-heraldic as patriotic emblems were used at the start of the Hundred Years War, 41.5mm x 31.5mm - *Ipplepen*.
564: shield-shaped, probably pseudo-heraldic, two bands of engraved zigzags between two transverse engraved lines, punched circles field on lower half, 46mm x 29mm - *Cockington*.
565: shield-shaped, very crude, pseudo-heraldic, three moulded oblique lines and crescents, hooked suspension loop, 47mm x 30mm - *Cockington*.
566: shield-shaped, remains of copper-alloy pin in suspension loop, 'on a chevron three roundels', perhaps an unrecorded variant (differenced) of the relatively minor Cornwall family arms, 43mm x 25mm - *Ringmore*
567: shield-shaped, metal martlets on traces of red field in bars; possibly blazoned '?, on three bars gules six martlets ?, 3, 2, 1.', 47mm x 27mm - *Ringmore*.
568: shield-shaped, royal arms of England, gilt lions on enamelled red field and blue enamelled label of three points (perhaps 5

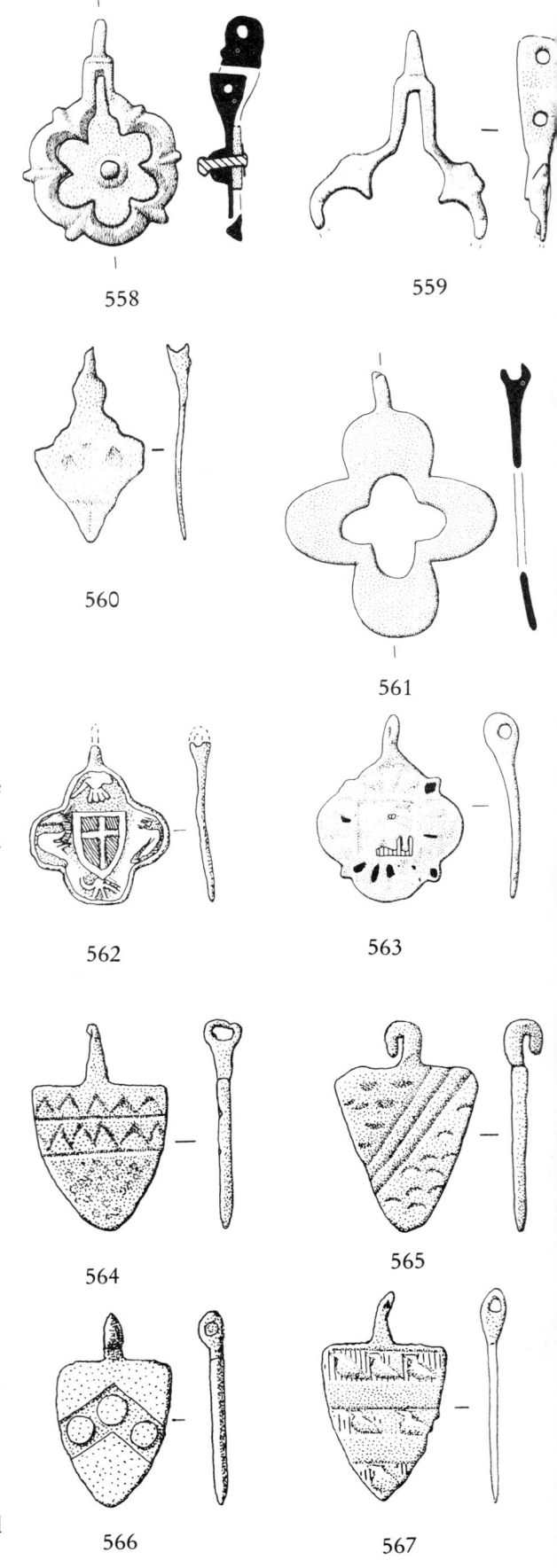

The Middle Ages

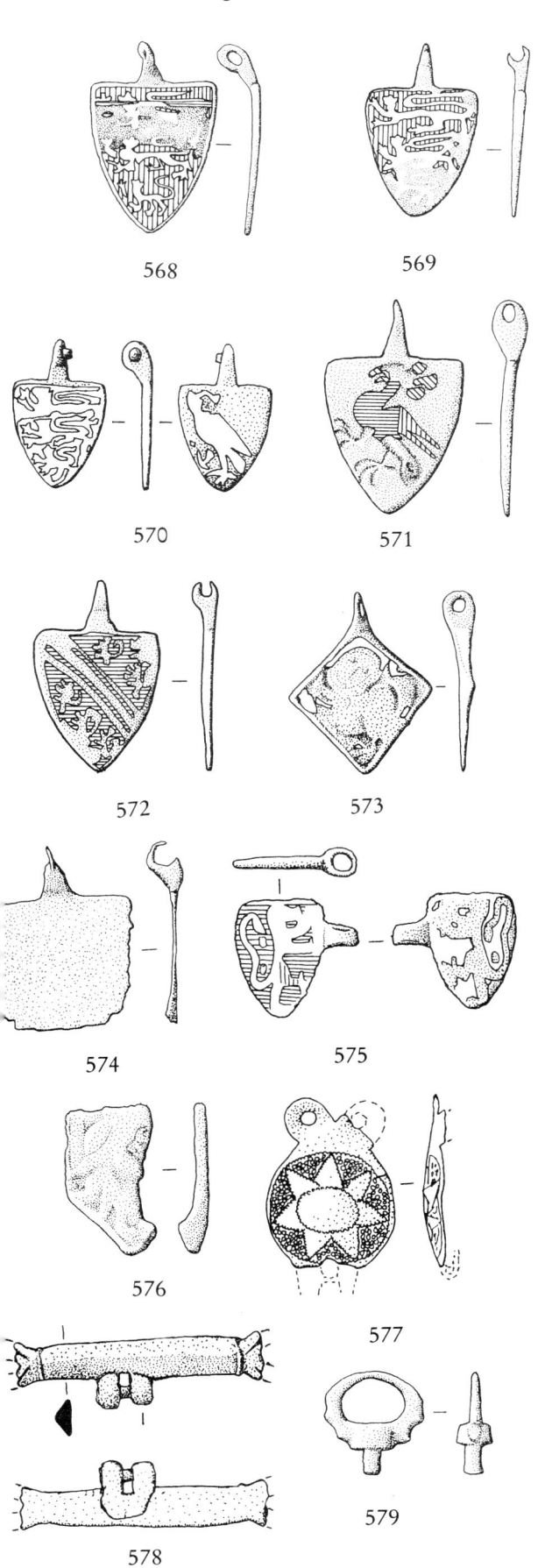

but that would be unusual), therefore blazoned 'gules, three lions passant guardant in pale or with a label of three ? 3 points azure'. The mark of an eldest son, perhaps connected with Edward II as prince, therefore c1300, 44mm x 27mm - *Colaton Raleigh*.

569: shield-shaped, fragmented suspension loop, royal arms of England, gilt lions on enamelled red field, therefore blazoned 'gules, three lions passant guardant in pale or', 38.50mm x 24.5mm - *Kingskerswell*.

570: shield-shaped, remains of copper-alloy pin, one side with probable royal arms of England, gilt lions on enamelled red field, therefore blazoned 'gules, three lions passant guardant in pale or', other side with white enamelled possible peacock on possible silver or gold field. Double-sided shields are nonsensicle and in this instance may represent the re-use of a redundant (?) England pendant, 33mm x 20mm - *Exeter*.

571: shield-shaped, probably pseudo-heraldic; stylised red, blue and green enamelled peacock. Frequently used as a sign of wealth, although it may be the unrecorded badge of some family, 49mm x 30mm - *Kingskerswell*

572: shield-shaped, fragmented suspension loop, six gilt rampant lions with a silver bend edged in gilt on blue enamelled field, therefore blazoned 'azure, a bend argent cotised or between six lyonceux rampant of the last'. The arms of the de Bohun family, Earls of Hereford, a major family with estates all over the country, e.g. Humfrey de Bohun, Earl of Hereford and Constable of England at the Siege of Caerlaverock, 1300, also at the 1st Dunstable tournament in 1308, 42.5mm x 27mm - *Otterton*.

573: lozenge-shaped, traces of silver field, possibly a hominoid-headed lion which perhaps is a strange depiction of St Mark whose emblem was a winged lion, or other mystical beast or a harpy, 40.5mm x 31mm - *Clyst St Mary*.

574: square, abraded edges, traces of gilt, fragmented suspension loop, 41mm x 28.5mm - *Cullompton*.

Cast copper-alloy side-looped rotating pendant, 14th century

575: shield-shaped, double-sided, heraldic or pseudo-heraldic, one side with a rampant lion in traces of red enamel on a gilt and blue enamelled field (which may be corrosion products), the other side a metal rampant lion with no colouring in the field, if the field is gilt, which it should be, then it is blazoned 'or, a lion rampant gules', 26mm x 26mm - *Coffinswell*.

Cast copper-alloy possible pendant, c14th century

576: possibly shield-shaped, fragmented, moulded beast, perhaps a mount, 13.5mm x 18.5mm - *Stokeinteignhead*.

Sheet copper-alloy pendant-mounts, 13th-14th century

577: oval, gilt, convex, fragmented, engraved seven-point star, punched circles field, 39mm x 28mm - *Stokeinteignhead*.

Cast copper-alloy pendant bar-mount, 13th-14th century

578: asymmetrical, gilt, triangular cross-section, central suspension lugs, copper-alloy pin, both terminals with rivet holes lost, 53mm x 15mm - *Stokeinteignhead*

STRAP JUNCTIONS

The several sections of medieval horse-harness were linked by forged iron or cast and/or forged copper-alloy junctions. Typically these are simple rings of varying size, however, more elaborate types were current. Other than horse-harness, it is now thought that straps used, for example, as dog or other animal leads may also have incorporated similar metal junctions.

A small group of very elaborate Romanesque junctions attributed to no later than the mid-12th century have now been recorded. All are cast copper alloy, some having hollow globular construction with intricate openwork formed from moulded lattice or foliate. A globular example from Somerset has a robust separate swivelling pin at each end. One pin has a separate pivoting penannular link with zoomorphic terminals attached. The link from the other pin is lost. Yet another, possibly from Gloucestershire, is perhaps one hemisphere of a globular type and has attached to its centre a separate zoomorphic-terminal annular link with integral swivelling pin. Provenanced from Gloucestershire is an example with a triangular body formed from two three-dimensional winged dragons joined by a transverse bar. A long separate robust pin passes through the body and is free to swivel. The top end of the pin has a separate pivoting penannular link with zoomorphic terminals. Attached to the transverse bar are two more separate swivelling pins, each with a separate zoomorphic-terminal pivoting penannular link. The last junction of this group comprises a pair of annular links, one of which has an integral pin that fits into a hole in the base of the other, and thereby swivels. A junction of the latter type from Wiltshire has zoomorphic terminals.

Frequently and erroneously credited as Romano-British, another type of junction comprises an annular ring with four equidistant lateral semi-circular or sub-triangular cross-section arms, each having a lozenge-shaped or circular coupling with circular openwork. Invariably lozenge-shaped couplings have lobed knops on the angles. Similar junctions are one-armed with both ends having either lozenge-shaped or circular couplings. Alternatively they may have one lozenge-shaped and one circular coupling.

Yet another form is identical to some pendant bar-mounts, but instead of a pair of pierced lugs they have either an annular rectangular female coupling or lateral flattened rectangular male coupling on one end. One of each makes a pair of junction pieces; the male coupling is passed through the female coupling and then twisted, thereby locking together the two sections of harness.

A rarer but probable strap junction is hollow-domed and circular with four equidistant loops. Each of the few known examples has an engraved cross on the domed body. The size of the circular orifice on each loop is quite small, therefore it is probable that each strap was linked by a metal hooked strap-end or was riveted. Quite possibly each of these three forms of strap-junction were also fitted to harness worn by dogs or other animals

Cast copper-alloy strap-junction, Romanesque, 12th century
579: annular, integral pin, moulded terminals, 23mm x 21.5mm - *Musbury*.

Cast copper-alloy strap-junctions, 13th-15th century
580: triangular cross-section arm, moulded waist below circular

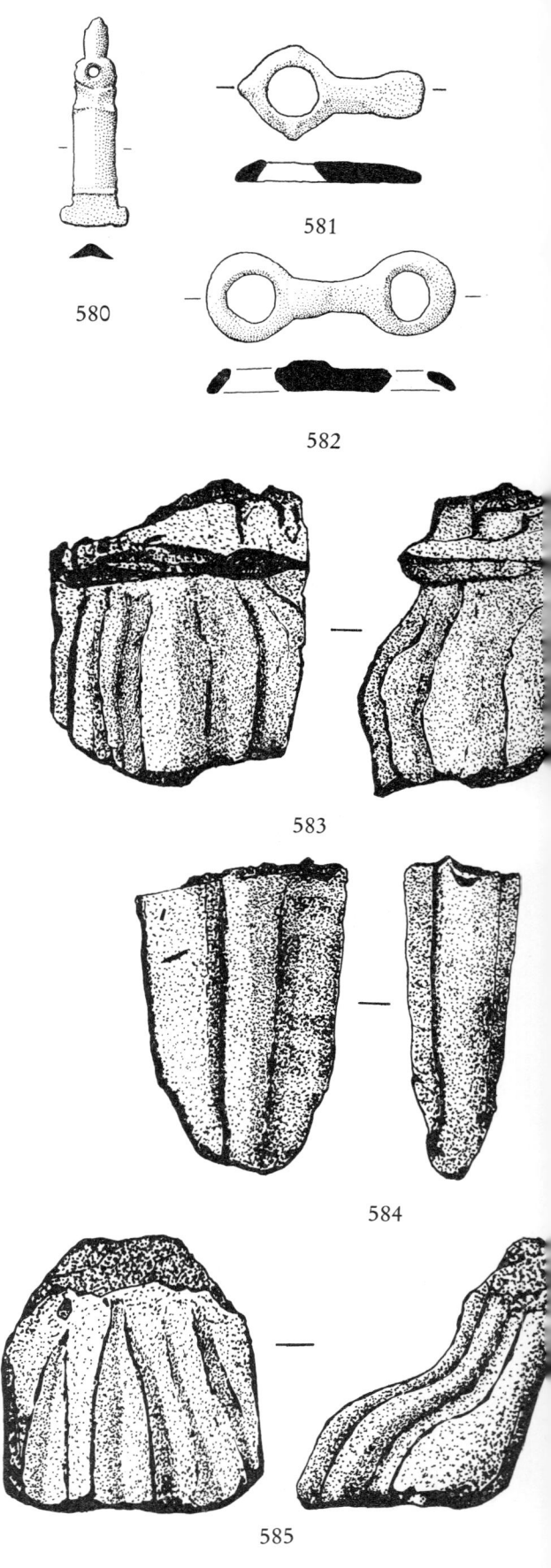

The Middle Ages

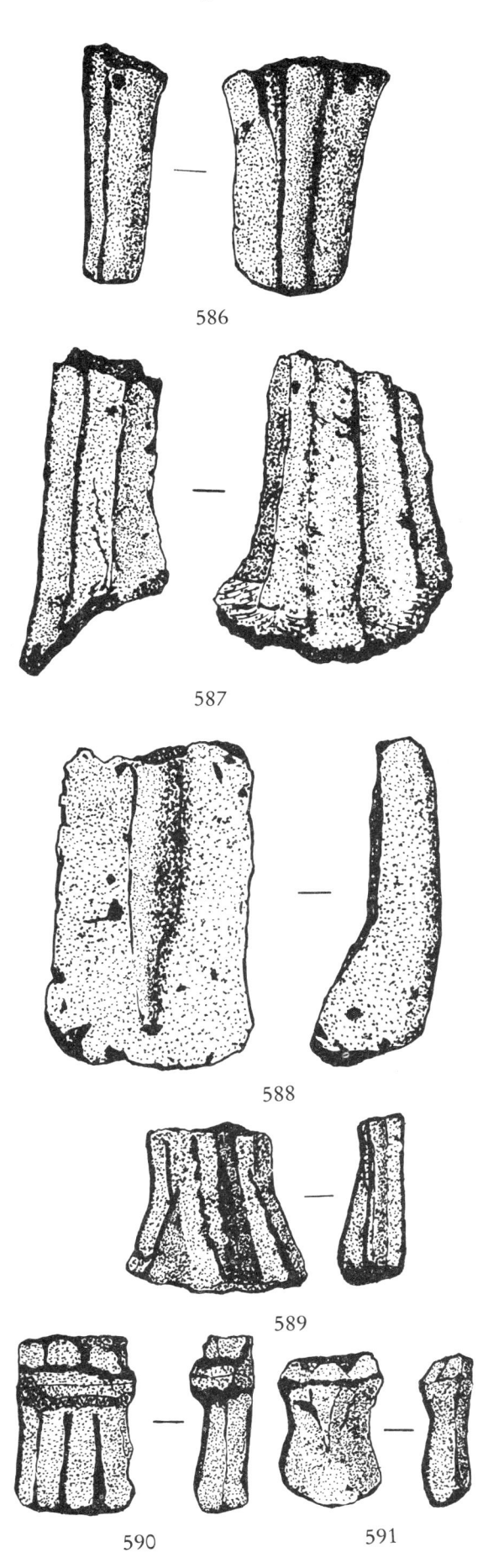

terminal with rivet hole, lobed knop, lateral flattened rectangular male coupling, 47mm x 15mm - *Bicton*.
581: fragment, sub-triangular cross-section arm, lozenge-shaped coupling with lobed knops on angles, circular openwork, 39.5mm x 22mm - *Coffinswell*.
582: circular cross-section arm with moulded subrectangular protrusion on one end, circular coupling on both ends, 53.5mm x 20mm - *Coffinswell*.

RECEPTACLES

In classical times, drinking-vessels, bowls, plates and jugs were often crafted from gold or silver, although lead/tin alloy and copper alloy were more common. The use of forged iron or cast or forged copper alloy for cooking-vessels had also been current for centuries prior to the early Middle Ages when it died out in favour of pottery. It became fashionable again late in the 13th Century.

Complete metal receptacles of the medieval period from non-associated contexts are rare, however, lead/tin-alloy or copper-alloy fragments are plentious. The former are invariably parts of bowls or dishes, and the latter, legs of cauldrons, skillets, jugs or ewers. Invariably the only method of attributing such pieces is by metal analysis or comparison with complete artefacts. With regard to legs, comparison is unreliable, for styles remained similar from the late medieval period until the 17th century. Because of this difficulty, it is probable that some examples depicted herein are not strictly attributable to the Middle Ages. Not uncommon finds are copper-alloy zoomorphic spouts which have become detached from ewers or jugs.

Cast copper-alloy receptacle legs, 13th-17th century
583: 67mm x 56mm - *Stokeinteignhead*.
584: 72mm x 45mm - *Stokeinteignhead*.
585: 61mm x 56mm - *West Ogwell*.
586: 56mm x 38mm - *Stokeinteignhead*.
587: 78mm x 54mm - *Cockington*.
588: 76mm x 47mm - *Haccombe*.
589: 39.5mm x 41mm - *Stokeinteignhead*.
590: 41.5mm x 27mm - *Chudleigh*.
591: 36mm x 24.5mm - *Stokeinteignhead*.
592: 61mm x 41mm - *Cockington*.
593: 62mm x 49mm - *Stokeinteignhead*.
594: 54mm x 40mm - *Cockington*.
595: 57mm x 44mm - *Watcombe*.
596: 98mm x 33mm - *Cockington*.
597: 40mm x 24mm - *Haccombe*.
598: 41mm x 27.5mm - *Stokeinteignhead*.
599: 42mm x 33mm - *Cockington*.
600: 34.5mm x 60.4mm - *Haccombe*.
601: 71.5mm x 16mm - *Exeter*.

Cast copper-alloy ewer spout, c14th-15th century
602: three-dimensional zoomorphic terminal, perhaps a bat, 49mm x 20mm - *Stoke Canon*.

BARREL TAPS

Wooden barrels or casks were current in the Middle Ages and later periods for holding water, wine, beer, cider, oils, brine or

592

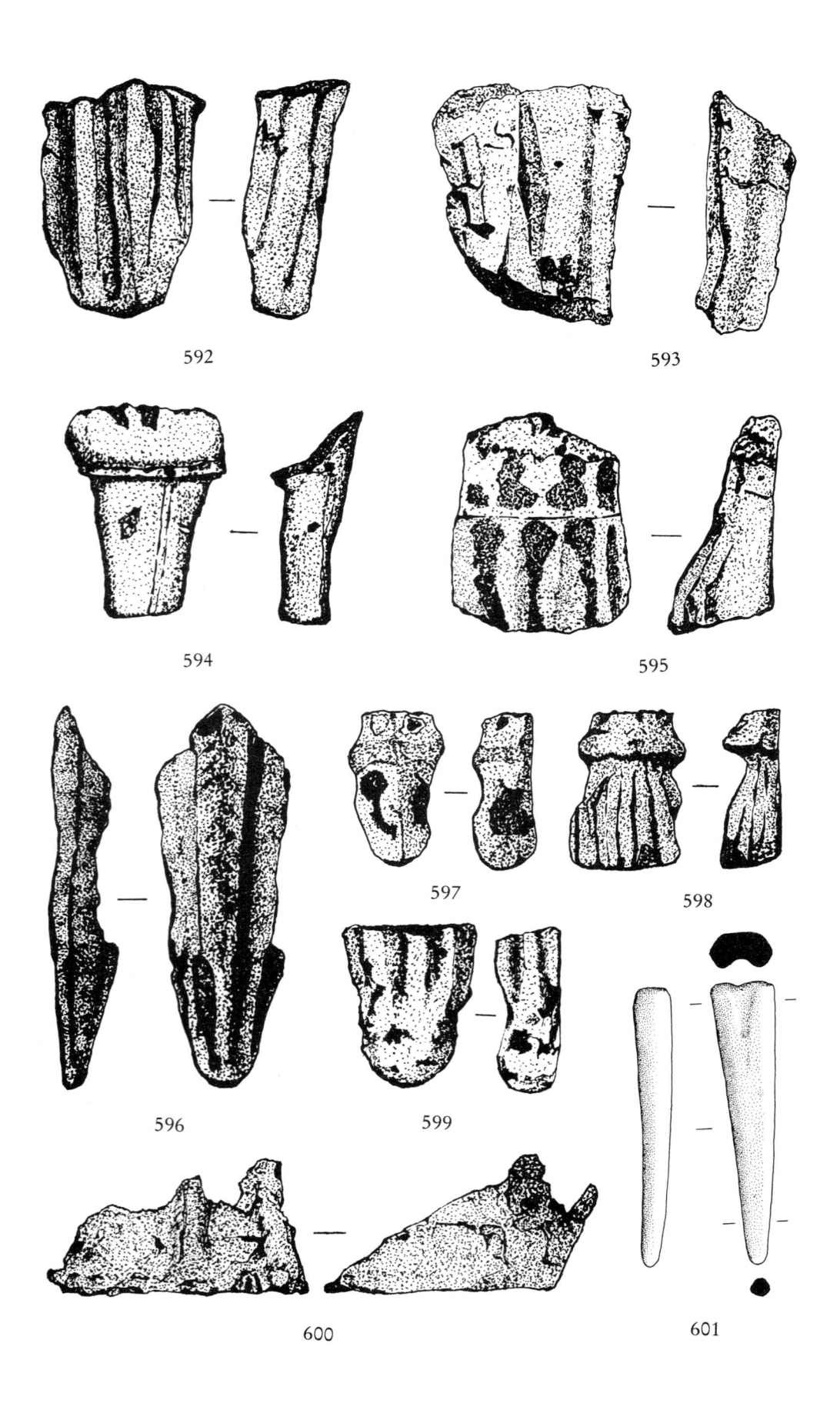

593

594

595

596

597

598

599

601

600

The Middle Ages

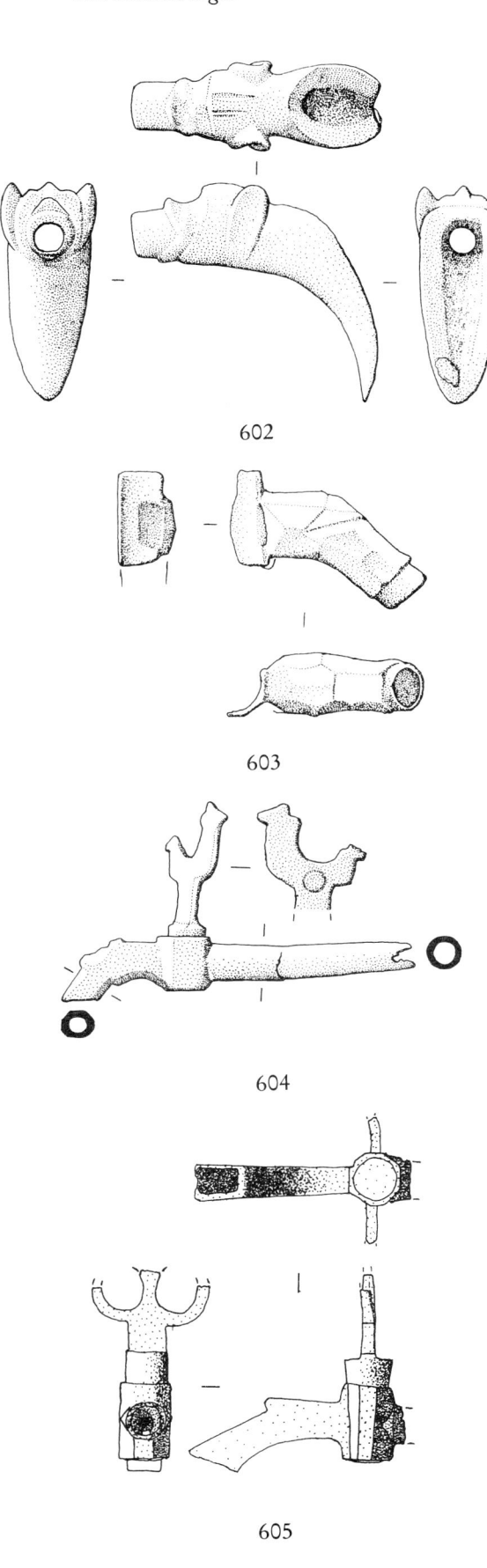

vinegar. Removal of the liquid was controlled by copper-alloy taps the earliest of which had irremovable keys. One end of the tap has a downturned spout and at the other, a spigot. Initially spigots were open-ended but later these were sealed and, instead, liquid flowed through a large number of small circular holes thereby acting as a filter. From around the 18th century barrel-taps were made with removable keys which prevented surreptitious removal of a container's contents.

The earliest barrel-taps, which are small in comparison to later examples, are attributed to the later Middle Ages and Tudor period and are characterised by keys of fleur-de-lis, zoomorphic or openwork trefoil form.

Cast copper-alloy barrel-taps and keys, c15th-16th century

603: fragmented, circular cross-section spout with moulded multi-facets, L. 42mm - *Stokeinteignhead*.
604: octagonal cross-section spout, circular cross-section spigot cracked and open-end fragmented, cockerel-shaped key, 75mm x 42mm - *Cockwood*.
605: fragmented, subrectangular cross-section spout, openwork trefoil-shaped key fragmented, 44mm x 47mm - *Haccombe*.

AVIARY AND CAGE-BIRD FEED AND WATER-TROUGHS

Small lead or lead/tin-alloy receptacles regularly found throughout the country have been variously described as medieval: 'bells', 'inkwells', 'holy water containers', 'blood-letting cups', 'dice shakers' or 'troughs for holding bird seed or water'. There is no stratified archaeological evidence for any of these uses.

The brim of one medieval trough recovered from the River Thames in London had apparently been deliberately squeezed together and when opened was found to contain leguminous seed thought to be vetch. Moreover, another Thames-foreshore squashed example of similar attribution enclosed 24 tiny bone false dice. Despite this confusion the current antiquarian consensus of opinion is that these receptacles were probably aviary or cage-bird feed and water-troughs. The earliest record of such troughs is the 1390s in Paris, however, although they remained current into the 17th century, the aforementioned from London are attributed to around the 15th century.

Troughs of medieval origin are thin-section cast lead/tin alloy. Essentially they have a curved front, flat back, and flat D-shaped base which tapers up to an open D-shaped top. Occasionally troughs have pronounced flared tops. Varying sizes are known. Frequently medieval troughs have moulded heraldic devices on the front and occasionally the back is similarly decorated. Small holes are sometimes provided a little below the rear brim through which a cord was passed for lashing the trough to the wickerwork cage. Alternatively an integral projecting annulet on each side served the same purpose. Another kind of medieval trough has a conical rounded base and two downturned integral brackets or hooks on the rear for hanging the trough over a horizontal bar.

Cast lead/tin-alloy aviary or cage-bird feed or water-trough, c15th century

606: flat bottom, fragmented back, flared top with moulded rim, 36mm x 61.5mm - *Poltimore*.

CANDLESTICKS

Domestic candlesticks of pre-1400 English manufacture are rare. However, they were probably widely used alongside those of Continental origin, possibly Normandy. Attribution of provenance is often difficult.

One c13th-14th-century candlestick is the pricket-type made from forged iron or forged and cast copper alloy which comprises a column with tripartite folding legs and a sharp pointed top whereby a wax candle was impaled. A double-ended lateral projection affixed to the column has on one end a ring-socket and on the other a chevron terminal. The socket probably held a rush, but the precise function of the chevron remains unknown. Another of similar period is forged iron and has fixed tripartite legs but in this instance the column lies almost horizontal. Riveted or brazed to the top of the column is a section of iron tube flattened in the centre and with one end bent up laterally, thus forming a socket for the candle.

Two types of c14th-century English spiked-base candlestick are known, both of which were simply inserted into any convenient crack in stone or wood walls or even furniture. One is cast copper alloy with a conventional socket, whilst the other has a cast copper-alloy spike, a separate folded sheet copper-alloy arm and a sheet copper-alloy tapered socket. Where the arm is folded it forms a loop which swivels on a lateral projection at the top of the spike. The socket is riveted to the other end of the arm. As this latter candlestick could be folded up, it probably found favour with travellers.

Other likely Continental socketed-candlesticks, of various forms, characteristically have a pair of rectangular or subrectangular slots in the sides of the socket which assisted removal of the candle-end.

From the 15th century English-made candlesticks were based upon the Continental tripod-type, i.e. with three short legs, each with a laterally outward bent foot. Next came the circular-based bunsen-burner type without legs. Variations of this style were current into the 16th century.

Cast and forged copper-alloy possible Continental socketed-candlestick, 14th-15th century
607: tapered socket with two rectangular holes, lateral arm with fragmented annular ring, circle with 'spokes' of punched dots on socket base, 69mm x 44mm - *Exeter*.

TRADE WEIGHTS

Multi-shaped cast lead trade-weights without official marks remained current throughout the Middle Ages. Of these the free-standing conical with integral loop variety is perhaps the most ubiquitous. One type of the latter, which is probably attributable to the 12th and 13th centuries, has oblique moulded grooves around the body, whilst another of similar form has a fluted body. Circular-flat types with a moulded floriated cross are thought to date from the same period. Shield-shaped lead weights, with or without a small hole in the top, bearing a moulded rampant lion, three lions passant or a lis surmounted by a crown, may be c1380-90. Flat-circular lead weights stamped with an incuse plantagenet crown appeared c1400, whilst around the late 14th century copper-alloy trade-weights came into use. Likewise these are also stamped with an incuse crown, the type of which seems to vary.

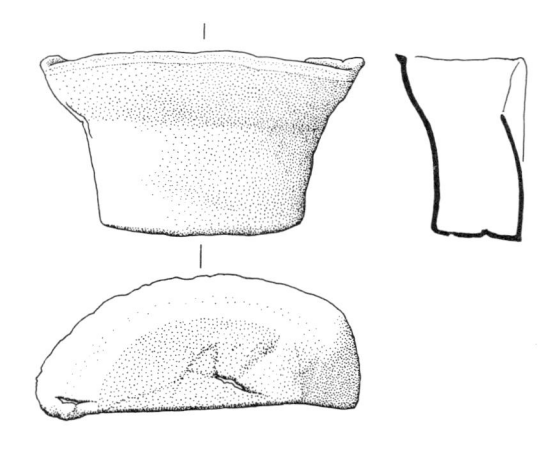

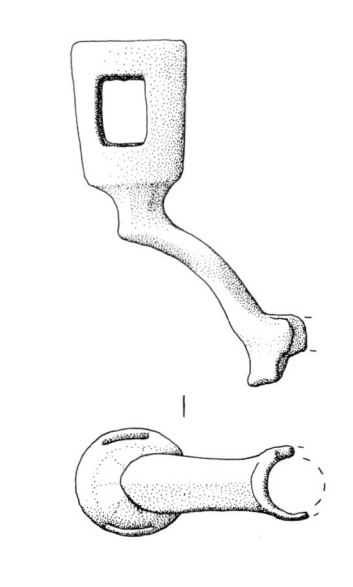

The Middle Ages

A common type of medieval weight, but now very rare, is the lead-filled copper-alloy globular steelyard-weight which are attributed to the second half of the 13th century. These weights have a triangular projection on top pierced by a circular hole by which means the weight was suspended. Two types of steelyard weight are known, viz: those having moulded heraldic shields and arms, and those with moulded heraldic shields and arms incuse. Both forms invariably have a band of incised decoration around the top, frequently chevrons.

Large weights especially for weighing wool were current from at least the time of Edward I until George III's reign. Initially they were cast lead, shield-shaped, with similar moulded marks as found on smaller shield-shaped trade weights. In the Elizabethan period copper-alloy shield-shaped wool weights came into being; henceforth they had the coat of arms of the reigning monarch or the Commonwealth respectively. Official marks as used on other types of trade-weight will normally be found on copper-alloy wool weights. Both lead and copper-alloy wool-weights have a suspension hole provided in the top through which a strap was secured before slinging them over a pack-horse's back, one either side. The mass of such weights is 7lbs (the clove) or 14lbs (the stone).

Cast lead trade-weight, probably c12th-13th century
608: 2 ounce, fluted conical, free-standing, integral loop, 43mm x 29mm - *Axminster*.
609: 1? ounce, octagonal and slightly conical, integral loop, 37.5mm x 18mm - *Axminster*.

COIN WEIGHTS AND BALANCES

Medieval hammered coinage was subject to the illicit practice of clipping or filing which Henry III tried to stop in 1247 by introducing the Long Cross penny. This coin had a cross that extended to the edge of the flan which it was hoped would prevent the removal of metal. For a while it did so, however, before too long it recommenced

Coins that had been in circulation for a long time became abraded which made them lighter; percentage wise this was a relatively small part of the total mass, whereas clipping or filing had an immediate and obvious effect. Usually it was apparent to the more keen-eyed person whether a coin had been tampered with, for the legend would be partially or wholly removed. However, poor striking frequently meant the impression was not central on the flan which gave a similar appearance.

In an unsuccessful attempt to overcome this problem, a simple balance known as a 'tumbrel', was devised. This operated without the need for weights, but precisely when this was introduced isn't known. Possibly it was in 1205 in the reign of King John, when a 'penny-poize' is chronicled, although this may be a reference to a coin-weight (Withers lists a silver penny-weight attributed to 1205). The first documentation of the word 'tumbrel' is in Edward I's 1292 Statute of Money. A later medieval hand-held coin-balance, made of copper alloy, comprises a horizontal double-sided bar, riveted together, with a central hole by which means a suspension chain or cord was attached. At each end of the bar another hole allowed a pivoting arm with a looped terminal to fold laterally when not in use. A small copper-alloy tray hung by means of triple cords from each arm; one held a coin and the other a weight.

In Edward I's reign a cast circular uniface lead weight with a moulded rim and a Long Cross with three pellets on each terminal was struck to weigh five shillings. He also issued a cast lead groat-weight which is square and uniface with a moulded crowned head within a lozenge and a pellet in each corner, a cast lead square uniface half-groat weight with a moulded Long Cross within a circle and three pellets in each angle, a cast lead rectangular uniface half-groat weight with moulded markings similar to the groat weight, a cast circular lead/tin-alloy possibly uniface penny-weight with a moulded facing crowned head within a beaded circle, and tiny cast lead/tin-alloy square weights for the round farthing with four moulded annulets within a square on the obverse and moulded diagonal cross-hatching on the reverse.

Edward III's minting of gold nobles and its fractions in 1344 prompted the issue of cast lead or lead/tin-alloy uniface square coin-weights depicting a moulded ship. Cast lead/tin-alloy square weights with a similar moulded ship on the obverse and moulded St George's cross on the reverse were produced around the same date. Some of the uniface weights bear a circular counterstamp with embossed cross-hatching on the reverse. Cast copper-alloy circular weights replaced the earlier issues in 1421-2, though a cast lead circular weight also circulated. The latter type are stamped incuse with a fleur-de-lis surmounted by a crown. Many of these weights are bordered with one or more incuse concentric circles and one is known with similar circles on the reverse. Two weights of this series have incuse grooves around the the edge. Other varieties undoubtedly exist. It wasn't until after 1465 that coin-weights represented a poor facsimile of the coin reverse. All such weights are uniface and mostly circular, though a few are square. The noble and ryal series are embossed with a ship, some with king, shield and rose, whilst the angel series embossed with St Michael and dragon. Weights for checking foreign coins circulating in this country were widely used. Of either circular or square form most are uniface. For the florin they are embossed with a fleur-de-lis, whilst the florin - ecu has a reverse of an embossed crown. Similarly, ecu weights are circular or square with an embossed crowned shield enclosing three lis. Lastly, the ecu au soleil weights are square or circular and uniface. Commonly they are embossed with a crowned shield with most having a sunburst within; however, one has three lis and a sunburst over the crown.

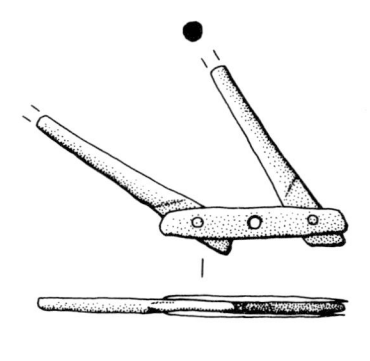

Forged and sheet copper-alloy coin-balance, c13th-14th century

610: subrectangular body formed from two sheets held by two separate copper-alloy rivets, central suspension hole, a tapered circular cross-section arm with flattened and angled inside end pivots on each of the rivets, terminals of both arms are lost, 106mm x 6mm - *Newton Abbot*.

Cast copper-alloy coin-weights, post 1464

611: Edward IV, ryal, (rose-noble), circular, uniface; embossed ship with rose on side and king standing facing holding shield in left hand and sword in right hand, flag inscribed E on stern, beaded circle, D. 18mm - *Coffinswell*.

612: Edward IV, half- or quarter-ryal, circular, uniface, as before, D. 11.5mm - *Cockwood*.

613: Low Countries, rose-noble, circular, uniface, embossed ship with rose on side, D. 16.5mm - *Cockwood*.

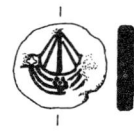

The Middle Ages

614: probably French, Mouton d'or, late medieval, circular, uniface, embossed paschal lamb within a beaded circle, Lombardic legend probably POIS DAGNIEL, D. 13.5mm - *Stokeinteignhead.*

615

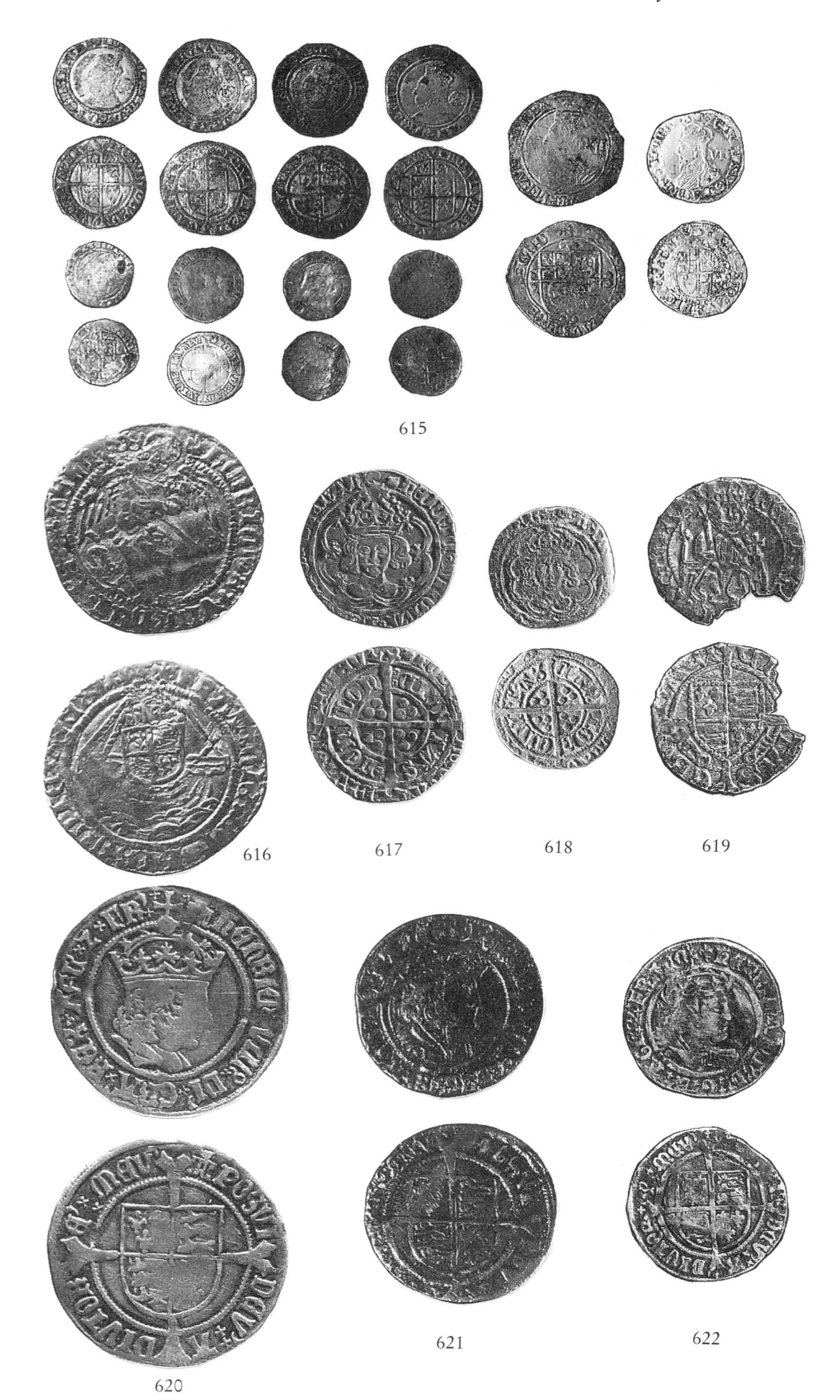

616   617   618   619

620   621   622

Chapter Six
The Tudor Period

623

624

625

It was during the Tudor period - particularly the reign of Elizabeth - that an economic boom led to a dramatic expansion in Devonshire's population. This explosion of humanity was so spectacular that apart from Yorkshire, Devon was able to muster more men for military duty than any other English county. Much of this increase in the populace was attributable to the growth of the woollen and fishing industries which attracted manpower from outside the county. Towns such as: Crediton, Uffculme, Ottery St Mary, Cullompton, Culmstock, Tiverton, Ashburton and Totnes grew fat on the woollen trade. Home-based lacemaking is thought to have been started at Honiton by Flemish refugees in Elizabethan times, and with the queen's support the industry flourished. To meet the food requirements of this enlarged workforce the agricutural community also expanded dramatically.

Throughout southern Devonshire considerable extant architectural evidence provides an insight into Tudor life. Tucked away in the folds of the rolling landscape are a goodly number of country houses and castles - some of which are rooted in earlier centuries - but many constructed at this time. East Budleigh's Hayes Barton, Sir Walter Raleigh's birthplace, is a particularly pleasing thatched example. In addition, many farmhouses were built or remodelled during the Elizabethan era. Totnes is one of England's finest examples of a late medieval and Tudor town, and after Exeter was the county's wealthiest. Devon's third richest was Plymouth, followed by Colyton. Downriver from Totnes, within sight of the sea, beautiful Dartmouth retains a number of fine Tudor buildings.

COINS

There was little difference in the coinage for the first four years of the Tudor period, however, in 1489 Henry VII issued a new gold pound coin called a 'sovereign' and on a limited scale, 'double' and 'treble-sovereigns'. The only other changes of this reign were a new style of gold angel, the gold ryal was reissued after an absence of about 16 years and soon after the beginning of the 16th century, for the first time, 'shillings' were struck. This new silver coin was known as the 'testoon'.

The reign of Henry VIII was a turbulent period for England's fiscal system as he was responsible for debasing the coinage on four occasions. In 1526 gold coins were increased in value by 10%; 1544 saw a reduction in fineness to 23 carat and similarly, silver coins from 0.925 to 0.750. Gold coins suffered a further decrease to 22 carat in 1545 and finally 20 carat; concurrently silver was also reduced to 0.500 and then 0.333. Four new gold coins were introduced in 1526 the first of which, the 'crown of the rose', was short lived and after several months was superseded by the 'crown of the double rose' and its 'halfcrown', and lastly the 'George noble' 'half-sovereigns' were first struck between 1544-7.

In 1549, in Edward VI's reign, the silver content of silver coins was raised to 50% and gold coins were increased in standard to 22 carat. Nonetheless, in 1550, an issue of base silver shillings was made, though these poor-quality coins were replaced in 1551 when a new higher-weight silver coinage was struck along with fine grade gold coins. This issue of silver coins included the 'crown', 'halfcrown', 'sixpence' and 'threepence' - four new denominations. Coins of this reign were the first to have dates marked, but in Roman numerals.

Nothing of consequence occurred to the coinage during Mary's or Philip and Mary's reign, although minting of gold crowns and halfcrowns was suspended and not restarted until Elizabeth ascended the throne. Edward VI's base silver shillings still circulated but in 1559 they were countermarked and reduced in value to fourpence-halfpenny and twopence-farthing respectively. The standard of silver coins was returned to 0.925 between 1560-77 but betwixt 1578-82 the standard was again slightly reduced, however, in 1582 it was restored to 0.925. The fineness of gold coins was also decreased between 1578-82. A weight reduction was made to gold and silver issues in 1601. 'Threehalfpence' and 'threefarthing' silver coins made an appearance in 1601. Milled silver coins were minted from 1561 but production ceased in 1572.

Of all Tudor monarchs' hammered coinage that of Elizabeth I is the most frequently found in the area, however, denominations above a shilling haven't been recorded. Issues of Henry VII, Henry VIII and Mary are elusive, whilst those of Edward VI have proved extremely rare. This predominance of Elizabethan coins appears to confirm that, for Devon, this part of the Tudor period was the most affluent.

A small mixed period hoard of two Elizabeth I, three James I and six Charles I silver coins (types unknown) was found at Manaton in 1879 which probably can be attributed to a Civil War secretion. In 1982 scrubland at Aller near Newton Abbot revealed a small hoard of mixed Tudor and Stuart coins - comprising four sixpences and four threepences of Elizabeth I, and one shilling and one sixpence of Charles I - likewise probably concealed during the Civil War. This is the only recorded hoard of largely Tudor coins found in South Devon.

Four silver coins found in southern Devon conjure up evocative images of the Spanish Main - Phillip II's 'pieces-of-eight, 'four' and 'one'. Such coins were minted in the Americas - either South America or Mexico, and were made rather crudely from irregular-shaped sections of silver bullion bar. The obverse and reverse die impressions were hammered on, usually in the most haphazard fashion. It is uncommon for these coins to have a fully discernable impression on both sides of the flan.

615: Hoard of Tudor and Stuart silver coins - Aller. Elizabeth I
    sixpence, 1566, mm portcullis.
    sixpence, 1567, mm coronet.
    sixpence, 1572, mm ermine.
    sixpence, 1593, mm tun.
    threepence, 1561-5, mm pheon.

626

627

628

629

The Tudor Period

630

631

632

633

634

635

637

636

threepence, 1577, mm eglantine.
threepence, (?) date, mm illegible.
threepence, 157[.], mm illegible.
Charles I
shilling, 1640-1, mm star.
sixpence, 1636-8, mm tun.
Gold coin
616: Henry VIII, 1544-7, quarter-angel, mm lis - *Cockington*.
Silver coins
617: Henry VII, 1493-5, groat, Canterbury - *Cockington*.
618: Henry VII, 1495-8, halfgroat, Canterbury - *Cockington*.
619: Henry VII, 1485-1509, sovereign type penny, York - *Cockington*.
620: Henry VIII, 1509-26, groat, mm castle, London - *Honiton*.
621: Henry VIII, 1526-44, groat, mm Lis, Canterbury or Durham, gold-coated as a forgery - *Poltimore*.
622: Henry VIII, 1526-44, groat, mm Lis, London - *Haccombe*.
623: Henry VIII, 1544-7, halfgroat, Tower - *Stokeinteignhead*.
624: Henry VIII, 1547-51, posthumous penny, no mm, London *Haccombe*.
625: Edward VI, 1550-1, shilling, Tower - *Cockington*.
626: Edward VI, 1551-3, shilling, mm tun - *Cockwood*.
627: Mary, 1553-4, groat, mm pomegranate - *Whilborough*.
628: Elizabeth I, 1560-1, shilling, mm cross crosslet - *Newton Abbot*.
629: Elizabeth I, 1580, sixpence, mm latin cross - *Coffinswell*.
630: Elizabeth I, 1560-1, groat, mm cross crosslet - *Abbotskerswell*.
631: Elizabeth I, 1575, threepence, mm eglantine - *Cockington*.
632: Elizabeth I, 1595-8, halfgroat, mm key - *Bishopsteignton*.
633: Elizabeth I, 1582-3, penny, mm bell - *Cockington*.
Continental silver coins
634: Anne, Duchess of Brittany, 1488-91, billon blanc - *River Teign, Ringmore*.
635: Phillip II, Spain, c1560, eight real's - *Churston*.
636: Phillip II, Spain, c1560, four real's - *Honiton*.
637: Phillip II, Spain, c1580, one real - *Coffinswell*.

JETONS

French-struck copper-alloy jetons remained current in England until c1580, though from c1450 they had thicker flans and are called 'piefort' jetons. Likewise, copper-alloy jetons of the Low Countries also circulated until the 1550s, whilst Nuremberg copper-alloy jetons continued their dominance through to the Stuart period.

During the 16th century, and right through the 17th, the use of jetons diverged from purely reckoning-counters into presentation gifts and gaming counters, however, they are all classified under the general term 'jetons'. In the reign of Charles I calculations by the written method began to replace counter reckoning and before the end of the 17th century jetons largely were confined to presentation or gaming pieces. Some jetons were struck in silver and given to governmental and commercial employees and members of learned societies as New Year presentation pieces, though jetons made from this metal were used as reckoning counters. Silver presentation jetons remained popular right

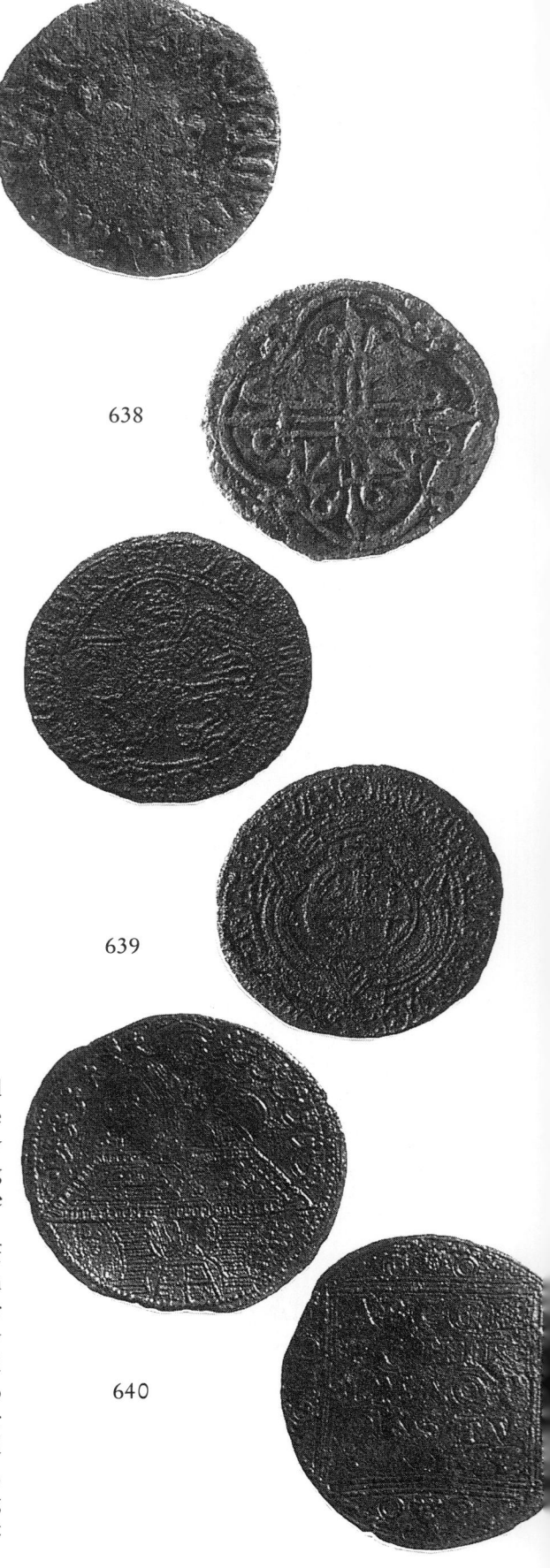

The Tudor Period

through the 19th century and declined in recent times. Gaming houses appeared during the 16th century wherein copper-alloy gaming counters were used - a practice that remained current until the beginning of the 20th century.

French, copper-alloy Crown type variant jeton, late 15th - early 16th century

638: Obv. royal crown, AVE GRACIA MARIA.
Rev. triple-stranded straight cross fleuretty with Tay crosses in spandrels, four-arched tressure with rosettes in hollows. - *Exeter*

German, Nuremberg, copper-alloy Lion of St Mark jeton, probably anonymous issue, c1500-70

639: Obv. rosette within halo which almost touches inner circle: crown, (?) RVE[...]
Rev. large orb, [....],- *Exeter*

German, Nuremberg, Hans Zwingel, copper-alloy Rechenmeister jeton, 1553-86

640: Obv. the Rechenmeister has jetons to one side and a counting grid to the other side.
Rev. in rectangular frame, with 'o 3-foil o' outside: ABCDE /FGHIK / LMNOP / QRSTV / : XYZZ (D reversed). (Zwingel's signature is the extra letter Z) - *Clyst St Mary*.

German, Nuremberg, Hanns Krauwinckle II, copper-alloy Rose / orb jetons, 1586-1635

641: Obv. 3 crowns and 3 lis arranged arround a central 8-petal rose, * HANNS KRAVWINCKEL . IN . NVR
Rev. Imperial orb surmounted by a cross patty, within a tressure with 3 main arches, * HEVT . ROT . MORGEN . TODT - *Bicton*.

642: Obv. as previous, DAS WORT GOTES BLEIBT EWICK *
Rev. as previous, HANNS KRAVWINCKEL IN NVRNB: - *Exeter*.

LEAD TOKENS

Cast lead or lead/tin-alloy tokens were current in medieval and Tudor England, presumably used for small change. The subject matter of the design on either side of the flan is either moulded, incised or incuse stamped. Little is known about such tokens at present, however, research by Robert Alvey of the University of Nottingham has been ongoing for some years now, but until concluded and published we can only speculate on the origins of many.

Cast lead circular token, 1563

643: moulded, Obv. crossed spade and mattock, 1563, beaded circle; Rev. BY LABOUR A[....], beaded circle, D. 17.5mm - *Exeter*.

BUCKLES

It was during the Tudor period that single-loop buckles were largely phased out, with the double-loop type becoming predominant (notwithstanding, some 17th-century buckles are single-loop). Shapes of single-loop buckles until c1600 were D, square or rectangular with the latest having decorative knops and mouldings. A feature of square buckles is a pronounced splayed foot on each of the sides, some of which have a small, lobed projection. Double-loop buckles current from c1500-1600 are found in square, rectangular, oval, asymmetrical or trapezium shapes.

Copper alloy, lead/tin alloy or iron were current for buckle manufacture at this time, although as with their medieval counterparts few iron examples have survived well. Silver buckles were still favoured by nobility and royalty but these are also extremely rare. Gilding and silvering of copper-alloy or silver buckles was commonplace, whilst ferrous or copper-alloy specimens are frequently tinned or bituminous paint coated.

Cast copper-alloy single-loop buckles, 1485-1600
644: subrectangular, concave sides; pointed, notched front, 32mm x 30mm - *Stokeinteignhead.*
645: rectangular; pointed, notched front, 27mm x 29mm - *Combeinteignhead.*

Cast copper-alloy single-loop buckles, c1485-1510
646: D-shaped, moulded oblique grooves, 33mm x 24mm - *Bicton.*
647: D-shaped, serrated edge, copper-alloy tongue, 33mm x 22mm - *Bicton.*

Cast copper-alloy single-loop buckles, c1500-1600
648: subrectangular, rounded notched front with engraved oblique lines, lobed terminals with engraved oblique lines, 25mm x 26mm - *River Teign, Ringmore.*
649: D-shaped, moulded transverse grooves, 27.5mm x 23mm - *Haccombe.*
650: subrectangular, slightly concave sides with expanded lobed terminals; rounded, notched front, narrowed strap-bar, 32mm x 31.5mm - *Cockington.*
651: rectangular, slightly concave sides with lobed expanded terminals and lobed knops, lozenge-shaped front knop with engraved lozenge-shape, narrowed strap-bar, 23.5mm x 38.5mm - *West Ogwell.*
652: subrectangular, slightly concave sides with expanded lobed terminals, rounded front with ovoid knop and engraved curvilinear, narrowed strap-bar, 34mm x 35.5mm - *Cockington.*
653: subrectangular, concave sides with expanded terminals and lobed knops, notched rounded front with oval and lobed knops, narrowed strap-bar, 30mm x 39mm - *Cockington.*
654: subrectangular, concave sides with moulded collars and expanded lobed terminals; rounded, notched front with engraved curvilinear, narrowed strap bar, 24mm x 30mm - *Cockington.*
655: subrectangular, concave sides with expanded lobed terminals, notched front with oblique corners and engraved curvilinear, 26mm x 30mm - *Newton Abbot.*
656: rectangular; sides with expanded terminals, lobed knops and transverse moulded lines, bifid front knop with moulded oblique lines, narrowed strap-bar, trace of iron tongue, 39mm x 38mm - *Newton Abbot.*
657: asymmetrical, concave sides, rounded front with lobed knop, narrowed strap-bar, 36mm x 39mm - *Newton Abbot.*
658: asymmetrical, concave sides, rounded front with lobed knop, narrowed strap-bar, 27mm x 27.5mm - *Cockington.*
659: asymmetrical, tinned, concave bifid sides; rounded, notched front, 26mm x 28mm - *Cockington.*
660: asymmetrical, concave sides; rounded, notched front,

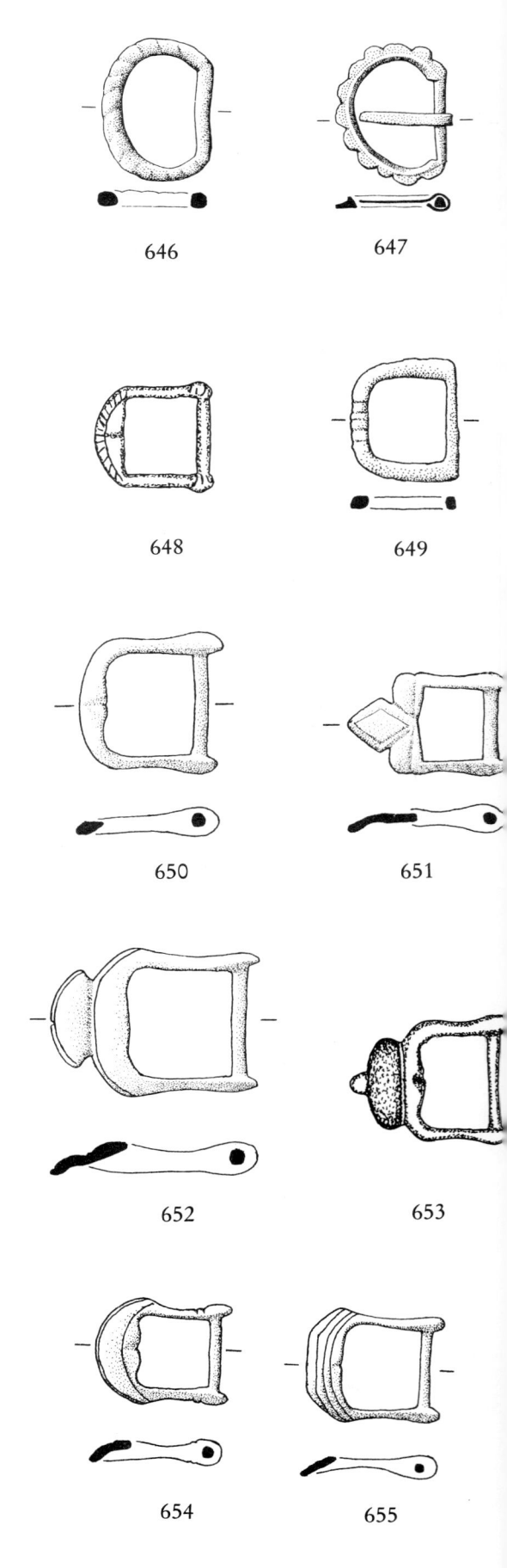

The Tudor Period

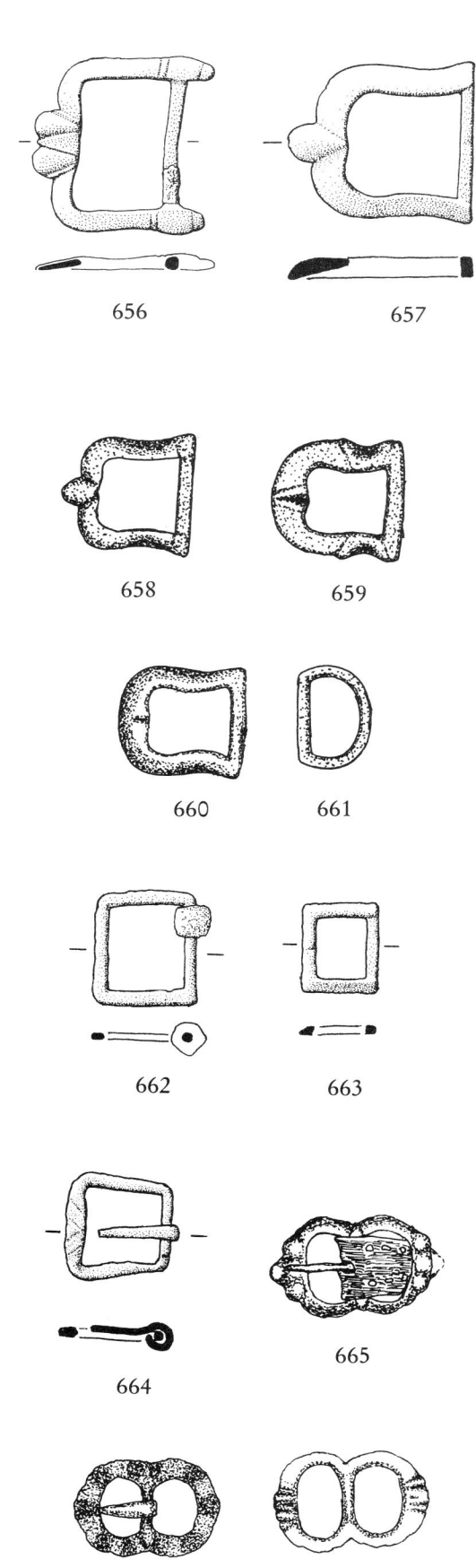

24.5mm x 27mm - *Newton Abbot*.
661: D-shaped, 23mm x 15.5mm - *Cockington*.
662: rectangular, fragment of iron tongue on back bar, 25mm x 22mm - *Cockington*.
663: rectangular, notched front, narrowed strap-bar, 20mm x 16mm - *Cockington*.
664: trapezium-shaped, engraved oblique lines on front, fragmented copper-alloy tongue, 23.5mm x 24.5mm - *Ringmore*.

Cast copper-alloy double-loop buckles, c1485-1600

665: oval, three moulded roundels and lobed knop on each loop, copper-alloy tongue, fragment of leather strap, 22mm x 26mm - *Alphington*.
666: oval, four roundels on each loop, copper-alloy tongue, 21mm x 31mm - *Cockington*.
667: oval, moulded quatrefoil on each loop, 21mm x 33mm - *Alphington*.
668: oval, copper-alloy tongue, 25.5mm x 37mm - Cockington.
669: ovoid, notched loops, copper-alloy tongue, 23.5mm x 37.5mm - *Cockington*.
670: fragment, oval, pointed loop, copper-alloy tongue, 33mm x 29.5mm - *Haccombe*.
671: oval; lobed knop on one loop, pointed knop on the other, slightly raised central bar, fragment of copper-alloy tongue, 30.5mm x 49.5mm - *Kingskerswell*.
672: oval, lobed knop on ends of each loop, 28.5mm x 33mm - *Cockington*.
673: oval, lobed knop on ends of each loop, one loop notched, 29.5mm x 33.5mm - *Kingskerswell*.
674: vesica-shaped, wedge-shaped protrusion on ends of central bar, 27mm x 52.5mm - *Cockington*.
675: vesica-shaped, protrusion on ends of central bar, copper-alloy tongue, 32mm x 51mm - *Cockington*.
676: oval, protrusion on ends of central bar, copper-alloy tongue, 24mm x 32mm - *Cockington*.
677: oval, protrusion on ends of central bar, 23mm x 37mm - *Haccombe*.
678: oval, protrusion on ends of central bar, 23mm x 27.5mm - *Cockington*.
679: oval, moulded roundel on each loop, protrusions on ends of central bar, 21mm x 31mm - *Haccombe*.
680: ovoid, notched ends, six moulded depressions on each loop, copper-alloy tongue, 22mm x 38mm - *Exeter*.
681: oval, six lobed-knops on each loop, protrusion on ends of central bar, 36mm x 48mm - *Haccombe*.
682: oval, each loop ornately moulded with curvilinear and transverse lines, moulded hominoid protrusion on ends of central bar, 38.5mm x 48mm - *Combefishacre*.
683: oval, trefoil knop with moulded fleuret on each loop, protrusion on ends of recessed central bar, 37mm x 49mm - *Alphington*.
684: oval, moulded fleuret knop on each loop, protrusion on ends of central bar, 29.5mm x 41mm - *Cockington*.
685: oval, moulded fleuret knop on each loop, protrusion on ends of central bar, 23.5mm x 37mm - *Cockington*.
686: oval, moulded fleuret knop on each loop, fleuret protrusion on ends of central bar, 30mm x 48mm - *Cockington*.

668 669 670

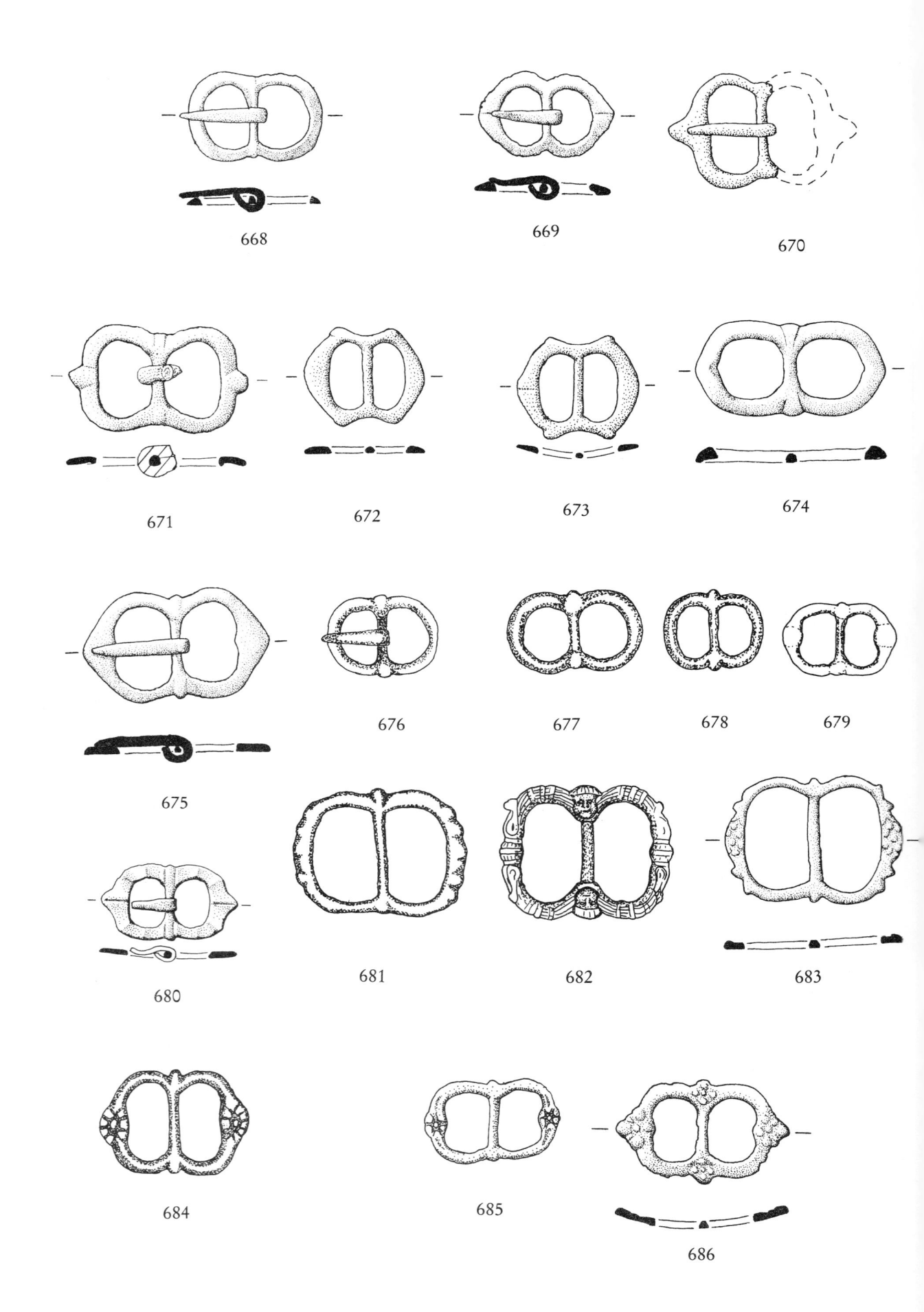

671 672 673 674

675 676 677 678 679

680 681 682 683

684 685 686

The Tudor Period 111

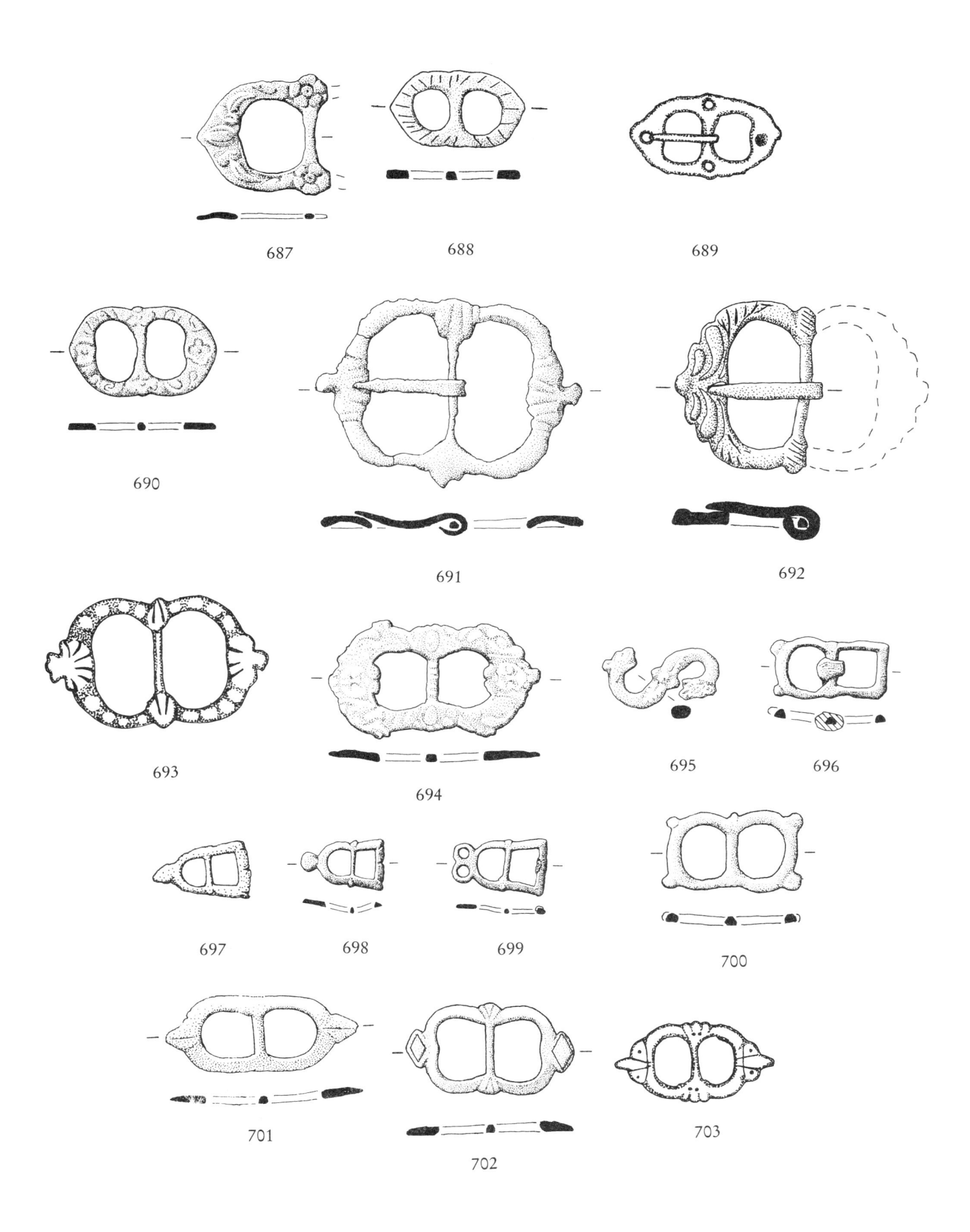

687 688 689

690 691 692

693 694 695 696

697 698 699 700

701 702 703

687: vesica-shaped, fragment; moulded foliate, moulded fleuret protrusions on ends of central bar, 35.5mm x 37mm - *Kenn*.
688: vesica-shaped, slight protrusions at ends of central bar, engraved oblique and transverse lines, 22mm x 38mm - *Newton Abbot*
689: vesica-shaped, slight protrusions at ends of central bar, three circular openwork and one blind hole, copper-alloy tongue, 25mm x 42.5mm - *Cockington*.
690: vesica-shaped, slight protrusions at ends of central bar, moulded foliate and fleurets, 26.5mm x 41.5mm - *Newton Abbot*.
691: oval, abraded, moulded escallop knop on each loop, moulded probable escallop protrusions on ends of central bar, copper-alloy tongue, 55.5mm x 74mm - *Newton Abbot*.
692: oval, fragmented, cinquefoil knop with moulded and engraved curvilinear and oblique lines, protrusions on end of central bar with engraved oblique lines, copper-alloy tongue, 49mm x 39mm - *Newton Abbot*.
693: oval, moulded and engraved scallop shell and eight roundels on each loop, protrusion with engraved oblique lines on ends of central bar, 38mm x 63mm - *Chudleigh*.
694: oval, loops with trefoil ends and central abraded bifid knops, moulded hominoid faces and foliate, 35mm x 59.5mm *Exeter*.
695: S-shaped, moulded beast heads terminals, lobed protrusions at centre, abraded moulded foliate, 18mm x 32.5mm - *Exeter*.

Cast copper-alloy double-loop buckles, late 16th early 17th century

696: asymmetrical, two lobed knops on rounded end, slight protrusions at ends of central bar, fragment of copper-alloy tongue, 18.5mm x 33.5mm - *Exeter*.
697: asymmetrical, pointed knop on rounded end, transverse grooves on subrectangular end, 17mm x 28mm - *Cockington*.
698: asymmetrical, lobed knop on rounded end, oblique grooves on subrectangular end, protrusions on ends of central bar, 15mm x 22mm - *Uffculme*.
699: asymmetrical, bifed knop with circular openwork on rounded end, protrusions on ends of central bar, trace of iron tongue on subrectangular end, 17mm x 26mm - *Uffculme*.
700: oval, two lobed knops on each loop, protrusion on ends of central bar, 24mm x 39mm - *Newton Abbot*.
701: oval; pointed, notched knops on each loop, 22mm x 54.5mm - *Newton Abbot*.
702: oval, lozenge-shaped knop with moulded lozenge on each loop, moulded trefoil protrusion on ends of central bar, 27mm x 47mm - *Cockington*.
703: oval, moulded trefoil knop with blind holes on each loop, moulded trefoil protrusions with blind holes on ends of central bar, 23.5mm x 45mm - *Cockington*.
704: oval, trefoil knop on each loop, narrowed central bar, 23.5mm x 44mm - *Cockington*.
705: oval, moulded trefoil on each loop, moulded trefoil protrusions at ends of central bar, 23mm x 40mm - *Cockington*.

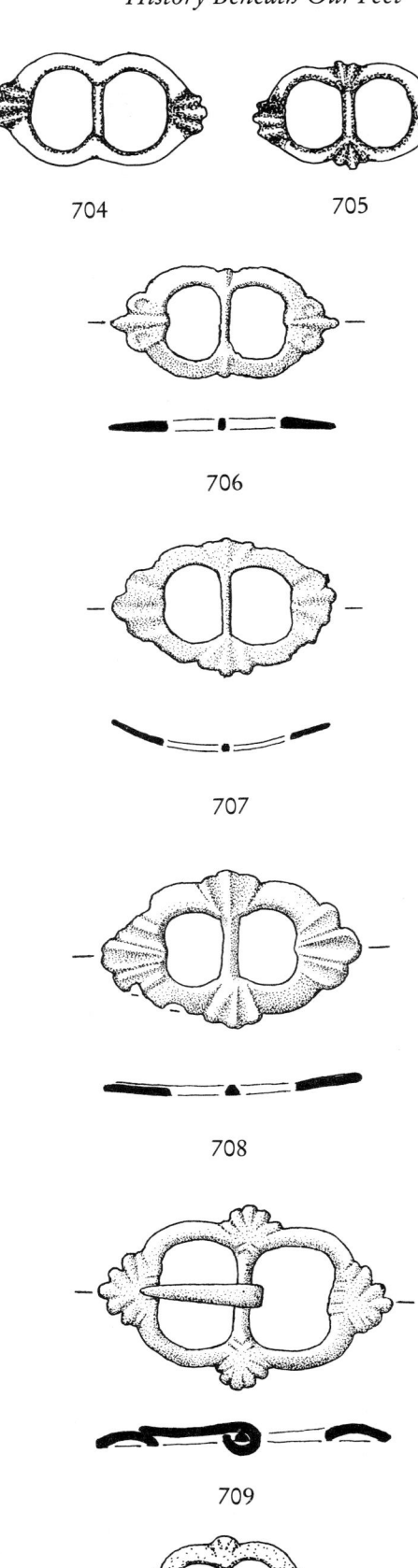

704

705

706

707

708

709

710

The Tudor Period

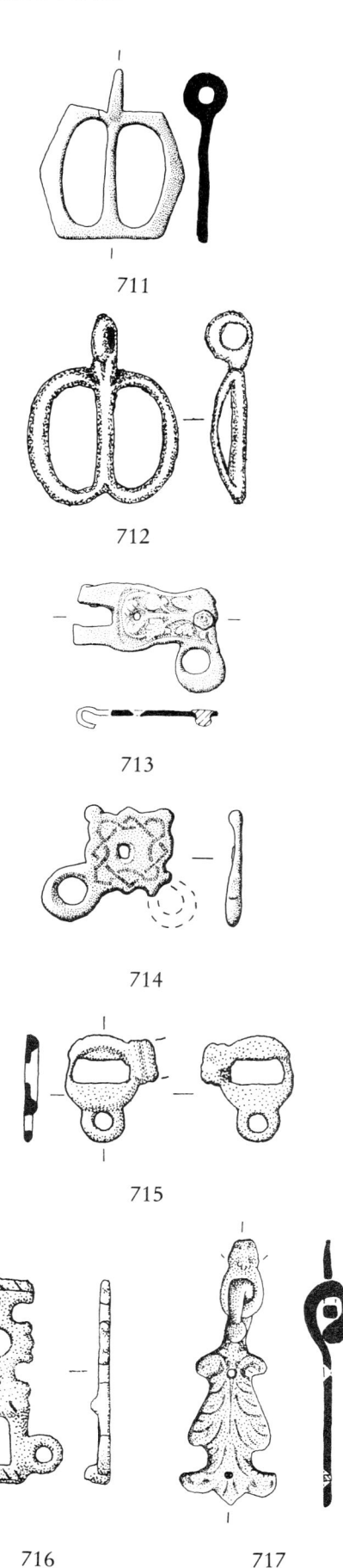

706: oval, moulded trefoil knop on each loop, protrusion at ends of central bar, 23.5mm x 45.5mm - *Stokeinteignhead*.

707: oval, moulded trefoil knop on each loop, moulded trefoils at ends of central bar, 29mm x 44mm - *Cockington*.

708: oval, moulded trefoil knop on each loop, moulded trefoils at ends of central bar, 33.5mm x 52.5mm - *Cockington*.

709: oval, moulded cinquefoil knops on each loop, moulded cinquefoil protrusions on ends of central bar, copper-alloy tongue, 38mm x 60mm - *Cockington*.

710: oval, semi-circular knops engraved with oblique lines, semi-circular protrusions at ends of central bar engraved with oblique lines, 13.5mm x 34.5mm - *Cockington*.

Cast copper-alloy sword belt hangers, 16th century

711: sexfoil, circular lateral suspension loop, 39mm x 32mm - *Exeter*.

712: oval, circular lateral suspension loop, 44.5mm x 33mm - *Cockington*

MOUNTS

Metalwork appliqués with integral or separate rivets remained current on strapwork throughout the Tudor period, though there was a tendancy towards blunt or pointed lugs which were inserted through the leatherwork and then bent over. Nail-like stud-mounts with ornate heads were in vogue on thick leather or wooden effects. Similarly, caution is advised concerning attribution; here, they are all classified under the general term 'mounts'. Some types undoubtedly carried over well into the 17th century.

Cast and forged copper-alloy hinged mount with integral loop and separate rivets, late 15th-16th century

713: asymmetrical, fragmented, engraved foliate and floriate, two rivet holes, one copper-alloy rivet, 25mm x 31mm - *Kingskerswell*.

Cast copper-alloy mounts with integral loops and separate rivets

714: late 15th-16th century, asymmetrical, fragmented, lobed knops on top angles; points on top and bottom, one rivet hole, engraved intertwined lozenge and quatrefoil, 26.5mm x 29mm - *Exeter*.

715: 16th century, asymmetrical, fragmented, subrectangular openwork, 24.5mm x 20mm - *Stokeinteignhead*.

716: 16th century, subrectangular, circular and asymmetrical openwork, two moulded transverse ribs, engraved oblique lines, two rivet holes, 47mm x 22mm - *Gappah*.

717: suspension loop of girdle-mount with separate symmetrical hooked mount suspended, trefoil bottom, bifid sides, globular knop, two rivet holes, remains of one iron rivet, engraved curlicues, 60mm x 12mm - *Exeter*.

Cast copper-alloy hooked mounts with separate rivets, with or without pendant annular rings, c.late 15th-c16th century

718: symmetrical, conjoined discs, fragmented, each disc with trefoil sides and engraved intertwined square and quatrefoil, lobed knop at top, two rivet holes, 57.5mm x 17.5mm - *Stokeinteignhead*.

719: triangular, fragmented, two rivet holes (one partially lost), 27mm x 11mm - *Stokeinteignhead*.

The Tudor Period
Distribution of metal detector finds in Southern Devon

1. Abbotskerswell (**MC, MA**)
2. Alphington (**MA**)
3. Aller (**HC**)
4. Ashburton (**A**)
5. Axminster (**MA**)
6. Bicton (**C, MA**)
7. Bigbury Beach (**A**)
8. Bishopsteignton (**MC, MA**)
9. Broadsands Beach, Paignton (**C**)
10. Chudleigh (**MC, MA**)
11. Churston (**C**)
12. Clyst St George (**A**)
13. Clyst St Mary (**A**)
14. Cockington (**MC, MA**)
15. Cockwood (**MC, MA**)
16. Coffinswell (**MC, MA**)
17. Colaton Raleigh (**A**)
18. Combefishacre (**A**)
19. Combeinteignhead (**MC, MA**)
20. Exeter (**MC, MA**)
21. Exmouth (**A**)
22. Gappah (**MA**)
23. Goodrington Beach, Paignton (**C**)
24. Haccombe (**MC, MA**)
25. Honiton (**C**)
26. Ipplepen (**A**)
27. Kenn (**A**)
28. Kingskerswell (**MA**)
29. Lympstone (**A**)
30. Maidencombe (**C**)
31. Mamhead (**A**)
32. Marldon (**A**)
33. Newton Abbot (**MC, MA**)
34. Paignton (**C**)
35. Poltimore (**C, A**)
36. Ringmore (**MA**)
37. River Teign, Ringmore (**C, A**)
38. Shaldon (**C**)
39. Sherford (**A**)
40. Starcross (**A**)
41. Stokeinteignhead (**MC, MA**)
42. Teignmouth (**A**)
43. Uffculme (**C, MA**)
44. West Ogwell (**A**)
45. Whilborough (**MC, A**)
46. Wolborough, Newton Abbot (**MC, MA**)

Key: **C** = single coin   **MC** = multiple coin   **HC** = hoard of coins
         A = artefact   **MA** = multiple artefact

720: triangular, two rivet holes, two copper-alloy rivets, 41.5mm x 12mm - *Exeter*.
721: triangular, two rivet holes, 29mm x 12mm - *Haccombe*.
722: triangular, fragmented hook, two rivet holes, remains of two iron rivets, traces of iron on back, 30mm x 14mm - *Cockington*.
723: symmetrical, bifid top, two rivet holes, two copper-alloy rivets, 39mm x 22mm - *Ringmore*.

Cast copper-alloy mounts with separate rivets

724: c.late 15th - early 17th century, asymmetrical, bifid (?) lower edge, moulded curvilinear, three rivet holes, remains of two iron rivets, 23mm x 29.5mm - *Axminster*.
725: c16th-17th century, quatrefoil, gilt; curvilinear of punched dots forming a (?) hominoid face within a quatrefoil linear border, three rivet holes, remains of three iron rivets, 28mm x 60mm - *Stokeinteignhead*.

Cast copper-alloy mount without rivets, 16th-17th century

726: asymmetrical, convex, moulded hominoid face, 19.5mm x 21mm - *Exmouth*.

Sheet copper-alloy mounts without rivets, 16th century

727: cinquefoil, moulded fleuret, traces of solder on back, D. 29mm - *Exeter*.

Sheet copper-alloy mount with separate soldered rivet, 1485-1540

728: cross-crosslet, turned-over edges, square openwork, one rivet, punched dot border, 22mm x 23mm - *Exeter*.

Cast copper-alloy mounts with integral rivets, c16th century

729: rectangular, gilded, probably two semi-circular side-loops each end (three lost) with crescent-shaped openwork, moulded fluting, two rivets, 27mm x 30mm - *Cockington*.
730: rectangular, gilded, probable side-loops lost, moulded fluting, two rivets, 25.5mm x 35mm - *Cockington*.
731: quatrefoil, quatrefoil openwork, two rivets, 33.5mm x 18.5mm - *Exeter*.
732: subrectangular, two moulded ribs, two rivets, 26.5mm x 8.5mm - *Cockington*.
733: asymmetrical, semi-circular cross-section, one rivet, 19.5mm x 8.5mm - *Cockington*.
734: asymmetrical, moulded fleuret and foliate, oval openwork, two rivets, 18mm x 14mm - *Clyst St Mary*.

Cast copper-alloy stud-like mounts, c16th century

735: cinquefoil, domed, moulded fleuret, D. 13mm - *Exeter*.
736: lozenge-shaped, pyramidal, gilded, punched circles forming a cross within a punched square and an engraved square, blind semi-circles border, 17mm x 17mm - *Cockington*.
737: moulded multi-foil, domed, unfettled, D. 12mm - *Cockington*.

Cast copper-alloy mounts with integral pointed or blunt lugs, c16th-17th century

738: circular, circular and semi-circular openwork, blindholes, engraved St Andrew's cross, D. 26mm - *Exeter*.
739: circular, pointed projection at one end and a broken (?) hook at the other, blue and white enamelled floriate, 63mm x

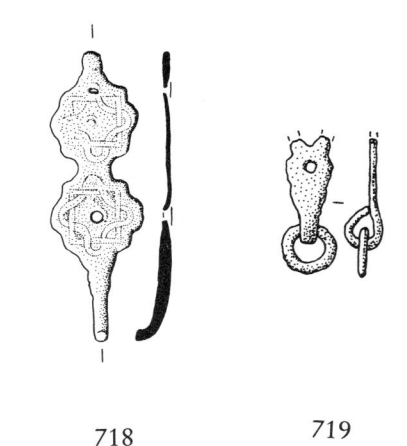

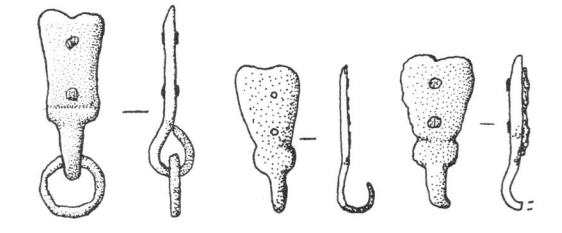

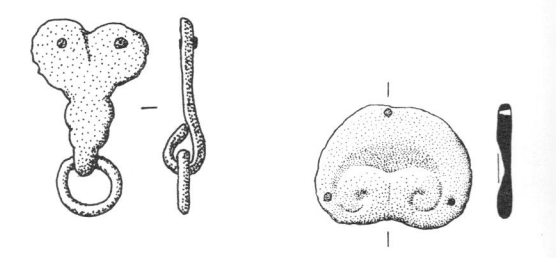

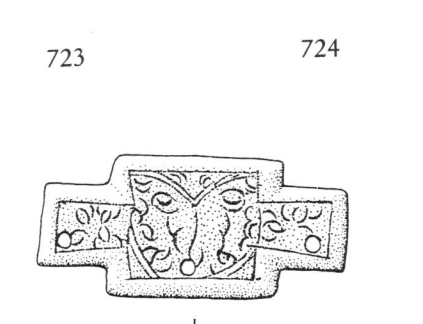

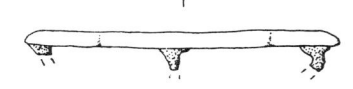

The Tudor Period 115

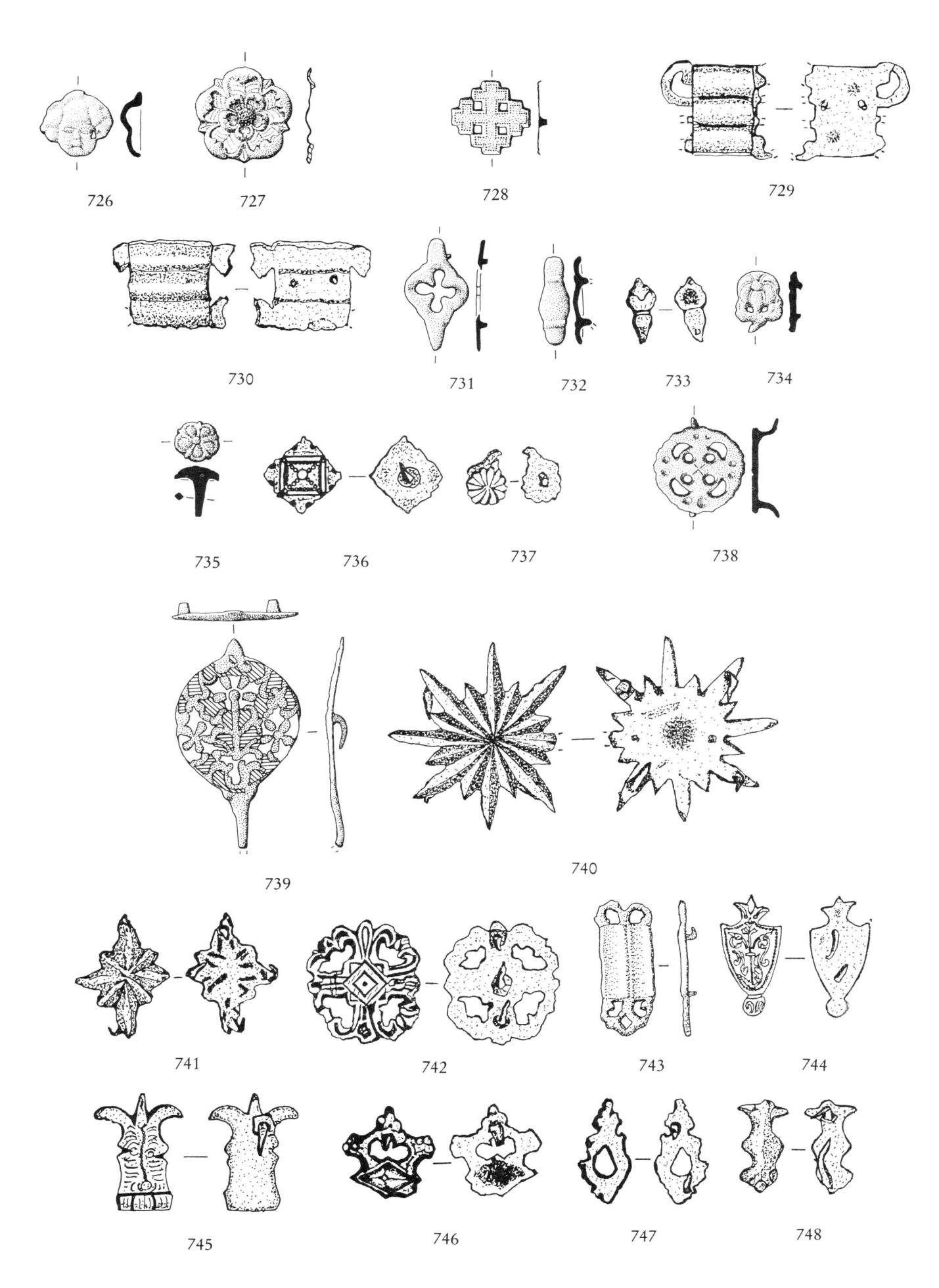

726 727 728 729

730 731 732 733 734

735 736 737 738

739 740

741 742 743 744

745 746 747 748

37mm - *Axminster.*
740: multi-point star, moulded chevron grooves, D. 59mm - *Cockington.*
741: multi-point star, tinned, moulded chevron grooves, 37mm x 27mm - *Cockington.*
742: oval, gilded, trefoil openwork forming a cross with fleur-de-lis top and square centre, moulded lozenges and square, 36mm x 33mm - *Coffinswell.*
743: subrectangular, gilded, moulded fluting, lozenge and crecent-shaped openwork, 41mm x 17mm - *Cockington.*
744: shield-shaped, gilded, trefoil knop, lobed bottom knop, engraved foliate and fleuret, punched beaded border, 36mm x 18mm - *Coffinswell.*
745: asymmetrical, trefoil top, bifid sides, moulded transverse bottom bar, longitudinal punched beaded band, engraved curlicues and transverse lines, 35mm x 26mm - *Cockington.*
746: asymmetrical, fragmented, tinned, asymmetrical openwork, trefoil top with moulded fleuret knops, moulded pyramidal lozenge, 27mm x 27mm - *Newton Abbot.*
747: asymmetrical, tinned, asymmetrical openwork, 31mm x 15mm - *Haccombe.*
748: asymmetrical, 28mm x 15mm - Stokeinteignhead.
749: asymmetrical, lobed top knop, trefoil bottom, moulded crescents, 23mm x 12mm - *Haccombe.*
750: asymmetrical, trefoil top with moulded chevron grooves, trefoil bottom, 26mm x 14mm - *Stokeinteignhead.*
751: sub-triangular, trefoil top, bifid sides, moulded oblique grooves, angled sides, 25mm x 20mm - *Stokeinteignhead.*
752: subrectangular, longitudinal bands of engraved crescents and punched dots, 28mm x 10mm - *Alphington.*
753: sublozenge-shaped, engraved linear border, 20mm x 12mm - *Cockington.*
754: circular, domed, gilded, fleuret formed from punched dots, D. 35.5mm - *Mamhead.*
755: cordate, gilded, fleuret formed from punched dots and circles, punched circles border, 33mm x 33mm - *Mamhead.*
N.B. Three of No.717 hung from copper-alloy triple-looped belt-mounts; all three hooks were rivetted to a third member from which a sword or dagger probably hung.

BUTTONS

Archaeology has shown that the earliest evidence for the use of buttons in Britain is by Bronze Age folk. Two types are attributed to this period, viz: cast copper-alloy one-piece, flat circular, moulded with concentric circles; and shale gold-covered conical with engraved zigzags, concentric circles and chevrons. Notwithstanding, there is nothing to suggest that the use of buttons was widespread during the Bronze Age. It is known that buttons were introduced into Sweden from the Far East around the 9th century. The current consensus of opinion is that in England, and Europe generally, they probably became fashionable early in the 13th century.

Archaeologically dated medieval metal buttons from London show that they are somewhat similar to metal buttons from later periods, therefore regarding attribution caution is advised unless from a datable deposit. Buttons made from cloth were also current during this period but are not considered here.

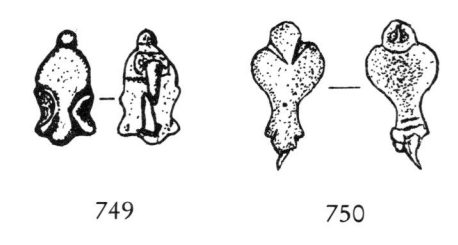

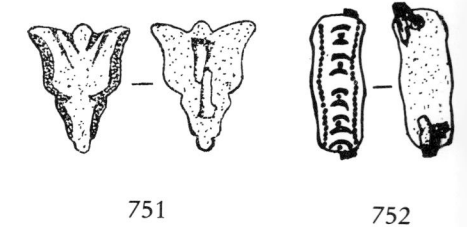

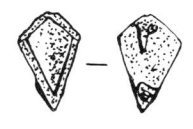

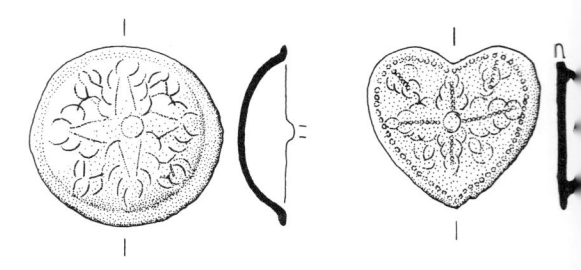

The Tudor Period

One form of medieval metal button is of cast solid construction which is either two-piece copper alloy, i.e. with a separate wire shank, or one-piece lead/tin alloy or tin, i.e with an integral shank. Another type of button comprises two pieces of sheet copper alloy pressed into hemispheres and then soldered together. Before the two halves are joined, a wire shank is passed through a hole in the top half and soldered into place. Yet another type has four pieces of sheet copper alloy soldered together and a separate wire shank similarly soldered before assembly. Copper-alloy buttons of this period are frequently tinned. Shapes are mainly spherical, biconvex, plano-convex or flat circular. Many medieval buttons, especially spherical or biconvex-types, are plain, however, others frequently have moulded or punched decoration, and openwork forms were also current. Gold or silver buttons of this era are known but are rare, as are those inset with gemstones; however, glass appliqués are fairly ubiquitous. Gilt or silver applied-surface decoration was also current.

Types of metal-button current in the later medieval period remained in use throughout the late 15th and 16th centuries. During Elizabeth's reign, however, flamboyant wealthy people wore not only base metal buttons but increasingly buttons made of gold or silver, some set with precious or semi-precious gemstones. Spherical openwork buttons or those decorated with wire appliqués were also in vogue. A cast copper-alloy one-piece solid-domed circular variety, with an extremely long shank, found favour in the 16th century. Characteristically these have moulded decoration and are sometimes tinned. Buttons at this time were frequently worn purely as extravagent adornment rather than for practical purposes.

Cast copper-alloy solid two-piece spherical button, c.late 15th - 16th century
756: tinned, copper-alloy wire shank, D. 10mm - *Abbotskerswell.*

Cast copper-alloy one-piece circular solid-domed long-shanked buttons, 16th century.
757: moulded eight-petalled fluret, 17mm x 14mm - *Newton Abbot.*
758: moulded roundels, 14mm x 12mm - *Stokeinteignhead.*

CLOTHING FASTENERS

Hooked forms of clothing-fastener have been used for thousands of years. Some hooks are extremely sharp-pointed which simply pierced the garment direct, whilst others are blunt and were used in conjunction with an eyelet. Sheet or cast metal was the normal material of manufacture, although other substances are known, e.g. bone. Some clothing-fasteners are exquisite works of art whilst others are plain.

During the Tudor period a particularly common form of copper-alloy or silver (frequently gilded) clothing-fastener comprised three hemispheres richly decorated with twisted wire appliqués and joined together to form a triangle. Soldered to the back was a sharp hook and a transverse rectangular loop. Apparently this type of fastener was secured to the garment by either sewing the loop direct or by affixing a fabric or leather strap to the loop. A variation of this style is known - a single hemisphere or hemi-ovoid. Frequently, clothing-fasteners with twisted wire appliqué decoration are erroneously attributed to the late Anglo-Saxon period.

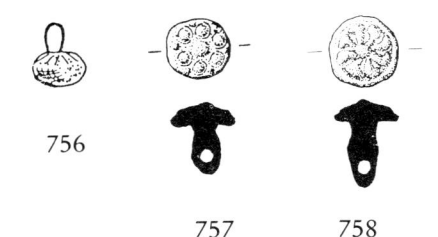

A clothing-fastener current from the late 15th century well into the 17th, is the cast copper-alloy sharp-pointed type which had rectangular or circular convex or flat body with integral rectangular, subrectangular or circular loop. Moulded or openwork ornamentation was commonplace and gilded or silvered examples are known. A fabric or leather strap was attached to the garment and the other end was sewn or riveted to the loop.

Similar to the former type of copper-alloy clothing-fastener, but somewhat larger, is the blunt-hooked variety which was used concurrently with a matching eyelet. Attachment to the garment was achieved by sewing through either integral lobed eyelets or holes in the body.

Sheet copper-alloy clothing-fasteners, which perhaps originated in the later Middle Ages, with a separate sharp-pointed dual hook rivetted to the back appear to have been less widely used in the Tudor period, for they are less common finds. Two styles are apparent, viz: lozenge-shaped with engraved decoration or incorporating a coin or jeton. Fastening was achieved by hooking each end directly into the garment.

Cast lead/tin-alloy or copper-alloy clothing-fasteners of circular form with moulded, engraved or openwork decoration are known from the 16th-17th century. This type was sewn direct to the garment.

Clothing-fastener eyelets attributable to this period, for some reason are relatively uncommon finds compared to hooked sections. However, several types are known, viz: two-piece, comprised of a copper-alloy wire trefoil-shaped eyelet and a separate single folded sheet copper-alloy plate with rivet holes; oval sheet copper-alloy plate with rivet holes and integral oval eyelet; and circular or oval sheet or cast copper-alloy with a rectangular eyelet and small circular projecting loops. Presumably the first was riveted to a strap, whilst the second was either riveted or sewn direct, and the third was sewn direct. The two former types are undecorated, whilst the latter, which is probably c16th century, frequently had moulded or punched ornamentation and occasionally enamelling.

Cast copper-alloy sharp-pointed clothing-fasteners, 15th-17th century

759 quatrefoil, asymmetrical openwork, subrectangular loop, fragmented hook, 33mm x 19mm - *Haccombe*.
760: circular, convex, moulded IHS within a border of pellets, subrectangular loop, fragmented hook, 32m x 14mm - *Cockington*.
761: circular, moulded (?) crowned bust within a fleurets border, unfettled rectangular loop, fragmented hook, 35mm x 18mm - *Cockington*.
762: circular, moulded pellets within a grooved circle, semi-circular loop, 33mm x 15mm - *Cockington*.
763: circular, gilded, moulded and grooved cross with circular holes in spandrels, subrectangular loop, fragmented hook, 32mm x 18mm - *Cockington*.
764: circular, engraved cross with circular holes in spandrels, fragmented hook, 30mm x 15mm - *Cockington*.
765: oval, moulded bust within a border of oblique lines, subrectangular loop, 38mm x 14mm - *Exeter*.

Sheet copper-alloy two-piece dual sharp-pointed clothing-fastener, 15th-17th century

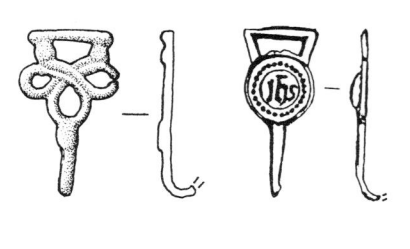

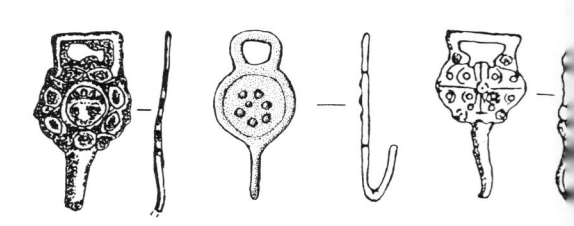

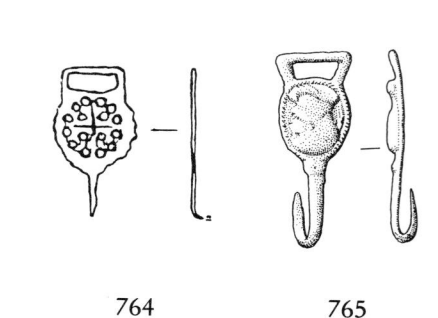

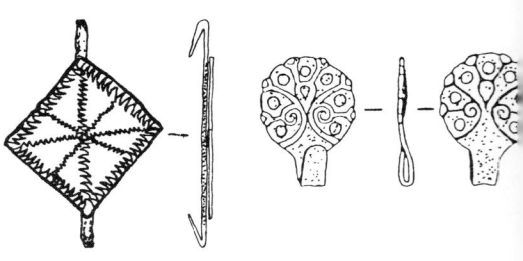

The Tudor Period   119

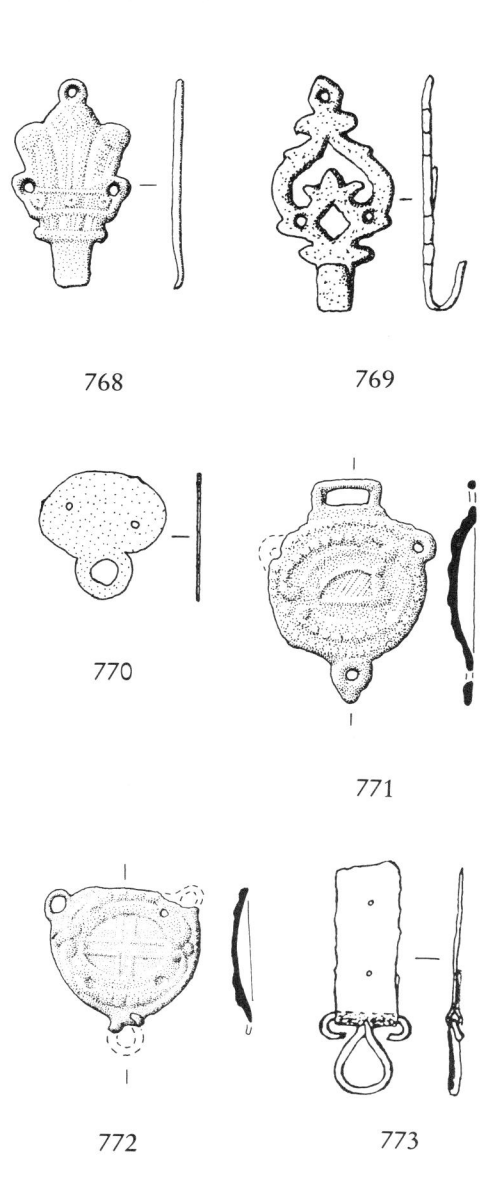

766: lozenge-shaped, one rivet hole; engraved zigzag border, eight-point zigzag star, separate dual-point hook with single rivet hole rivetted to front plate with a copper-alloy rivet, 30mm x 44mm - *Stokeinteignhead*.

Cast lead/tin-alloy double-sided clothing-fastener, 16th-17th century

767: circular, concave, moulded escalloped edge, seven circular holes, engraved curvilinear and crescents on front, moulded curvilinear and crescents on back, 25mm x 18mm - *Cockington*.

Cast copper-alloy blunt-hooked clothing fastener, 16th-17th century

768: symmetrical, fragmented, moulded Prince of Wales feathers, three semi-circular attachment loops, 41mm x 12.5mm - *Lympstone*.

Sheet copper-alloy blunt-hooked clothing fastener, 16th-17th century

769: symmetrical, lozenge-shaped and symmetrical openwork, three attachment holes, 46.5mm x 23.5mm - *Gappah*.

Sheet copper-alloy clothing-fastener eyelet, 15th-17th century

770: oval, circular eyelet, two attachment holes, 25mm x 24mm - *Cockington*.

Cast copper-alloy blunt-hooked clothing-fastener eyelets, 16th-17th century

771: oval, fragmented, convex, semi-circular attachment loops, moulded voided cross within a wreath, traces of red enamel in cross, three circular blind-holes and one circular hole, 28mm x 29mm - *Uffculme*.

772: circular, fragmented, convex, rectangular eyelet, semi-circular attachment loops, moulded harp within two beaded concentric circles, 44mm x 32.5mm - *Clyst St George*.

Copper-alloy folded sheet and wire two-piece clothing-fastener eyelet, 15th-17th century

773: trefoil eyelet, two rivet holes, 45mm x 17mm - *Cockington*.

FINGER RINGS

The wearing of finger rings remained fashionable throughout the later Renaissance period, and, as in the Middle Ages, on all joints of all digits. Vanity prevailed, for wealthy people often displayed their finger-rings through incisions in the glove and they were even worn on necklaces or hat-bands.

Many types of finger-ring current at this time are similar to those of the medieval period. Bezels with foil-backed engraved crystals or other white gemstones resumed favour. Seal finger-rings, although somewhat heavier than their antecedents, appear to have been dominant. Directly engraved devices remained fashionable; early examples frequently were engraved with a crowned letter or letters (probably representing the owner's initial or initials) or the sacred cipher IHC or IHS invariably surmounted by a crown.

It was the 16th century which saw the start of more complicated and elaborate gem-cutting which assisted the popularity of ostentatious finger-rings, especially richly-enamelled types with large circular or rectangular bezels inset with gemstones. Early finger-rings of this period invariably have a single large gemstone, but from the end of the 16th century there was a progression into a number of smaller stones. Frequently finger-rings of the latter style have a central larger gemstone surrounded by smaller stones.

Gold, bezel finger-ring, late 16th early 17th century
774: semi-circular cross-section hoop, size E, internal D. 13mm, shoulders and hoop engraved with stylised floriate and scrollwork, underside of circular bezel engraved with crosses and a fleuret, settings for eight peripheral small gemstones and a large rectangular central gemstone, five peripheral faceted-rubies - three lost, central gemstone lost - probably this was a diamond - *Cockington*.

Gold, posy finger-ring, late 16th early 17th century
775: semi-circular cross-section hoop, size E?/F, internal D. 14mm, outside of hoop engraved with foliate and floriate, inside of hoop inscribed NO TREASURE TO A TRUE FREND - *Cockington*.

Copper-alloy finger-rings
776: c.late 15th - 16th century, fragmented, gilt, oval cross-section hoop moulded quatrefoil shoulders, flat square bezel, external D. 16.5mm, internal D. 15.5mm - *Ipplepen*.
777: 16th century or later, circular cross-section hoop, circular bezel set with a green glass faceted stone, external D. 20mm, internal D. 17.5mm - *Ashburton*.

N.B. It is reasonable to believe that Nos. 774 and 775 formerly belonged to a child. This is a possibility, for it was custom for wealthy people to dress their children, including jewellery, as replicas of adults. It was also custom for women to be married at a very early age, even as young as twelve. However, in this instance, due to their high intrinsic value, it is probable that both finger-rings were worn on the little finger of an adult female.

Each finger-ring is a quality piece, and would have been purchased by a person of considerable wealth. Their similar size makes it a possibility that they were made for the same person, and as they were found adjacent to Cockington Court, the chances are they belonged to a young lady or ladies of the Cary family.

George Cary esq married Wilmotta Gifford of Yeo, near Clovelly, in 1561; both were 21-years of age. This was her second marriage, her first was at barely 13 to John Bury of Collaton which was annulled, unconsummated.

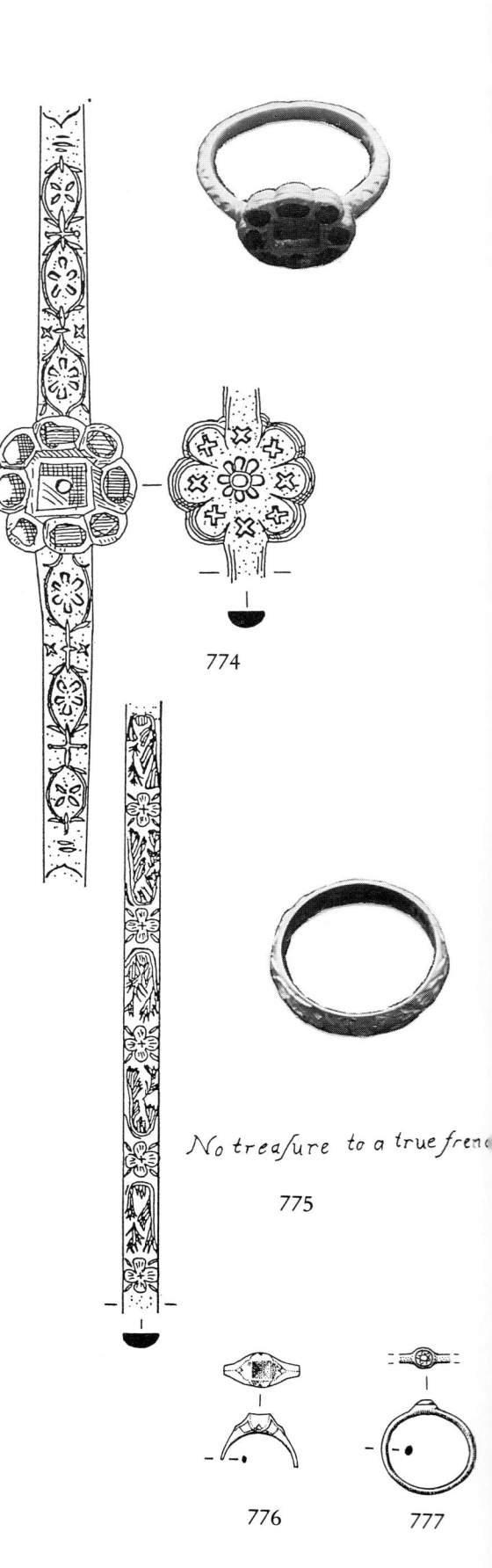

Wilmotta bore George Cary five children, three daughters and two sons. Records of births and deaths of theses children are either non-existent or extremely contradictory. One reference states that all the children, except the eldest boy, died at an early age, how early is not clear. It is known that two of the daughters were named Jane and Anne respectively, the name of the third daughter is unrecorded. Another document indicates that Jane died unmarried, but no date of death is given. The same document states that Anne married Sir Richard Edgecumbe and that their union remained childless and she died in 1625. Yet another chronicle says that two daughters of Sir George Cary were buried at Cockington in 1581, which two it doesn't state. A number of possibilities arise. Perhaps the finger rings were owned by Wilmotta before her marriage to George Cary, and she kept them afterwards, or they came into her possession after they were married. However, they could have belonged to one or more of their daughters.

After 21-years of marriage Wilmotta died in 1581, and, as the Carys did not have a family vault in Cockington Church (St George and St Mary), she was laid to rest in St Saviour's Church, Tormohun. After her death George Cary had a family vault built in Cockington Church. A monumental brass on Wilmotta's tomb depicts her and her three daughters; the two sons were once also shown but have been obliterated. The three girls are depicted all of similar size in characteristic adult-style dress, but obviously children. If the record of Wilmotta having died in 1581 is correct, why wasn't she also buried in the family vault at Cockington with her two daughters who were supposedly interred therein in 1581? Another document states that two of the Cary girls were buried in Cockington Church, one in 1581 and the other in 1601. The two most obvious sources of solving this enigma are the family vault and the burial register. However, the burial register for this period no longer exists as it was probably destroyed during the Civil War, and the vault is located beneath the floor immediately in front of the High Altar and is now impossible to see as the floor level was raised in 1933 when the altar was rebuilt. There is no inscription on the vault cover referring to any of the Carys interred within.

George Cary and his wife moved into Cockington Court in 1567, six years after their marriage. How many children they had at this time is not known, however, it can be safely assumed they had some. Almost certainly, the reference to two daughters being buried at Cockington in 1581 is incorrect, the dates 1581 and 1601 are more realistic. The family vault must have been built too late for Wilmotta to be buried in it.

Comparison of all available dates provides a guide to the possible maximum ages of all three daughters at their deaths:
Marriage of George and Wilmotta - 1561
Confirmed death of Anne - 1625 = 64 years
Burial date of Jane - c1601 = 40 years
Burial date of other girl - 1581 = 20 years
It is probable that Jane and the unidentified daughter lived at Cockington Court for the whole of their lives, whereas Anne left when she married Sir Richard Edgecumbe.

This hypothesis of the female members of George Cary's family implies that the two finger-rings could have belonged to any one of them, or perhaps two. Of course, the Court would have received wealthy visitors from time to time who may have lost the finger rings, however, the chances of one guest losing two of them, or conversely, two guests each losing one, each of similar size, is less likely.

PENDANT NECK-JEWELS

Jewels in the form of neck-pendants have been current for thousands of years. Some were suspended singly from a simple necklace, such as a metal chain or fabric or leather cord, whilst others hung singly or in multiples from an elaborate metal necklace. Other than gold or silver, neck-pendants are found in base metal, as well as non-metalic materials. Frequently applied-surface decoration is found on metal examples, e.g: gilt, silver, tin, enamel, niello, paint, wire, intaglio, glass, glass past, and precious or semi-precious gemstones. Engraved or repoussé decoration was fashionable during some periods. Shapes of pendants are diverse, with the cross being especially favoured from the time of Christ. Cordate lockets have been popular for centuries and remain so today. Apart from personal beautification, neck pendants sometimes represented a badge of office or were used as reliquaries, amulets or seals.

778: **The Torre Abbey Memento Mori pendant Jewel, c1540-50**
English, three-dimensional gold skeleton lying in a gold coffin, separate gold lid, white, black, opaque white and pale blue, dark blue and translucent green champlevé enamel, inscribed around the outside of the coffin THROUGH. THE. RESVRRTION. OF. CHRISTE. WE. BE. ALL. SANCTIFIED. - *Torquay*.

N.B. A member of the Ridgeway family who resided at Torre Abbey, dug up this rather macbre jewel in the Abbey grounds in the 17th century. The pendant was passed to the Cary family when they acquired Torre Abbey. In 1856 Robert Sheddon Sulyarde Cary sold the jewel to the Victoria and Albert Museum for £21.00, where it is still displayed in the jewellery gallery.

CLOTH SEALS

From the 13th century it was custom for cloth-producers and government inspectors (alnagers) to afix lead seals to newly-woven cloth which denoted it complied with the expected weight and size and that the necessary tax had been paid to the Crown. Apart from weavers and clothiers, who applied their seal at the place of origin which was either in this country or on the Continent, a seal was often affixed after completion of other processes, e.g. dying. Such seals vary in size and comprise a pair of cast conjoined discs, one with a rivet hole and the other an integral lead rivet (others have four or six discs), which were folded over before inserting the rivet through the hole. Dies, one or both of which created an embossed impression, were then placed either side and struck with a heavy hammer. Devices may be a weaver's or clothier's mark or name, town or city name, coat of arms, date or other motif. Gilded or painted examples are known. Oval, square, rectangular, or lozenge-shaped seals were also current. It seems that at least one series of cloth-seal were cast with moulded devices.

Cast lead circular cloth-seals

779: 1558-1727, half only, triple rose surmounted by a crown within a border of oblique lines, traces of (?) red paint field, D. 37mm - *Newton Abbot*.

780: 1558-1727, arms of the realm, blundered Old French legends HONI . SOIT . OUI . MAL . Y . PENSE (evil to him who evil thinks) DIET ET NON DROIT (God and my right), triple rose surmounted by a crown, 55mm x 38.5mm - *Newton Abbot*.

781: 16th - early 17th century, fragmented, German, Augsburg, A with annulet below and right, pine-cone on tripartite base, D. 20mm - *Exeter*.

782: possibly late 16th - early 17th century, uniface; perhaps

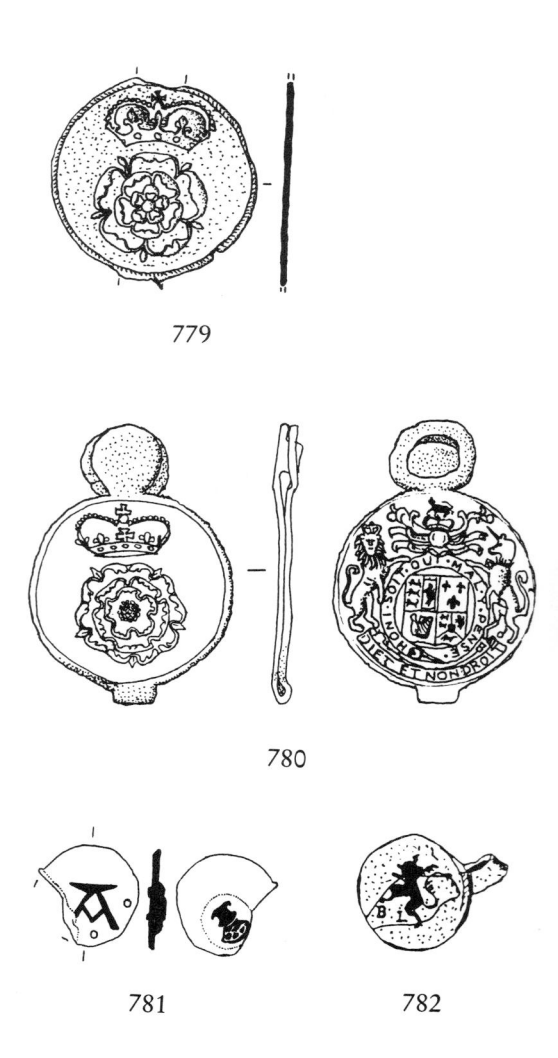

The Tudor Period

Continental, Belgium; (?) lion rampant surmounting BL, D. 22mm - *Cockington*.

THIMBLES

It was the 16th century which saw the introduction of silver thimbles. Until the 15th century Europe's silver came mainly from German mines. However, Spanish exploration and exploitation of South and Central America in the 16th century provided a copious supply of silver for European silversmiths and specialist thimble-makers.

Although some were English, during the first half of the 16th century most copper-alloy or silver thimbles were manufactured on the Continent, especially at Nuremberg, by either the cast or hammered method. Thimbles of this period are characterised by their hand-punched indentations, some of which start from the base and spiral up the sides and over the crown, though others have regular rows on the sides and concentric circles on the crown. Frequently both English and Nuremberg spiral indentation-type thimbles have a maker's mark stamped where the spirals begin on the base; however, no record is extant of touchmarks, therefore they do not assist with attribution.

Later in the century Nuremberg craftsmen developed the technique of making two-piece thimbles from sheet cylinders with separately soldered caps. Some thimbles of this type of have a wide border with engraved decoration. Early cast or hammered Nuremberg thimbles are fairly short and have pointed crowns, whilst two-piece thimbles are tall and slim with flat crowns. Open-top sewing rings of this period frequently have a bottom and top, or just bottom band of tiny punched dots or engraving. One particular form has a thick bottom-rim and a slightly thinner top-rim. Indentations are generally in transverse or vertical bands varying from fairly small to large and may be circular or triangular.

A particular kind of silver thimble of this period is the so-called filigree type which has a smooth body covered by a decorative wire appliqué. Highly ornate silver miniature thimbles were also current which were not really functional but rather novelty items. Despite being produced in their thousands, 16th-century silver thimbles are nowadays extremely rare.

Cast copper-alloy thimbles, 16th century
783: flat crown, spiral of large circular indentations on sides and crown, punched shield-shaped cartouche with embossed reversed K maker's mark, 22mm x 20mm - *Cockington*.
784: flat crown, regular bands of large circular indentations on sides, concentric circles of smaller circular indentations on crown, 20mm x 18mm - *Stokeinteignhead*.

Cast copper-alloy sewing rings, 16th century
785: thick bottom-rim, thinner top-ring, regular bands of large triangular indentations, 15.5mm x 20mm - *Wolborough, Newton Abbot*.
786: top and bottom band of tiny punched dots, vertical bands of circular indentations, 12mm x 17.5mm - *Cockington*.
787: bottom band of tiny punched dots, transverse bands of large circular indentations, 13.5mm x 15.5mm - *Axminster*.

SPOONS

Spoons of the late 15th-16th century are made of cast and

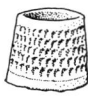

forged silver, copper alloy or lead/tin alloy, and generally have circular or rectangular cross-section stems with fig or pear-shaped bowls. Diamond-point, maidenhead, writhen, lion sejant or Apostle knops were current on early spoons of this period, however, towards the end of the 16th century the seal-top became dominant. This name appears to be a misnomer, for there is no evidence of such knops having engraved devices which could be used as seals, however, scratch engraved or pricked inscriptions were current. These are frequently a date and two sets of initials which probably represent a betrothed couple and the year of their marriage. The slip-top appeared around the late 15th century and this simple obliquely-cut stem was used on precious as well as base metal spoons.

Knops of silver seal-top spoons, which frequently are gilded, are invariably separate, often made by a different craftsmen, and soldered to the stem by means of a stepped or V-joint. Both silver or base metal spoons sometimes have a maker's touch mark stamped on the inside top end of the bowl or, alternatively, on the top end of the back of the bowl. Silver spoons frequently are hallmarked on the lower part of the reverse of the stem and have the town mark stamped inside the bowl at the top end.

Cast and forged silver seal-top spoon, c1590-1600
788: fig-shaped bowl with embossed crowned X maker's mark stamped inside and inscribed IR 1612 on back, hexagonal cross-section stem, hallmarked, made at Exeter by Richard Osborne, gilded seal-top knop inscibed I.G made by Robert Tite of Salisbury, L. 172mm - *Alphington*.

N.B. Richard Osborne was made a Freeman of the City of Exeter in 1559, he died in 1607.

DAGGERS AND KNIVES

The 16th century saw a revival of the ornate type of moulded knife-terminal which disappeared along with Romanisation. End-plates, as they are now called, are solid cast and three-dimensional zoomorphic, hominoid or other moulded design. Some have engraved or punched decoration. A characteristic of this style of knife-furniture is a slotted base into which fitted the tang. Concurrent with the slotted type was a form with an integral male member which fitted into a corresponding female orifice in the haft. Other knives of this period have cast lead/tin-alloy hafts with integral pommels and moulded decoration. These are often embellished with a spiral of inlaid twisted wire.

Cast lead/tin-alloy dagger handle, late 16th century
789: fragmented, integral spherical pommel, spiral moulding which originally had an inset twisted wire, 79mm x 16mm - *Cockington*.

Cast copper-alloy three-dimensional knife-end stops, late 16th - 17th century
790: neck and head of a horse, integral abraded male member, 30mm x 27mm - *Alphington*.
791: a bird, engraved zigzags, slotted, remains of iron tang, 22mm x 18mm - *Kingskerswell*.
792: asymmetrical; moulded concentric circles, oblique and transverse lines and chevron grooves on both sides, slotted, remains of iron tang, 23.5mm x 19.5mm - *Cockwood*.
793: asymmetrical, trefoil top with moulded collar beneath, three

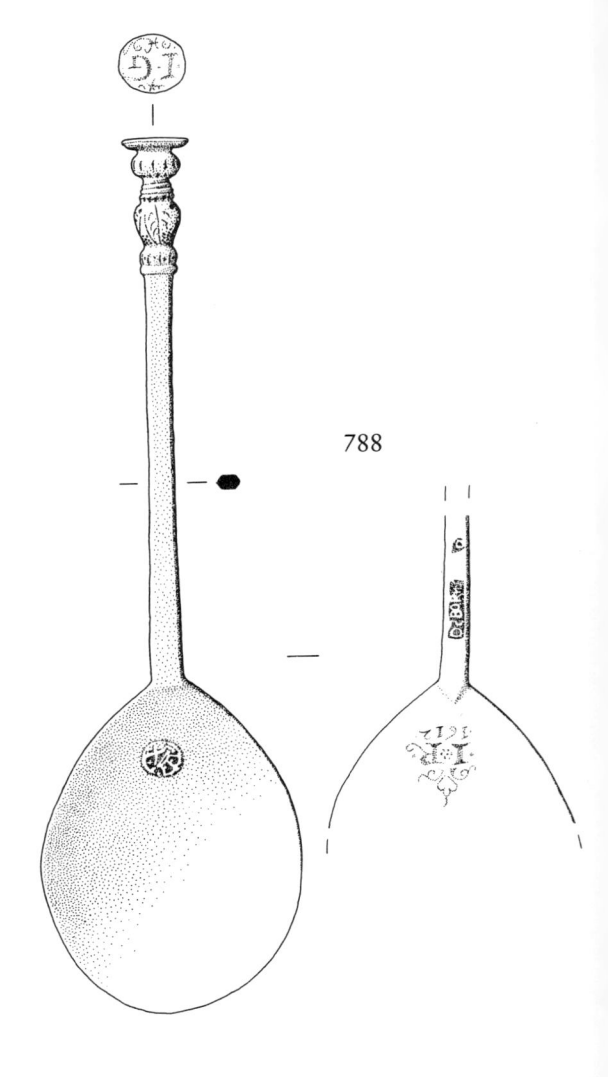

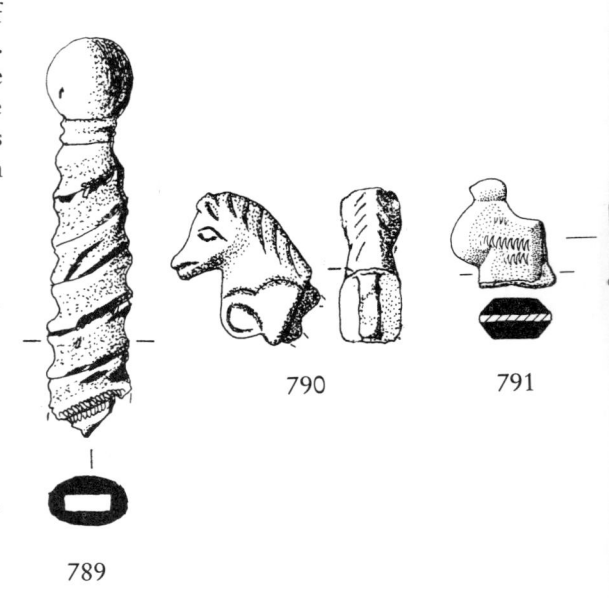

The Tudor Period 125

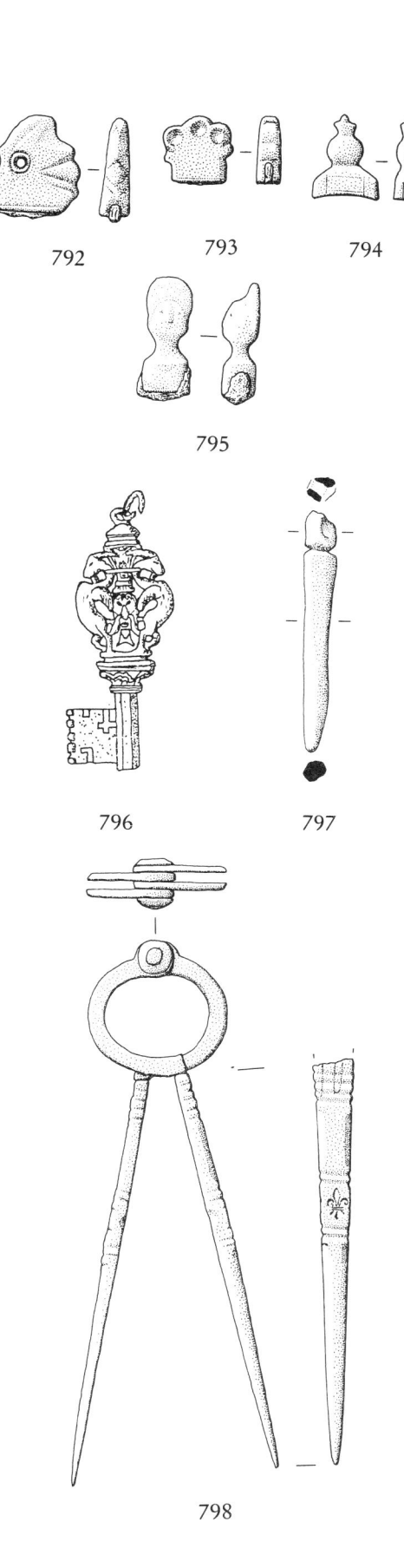

blind holes each side, slotted, remains of iron tang, 15.5 x 15mm - *Cockwood*.
794: symmetrical, crescent-shaped base surmounted by a pineapple-type knop, rectangle of punched dots each side, slotted, remains of iron tang, 19mm x 14.5mm - *Stokeinteignhead*.
795: female bust, slotted, remains of iron tang, 28mm x12mm - *Stokeinteignhead*.

KEYS

At the commencement of the Tudor period the simple forged iron or cast copper-alloy kidney-shaped bow key was prevalent and remained so up until the Elizabethan era which saw the inception of elaborate keys for use with warded locks. Late Renaissance keys were utilised for precisely the same purposes as their antecedants, and similarly they vary in size accordingly. Primarily iron was the metal used for door and chest keys whereas casket keys invariably were made from copper alloy. Many of these keys, of both types, have ornate openwork bows. Likewise, bits are frequently extremely ornate with intricate clefts and bullets. The most ornamental of all are the 'masterpiece' keys made as apprentice pieces, a type which carried over into the 17th century. Invariably these have intricate representational bows of either: foliate, floriate, hominoid, animals, birds or heraldic devices.

Cast copper-alloy casket-key, late 16th century
796: French, traces of gilt, bow formed from an outward facing rampant winged ram left and right of a moustached and bearded effigy, fluted stem, no clefts, circular suspension loop with a separate copper-alloy split ring, 60mm x 22mm - *Cockington*.

STYLI

Used for scribing on slate tablets, lead styli were current from the Middle Ages through to the 19th century. Though varying in length and diameter, frequently they are simply a length of circular or subrectangular cross-section roughly cast rod and easily mistaken for a piece of scrap lead. However, some were more precisely made, with a gentle taper and occasionally a suspension loop. Attribution can be difficult unless from a dateable deposit.

Cast lead styli, possibly c16th-17th century
797: tapered circular cross-section, moulded globular knop pierced as a suspension loop, L. 55mm - *Cockington*.

NAVIGATIONAL DIVIDERS

Dividers or compasses have cetainly been around for several thousand years, used in general building and engineering work. However, precisely when this essential instrument was first employed for navigational chart work is uncertain.

Irrespective of application, dividers were cast and/or forged from copper alloy or iron and comprised a looped handle and a pair of sharp-pointed legs, often with moulded decoration and are even known shaped as three-dimensional human legs. Each leg of navigational dividers attributed to the 16th century is usually decorated with moulding, engraving, punchwork or filework and has one end of a semi-circular handle of two separate pieces of copper alloy soldered and morticed and tennoned to the top. The other ends of the two parts of each handle have a rivet hole and are slotted together and riveted, thereby forming a hinge.

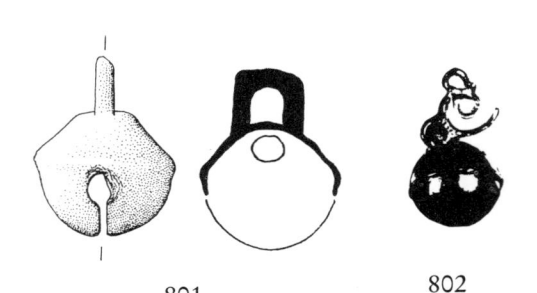

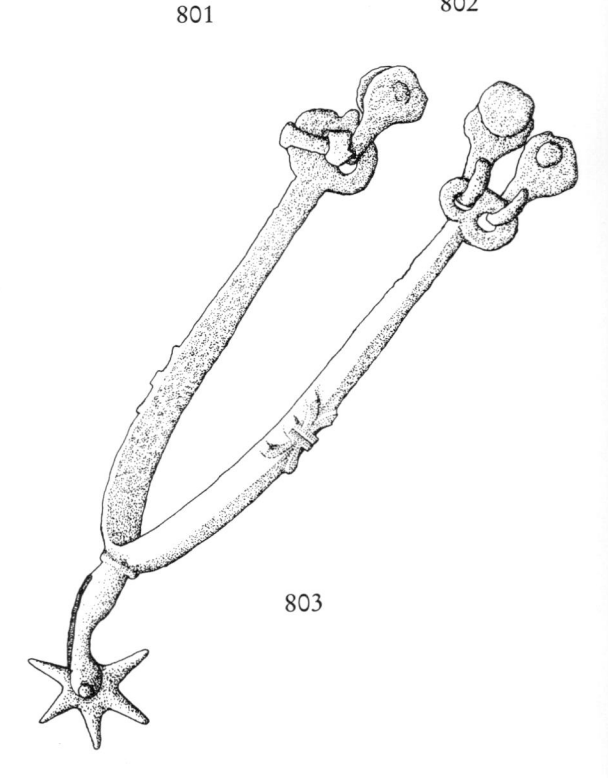

Cast and forged copper-alloy navigational dividers, 16th century

798: probably Spanish, each leg fractured at juncture with semi-circular handle, both legs tapered semi-circular cross-section and two panels of rectangular cross-section with filed nicks and transverse ribs on fronts and sides, incuse stamped fleur-de-lis on outside of one leg, L. 121mm - *Bigbury Beach.*

N.B. No.798 probably came from a wrecked Spanish galleon that lies just offshore in the mouth of the River Erme.

CROTAL BELLS

Globular crotal bells remained current throughout the 16th and 17th centuries much the same as before. Though smaller types continued to be fashioned from sheet silver or copper alloy, with either sheet or wire suspension loops, for uses such as hawking, predominantly they were cast in copper alloy (bell metal) by bell-founders and comprise two parts, the bell proper and a separate elongated iron pea. Moulded decoration of one or both sections is commonplace. The top half has a circular sound-hole, whilst the bottom is provided with a pair of slightly smaller circular holes conjoined by a slit which served the same purpose. The pea was inserted through the upper hole. Before the passing of the 17th century the name crotal appears to have been replaced by 'rumbler' for globular bells.

Cast copper-alloy crotal bells, late 16th - 17th century
799: corroded iron pea, 45.5mm x 35mm - *Cockington.*
800: corroded iron pea, 38mm x 28mm - *Bishopsteignton.*
801: 36mm x 27mm - *Newton Abbot.*

Sheet and wire silver crotal bell, late 16th - 17th century
802: possible silver pea, separate silver suspension wire attached to loop, 19mm x 15mm - *Stokeinteignhead.*

SPURS

The long-necked rowel-spur remained current from the mid-15th century well into the first half of the 16th century. However, early in the 16th century fashion changed to a spur with a much shorter, drooped neck. During this transitional period and onwards, rowels ranged from medium seven-point, large long five-point to large short seven-point. Gilded spurs were fashionable for the wealthy, whilst those worn by retainers were usually silvered or tinned. Towards the end of the 16th century rowel-spurs became more ornate, the sides, neck and crest often have engraved or moulded decoration.

Forged iron rowel-spur, c1590-1640
803: probably English, worn on left foot, short moulded neck, drooped rowel-box; small, long six-pointed rowel; straight sides with lateral figure-eight terminals (one larger than the other), two mushroom-headed stud attachments on each, moulded Ferde-moulin (mill-rind) on each side, two spur-leathers (one broken), L. 132mm - *Cockington.*

N.B. Found on 23 October 1914 when a concealed squint in Cockington Church was re-opened and is probably part of Sir George Cary's funerary achievement.

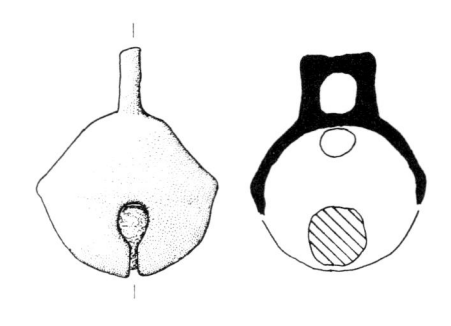

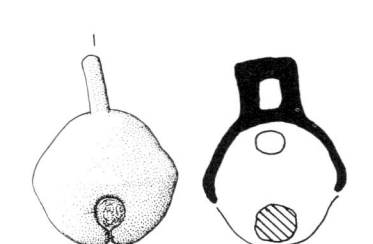

The Tudor Period

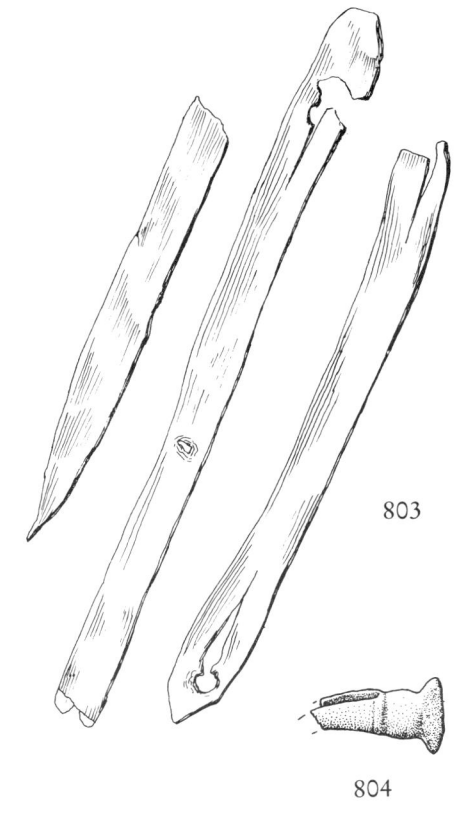

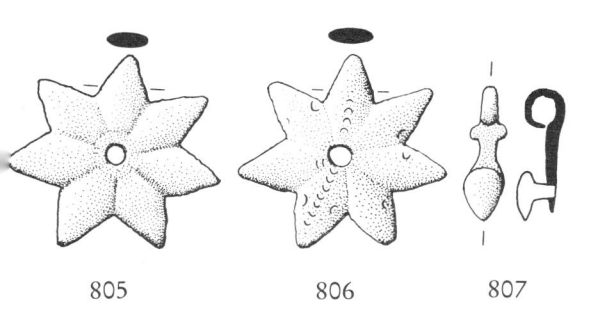

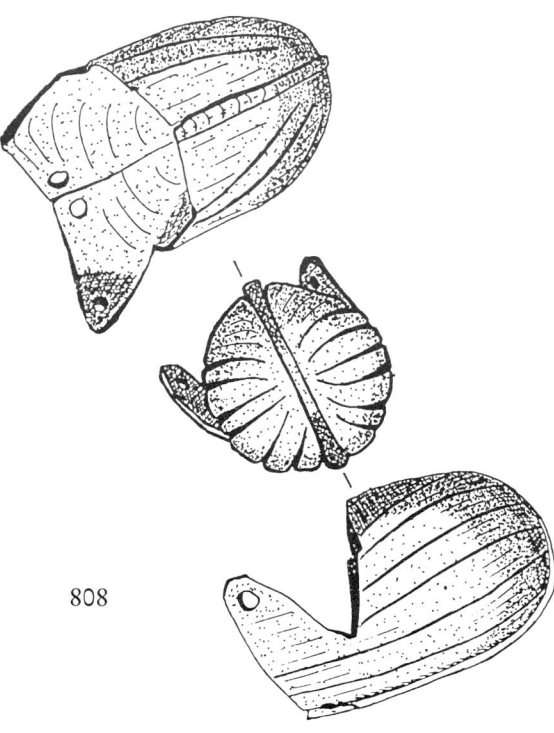

Cast and forged copper-alloy rowel-spur, possibly late 16th - 17th century
804: fragmented, short moulded neck, drooped rowel-box, L. 25mm - *Exeter*.

Cast copper-alloy spur rowels, 16th-17th century
805: large, short seven-point, moulded oblique grooves and central circle, D. 41mm - *Cockington*.
806: large, short seven-point, traces of gilt, moulded oblique grooves and punched crescents, D. 39mm - *Exeter*.

Cast and forged rowel-spur stud-attachment, 16th-18th century
807: ovoid stud, L. 26.5mm - *Cockington*.

SADDLE POMMELS

From the later Middle Ages until the 17th century many saddles were large and robust, a necessity as they were designed to carry a man dressed in full or partial armour. Heavy-duty saddles were wooden-framed and leather-clad. A separate cast, one or two-piece copper-alloy decorative pommel was riveted to a wooden protrusion on the front of the frame, to which the reins could be secured. The usual type of pommel is bulbous, though a more flattened version is known. Both forms have two or three wings and one or more nail holes, normally one in each wing. Although some pommels are undecorated, ornate moulded or engraved designs usually cover much of the surface. Saddle pommels which antecede the Tudor period are rare.

Cast copper-alloy saddle-pommels, 16th-17th century.
808: two-piece, tinned, two wings, moulded band along seam, moulded longitudinal grooves, four nail holes, 60mm x 40mm - *Bishopsteignton*.
809: one-piece, three wings (one lost), punched dots field, bands of engraved curvilinear, lozenges and chevrons formed from punched crescents, punched circles and crescents, 50mm x 33mm - *Bicton*.
810: two-piece, fragmented, flattened type, two nail holes, 51.5mm x 39mm - *Marldon*

AVIARY AND CAGE-BIRD FEED- AND WATER-TROUGHS

Post medieval aviary and cage-bird feed- and water-troughs are more substantially cast from lead and are flat-bottomed, thereby free-standing. They lack holes or annulets and invariably are undecorated, although the front of the body is frequently divided into broad stepped bands. A particularly fine example from Lincolnshire has a moulded fruit-laden tree depicted on the front which perhaps represents the tree of life.

Cast-lead aviary and cage-bird feed- and water-troughs, 16th-17th century
811: flat bottom, slightly flared top with a pronounced rim, numerous transverse and oblique grooves on bottom, 24mm x 52.5mm - *Poltimore*.

TRADE WEIGHTS

It is probable that cast lead shield-shaped official trade-weights remained current until the end of the 15th century, however, their flat-circular counterparts continued in use well into the 19th.

From c1588 the Plumbers Company were empowered to stamp their mark, St Michael holding a sword in the right hand and scales in the left, on lead weights or iron weights with lead weight-adjustment plugs in the City of London. Lead weights, from c1590, invariably carry an incuse stamp of the City of London Sword of St Paul and a moulded royal cipher surmounted by a crown. Numerous provincial verification marks found on official lead trade-weights have been identified, however, many marks, which may be authentic or otherwise, remain an enigma.

Towards the end of the 15th century cast copper-alloy flat-circular official trade-weights were stamped with variations of a Lombardic h surmounted by a crown. Apparently the use of this mark extended well into Henry VIII's reign. In 1588 the Founders Company, in London, were authorised to stamp copper-alloy trade-weights with their mark of the ewer (or laverpott), whilst from c1590 they carry the Sword of St Paul, crowned royal cipher, and Averdepois A. London-made copper-alloy trade-weights from c1590 until 1826 carry all four of these marks or a variation of them. Denominations of below two ounce invariably have the Averdupois A missing, whilst on X and 1/16 ounce weights the sword is absent. The royal cipher comprises the respective monarch's initials and for Queen Elizabeth is EL.

From the 15th century cast copper-alloy bell-shaped official trade-weights were used alongside flat-circular types, although those which antecede Elizabeth I are extremely rare. Usually bell-shaped weights are stamped on the shoulder. The aforementioned large wool-weights continued in use throughout the period, although from Elizabeth I's reign they were made from cast copper-alloy moulded with the royal arms. They are shield-shaped with a suspension hole in the top.

Cast lead flat-circular trade-weights, late 15th-16th century

812: 1lb; embossed A, Tudor rose and possible I, incuse (?) 1, D. 54.5mm - *Haccombe*.

813: 2oz, two incuse hearts, embossed Tudor rose, D. 29mm - *Uffculme*.

Cast copper-alloy flat-circular trade-weights, 16th century

814: 4oz, embossed crowned Lombardic h, central circular hole filled with iron corrosion, D. 61mm - Totnes.

815: 2.83 grammes, embossed crowned Lombardic h, D. 17.5mm - *Stokeinteignhead*.

816: 2oz; embossd crowned EL, sword of St Paul and ewer, D. 42mm - *Coffinswell*.

COIN WEIGHTS

For the reigns of all Tudor monarchs up until Elizabeth I, coin-weights current before or during Henry VII's reign remained in use. It is possible that weights for the George noble and half-noble were struck by Henry VIII but none are known to be extant. None are known for Mary or Edward VI.

Elizabeth I possibly issued a square copper-alloy weight for the half-noble with an embossed ship on the obverse and embossed crowned VI.S VIII.D. on the reverse. Square copper-alloy weights for the sovereign and half-sovereign were struck either by Elizabeth I or James I. They are embossed on the

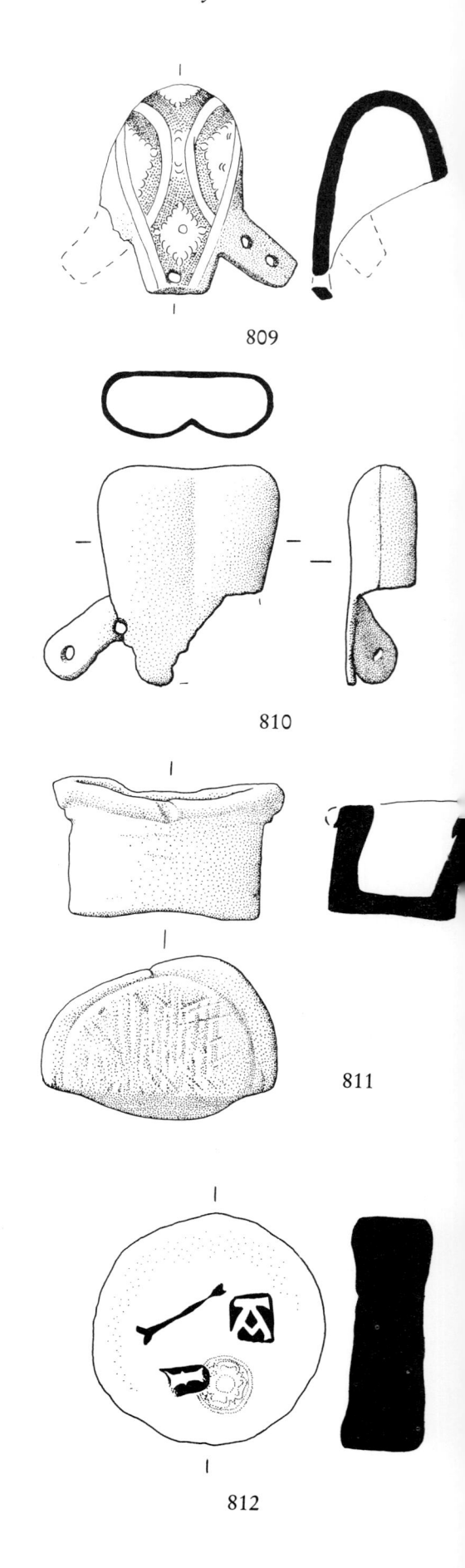

The Tudor Period

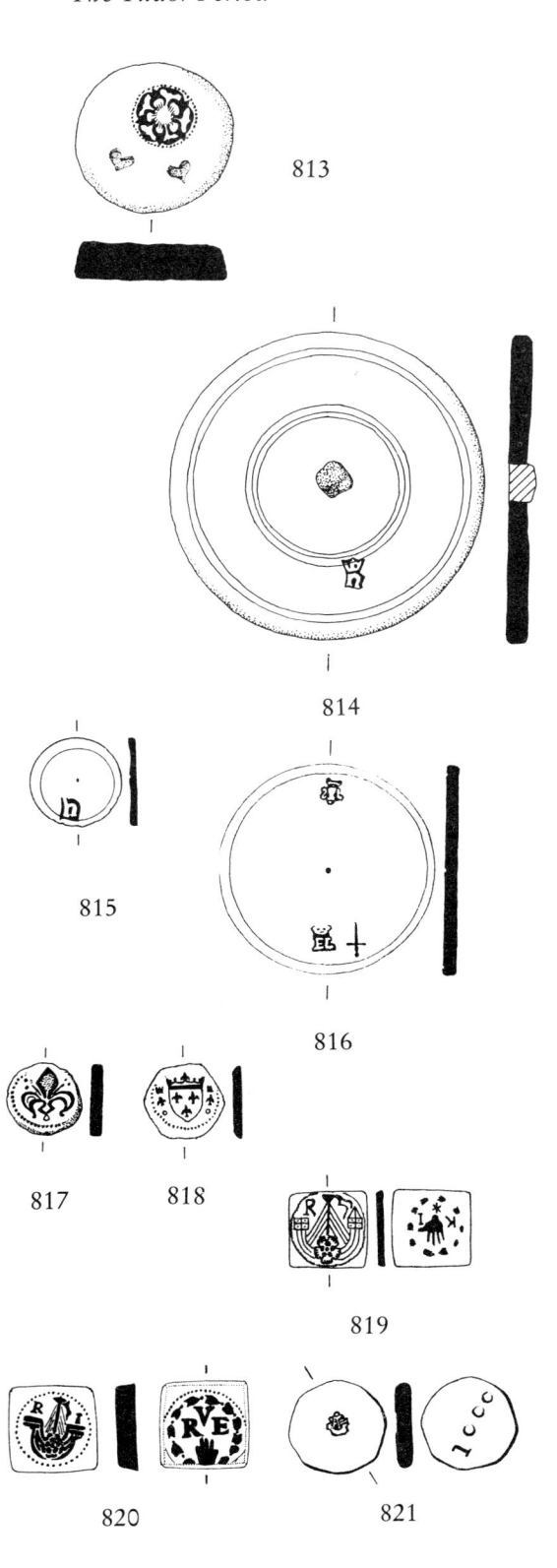

obverse with Henry VIII crowned and enthroned, whilst the reverse has embossed variations of crowned Xs, crowned HR or crowned HXR according to denomination and issue. A square copper-alloy weight for the crown was issued by Elizabeth I. It has an embossed crowned rose enclosed by a beaded circle on the obverse and an embossed V surmounted by a crown and an s below the crown. James I issued a set of crown weights, all of which have an embossed crowned Henry VIII enthroned obverse, and embossed reverse of a crowned HR.

All copper-alloy weights struck for coins of Elizabeth I, some of which were issued by James I and are countermarked I on the reverse, are square with embossed designs on both sides. The fine sovereign weight has an obverse of a rose with a central shield and a reverse of XXX with a crown above and s below. For the angel and its quarter the obverse is St Michael spearing a dragon, and reverse of a crowned X with s below or crowned II.S with VI.D below respectively. Weights for the pound and its fractions are marked according to denomination with either Elizabeth's crowned bust or a crowned shield enclosing three lis on the obverse. Again reverses vary according to denomination from: crowned E.R., crowned X with s below, crowned V with s below, crowned II.S with VI.D below, crowned VI with s below or crowned VI.S.

There were numerous copper-alloy square coin-weights used in this country in the 16th century which were made in Antwerp. They are characterised by a moulded hand on the reverse.

Cast copper-alloy circular coin-weight, 16th century
817: florin, uniface, moulded, fleur-de-lis within a beaded border, D. 14mm - *Haccombe*.

Cast copper-alloy hexagonal coin-weight, 16th century
818: French, ecu (crown), uniface; embossed three fleur-de-lis within a shield surmounted by a crown, W fleur-de-lis O each side of shield, beaded circle, D. 15mm - *Cockington*.

Cast copper-alloy Antwerp-made square coin-weights, c1580
819: rose-noble, moulded; Obv. ship with rose in centre and R (rose) and I at side of mast, beaded circle; Rev. hand surmounted by RVE (maker Reynier van Etterson) within a wreath and beaded circle, 17mm x 17mm - *Colaton Raleigh*.

820: rose-noble, moulded; Obv. ship with rose in centre and R (rose) at side of mast, beaded circle; Rev. hand with a star below and unknown makers mark KI within a wreath, 15mm x 15mm - *Sherford*.

Cast copper-alloy octagonal possible coin-weight, c16th-17th century
821: 2.8 grammes, unidentified, traces of tinning or silvering on obverse, incuse, Obv. ship, Rev. 1000, D. 17mm - *Haccombe*

823

Chapter Seven
The Stuart Period

822

Many of the towns and villages that had flourished under the House of Tudor continued to do so for much of the Stuart era, although Totnes, in particular, suffered due to a decline in the woollen industry. In Henry VIII's reign it was the second wealthiest town in the county, but had fallen to about tenth position by the time of Charles II's restoration in 1660. Nonetheless, it continued as a prosperous community. Ashburton remained an important cloth-producing town, although it suffered from a contraction in the tin trade in the first quarter of the 17th century. In the east of the county, at: Honiton, Uffculme, Culmstock, Ottery St Mary and Tiverton, the woollen trade thrived for the whole of the 17th century and into the 18th. Similarly, still under royal patronage, lacemaking proved ever profitable at Honiton and Bradninch.

The great rebuilding programme that started in the last half of the 16th century continued right up until 1645. We can delight in looking at many of these architectural wonders which still exsist today. Dartmouth expanded, many fine buildings were erected on the reclaimed land gained as a result of the infilling of Mill Pool - the famous 'Butterwalk' is especially enchanting. In the case of farmhouses, the great majority of which continue as private homes, they provide a feast of 17th-century features

The Civil War of 1642-9 affected Devon as much as the rest of the country. Military actions that occurred in the area are well recorded, it is said, better than anywhere else in England. Much structural damage was occasioned to some large country-houses and many farmhouses, villages and towns during this long, tragic, and bitter struggle. Some were wholly or partially destroyed by fire, having been deliberately torched, whilst others were damaged by cannon and small arms shot.

Regretably, until now, little by way of small common objects have survived to provide an insight of into everyday life during the 17th century. It is noteworthy that this unsatisfactory situation has been somewhat rectified due to the hobby of metal detecting. There is now available for study by students of the period, a diversity of numismatical and metal artefactual evidence.

Alloys of copper continued as the metal most used for the manufacture of small objects. Lead/tin-alloy was current also, however, it seems to have increased towards the end of the Stuart period. Precious metals remained popular with the more affluent members of society, particularly for jewellery, whilst gilding, silvering and tinning was fashionable for buttons, buckles and horse furniture.

824

825

826

828

827

The Stuart Period

829

830

831

832

833

834

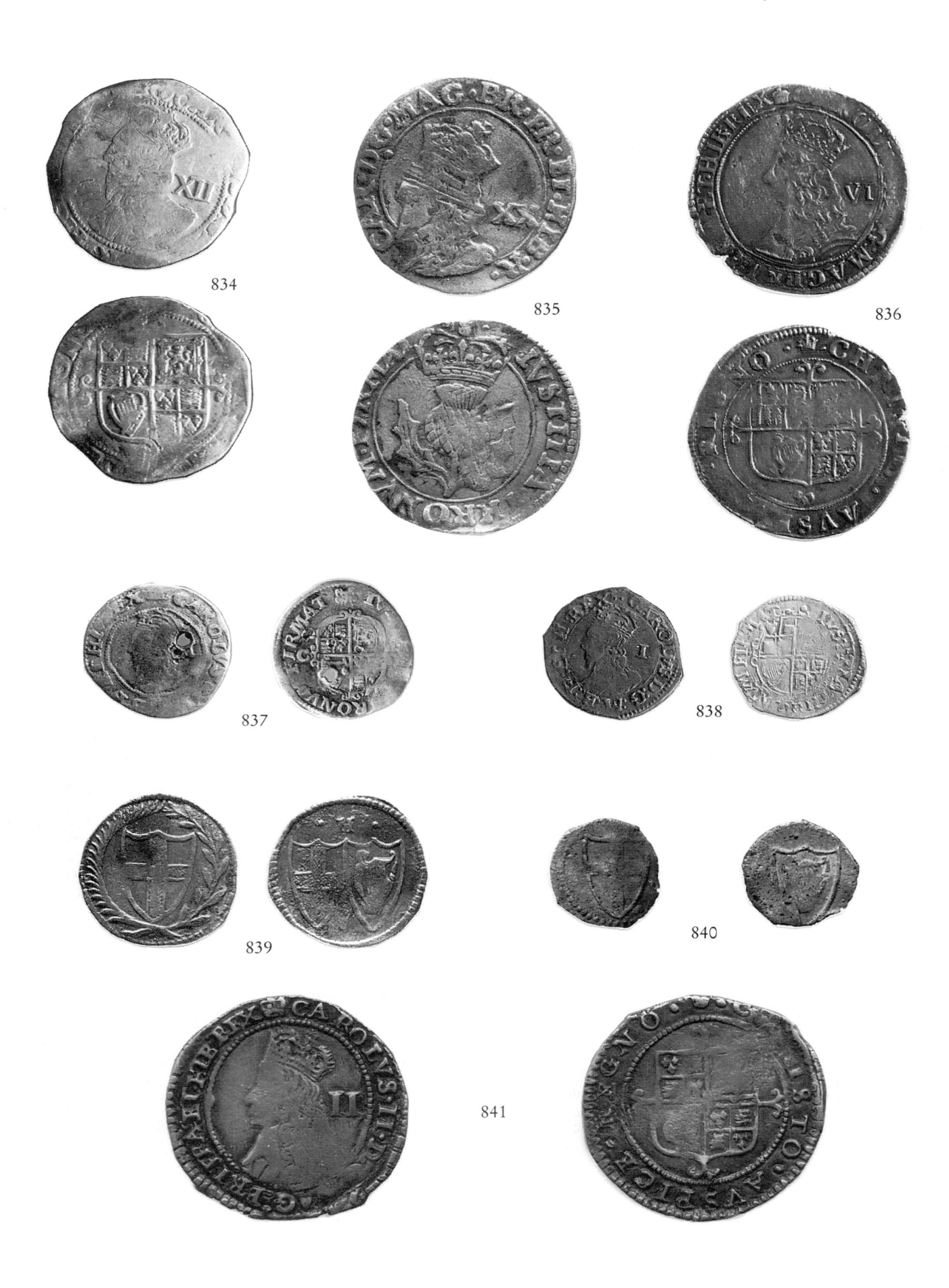

835

836

837

838

839

840

841

The Stuart Period 135

842

843

844

845

846

847

848

849

COINS

After James I's accession in 1604 the gold sovereign was reduced in weight and renamed the 'unite'. Between 1604-19 gold coins known as: 'rose-ryals', 'spur-ryals', 'angels', 'half-angels', 'Britain crowns' and 'thistle crowns' respectively, appeared, and in 1619 the unite was replaced by the lighter 'laurel' and its fractions, the 'half' and 'quarter-laurel'. From 1613 copper farthings were minted under licence by Lord Harrington, the coining of which was later transferred to the Duke of Lennox.

Charles I's most notable coins are the irregular-shaped silver 'siege pieces', gold 'triple-unites' and silver 'pounds' and 'half-pounds' struck at several provincial mints during the Civil War. Another attempt at machine-milled coins was made between 1631-9, this time by Nicholas Briot. This was also abandoned for being too slow. Under licence the Duchess of Richmond, followed by Lord Maltravers and several others, continued striking copper 'royal' and 'rose farthings' until 1644.

The royal arms were replaced on some Commonwealth gold or silver coins by St George's cross on the obverse and St George's cross and the Irish harp on the reverse, however, others have an obverse of Oliver Cromwell's bust and a crowned shield reverse. Farthings are known with other reverses. This was the last occasion that silver halfpennies were struck.

Other than the silver crown, hammered gold and silver coins of Charles II were struck until 1662 when they were superseded by Roettiers milled coinage. Larger denominations have an inscribed edge, whilst the edges of lower denominations are grained - this was to prevent clipping or filing. As the gold of some of the new gold coins came from Guinea in West Africa they were named 'guineas', and were issued as 'five guineas', 'guineas' and 'half-guineas'. The first regal copper halfpennies and farthings were issued in 1672, and in 1684 and 1685 tin fathings with a copper plug were struck.

Copper-plugged tin farthings and newly struck similar halfpennies remained current through James II's three-year reign. Gold denominations remained as before. After William and Mary's accession the silver coinage was deemed to be much underweight through clipping and abrasion, therefore by 1694 the guinea was valued for up to 30 shillings. In the same year copper halfpennies and farthings replaced the earlier tin issues. In 1696 William III undertook his great re-coinage whereby the poor condition hammered coinage that still circulated was withdrawn and smelted. As long as they had been officially pierced in the centre some hammered coins remained current for a short time. Only three major changes to the currency occured in Queen Anne's reign. After the Act of Union of 1707 the royal arms were changed to welcome Scotland, 'VIGO' was marked below the queen's portrait on coins minted from prize-bullion seized at Vigo Bay, and copper halfpennies were not struck.

Regarding hoards of Stuart or partially comprising Stuart coins, four which antecede the metal detector are chronicled, albeit scantly. The first (1879) was mentioned in the Tudor chapter, whilst Barton Old Hall near Newton Abbot was the find-spot in 1880 for 72 silver coins, the latest date of which was 1644-5 (Charles I). The only location in the area which now fits this description is Barton Hall, now a holiday camp, which is nearer Torquay. Lastly, at Buckfastleigh on an unrecorded date, 36 silver coins turned up, the latest being an Exeter halfcrown

850

851

852

The Stuart Period

dated 1644.

822: Hoard of seven Stuart gold coins - Chudleigh
James I
unite, 1604-5, mm lis.
unite, 1612-3, mm tower
unite, 1613-5, mm tun.
unite, 1613-5, mm tun.
unite, 1613-5, mm tun.
unite, 1615-6, mm closed book.
unite, 1617-8, mm plain cross.

N.B. Hoards of James I coins are rare, due to the stable political climate during his reign. Only two other hoards of this reign comprising gold coins alone are recorded from the United Kingdom. The Chudleigh coins, which are in very fine condition, were found by Val MacRae in March 1986 scattered down the steep bank of an ancient hollow way. Whether or not they comprise a true hoard is open to conjecture, for no evidence of a container was found. Possibly they were the contents of a purse which was lost, the purse subsequently rotting away. However, at a Treasure Trove inquest held on 9 July 1986, the coins were declared Treasure Trove. Eventually they were acquired by EM for £1,650.00.

823: Hoard of six Stuart silver coins - Cockington Charles I
Scotland thirty shillings, 1625-36, mm thistle.
halfcrown, 1634-5, mm bell.
halfcrown, 1639-40, mm triangle.
halfcrown, 1645-6, mm sun.
halfcrown, 1645+, (?) mm.

Charles II
crown, 1663, mm crown.

N.B. The five Charles I coins are very abraded and clipped. They, along with the Charles II crown, were found scattered over several square meters and were lying just beneath the surface. No evidence of a container was recovered. Probably they were the contents of a lost purse. An inquest was not held.

Silver coins

824: James I, shilling, 1603-4, mm thistle - *Offwell*.
825: James I, shilling, 1607-9, mm coronet - *Cockwood*.
826: James I, sixpence, 1604, (?) mm - *Alphington*.
827: James I, Ireland, sixpence, 1606-7, mm escallop - *Haccombe*.
828: James I, penny, 1603-4, mm thistle - *Abbotskerswell*.
829: James I, penny, 1605-6, mm rose - *Cockington*.
830: Charles I, halfcrown, 1640-3, clipped, (?) mm - *River Teign, Coombe Cellars*.
831: Charles I, halfcrown, 1636-8, mm tun - *Uffculme*.
832: Charles I, halfcrown, 1640-1, mm star - *Uffculme*.
833: Charles I, shilling, 1643-4, mm (P) - *Offwell*.
834: Charles I, shilling, 1643-4, mm (P) - *Stokeinteignhead*.
835: Charles I, Scotland, twenty pence, 1637-42, mm none - *Cockwood*.
836: Charles I, sixpence, 1635-6, mm crown - *Offwell*.
837: Charles I, halfgroat, 1633-4, mm portcullis - *Goodrington Beach, Paignton*.
838: Charles I, penny, 1625-42, mm two pellets - *Haccombe*.

839: Commonwealth, halfgroat, 1649-60, mm none - *Exeter*.
840: Commonwealth, halfpenny, 1649-60, mm none - *Uffculme*.
841: Charles II, halfgroat, 1660-85, third issue, mm crown - *Cockwood*.
842: Charles II, penny, 1660-2, mm crown *Combeinteignhead*.
843: James II, threepence, 1686 - *River Teign, Coombe Cellars*.
844: William and Mary, threepence, 1689 - *Exmouth*.
845: William III, sixpence, 1696 - *Goodrington Beach, Paignton*.

Copper, tin or gunmetal coins

846: Charles I, rose farthing, sceptres below crown, 1625-49 - *Uffculme*.
847: James II, halfpenny, (?) date - *Seaton*.
848: James II, Ireland, gunmoney shilling, 1689 - *Exeter*.

American silver coin

849: Massachusetts, New England, oak tree twopence, 1662 - *Plymouth*.

Continental gold coin

850: Ferdinand III, United Provinces of the Netherlands, ducat, 1674 - *Beesands Beach*

Continental silver coins

851: Netherlands, provence of Campden, one gilder, 1618 - *Beesands Beach*.
852: Louis XIIII, France, 20 sols, 1707 - *Cockington*.

Continental copper coins

853: Phillip III or IV, Spain, eight maravedis, (?) date - *Kingskerswell*.
854: Phillip IV, Spain, eight maravedis, 1621-9 - *Maidencombe*.
855: Phillip IV, Spain, countermarked eight maravedis, 1625-65 - *Stokeinteignhead*.
856: Phillip IV, Spain, eight maravedis, c1660-5 - *Maidencombe*.

N.B. No.849 is particularly noteworthy, for it is one of the earliest hammered coins struck in America and is an extremely rare find in this country.

TOKENS

Between 1648-72, particularly the Commonwealth period, small denomination regal coinage was in short supply. In order to overcome this problem individual towns and traders decided to issue small change in the form of copper tokens. Most were halfpennies or farthings, with a lesser number of pennies, and were struck in a variety of shapes. The commonest is circular, but some are square, octagonal, lozenge or cordate. Unlike coins, iconography and inscriptions on trade tokens aren't standard throughout, however, one side usually depicts the date, the name of the town or trader or trader's initials, whilst the other side may show a coat of arms or other design and the denomination.

Devonshire was second only to Yorkshire in the number of different 17th-century trade-tokens issued. Despite this, few in a recognisable condition have been recorded from the county - no doubt due to the extremely acid ground destroying these wafer-thin pieces of hammered copper.

Small denomination coinage again became scarce in the 18th century and remained so until 1821 when coin-making was resumed after a period of restraint in the minting of silver and copper coins. This shortage led to the introduction in 1787 of copper trade-tokens which were struck by private traders in most

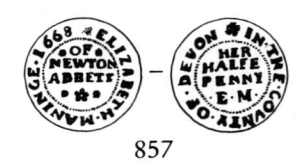

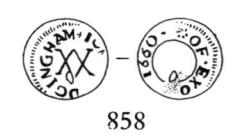

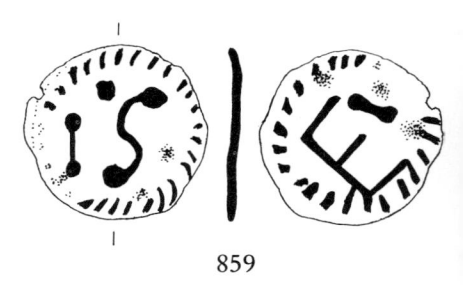

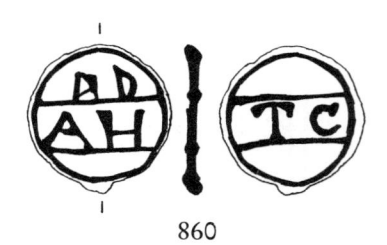

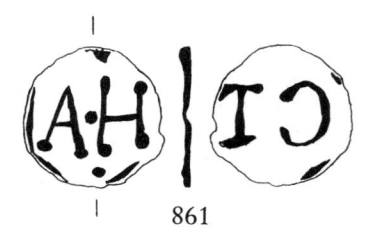

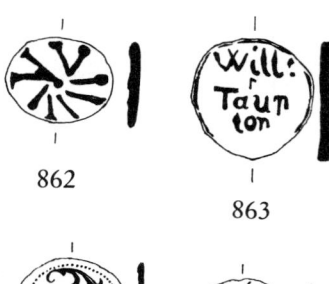

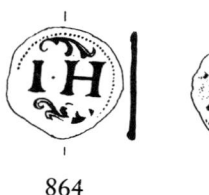

The Stuart Period

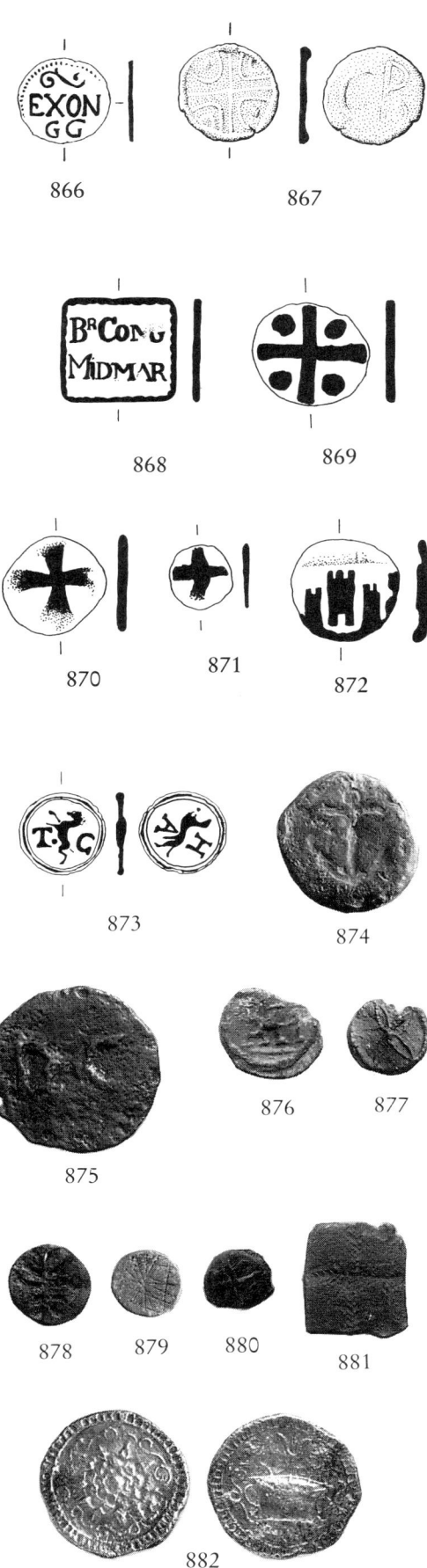

towns and cities throughout the land. During the Napoleonic wars small change was particularly thin on the ground which led to the introduction of trade tokens once more: on this occasion silver as well as copper tokens were issued.

The 17th century saw an upsurge in the use of lead or lead/tin-alloy tokens. Invariably tokens of this period are cruder than their antecedents, and in the main are uniface and circular, though oval or rectangular examples are known, some of which are multi-face. Notwithstanding, it seems that attribution between the 1690s and 1780s is justified.

Tokens made from worn-out coins, especially sixpences, shillings and halfpennies, are widespread finds. Wealthy people even used gold coins, though none appear to be recorded as recovered by any method. The romantic custom of young men presenting their sweethearts with such tokens of affection was current during the 17th century and even earlier, particularly at the time of William III and soon after, for his sixpences are the dominant love token. These were deliberately bent into a distinctive Z-shape, and are said to be the origin of the crooked sixpence nursery rhyme. Other than symbols of love, tokens formed from bent coins were current from the 16th century as good luck talismans.

Copper trade-tokens, 17th century
857: 1668, halfpenny, Newton Abbot, Elizabeth Maning - Decoy, *Newton Abbot*.
858: 1660, farthing, Exeter, John Ledgingham - *Abbotskerswell*

Cast lead or lead/tin-alloy tokens, c17th century
859: circular, incuse, Obv. IS within a border of oblique lines. Rev. E within a border of oblique lines, D. 34mm - *Exeter*.
860: circular, embossed, Obv. AD AH between transverse lines within a linear border. Rev. TC between transverse lines within a linear border, D. 30mm - *Exeter*.
861: circular, embossed, Obv. A:H, Rev. CI, D. 27.5mm - *Exmouth*.
862: oval, uniface, embossed, AV and oblique lines, L. 20.5 - *Exeter*.
863: circular, uniface, incuse, Will: r Taunton, D. 23mm - *Exeter*.
864: circular, uniface, incuse, I.H and foliate within a beaded border, D. 22mm - *Exeter*.
865: circular, uniface, embossed, St Andrew's cross with chevrons in the spandrels, D. 18mm - *Exeter*.
866: circular, uniface, incuse, curlicue and EXON [Exeter] surmounting GG within a beaded border, D. 18.5mm - *Uffculme*.
867: circular, embossed, Obv. cross pattée with a pellet in each spandrel, Rev. CB, D. 22mm - *Uffculme*.
868: rectangular, uniface, embossed, BR CO [?] MG MIDMAR, 23mm x 24.5mm - *Newton Poppleford*.
869: circular, uniface, embossed, cross with pellet in each spandrel D. 15mm - *River Exe, Starcross*.
870: circular, uniface, embossed, cross pattée, D. 21.5mm - *River Exe, Starcross*.
871: circular, uniface, embossed, cross, D. 14mm - *River Exe, Starcross*.
872: circular, uniface, embossed, castle, D. 22.5 - *Exeter*.
873: circular, embossed, Obv. T. rampant horse G, Rev. a dog with H above A below, D. 19mm - *Exeter*.

874: circular, uniface, incuse, anchor - *Newton Abbot.*
875: circular, uniface, embossed, D C - *River Teign, Ringmore.*
876: circular, uniface, embossed, AH - *Alphington.*
877: circular, uniface, embossed, daisy - *Alphington.*
878: circular, uniface, embossed, (?) leaf - *River Teign, Ringmore.*
879: circular, uniface, incised, lines - *River Teign, Coombe Cellars.*
880: circular, uniface, embossed, St Andrew's cross with pellet in each spandrel - *River Teign, Coombe Cellars.*
881: rectangular, uniface, a cross formed from incuse chevrons - *Alphington.*
882: circular, embossed, Obv. Tudor rose and sunburst within a wreathed hoop, Rev. urn with flowers within a wreathed hoop - *River Teign, Ringmore.*

Silver love tokens
883: William III, sixpence - *Stokeinteignhead.*
884: Anne, shilling - *Kingsteignton.*

RELIGOUS MEDALLIONS

By the end of the 15th century the practice of undertaking a pilgrimage had largely died out. Nonetheless, souvenirs continued to be sold at shrines and other religous sites. One form of souvenir is the cast silver, copper-alloy or lead/tin-alloy pendant medallion, which was worn around the neck suspended from a chain, with an embossed iconographic representation on one or both sides. Suspension loops on some medallions of this type are somewhat similar to loops on medieval horse-pendants.

Cast copper-alloy religous medallion, 17th century
885: circular, moulded, Obv. possibly a standing saint and inscribed 'S' ELISA. .APG.PO., Rev. a group of standing figures, D. 15mm - *Haccombe.*

N.B. This inscription refers to either St Elizabeth of Hungary whose cult centred on the German town of Hesse, or St Elizabeth of Portugal.

BUCKLES

Stuart buckles are as varied as their antecedents, and some are very elaborate, frequently with ornate knops and protruding ends to the central bar. Single-loop buckles used in conjunction with personal costume had largely declined by the beginning of James I's reign in favour of the double-loop variety, though on horse harness they remained current for the duration of the 17th century. Metals of manufacture and types of applied-surface decoration are consistent with earlier periods.

Cast copper-alloy asymmetrical double-loop girdle buckles, 1600- 50
886: rounded front, slightly rounded back, 59mm x 41.5mm - *Exeter.*
887: rounded front, straight back, protrusions on ends of central bar, 38mm x 36.5mm - *Cockington.*
888: rounded front, straight back, protrusions on ends of central bar, 37mm x 32mm - *Kingskerswell.*
889: pointed front, slightly concave back, protrusions on ends of central bar, 45.5mm x 37.5mm - *Alphington.*

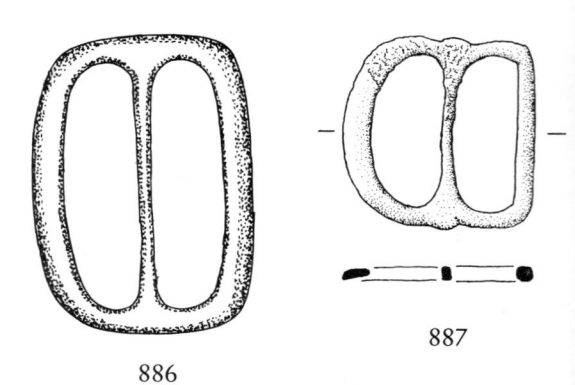

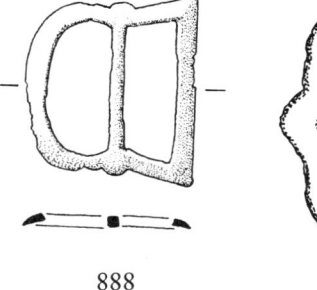

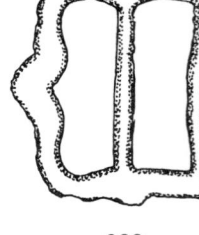

The Stuart Period

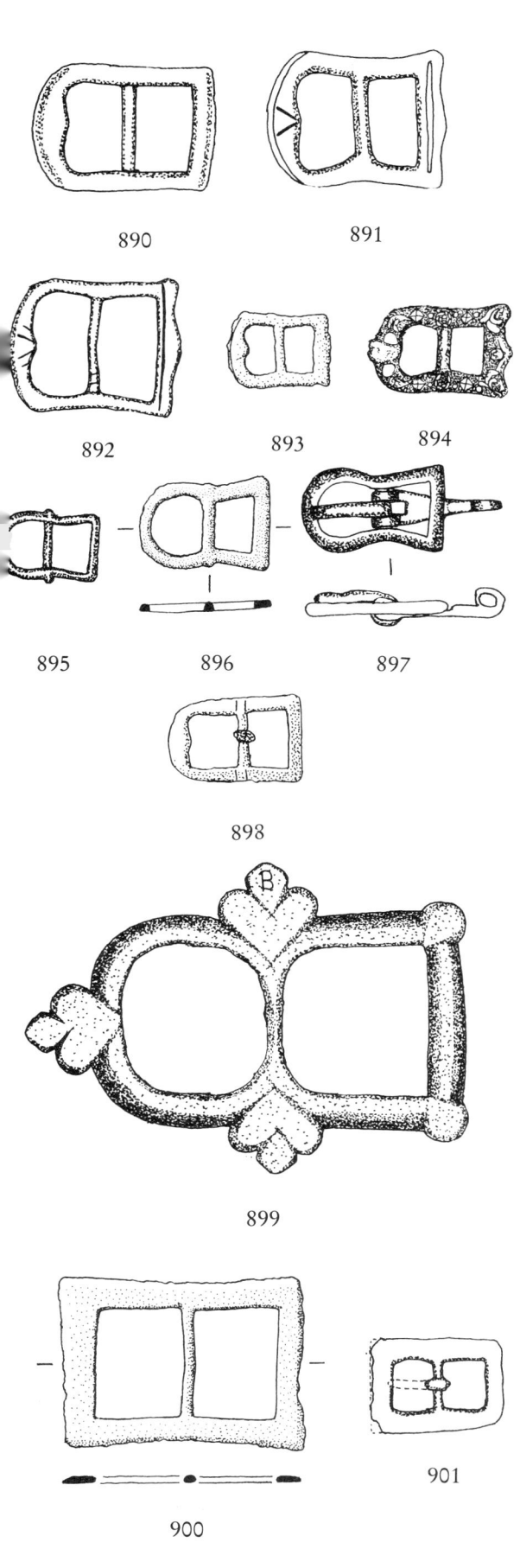

Cast copper-alloy asymmetrical double-loop spur-buckles, 1600-1700

890: rounded front, slightly convex back, narrowed central bar, 28.5mm x 40mm - *Cockington*.

891: rounded front with engraved oblique and border lines, trefoil back with transverse moulded groove, 31.5mm x 39.5mm - *Kingskerswell*.

892: rounded front with oblique engraved lines, raised trefoil back, narrowed central bar, 32mm x 37.5mm - *Cockington*.

893: rounded front with moulded groove, straight back, 17.5mm x 22.5mm - *Cockington*.

894: rounded front with bifid knop, trefoil back, narrowed central bar; moulded foliate, floriate and lozenges with St Andrew's crosses, 22mm x 32mm - *Cockington*.

895: rounded front, straight back, protrusions on ends of narrowed central bar, 16.5mm x 22.5mm - *Alphington*.

896: rounded front, straight back, slight protrusions on ends of central bar, 21.5mm x 29mm - *Cockington*.

897: rounded front, straight back, narrowed central bar, separate copper-alloy tongue and lateral eyed-chape, 20mm x 44mm - *Cockington*.

898: rounded front, straight back, slightly raised central bar, remains of iron tongue, 20mm x 29mm - *Newton Abbot*.

Cast copper-alloy asymmetrical double-loop (?) baldrick buckle, c1628-1700

899: rounded front with trefoil knop, straight back with lobed knops on angles; trefoil protrusions on ends of central bar, incuse stamped B, 70.5mm x 96.5mm - *Kingskerswell*

Copper-alloy rectangular or subrectangular double-loop girdle-buckles, 1600-1700

900: 39mm x 52mm - *Cockington*.

901: abraded edge, fragmented copper-alloy tongue, 21.5mm x 29mm - *Cockington*.

902: 24mm x 34mm - *Stokeinteignhead*.

903: 27.5mm x 29.5mm - Cockington.

904: 20.5mm x 23mm - *Haccombe*.

905: concave sides, protrusions on ends of central bar, copper-alloy tongue, 27mm x 31.5mm - *Alphington*.

906: concave sides, protrusions on ends of central bar, 20.5mm x 26mm - *Haccombe*.

907: concave sides, protrusions on ends of central bar, 15.5mm x 22mm - *Alphington*.

908: tinned, slightly rounded ends, abraded trefoil sides, narrowed central bar, 28mm x 41mm - *Cockington*.

909: pointed knops on ends, lobed protrusions on ends of central bar, engraved curlicues and oblique grooves, 41mm x 48m - *Exeter*.

910: asymmetrical openwork, engraved oblique grooves around edge, 33.5mm x 48.5mm - *Cockington*.

911: fragmented, elaborate frame, asymmetrical openwork, 50mm x 40mm - *Exeter*.

912: tinned, lobed protrusions on ends of central bar, asymmetrical openwork, moulded beaded border, copper-alloy tongue, 37.5mm x 58.5mm - *Haccombe*.

Cast copper-alloy subrectangular (?) spur-buckle, c1650

913: tinned, elaborate frame, asymmetrical openwork, 35mm x 52mm - *Cockington*.

Cast copper-alloy rectangular (?) spur-buckles, c1650-1700

914: lobed knops on angles, bifid knops on ends, bifid protrusions on ends of central bar, 27.5mm x 37mm - *Cockington*.

915: lobed knops on angles, trefoil knops on ends, wedge-shaped protrusions on ends of central bar, 32mm x 52mm - *Exeter*.

Cast copper-alloy oval double-loop buckles, with or without folded sheet copper-alloy plates, 1650-1700

916: stud hole in plate, 23mm x 38mm - *Cockington*.

917: moulded roundels, 23.5mm x 29mm - *Newton Abbot*.

Cast copper-alloy symmetrical double-loop (?) shoe- or spur-buckles, with or without folded sheet copper-alloy plate and stud chape, 1600-50

918: rounded ends, trefoil sides, raised frame at junctions of central bar, punched circles and fleurets, 28.5mm x 41.5mm - *Cockington*.

919: rounded ends, trefoil sides, raised frame at junctions of central bar, 27mm x 40mm - *Cockington*.

920: rounded ends, bifed sides, copper-alloy plate and stud chape, 22.5mm x 37.5mm - *Cockington*.

921: rounded ends, concave sides, raised frame at junctions of narrowed central bar, 21mm x 31mm - *Cockington*.

Cast copper-alloy symmetrical double-loop shoe-buckle, c1650-1700

922: rounded ends, narrowed central bar, moulded roundles, 22.5mm x 33mm - *Newton Abbot*.

Cast copper-alloy oval double-loop girdle buckles, 1600-1700

923: tinned, trefoil knops, trefoil protrusions on ends of central bar, circular openwork, 50mm x 85mm - *Exeter*.

924: trefoil knops on ends engraved with fleurets, trefoil sides, trefoil protrusions on ends of central bar, copper-alloy tongue, 46.5mm x 67mm - *Littlehempston*.

Cast copper-alloy trapezium-shaped double-loop girdle-buckles, c1600-1700

925: tinned, pointed ends, lobed knops around frame, asymmetrical openwork, copper-alloy tongue, 40.5mm x 83mm - *Chudleigh*.

926: pointed ends, bifid protrusions at ends of central bar, 34.5mm x 50mm - *Cockington*.

Cast copper-alloy trapezium-shaped double-loop spur-buckles, c1600-50

927: pointed ends, protrusions on ends of central bar, punched circles, crescents and fleurets, 24mm x 49mm - *Cockington*.

928: tinned, pointed ends, protrusions on ends of central bar, 22mm x 43mm - *Cockington*.

929: pointed ends, protrusions on ends of central bar, punched fleurets, 25mm x 47mm - *Newton Abbot*.

930: trefoil ends, slight protrusion on ends of central bar, engraved notch and transverse line on both ends, copper-alloy tongue, 27.5mm x 42mm - *Cockington*.

931: trefoil ends, protrusion on ends of central bar, engraved notch on both ends, 22mm x 33mm - *Chudleigh*.

932: trefoil ends, trefoil sides, bifid protrusions on ends of narrowed central bar, 28mm x 40mm - *Haccombe*.

933: bifid narrow end with lobed knops on angles, quatrefoil

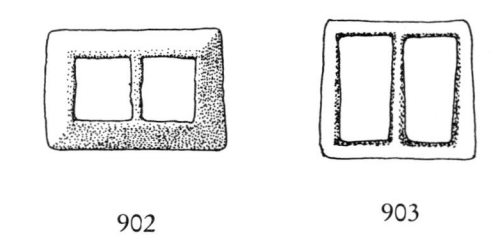

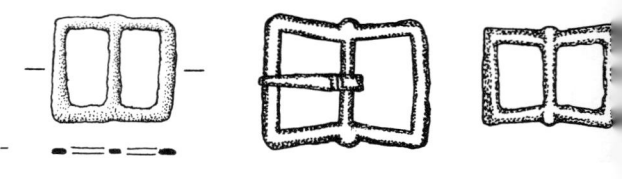

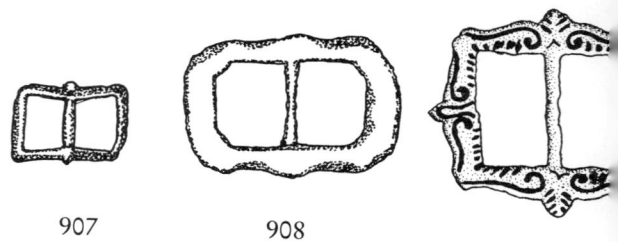

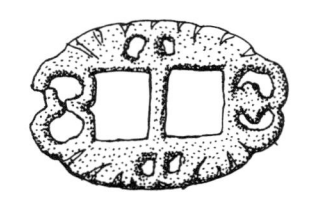

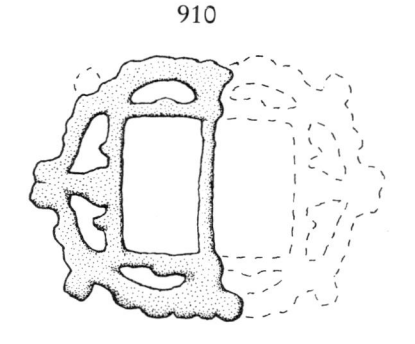

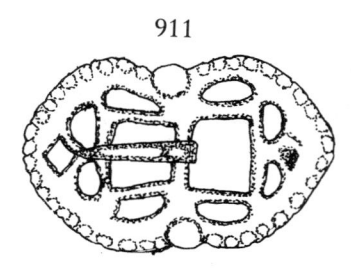

The Stuart Period 143

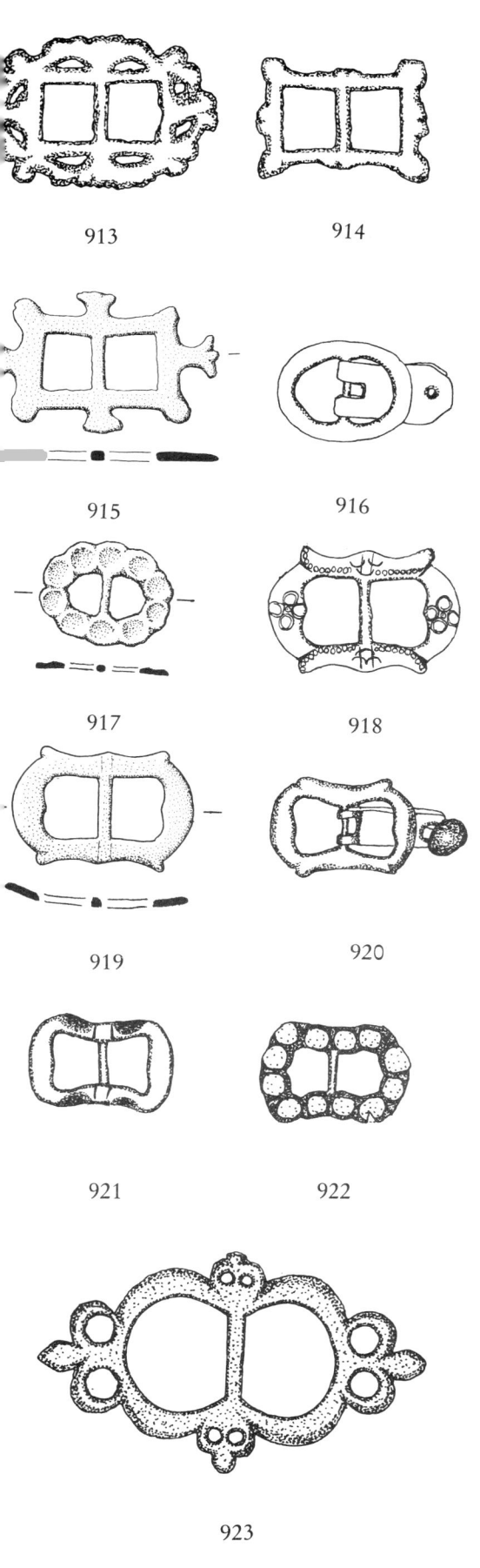

wide end with large lobed-knops on angles, 41mm x 27mm - *Exeter*.
934: 24.5mm x 24mm - *Exeter*.

Cast copper-alloy rectangular or oval double-loop sword-belt hanger, 1600-1700
935: rectangular, abraded lateral circular suspension loop, 49.5mm x 35mm - *Chudleigh*.

Cast silver asymmetrical buckle with drilled frame for separate spindle, 1660-1720
936: trefoil knop on each end, moulded foliate, 32mm x 43mm - *Aishe*.

Cast copper-alloy asymmetrical double-loop possible shoe- or knee-buckles with drilled frame for separate spindle, c1660-1720s
937: rounded front, lobed knops on straight end, slight protrusion at spindle holes, engraved circles, curvilinear and oblique lines, 26mm x 36mm - *Haccombe*.
938: rounded front, 25mm x 29.5mm - *Bishopsteignton*.
939: rounded front, 22mm x 27mm - *Newton Abbot*.
940: rounded front, copper-alloy spindle and tube with two spikes, 25mm x 22mm - *Exeter*.

Cast copper-alloy trapezium-shaped shoe-buckle with drilled frame for separate spindle, c1660-1720s
941: moulded quatrefoil knops on ends, embossd trefoil protrusions around spindle holes, copper-alloy spindle and fragmented stud-chape, maker's mark R.WH stamped on chape, 31.5mm x 53mm -*Haccombe*.

Cast copper-alloy trapezium-shaped or oval shoe- or knee-buckles with drilled frames for separate spindles, c1660-1720s
942: rounded notched-ends, moulded bifid protrusions around spindleholes, 24mm x 29mm - *Bishopsteignton*.
943: rounded ends, moulded collar each side of spindle holes, 21mm x 33mm - *Haccombe*.
944: rounded ends with moulded border line, notch with engraved oblique and longitudinal lines at both ends, raised frame above spindle holes; copper-alloy spindle, tongue and fragmented anchor chape, 18mm x 33mm - *Stokeinteignhead*.
945: moulded quatrefoil knops on ends, moulded bifed protrusions around spindle holes, 24mm x 34.5mm - *Teigngrace*.
946: rounded notched-ends, narrowed frame at sides, raised around spindle holes; copper-alloy spindle, tongue and anchor chape, 21.5mm x 42mm - *Haccombe*.
947: rounded ends with slightly lobed knops with engraved oblique lines, engraved oblique lines each side, 22.5mm x 33.5mm - *Bishopsteignton*.
948: rounded ends, moulded roundel each side of both spindle holes, 26.5mm x 37.5mm - *Kingsteignton*.
949: rounded ends, moulded collar each side of both spindle holes, 22.5mm x 36.5mm - *Haccombe*.
950: concave notched-ends, each with two circular openwork, bifid sides, 20mm x 33mm - *Haccombe*.
951: rounded ends with engraved oblique lines; copper-alloy spindle, tongue and anchor chape, 17mm x 23.5mm - *Exeter*.

952: quatrefoil ends; copper-alloy spindle, tongue and stud chape (stud lost), 14mm x 21mm - *Exeter*.
953: moulded wedge-shaped knop each end, moulded trefoil sides, 15.5mm x 22mm - *Exeter*.
954: moulded transverse and oblique lines on ends and sides, remains of copper-alloy spindle, 23mm x 30.5mm - *Haccombe*.
955: notched end; copper-alloy spindle and fragmented chape, 20mm x 32mm - *Newton Abbot*.

Cast copper-alloy subrectangular shoe-buckles with drilled frames for separate spindles, c1660-1720s
956: pointed ends, slightly trefoil sides, moulded collar each side of both spindle holes, 30.5mm x 47mm - *Haccombe*.
957: flattened cinquefoil ends, engraved oblique lines on inside ends of frame, slight moulded collar each side of both spindle holes, 30.5mm x 48.5mm - *Ringmore*.

Cast copper-alloy rectangular or subrectangular shoe- or knee-buckles with drilled frames for separate spindles, c1660-1720s
958: engraved oblique lines in angles, copper-alloy spindle and fragmented chape, 19mm x 26mm - *Haccombe*.
959: moulded groove around frame; copper-alloy spindle, tongue and fragmented chape, 18.5mm x 22mm - *Cockington*.
960: oblique corners, moulded line around ends; copper-alloy spindle, tongue and fragmented chape, 18mm x 21.5mm - *Cockington*.
961: pointed ends, engraved transverse lines; copper-alloy spindle, tongue and fragmented chape, 15.5mm x 24mm - *Newton Abbot*.
962: oblique corners, moulded lines on ends; copper-alloy spindle, tongue and stud chape, stamped maker's mark WW, 15.5mm x 31.5mm - *Exeter*.
963: copper-alloy spindle and remains of chape, 17mm x 21.5mm - *Cockington*.
964: copper-alloy spindle, tongue and stud chape, 16mm x 27.5mm - *Stokeinteignhead*.

Cast copper-alloy oval knee-buckles with drilled frames for separate spindles, c1660-1720s
965: engraved circles and curvilinear; copper-alloy spindle, tongue and stud chape (stud lost), incuse stamped maker's mark BoT on chape, 16.5mm x 18mm - *Haccombe*.
966: 18mm x 21.5mm - *Cockington*.
967: moulded oblique grooves, 30mm x 32mm - *Abbotskerswell*.

BUTTONS

Types of metal button current in the later Tudor period extended well into the 17th, however, several new kinds became fashionable. Pimple buttons regained their popularity in the middle of the 17th century and are either two-piece flat or three-piece hollow domed. Cast lead/tin-alloy one-piece flat buttons with moulded or engraved decoration were commonplace for much of the period as were large one-piece cast copper-alloy hollow or solid-domed buttons. Invariably the latter are ornamented with intricate engraved foliate, floriate or a cross and frequently gilded or silvered and occasionally enamelled. Variations of this button are known, viz. hexagonal or those with

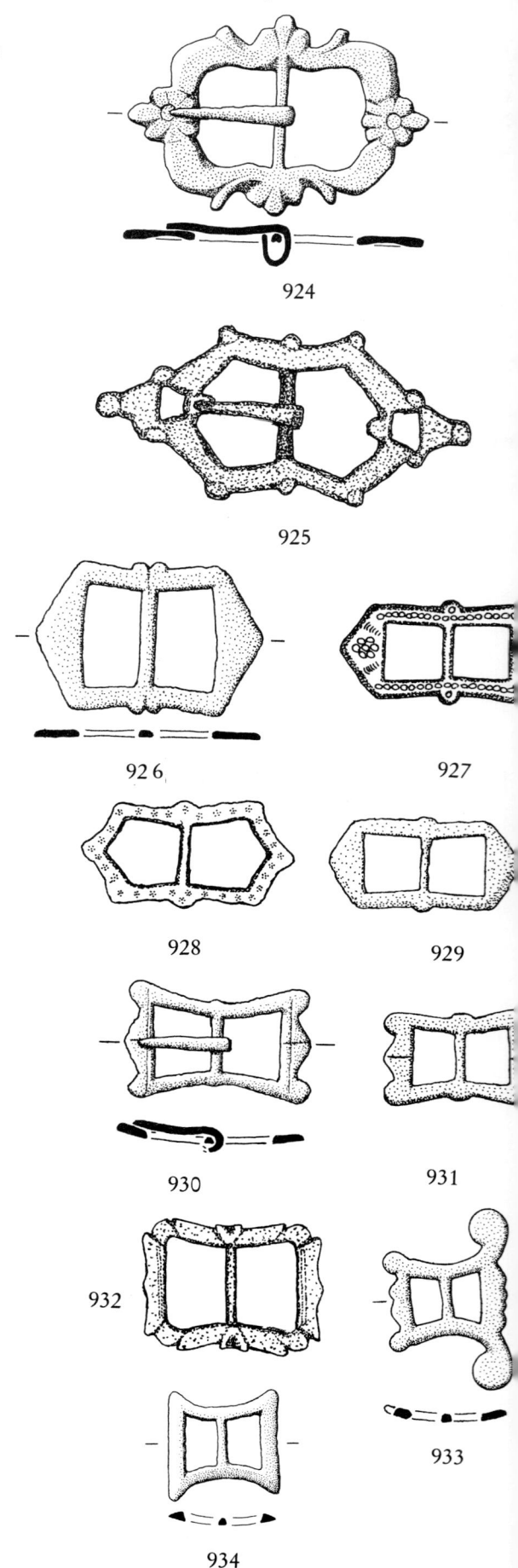

The Stuart Period

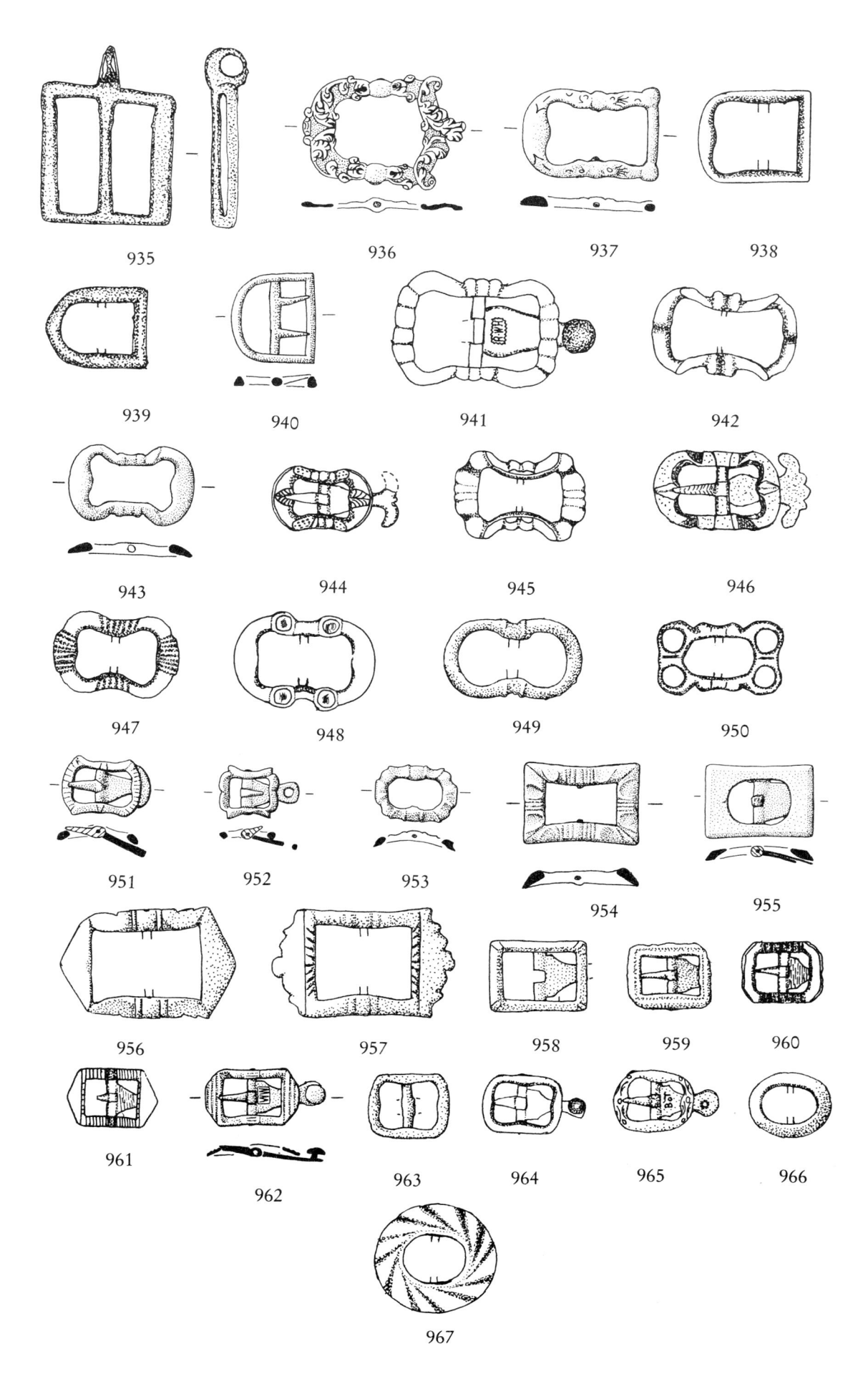

935 936 937 938
939 940 941 942
943 944 945 946
947 948 949 950
951 952 953 954 955
956 957 958 959 960
961 962 963 964 965 966
967

moulded decoration. Later in the 17th century plain or engraved flat two-piece buttons with separate copper-alloy wire shanks and iron-backed domed two or three-piece buttons, either solid or hollow, came into general use. One-, two- or three-piece solid or hollow silver spherical buttons and flat one- or two-piece silver buttons were widely used by the more wealthy.

Cast copper-alloy one-piece circular hollow-domed buttons, 17thcentury

968: engraved fleuret and foliate, border of small punched circles, D. 27mm - *Haccombe*.

969: engraved fleuret and foliate, border of small punched circles, D 25mm - *Combeinteignhead*.

970: abraded perimeter, engraved five-petal fleuret, border of small punched circles, D. 25.5mm - *Ringmore*.

971: abraded perimeter, traces of rust adhering to back and shank, engraved fleuret, border of small punched circles, D. 26mm - *Ringmore*.

972: engraved fleuret, D. 26mm - *River Teign, Shaldon*.

973: abraded perimeter, engraved curlicues, circles and lines, border of punched dots, D. 25mm - *Alphington*.

974: engraved voided cross, central concentric circles, bifids in spandrels, D. 29mm - *Cockington*.

975: engraved six-petal floret and fleurets, border of oblique lines, D. 26mm - *Cockington*.

976: engraved St Andrew's cross, crescents in spandrels, D. 22.5mm - *Coffinswell*.

977: St Andrews cross formed from small punched circles, each arm terminating in an engraved circle, engraved circles and crescents in spandrels, D. 26mm - *Ringmore*.

978: fleuret and border of small punched circles, D. 26mm - *Haccombe*.

979: moulded fleuret within a sexfoil, fragmented shank, D. 24mm - *Haccombe*.

980: moulded bust of a cavalier, abraded edge, D. 29mm - *Cockwood*.

981: moulded central and six peripheral roundels, each with a star and pellet, D. 28mm - *Stokeinteignhead*.

982: blue and white enamelled fleuret, D. 22.5mm - *Haccombe*.

Cast copper-alloy one-piece hollow-domed hexagonal button, 17th century

983: voided hexagon with six voided arms formed from punched dots, border of punched dots; circles, crescents and curlicues formed from punched dots between arms, fragmented shank, D. 25.5mm - *Marldon*.

Cast copper-alloy one-piece flat circular buttons, 17th century

984: engraved and punched quatrefoil and curvilinear, border of punched dots, D. 14.5mm - *Haccombe*.

985: downturned rim, slightly recessed, engraved fleuret, D. 20mm - *Cockington*.

986: engraved six-point star and fleuret within moulded circle, D. 14mm - *Cockington*.

987: moulded fleuret within a circle, D. 12mm - *Cockington*.

Cast lead/tin-alloy one-piece flat circular button, 17th century

988: turned-over edge, moulded multi-point star and concentric

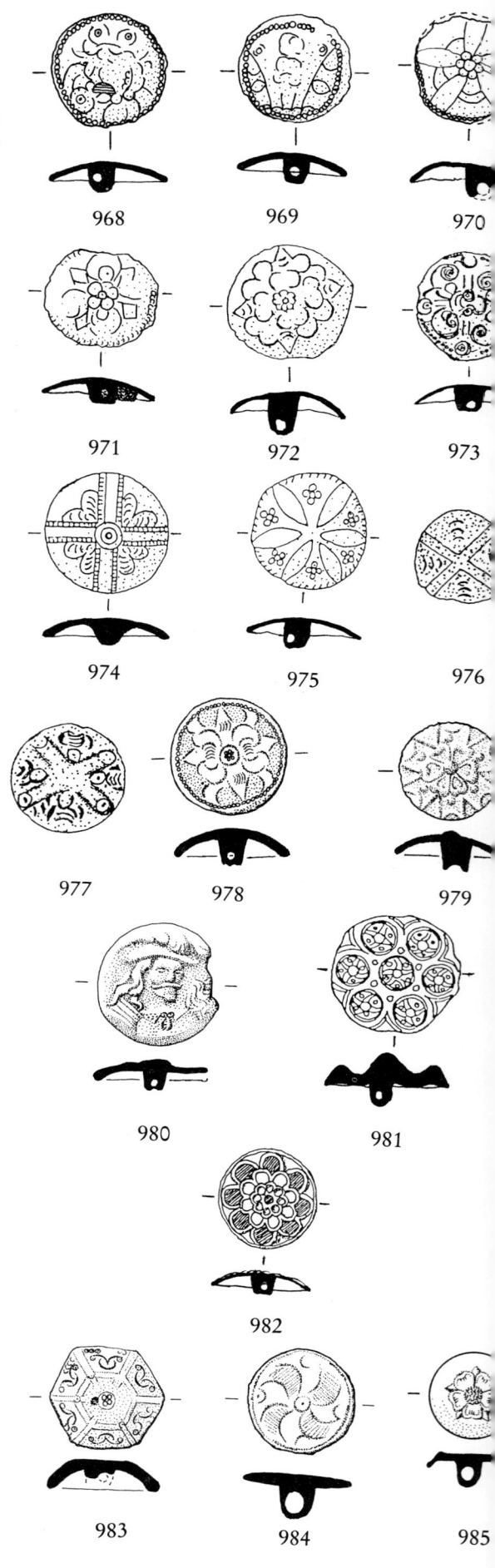

The Stuart Period 147

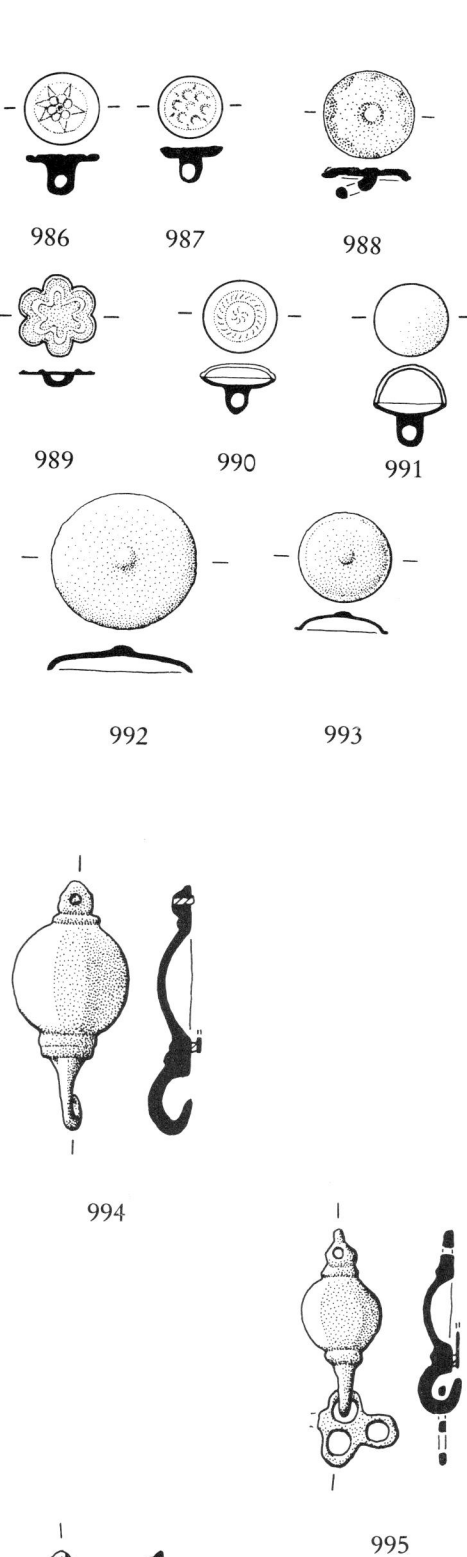

circles, D. 17mm - *Cockington*.

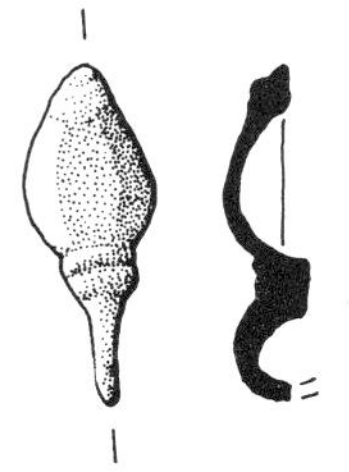

Cast lead/tin-alloy one-piece flat sexfoil button, 17th century

989: moulded concentric sexfoils, D. 14mm - *Cockington*.

Cast lead/tin-alloy two-piece biconvex button

990: punched dots forming concentric circles and curvilinear, D. 14.5mm - *Cockington*.

Cast copper-alloy and lead/tin-alloy two-piece biconvex button, 17th century

991: copper-alloy shank and base, lead/tin-alloy top, D. 14mm - *Cockington*.

Cast copper-alloy one-piece domed pimple-buttons, 17th century

992: shank lost, D. 28mm - *Haccombe*.
993: shank lost, D. 18mm - *Haccombe*.

CLOTHING FASTENERS

A type of fastener attributable to the 17th century is somewhat more robust than its antecedents. Though classified for use with clothing, precisely which kind of garment isn't known. Associated artefactual evidence implies they were multi-function fasteners used with leather or fabric straps, or costume, for one has a remnant of an eye attached to the hook, whilst another is known with a 17th-century spur-buckle similarly affixed.

Cast from copper alloy they come in several sizes and are either circular or oval. The body is always convex, invariably with three longitudinal facets, with a substantial integral hook on one end and frequently a moulded projection with a rivet hole on the other. Some fasteners of this type have only a slight projection, or indeed it is completely absent, therefore an integral copper-alloy rivet replaces the rivet hole. A separate sheet copper-alloy backplate is held by an integral or separate inset iron or copper-alloy rivet where the hook joins the body. Similarly a separate copper-alloy or iron rivet, which passes through the rivet hole in the projection, secures the backplate's other end. Attachment to the garment etc was achieved by trapping the material between the backplate and body and then riveting. Examples have been recovered with fragments of leather in situ between the backplate and body.

Cast copper-alloy convex clothing-fasteners, 17th century

994: circular, three longitudinal moulded facets, two moulded transverse collars at juncture of hook and body with integral rivet, lobed protrusion with rivet hole and moulded transverse collar, remains of iron rivet, backplate lost, 46mm x 22mm - *Bishopsteignton*.

995: circular, three longitudinal facets, moulded transverse collar at juncture of hook and body with integral rivet, lobed protrusion with rivet hole and moulded transverse collar, remains of iron rivet, fragment of sheet copper-alloy backplate, fragmented probable quatrefoil eyelet attached to hook, 34mm x 16mm - *Cockington*.

996: oval, three longitudinal facets, two moulded transverse collars at juncture of body and fragmented hook with integral rivet, lobed protrusion with remains of integral copper-alloy rivet, backplate lost, 33mm x 13mm - *Stokeinteignhead*.

The Stuart Period
Distribution of metal detector finds in Southern Devon

1. Abbotskerswell (**MC, MA**)
2. Aishe (**MC, MA**)
3. Alphington (**MC, MA**)
4. Axminster (**MC, MA**)
5. Beesands Beach (**MC, MA**)
6. Berry Pomeroy (**A**)
7. Bishopsteignton (**MA**)
8. Bovey Tracey (**MC, MA**)
9. Brixham (**A**)
10. Christow (**C**)
11. Churston (**C**)
12. Chudleigh (**HC, MC, MA**)
13. Cockington (**HC, MC, MA**)
14. Cockwood (**MC, MA**)
15. Coffinswell (**MC, MA**)
16. Combeinteignhead (**MC, MA**)
17. Colaton Raleigh (**A**)
18. Clyst St Mary (**A**)
19. Clyst St George (**A**)
20. Decoy, Newton Abbot (**MC, MA**)
21. Denbury (**MA**)
22. Exeter (**MC, MA**)
23. Exmouth (**MC, MA**)
24. Gappah (**C, A**)
25. Goodrington Beach, Paignton (**MC**)
26. Haccombe (**MC, MA**)
27. Harbertonford (**A**)
28. Kenn (**A**)
29. Kingskerswell (**MC, MA**)
30. Kingsteignton (**MC, MA**)
31. Littlehempston (**MA**)
32. Maidencombe (**MC, MA**)
33. Marldon (**A**)
34. Mamhead (**A**)
35. Mansands (**A**)
36. Musbury (**MA**)
37. Newton Abbot (**MC, MA**)
38. Newton Poppleford (**MC**)
39. Offwell (**MC**)
40. Pymouth (**MC, MA**)
41. Poltimore (**MA**)
42. Ringmore (**MC, MA**)
43. River Dart, Kingswear (**C**)
44. River Exe, Starcross (**MC, MA**)
45. River Teign, Teignmouth (**A**)
46. River Teign, Combe Cellars (**MC, MA**)
47. River Teign, Ringmore (**MC, MA**)
48. River Teign, Shaldon (**MA**)
49. Seaton (**C**)
50. Stantor Barton (**MC, MA**)
51. Stokeinteignhead (**MC, MA**)
52. Stoke Canon (**A**)
53. Teigngrace (**A**)
54. Totnes (**MC, MA**)
55. Two Mile Oak (**MC, MA**)
56. Uffculme (**MC, MA**)
57. West Ogwell (**C, MA**)
58. Wolborough, Newton Abbot (**MC, MA**)

Key: **C** = single coin **MC** = multiple coin **HC** = hoard of coins
     A = artefact **MA** = multiple artefact

R. EXE
R. CULM
R. CLYST
R. OTTER
R. AXE

56

52
41
22
3
18
19
39
4
36
49
38
17
TEIGN
10
28
34 44 23
12 14
8
24
53 30 7 45
37 46
58 20 16 47 42 48
57 26 51
21 55 1 29 15 32
R. DART
50 13
31 33
6
54
2
25
11
9
27
35
43

5

Scale = 1:316,000 (approx.)

5 miles
8 kilometres

Based upon Ordnance Survey mapping with the permission of the
Controller of Her Majesty's Stationery Office, © Crown copyright.

MOUNTS

Examples of metalwork mounts depicted here, are thought to be c17th century or later. Similar to earlier types, attribution of the smallest may be from personal costume straps and the larger from elsewhere. One form of mount which can be positively assigned is the bridle boss.

Mouth-piece ends of early medieval curb-bits were normally decorated with heraldic, pseudo-heraldic or decorative metal appliqués, but before the end of the 15th century another type of mount for bits came into being and remained fashionable throughout the Tudor period. These bridle-bosses are circular and made from sheet copper alloy in a pronounced umbonate-shape. Some are elaborately engraved and gilded and invariably have several rivet holes around the perimeter whereby securement was achieved to the mouth-piece end. Frequently, decorative copper-alloy moulded fleuret rivet-heads remain in situ. However, many bosses are quite plain apart from a number of moulded roundels. This type often have a central rivet hole or none at all; the latter were soldered to the mouth-piece end.

The Stuart period heralded cast copper-alloy or lead/tin-alloy bridle-bosses, frequently gilded or silvered, which invariably featured more elaborate shapes based on the circle with embossing and/or openwork. Affixing was achieved by riveting.

Cast copper-alloy flat mounts with integral lugs, 17th century

997: vesica-shaped, traces of gilt, bifid protrusions, lobed knop on one end, engraved foliate and fleuret, punched crescents border, 91mm x 32mm - *Exmouth*.

998: circular, rectangular side-projections (one lost), engraved foliate and fleuret, 33mm x 34mm - *Cockington*.

Cast copper-alloy flat mounts with integral lugs, c17th-18th century

999: subrectangular, tinned, pointed knops, fragment of leather attached to one lug, 39mm x 40mm - *Cockington*.

1000: rectangular, flat, engraved lozenges and oblique lines, 16mm x 11mm - *Stokeinteignhead*.

1001: cordate, flat, gilded, engraved oblique and vertical lines, lobed knop, 20.5mm x 14.5mm - *Cockington*.

Cast copper-alloy domed mounts with integral lugs, c17th-18th century

1002: sexfoil, triangular openwork, moulded oblique grooves, D. 28mm - *Cockington*.

1003: circular, engraved concentric circles, D. 17mm - *Cockington*.

Cast copper-alloy flat mount with lug and separate rivets, c17th-century

1004: shield-shaped, rectangular openwork, two rivet holes, 28.5mm x 27mm - *Cockington*.

Cast copper-alloy flat mount with integral annular ring, c17th-18th century

1005: abraded downturned edge, punched dots forming a fleuret and concentric circles, D. 30mm - *Stokeinteignhead*.

Cast and forged copper-alloy hooked mount with separate rivets, c17th-18th century

1006: oval, oval openwork, sprung clip, 38mm x 12mm - *Exeter*.

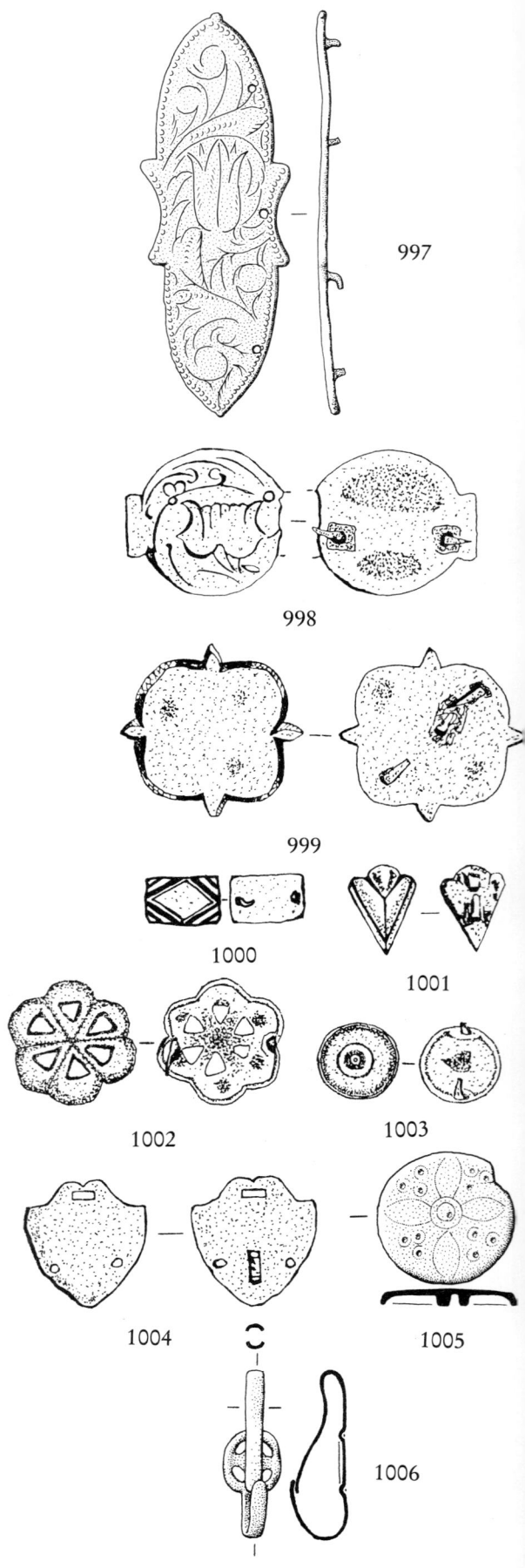

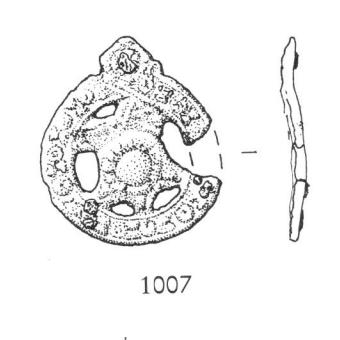

The Stuart Period   149

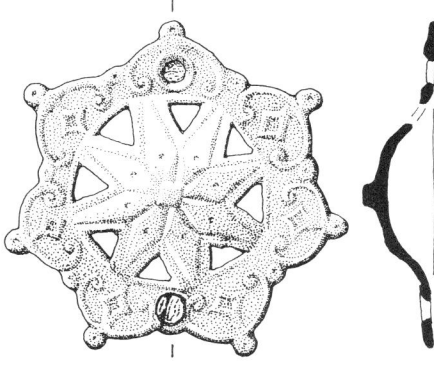

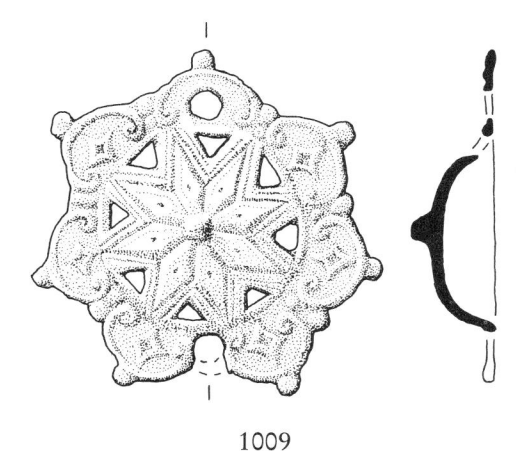

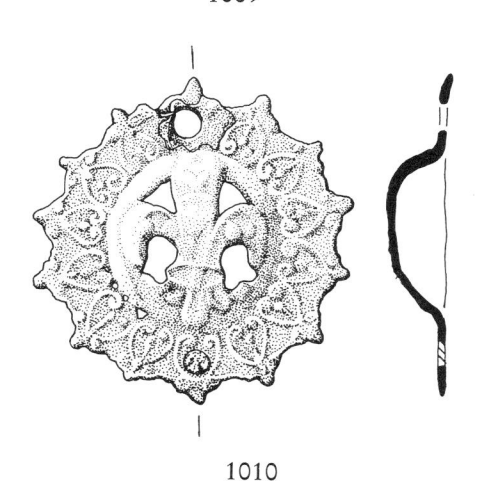

Cast lead/tin-alloy flat mount with separate rivets, c17th-18th century

1007: fragmented, pointed knop, moulded fleurets and curvilinear, asymmetrical openwork, three rivet holes, remains of three iron rivets, 40.5mm x 34mm - *Haccombe*

Cast copper-alloy umbonate bridle-bosses, 17th century

1008: septfoil, lobed knops, triangular openwork forming an eight-point star; moulded central lozenge, eight-point stars and dots; moulded curlicues and lozenges border, two rivet holes, remains of iron rivets, D. 64.5mm - *Exeter.*

1009: septfoil, similar to No.988, D. 65.5mm - *Cockwood.*

1010: multifoil, 14 lobed knops, triangular and asymmetrical openwork forming a fleur-de-lis with abraded moulding, moulded curlicues and dots border, two rivet holes, one iron rivet, D. 63mm - *Harbertonford.*

1011: multifoil, fragmented, probably 14 pointed knops, moulded central roundel and wavy-armed multifoil and border of chevrons, two rivet holes, D. 56.5mm - *Littlehempston.*

1012: octofoil, eight lobed knops, moulded hominoid face, abraded border of moulded ovals or subrectangles, three rivet holes, three copper-alloy rivets, D. 65.5mm - *Exmouth.*

1013: circular, irregular multi lobed-knops, moulded central fleuret, radiating arms, curvilinear, pellets and quatrefoils, two rivet holes, D. 63mm - *Clyst St Mary.*

1014: circular, abraded perimeter, asymmetrical openwork forming a fleur-de-lis with abraded moulding, moulded curvilinear and pellets, two rivet holes, D. 56mm - *Axminster.*

1015: multifoil, 18 abraded trefoil knops, asymmetrical openwork, moulded central fleuret, moulded cordates and curvilinear, two rivet holes, one iron rivet, iron corrosion around rivet holes, D. 66mm - *Musbury.*

1016: multifoil, abraded and fragmented perimeter, moulded fleuret, radiating pointed and ropework arms, ropework border, two rivet holes, D. 61.5mm - *Axminster.*

1017: multifoil, six large and six small rounded knops; cordate, circular and oval openwork, moulded star, curvilinear and ropework, two rivet holes, D. 47.5mm - *Mamhead.*

1018: multifoil, six pointed and six abraded trefoil knops, asymmetrical openwork; moulded curvilinear, concentric ovals and central fleuret, two rivet holes, D. 60mm - *Haccombe.*

1019: multifoil, abraded 12 large pointed knops and 12 small lobed- knops, asymmetrical openwork; moulded central roundel, curvilinear and pellets, D. 54mm - *Combeinteignhead.*

1020: multifoil, six lobed and six pointed knops, moulded bust and foliate, three rivet holes, three copper-alloy rivets, D. 64mm - *Cockington.*

1021: multifoil, ten lobed knops, triangular openwork; moulded central roundel, curvilinear, fleur-de-lis and transverse lines, (?) ten rivet holes, three copper-alloy rivets with moulded concentric circle and pellets head, remains of iron mouthpiece end, D. 54mm - *Haccombe.*

150

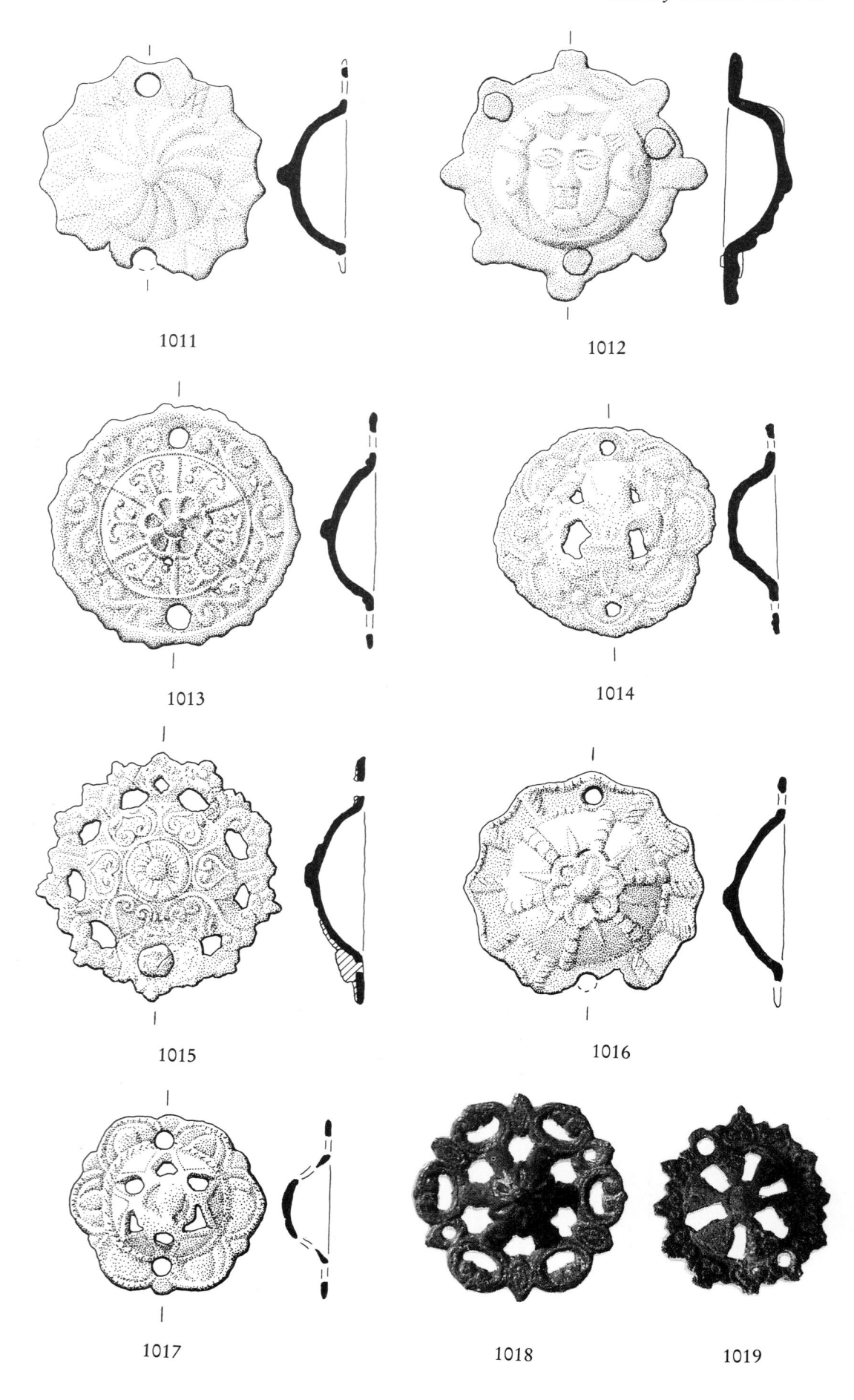

1011

1012

1013

1014

1015

1016

1017

1018

1019

History Beneath Our Feet

The Stuart Period

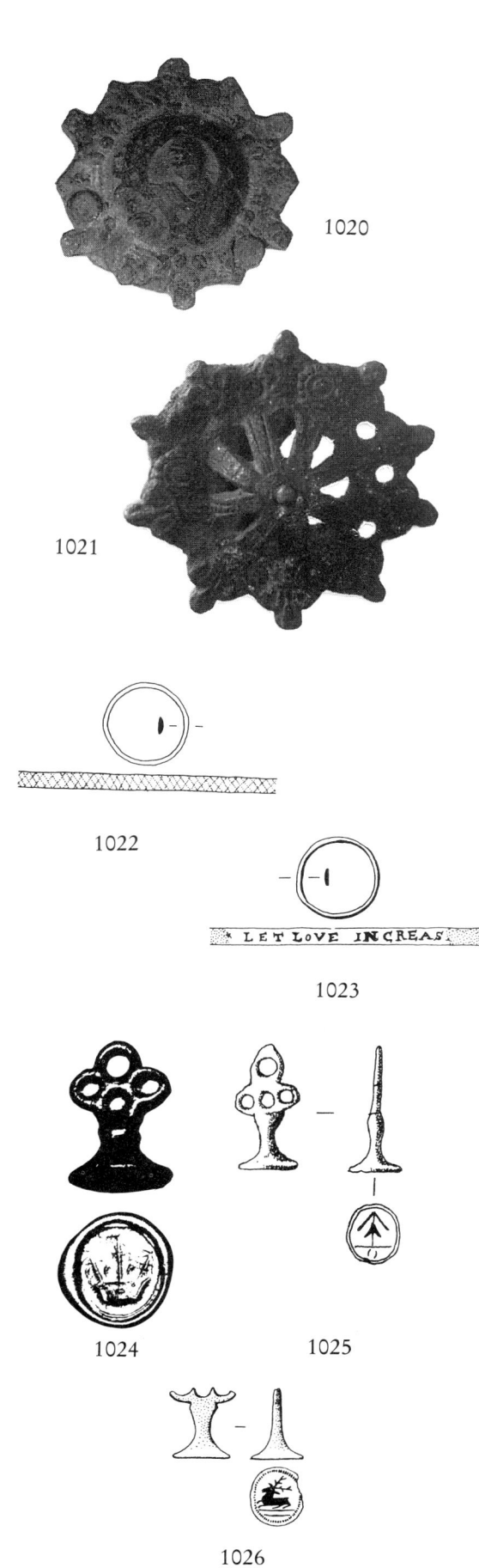

FINGER RINGS

In the 17th century precious metal finger-rings were confined to the wealthy, whilst lower classes wore base metal types which frequently were gilded. Finger rings embellished with large bezels of cut multi-gemstones, foil-backed glass or paste gems increased in popularity. Many bezel finger-rings of this period have richly engraved and enamelled shoulders or even the complete hoop so ornamented. Bezels are normally rectangular or circular, of which the former are occasionally set with a sharp-pointed diamond which was used for writing on glass, especially window panes.

Gold or silver-gilt posy finger-rings also became much more fashionable with ladies who wore them on the thumb as wedding rings. Hoops are usually plain, although decorated examples are known, with inscriptions engraved inside. More familiar types of gold finger-ring current as wedding rings have either a plain or decorated hoop. Several types of finger-ring popular in preceeding centuries remained current throughout the 17th, viz: signet, magical, decade, serjeants, commemorative and peasant. The latter class are base metal or low-grade gold facsimilies of contemporary or older styles of good-quality finger-ring and may have bezels set with semi-precious, glass or past gemstones.

Gold finger-ring, 17th century
1022: semi-circular cross-section hoop, cross-hatched engraving, size N, external D. 19mm, internal D. 16.5mm - *Cockington*.

Gold posy finger-ring, 17th century
1023: slightly semi-circular cross-section hoop, inscribed inside LET LOVE INCREAS[.], evidence of being enlarged which has obliterated most of the last letter E, external D. 18.5mm, internal D. 16mm - *Poltimore*.

SEAL MATRICES

Types of personal pendant seal matrices current throughout the later Middle Ages and Tudor period remained in vogue in the Stuart era when they were more correctly known as 'fob-seal' matrices. Made of precious or base metal, with either an integral or separate die, they were suspended from watch-chains or ribbons and carried in the breeches waistband fob-pocket. The more costly gold or silver fob-seals are sometimes provided with an intaglio or engraved gemstone, or have the device engraved direct. Base metal fob-seals are normally gilded or silvered and have directly engraved devices or devices engraved on semi-precious gemstones or glass dies.

One form of fob-seal matrice of this period has a revolving die with an engraving on each face, whilst another revolving kind has three die-faces on a triangular matrix. Both types have elaborate openwork bodies.

Die iconography is infinite, viz: the lion, marks of individual merchants, owner's initial/s surmounted by a crown, the sacred monogram IHC or IHS, other religous designs, miscellaneous obscure devices, occupational and name related designs, heraldic devices, and 'Sohou' hunting scenes. Legends may be Old French, Middle English or Latin, using lettering of Lombardic capitals, black letter, or Roman capitals.

A not uncommon 17th-century seal matrix is the cruciform which has quadruple circular-dies. This type is known in base metal or silver and usually has pseudo-heraldic or obscure devices, a different one on each face. Frequently, at the centre of the cross is circular openwork. A bipartite type, much the same as the former, is also known. The popularity of clay pipe smoking in the 17th century saw the development of a host of different types of copper-alloy or silver tamper (or stopper) for compressing tobacco in the pipe bowl. One form of tamper is integral with a finger ring, some of which have engraved devices on the bezel. Seal finger-rings of precious or base metal with engraved bezel-dies also remained popular.

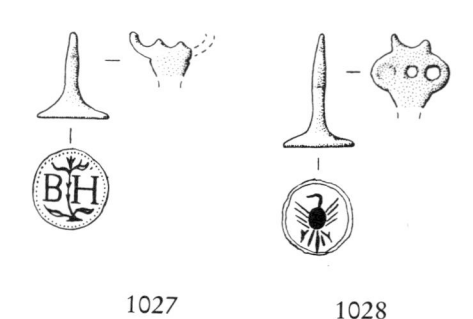

Cast copper-alloy fob-seal matrice, 17th century
1024: oval, ship, circular cross-section handle, quatrefoil suspension loop, 21mm x 18mm - River Teign, *Teignmouth*.
1025: oval, obscure conjoined arrows, circular cross-section handle, quatrefoil suspension loop, 29mm x 14mm - *Stokeinteignhead*.
1026: oval, stag within a beaded border, circular cross-section handle, fragmented quatrefoil suspension loop, 16mm x 13mm - *Stoke Canon*.
1027: oval, foliate and fleuret between B & H, circular cross-section handle, fragmented quatrefoil suspension loop, 17mm x 16mm - *Ringmore*.
1028: oval, stylised bird, circular cross-section handle, fragmented unfettled quatrefoil suspension loop, 22.5mm x 15mm - *Clyst St George*.

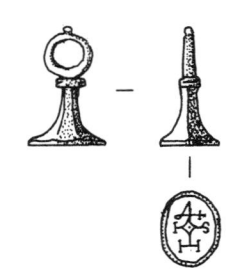

Cast silver fob-seal matrix, 17th century
1029: oval, stylised IHS, hexagonal cross-section handle, circular suspension loop, 23mm x 14mm - *Alphington*.

Cast copper-alloy multi-die matrice, c17th century
1030: cruciform-shaped, circular openwork, circular dies: swan, heart, two arrows and (?) eye, abstract star, (?) fleury, 32mm x 15mm - *Haccombe*.
1031: cruciform-shaped, circular openwork, circular dies (one lost), abraded devices, 39mm x 13.5mm - *Stantor Barton*.

Cast copper-alloy double revolving matrix, c17th century
1032: circular, bust of (?) Charles I and a standing female figure holding a sprig of foliate in her right hand and supporting an anchor with her left hand, crescent-shaped handle, circular suspension loop, 13mm x 18mm - *Abbotskerswell*.

N.B. No.1024 was possibly a merchant's seal and considering the die impression and the provenance, perhaps he was involved in local sea-trade. At the official opening of Newton Abbot Museum in 1982, the Mayoress of Newton Abbot used this seal to mark a letter of identification. No.1032 was found by a workman behind a fixed bench-seat in the Court Farm Inn.

CLOTH SEALS
The practice of marking newly manufactured cloth with lead seals remained current throughout the 17th century.

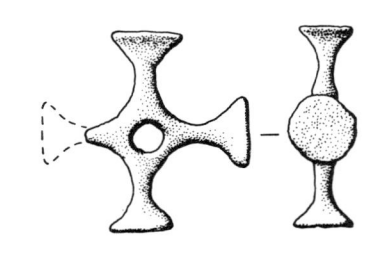

Cast lead circular cloth-seals
1033: post-1660, possibly Charles II, half only, paschal lamb and DAVID . ILLM (? Willm), D. 29mm - *Exeter*.
1034: post-1660 possibly James II, 1? surmounted by a crown,

The Stuart Period

1032

1033

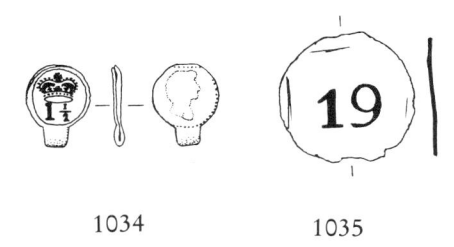

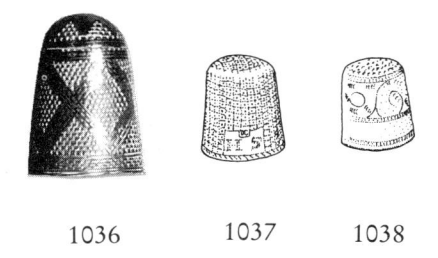

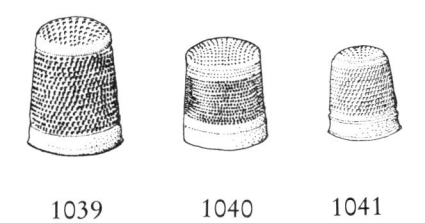

1034 1035

1036 1037 1038

1039 1040 1041

monarch's bust (abraded), 16mm x 7mm - *Exeter*.
1035: possibly 17th century, half only, perhaps Netherlands, Haarlem, 19, D. 25mm - *Exeter*.

THIMBLES

Seventeenth-century thimbles which antecede the English Civil War are similar to the squat late 16th-century type imported from Europe. Silver examples are rare, for many were melted down as bullion to finance both the Royalist and Parliamentarian causes.

Thimbles of copper alloy or silver made during the Commonwealth period are tall and slim and invariably two-piece. Indentations are either punched or knurled circles or waffles, whilst around the base is a fairly wide border frequently engraved with a Puritan religous motto. Some have sides ornamented with 'Z', cross-hatched or chevron strapwork. After the Restoration thimble-making continued along the same lines, although strapwork became more elaborate and crowns occasionally were engraved with a clock. Mottos of a sombre nature around the base also prevailed. Silver-gilt and silvered copper-alloy thimbles were also current. Another feature of mid-17th-century thimbles is a border of thin engraved lines, called 'matting'.

Later in the 17th century silver thimbles evolved into a squatter shape of two-piece construction. Indentations by now were solely knurled circles. Many of these thimbles feature a matted decorated broad border or cartouche personalised with engraved owner's name or initials and date. Sombre mottoes gave way to more lighthearted clichés. Silver commemorative thimbles appeared around 1662, but are rare

In 1688 Dutchman John Loftingh (later Lofting) moved to England. He started a factory at Islington, London, and under a patent of 1693 commenced cast thimble production. Soon afterwards he transferred the factory to a watermill-powered site at Great Marlow, Buckinghamshire, which manufactured more than 150,000 thimbles a month until the 1740s. Lofting's thimbles are of high quality and were cast in two parts then soldered, and are characterised by a wide border at the bottom and a band around the top. Indentations are knurled and quite small and uniform.

Sheet silver two-piece thimble, mid-17th century
1036: waffle-shaped indentations, cross-hatched strapwork on sides and crown, broad boarder and two narrower bands around top of sides, 30mm x 22mm - *Chudleigh*.

Sheet silver two-piece thimble, 1670-1730
1037: circular indentations, ropework band around base, cartouche inscribed E.H., maker's mark D.C., 18mm x 17mm - *Haccombe*.

Sheet copper-alloy two-piece thimble, probably English, 17th century
1038: circular indentations on crown, wide band of engraved curvilinear, three narrow bands of punched dots, 16mm x 14mm - *Haccombe*.

Cast copper-alloy two-piece probable John Lofting thimbles, late 17th century
1039: knurled small indentations, wide border, band around top, 21mm x 19mm - *Cockington*.

1040: knurled small indentations, wide border, band around top, 17mm x 16mm - *Stokeinteignhead*.
1041: knurled small indentations, wide border, band around top, 16mm x 15mm - *Haccombe*.

BODKINS

During the 16th and 17th centuries a metal tool called a bodkin formed part of a lady's sewing kit. Essentially bodkins are large-eyed long blunt needles used for threading tape through garment hems. They also had a secondary function as hairpins. Although copper-alloy bodkins are known, normally they are forged silver with rectangular or circular cross-sections. A less common type has part of the body as a barly twist. Some silver bodkins have a steel core and many have an ornate knop, of which the most common is spoon-shaped. Most bodkins have engraved decoration covering much of their length and, like thimbles, are frequently engraved or pricked with the owners initials and a date. Similar to early 17th-century silver thimbles, many bodkins disappeared to finance the Civil War.

Cast and forged silver bodkins, 17th century

1042: rectangular cross-section, annular looped knop, embossed collar, engraved scrollwork and punched dots, inscribed I.V. 1651, L. 164mm - *Two Mile Oak*.
1043: hexagonal and barly twist cross-section, iron core, eye and knop lost, L. 137.5mm - *Cockington*.
1044: rectangular cross-section, large and small eye, spoon-shaped knop, punched foliate, moulded collars and quatrefoils, L. 155mm - *Maidencombe*.

SPOONS

Knopped spoon manufacture ceased c1650 but was revived during the Restoration and then remained current until the end of the century. Many were destroyed or converted into slip-tops during the Commonwealth period. Of all the knops, the seal-top and apostle were perhaps the most prevalent. Lead/tin-alloy slip-top spoon production continued into the early 17th century and then halted; however, in the reign of Charles I this type was resurrected in silver or tinned-copper alloy. Bowls are a slightly more rounded form of the fig shape.

Puritan spoons of silver, lead/tin alloy or tinned-copper alloy appeared in the Commonwealth period and are characterised by their large elliptical bowls and slightly tapered rectangular cross-section stem. An engraved inscription is occasionally found on the stem's uppermost side. Silver 17th-century spoons of all types are usually hallmarked. Tinned-copper-alloy slip-top and puritan spoons invariably have the maker's touchmark stamped inside the bowl at the top end. Such marks usually comprise the maker's initials or the maker's initials either side of some other device, e.g. several spoons, encompassed by the words DOUBLE WHYTED (or WHITED), which means two coats of tin have been applied. Likewise, lead/tin-alloy puritan or slip-top spoons carry maker's touchmarks, although attribution of those made in London before 1666 is rarely possible.

After the Restoration the slip-top spoon evolved into the trifid spoon, the stem of which, at its juncture with the bowl, was lengthened into a rat-tail support, longitudinally for about half the bowl's length. The stem itself became much wider, of

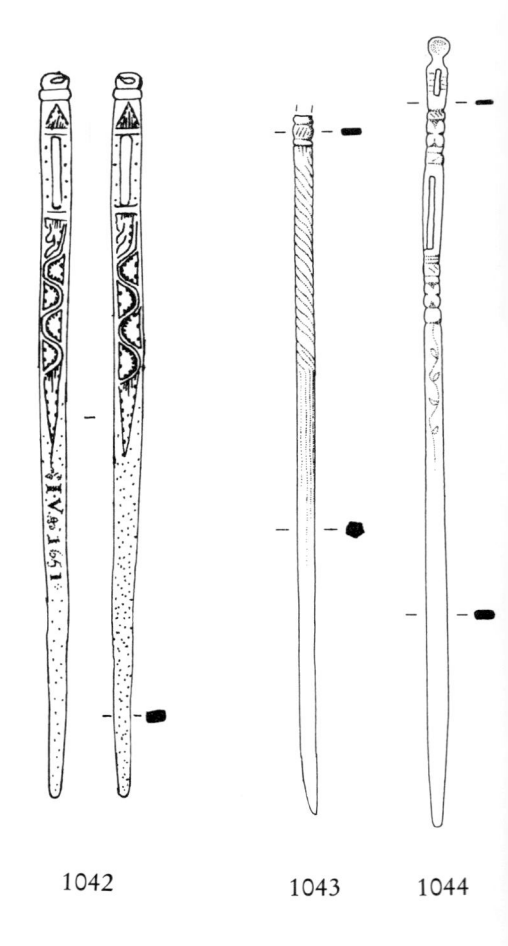

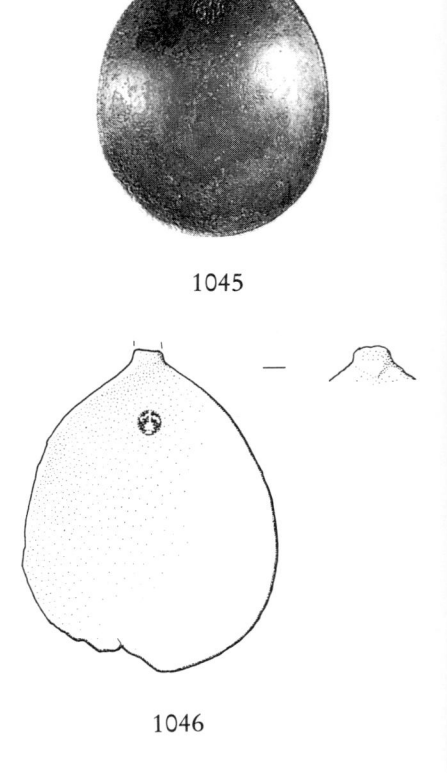

1042 1043 1044

1045

1046

The Stuart Period

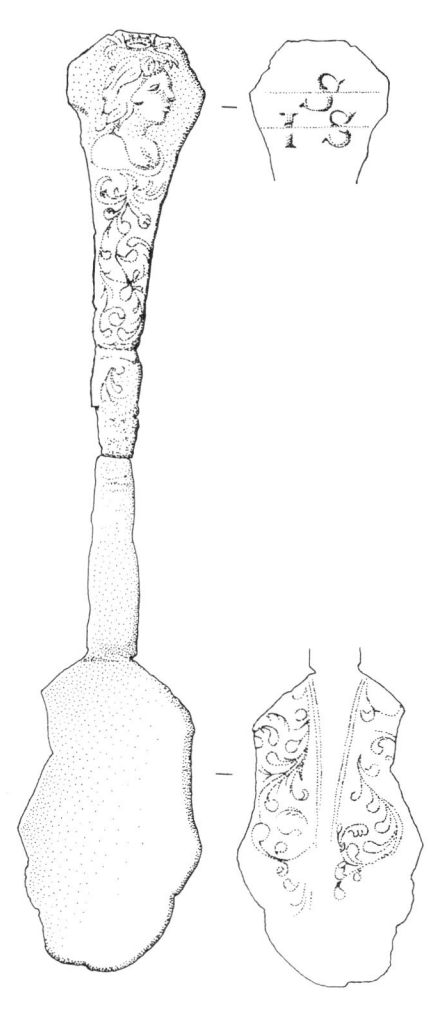

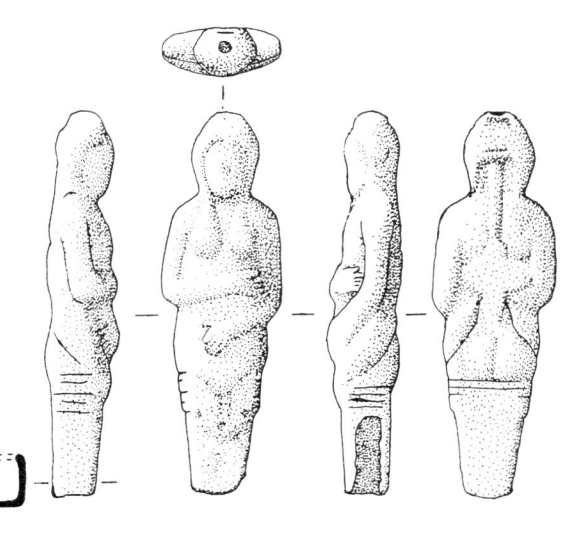

rectangular or subrectangular cross-section. Trifid terminal shapes vary; early examples have sharply indented apertures which by c1675 had decreased considerably, and before the turn of the century they were reduced to a gentle curve without apertures. Embossed lacework decoration on fronts of stems and backs of bowls of tryfid rat-tail spoons became popular c1680. Hallmarks or makers touchmarks may be found on the underside lower section of the stem on Trifid rat-tail spoons, and frequently the owner's initials are engraved or embossed on the underside of the stem at the top end. Some spoons of this type have embossed commemorative designs on the front top end of the stem, whilst a West Country silver varient has engraved multi-circles covering much of the stem front.

A silver spoon peculiar to 17th-century Devon is the Buddha-knop made mainly by Raleigh Clapham and hallmarked at Barnstaple. Another type of silver-spoon, made in Scotland and the north of England in the tryfid period, is the disc finial or 'memento mori', which are engraved with a skull or other design on the disc and an inscription on the stem front.

Specialist spoons re-emerged at the beginning of the 17th century. One is called the hoof spoon which was used for extracting spice from a table spice-box and normally was made of silver with an ovoid or oval bowl and a short wavy stem terminating in a horse's hoof. The silver sucket spoon, a combined spoon and fork, i.e. a spoon bowl at one end and a two-pronged fork at the other, became popular during the Commonwealth period, and is similar to the Saxon sucket spoon. It was used for eating sweetmeats, but not at the dining table. Engraved rat-tail spoons with a folding handle made a comeback c1660 and were used with matching forks. Around the same time the tea spoon and dessert spoon made their appearance, forms frequently richly engraved with foliate decoration. The marrow spoon also evolved during the tryfid period, the earliest of which is a normal table-spoon with a narrow stem provided with a longitudinal hollow which fitted conveniently inside a marrow bone. A custom started by 17th-century seamen was the presentation of metal, wood, bone or ivory love spoons which invariably were not functional. Some are over 600mm long.

Cast tinned-copper-alloy table spoons, 17th century
1045: fig-shaped bowl, maker's touchmark three spoons with G left and P right surrounded by DOUBLE WHITED, 55mm x 43mm - *Newton Abbot.*
1046: abraded fig-shaped bowl, fragment of stem, obscure maker's-touchmark, 63mm x 48.5mm - *Axminster*

Cast lead/tin-alloy rat-tail trifid laceback table spoon, c1680-1714
1047: abraded and fragmented, moulded foliate, floriate and (?) crowned bust on front of stem, moulded foliate on back of bowl and initials S I S on underside top end of stem, L. 185mm - *Cockington.*

KNIVES

Culinary knives current in the 17th century and later have sharp-pointed blades with a single cutting-edge and scale or whittle tangs. Hafts are made of either metal, bone, ivory or, more commonly, wood, and may be composite, solid or hollow. Three-dimensional hominoid hafts of hollow cast copper alloy were popular at this time, as were composite hafts with decorative end-caps.

Cast copper-alloy three-dimensional probable knife haft, 17th century
1048: abraded female figure, fragmented square socket, L. 75mm - *Beesands Beach*.

SPURS

Characteristic of many early to mid-17th-century rowel-spurs are their moulded bent necks and tapering mildly curved sides. Notwithstanding, some rowel-spurs of c1625-75 have fairly straight sides or unmoulded necks which rise sharply before bending almost laterally downwards. Other types of neck attributed to c1600-50 are the baluster, which lacks mouldings and is bulbous, and the wavy. Current from the later medieval period until c1650 was the cabled-arm rowel-spur, whilst between 1600-60 rowel-spurs with moulded wavy sides were fashionable. Straight-sided rowel-spurs were the dominant type by the end of the 17th century.

Terminals of some 17th-century rowel-spurs are the elongated two-ring type which occasionally may have additional central decorative openwork, whilst others are even or offset figure-8. Separate cast and forged copper-alloy or iron (or part iron part copper alloy) studs, which may be elliptical or lozenge-shaped, for attaching the spur leather, hooked through the terminal, whilst the stud passed through a slit in the leather strap. Rowels of this period vary from medium-sized seven-point, large long five-point to large short seven-point. English 17th-century rowel-spurs frequently are gilded and many exhibit decorative patterns formed from small punched circles, dots or crescents.

Prick-spurs enjoyed a revival during the 17th century, albeit on a restricted scale. Other than lacking goads their general shape is very similar to rowel-spurs contemporaneous with the same century.

Cast and forged copper-alloy rowel-spurs
1049: 1600-50, fragmented, subrectangular cross-section gently curved and moulded side, lateral figure-eight terminal, L. 63mm - *Berry Pomeroy*.
1050: possibly 1600-50, fragmented, short straight moulded neck and rowel box, oblique grooves form cabling on circular cross-section sides, L. 21mm - *Haccombe*.
1051: 1600-60, fragmented, gilt, short wavy neck with drooped rowel box, moulded wavy semi-circular cross-section sides, curlicues and lines of punched circles and dots, L. 69.5mm - *Stantor Barton*.
1052: 1600-75, fragmented, gilt, moulded short neck with drooped rowel-box, semi-circular cross-section sides engraved with curlicues and circles, punched dots, L. 72mm - *Colaton Raleigh*.
1053: c1640-70, fragmented, semi-circular cross-section straight and moulded side with engraved transverse and horizontal lines, cordate two-ring terminal, L. 37.5mm - *Cockington*.
1054: c1660-1740, fragmented, short neck with drooped rowel-box, semi- circular cross-section sides, L. 57mm - *Poltimore*.
1055: possibly 17th century, fragmented and distorted, neck lost leaving a lozenge-shaped area, triangular cross-section

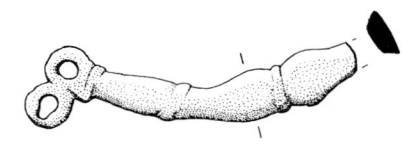

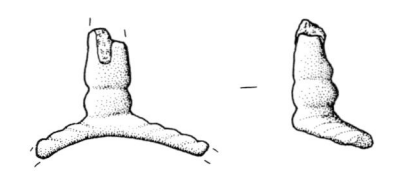

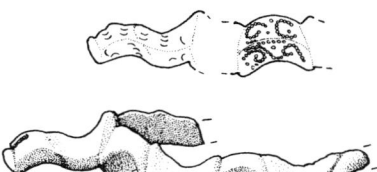

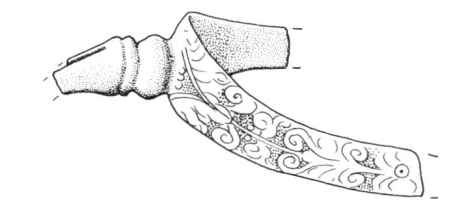

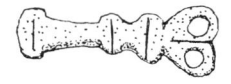

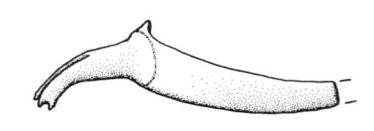

The Stuart Period

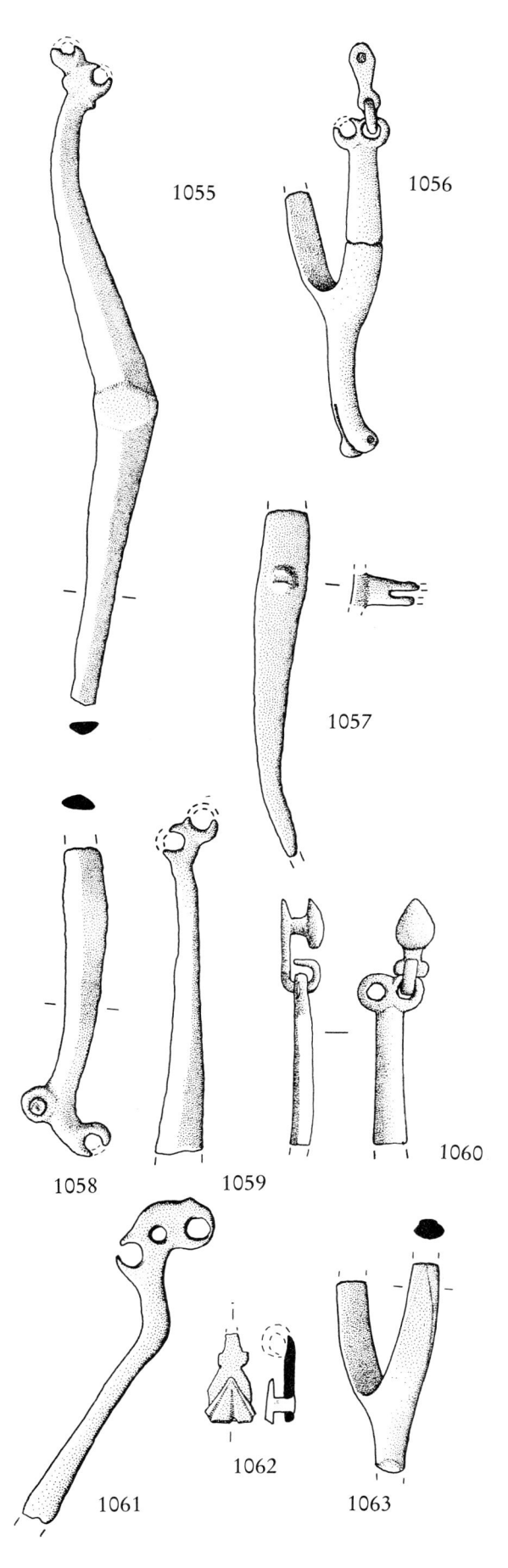

tapered sides, one oblique figure-eight terminal, L. 152.5mm - *Chudleigh*.

1056: 1660-1750, fragmented, long neck with drooped and expanded rowel-box, traces of iron rowel-pin, semi-circular cross-section straight sides, one lateral figure-eight terminal, one stud-attachment with stud lost, L. 77mm - *Poltimore*.

1057: probably 1650-1700, fragmented, very short straight neck and rowel box, semi-circular cross-section sides, L. 80mm - *Exeter*.

1058: probably 17th century, fragmented, triangular cross-section side, elongated oblique two-ring terminal, remains of iron stud in one hole, L. 71mm - *West Ogwell*.

1059: possibly 17th century, fragmented, triangular cross-section side, oblique figure-eight terminal, L. 77mm - *Poltimore*.

1060: mid-17th-18th century, fragmented, semi-circular cross-section side, lateral figure-eight terminal, ovoid stud-attachment, L. 39.5mm - *Exeter*.

1061: c.mid-17th century, fragmented, semi-circular cross-section, oblique figure-eight terminal with central hole, L. 82mm - *Exeter*.

1062: c1700, fragmented, vesica-shaped cross-section sides each with a moulded chevron, circular cross-section long neck, L. 44mm - *Cockington*.

Cast and forged copper-alloy spur-leather attachment, mid-17th century

1063: triangular stud, moulded longitudinal and border grooves, attachment loop lost, 20.5mm x 11.5mm - *Cockington*.

RECEPTACLES

In the 17th century types of copper-alloy or iron receptacle for domestic use remained much the same as in the later Middle Ages and Tudor period. Lead/tin-alloy-ware on a limited scale would be found in many households at the beginning of the Stuart era, however, there was an upsurge in its popularity, particularly plates, dishes and tankards, soon after the turn of the century.

As well as for storing, cooking or serving food and drink, specialist metal-receptacles were widely used during this period, e.g: tobacco, snuff, watch or jewellery boxes. These were made from gold or silver, although copper alloy or lead/tin alloy was more common. Similar objects were made from iron but rarely have survived.

Cast copper-alloy skillet, c17th century

1064: fragmented, handle, embossed scrollwork on upper side, three embossed transverse grooves on underside, 92.5mm x 27mm - *Denbury*.

Cast copper-alloy box lid, 17th century

1065: rectangular with obliquely cut corners, probable hinge on one end lost, small rectangular recess on opposite end, pivoted hooked catch (broken) held by a separate copper-alloy rivet, embossed horseman and foliate, 70mm x 38mm - *Stokeinteignhead*.

N.B. No.1065 perhaps was associated with the military.

BARREL TAPS

A style of barrel-tap with an unremovable key which has a bifurcate handle is regularly found in this country in random non-associated contexts and is frequently described as 18th century or even 14th. Though there is no archaeological confirmation for the latter, it definately antecedes the former, for identical examples have been recovered from 17th-century deposits at Jamestown, Virginia

Cast copper-alloy barrel-tap, 17th century
1066: fragment, bifurcate handle, lateral lip on top of each branch, oval and sub-lozenge-shaped cross-section, 14mm x 44mm - *Haccombe*.

TRADE WEIGHTS

Official flat, circular, lead trade-weights, as well as unauthorized types, remained current until the passing of the 17th century. Those made in the City of London are stamped with the Plumbers Company mark of St Michael, whilst provincial examples frequently have maker's or owner's marks and stamps of individual towns and cities. Both lead or copper-alloy flat circular 17th-century London-made trade-weights are stamped with the royal cypher surmounted by a crown, or the Commonwealth insignia, viz: James I - I; Charles I - C (CR lead); Commonwealth - shield of St George (St George's shield and the Irish harp lead); Charles II - C (CIIR lead); James II - I; William and Mary - WM; William III - W; Anne - A (AR lead).

Regarding the cyphers of James I and James II, trade-weights of the former have the crowned I, A, and sword at 1800 and the ewer is inverted and placed at 1200, whilst James II's crowned I, and the symbol : (see below), and sword are at 1200 and the ewer is upright at 1800. Confusion arises when differentiating Charles I and Charles II trade-weights, for both the crowned C, A, and sword are situated around 1200, whilst the ewer is at 1800. However, in the reign of Charles II the letter A was replaced by the symbol :, a mark which remained current until the latter part of William III's reign when the letter A was reinstated.

Cast copper-alloy shield-shaped wool-weights bearing the moulded arms of the respective monarch or the Commonwealth, and bell-shaped trade-weights remained current throughout the Stuart period.

Cast lead flat circular trade-weights, probably 17th century
1067: 1 ounce, possibly James I, embossed, fleuret, I, D. 29.5mm - *Axminster*.
1068: 4 ounce, embossed, 4 stars, obscure mark, D. 40mm - *Exeter*.
1069: 2 ounce, embossed, 2 fleurets, concentric circles, D. 25mm - *Axminster*.
1070: ? ounce, embossed, Long Cross and roundel, D. 21.5mm - *Musbury*.

Cast copper-alloy flat circular trade-weights, 17th century
1071: [ounce, James I, 1603-25, embossed and incuse, crowned I, sword of St Paul, ewer, D. 29mm - *Totnes*.
1072: 1 ounce, Charles I or II, 1625-85, embossed and incuse, crowned C, sword of St Paul, ewer, D. 36mm - *Cockington*.

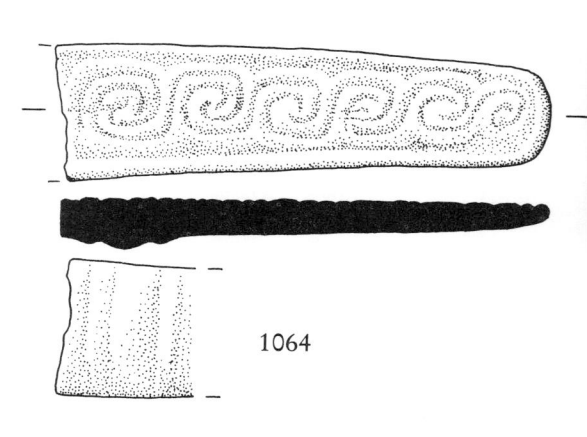

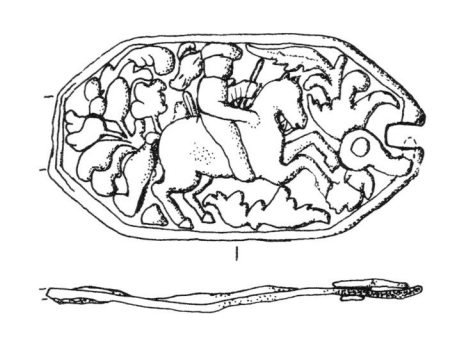

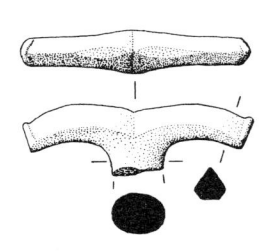

1064

1065

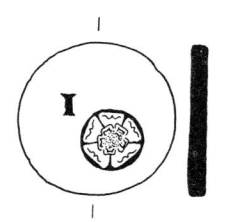

1066

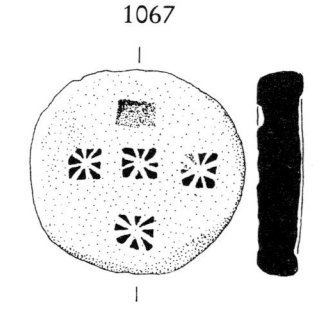

1067

1068

The Stuart Period

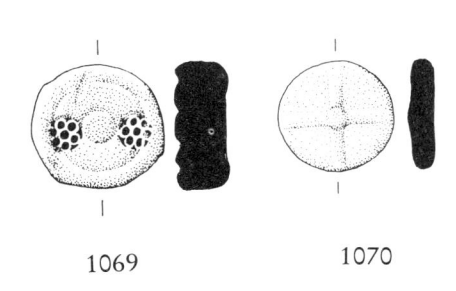

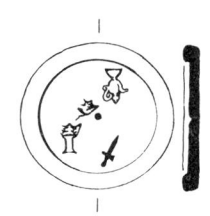

1069　　　　　1070

1071

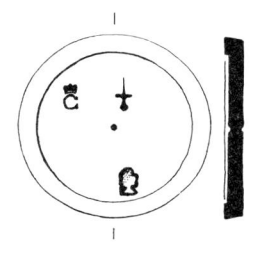

1072

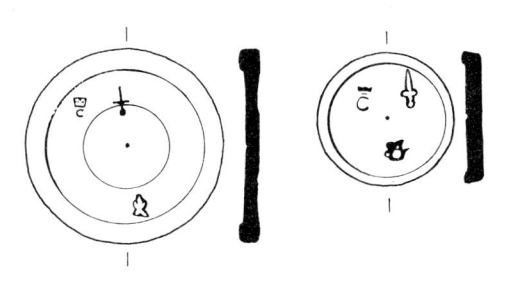

1073　　　　　1074

1073: 1 ounce, Charles I or II, 1625-85, embossed and incuse, crowned C, sword of St Paul, ewer, D. 37.5mm - *Cockwood*.
1074: ? ounce, Charles I or II, 1625-85, embossed and incuse, crowned C, sword of St Paul, ewer, D. 25mm - *Cockwood*.
1075: ? ounce, Charles I or II, 1625-85, embossed and incuse, crowned C, sword of St Paul, ewer, D. 26mm - *Cockington*.
1076: 1 ounce, Anne, 1702-14, embossed and incuse, crowned A, sword of St Paul, ewer, A, D. 31mm - *Cockington*.
1077: 1/2 ounce, Anne, 1702-14, embossed, crowned A, ewer, 14mm - *Haccombe*.

Cast copper-alloy cup-weight, possibly 17th century
1078: 1 ounce troy, embossed, lion passant (goldsmiths mark) and obscure shield-shaped mark on inside and underneath, obscure marks on rim, 16mm x 28mm - *Haccombe*.

COIN WEIGHTS

Between c1620-32 production of copper-alloy embossed square coin-weights increased considerably and their use became more widespread. Representing some sixteen types of gold coin, the obverse design of some of these weights corresponds to the respective denomination, and many have on their reverse the value surmounted by a crown. The last series of square weights to be struck has the denomination embossed on the obverse and variations of 'without grains', 'les 3 gr' etc within a beaded circle or lozenge on the reverse. One weight in this series has the denomination on both sides. Incuse stamped weights for this series also exist, either uniface with the denomination or denomination on both sides. Numerous coin-weights of this era are counterstamped on their reverse with the respective monarch's cypher surmounted by a crown, viz: an I for James I & II, and C for Charles I. Also current as counterstamps were the fleur-de-lis or, very infrequently, a date-letter of the London hallmark

Square coin-weights were banned in 1633 and replaced by official copper-alloy circular coin-weights. Obverse and reverse designs are similar to the immediately preceeding square weights. Although Nicholas Briot, the Mint's chief engraver, made the dies for some of the new circular coin-weights, other engravers also made dies and many of the weights carry a letter B which is not Briot's mark, but to whom it is attributed isn't known.

Charles I's coin-weights for gold coins are as follows (there are many varieties): angel - Obv. St Michael slaying a dragon, Rev. crowned Xs; unite - Obv. crowned, draped bust left, Rev. crowned XXs; double crown - Obv. crowned, draped and armoured bust, Rev. crowned Xs; crown - crowned and armoured bust left, Rev. crowned Vs; halfcrown - crowned and armoured bust left. Legends on the preceeding weights are variations of CAROLUS REX. Pennyweights and grain weights of 1603-49 are mainly square or circular copper alloy. For pennyweights the denomination is embossed on the obverse and/or reverse in Roman numerals, some with a crowned C. Grain weights have embossed annulets representing the number of grains and are uniface. Many are countermarked with either a lion, crowned I or C. An irregular-shaped five grains copper weight, also uniface, apart from five annulets and crowned CR, is marked with a rose,

B and a double line square border.

Marks on weights for Charles I's silver coinage again are varied and complicated but are in three groups. The main points are as follows. WC GROUP: ducatoon - Obv. 15 armoured bust right 79, PHILLIPVS REX HISPANIARVM (N reversed), Rev. 5s 6d A: DVCK ATOVNE W C, or Obv. similar to former, Rev. [...] DVCKA TOONE WW; half-ducatoon - Obv. similar to former, Rev 2s 9D HALFE:A: DVCKATO VNE W.C; halfcrown - Obv. king on horseback, Rev. crowned CR, crowned XXX or with out grains within beaded circle; shilling - Obv. C lis R XIID with out grans, Rev. R XII D WITHOVT GRAINS WC; or crowned XII, lis left, D right; or crowned XII, lis left, g right; sixpence - Obv. crowned VI, lis left, D right, Rev. VI D WITHOVT GRAINS W C. TR GROUP: halfcrown - Obv. crowned C, XXX left, D right, Rev. crowned R, II left, VI right; shilling - crowned C, I left, S right; Rev. crowned R, XII left, D right; sixpence - crowned C VI left, D right.

LION AND ROSE GROUP: halfcrown - Obv. king in armour mounted left over two lions, WITH. OVT. .GRANNS., Rev. crowned CR, above rose XXX rose and lion rampant, crown right, D left; shilling - Obv. crowned rose, WITH.OVT. GRANES, Rev. crowned CR over XII and lion rampant, rose left and right, crown left, D right; sixpence - Obv. crowned rose, WITH.OVT. .GRANS., Rev. crowned CR over VI, lion rampant and pellet, rose left and right, crown left, D right; mule shilling - Obv. crowned rose, WITH.OVT. .GRANS., Rev. crowned CR over XII, pellet left and right, lion rampant, rose left and right. Similar halfcrowns, shillings and sixpences to the immediately previous have no legends. The halfcrown obverse also has no lions below the horse and the shilling and sixpence obverse has a small lion left and right.

LION GROUP: halfcrown - Obv. lion rampant, Rev. crowned CR over XXX and lion rampant with a pellet either side, rose left and right, crown left, D right; shilling - Obv. lion rampant, Rev. crowned CR over XII and lion rampant with a pellet either side, rose left and right, crown left, D right; sixpence - Obv. lion rampant, Rev. crowned CR over VI and lion rampant and pellet, rose left and right, crown left, D right.

Coin-weights depicting Charles II's crowned portrait facing left and title CAROLVS II REX on the obverse were made for weighing the newly minted guineas and half-guineas. Reverses depict a crowned XXS or XS. Countermarked James II weights were used for weighing James I and Charles I coins still circulating, but weights without countermarks were for use with his own coinage. All bear on the obverse his bust facing right, some with and some without the legend IACOBVS. II.REX. Reverses depict a crown over the denomination, e.g. XXs.

William and Mary weights were for guineas and half-guineas have their portraits and variations of the legend GVLIELMVS. ET. MARIA. on the obverse, and the value in words surmounted by a crown and sceptres on the reverse.

The above types of coin-weight remained current in the reigns of William III and Anne, however, a new series of coin-weights were made by the Founders Company for the French coin, the pistole, which circulated in Britain at this time. Some of these weights carry William III's bust on the obverse, although the majority depict Louis XIV. The denomination surmounted by a crown is carried on the reverse of William III's coin-weights,

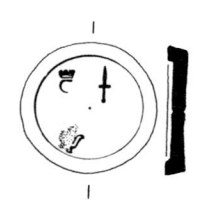

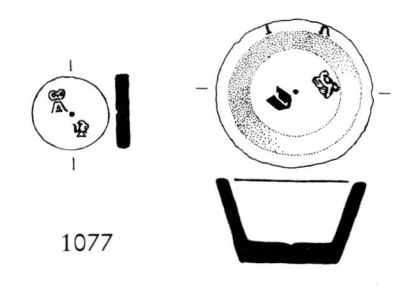

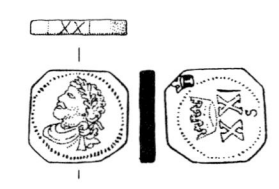

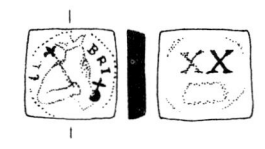

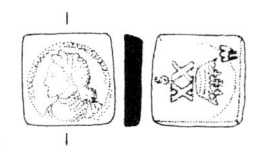

The Stuart Period

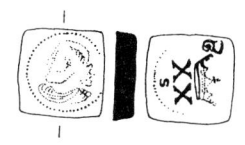

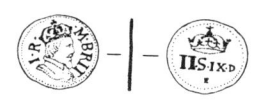

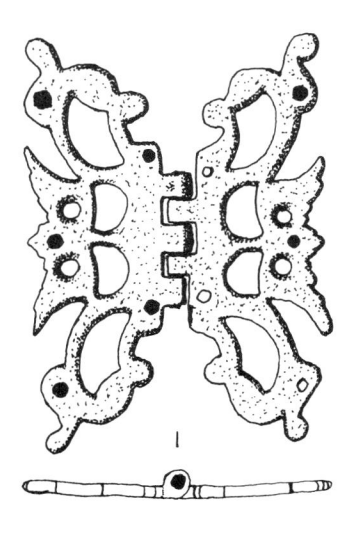

whilst Louis XIV's depict the word pistol with a number and three fleur-de-lis above. There is also a group of incuse stamped pistol weights. Embossed pennyweights were struck with a large V or III on the obverse and a large rose on the reverse. Some Founders Company-made weights are stamped with the ewer and carry the maker's initials. Additionally many weights bear the seller's name or initials. A group of weights for silver coinage are stamped incuse or embossed with the denomination, e.g. XII D. Some are uniface whilst others are double-sided. Other marks may be found on these.

Coin-weights of Anne are scarce. They carry her portrait facing left and variations of the legend ANNA.DEI. GRATIA on the obverse, whilst the reverse is crown and scepters over the denomination in words and a W.

Cast copper-alloy square coin-weights, 17th century

1079: James I, 1603-25, laurel, embossed, modified by removing corners to weigh a guinea, Obv. laureate bearded bust of king left, beaded circle; Rev. crowned XXS, counterstamped incuse I, crowned I certification mark embossed stamped on a lead plug, beaded circle, XX incuse stamped on edge - *Haccombe*.

1080: James I, c1620, unite, embossed; Obv. crowned bust of king right, holding orb and sceptre, I.R. BRI., beaded circle; Rev. crowned XX, beaded circle, 17.5mm x 17.5mm - *Brixham*.

1081: James I, c1620, laurel, embossed: Obv. laureate bearded bust of king left, beaded circle; Rev. crowned XXS, embossed stamped crowned I certification mark, beaded circle, 18mm x 18mm - *Haccombe*.

1082: James I laurel, c1630, embossed; Obv. laureate bearded bust of king left, beaded circle; Rev. crowned XXS, embossed stamped crowned C certification mark of Charles I, 17mm x 17mm - *Cockington*.

Cast copper-alloy circular coin-weights, c1632-62

1083: Charles I or II, two shillings and ninepence, embossed, Obv. bust of king right, I.R. .M.BRIT, beaded circle; Rev. crowned II.S.IXD, beaded circle, D. 14mm - Wolborough, *Newton Abbot*.

1084: c1700, French Louis or pistol, embossed; Obv. bust of Louis VIII right [......... D.G. ...], beaded circle, Rev. I PISTOL W surmounted by three lis, D. 19.5mm - *Exeter*.

DOOR & FURNITURE FITTINGS

Through the ages important buildings had forged iron hinges, decorative studs, escutcheons, bolts, knockers and handles fitted to doors. At times, particularly on internal doors and furniture, similar metalwork embellishments were either sheet, cast or forged copper alloy.

A particular form of 17th-century cast copper-alloy or lead/tin-alloy drawer-pull has an embossed fleuret handle with an integral bolt which was secured with a nut. Another bolt-type has a separate drop-handle hanging from an eyed bolt which passes through a septfoil fleuret escutcheon. Other drawer-pulls of this period feature an annular split-ring handle.

Cast gilt-copper-alloy decorative furniture-mounts started to become popular during this period. Invariably they represent foliate, floriate, scrollwork or animals and have either nail holes or a stud-like rear projection by which means they were secured to the woodwork.

Hinges of forged iron or cast and forged copper alloy were used on doors in structures as well as on furniture, therefore they vary in size considerably. Seventeenth-century hinges are frequently asymmetrical with ornate outline and openwork. Nail holes are provided for pinning to the door.

Sheet copper-alloy hinge, late 17th century
1085: asymmetrical, asymmetrical openwork, copper-alloy pin, ten nail holes, remains of sevon iron nails, 81mm x 59mm - *Haccombe*.

Cast and forged copper-alloy drawer-pull, 1660-1710
1086: four-piece, sexfoil plate with embossed oblique lines and rectangular bolt-hole, fragmented drop handle, looped-bolt and nut lost, plate D. 34.5mm, handle 26mm x 29mm - *Cockington*.

AMMUNITION

Undoubtedly some of the ubiquitous lead ball bullets found by metal detectors antecede the 17th century, however, the majority may be attributed to c1600-c1850 (notwithstanding, latterly, there has been a revival in blackpowder shooting which may account for some).

Musket balls or shot were fired from smoothbore muskets or pistols, the bore of which varies. The largest, 0.753 calibre, were used with 18th-century military firearms such as the 'Old Army-Musket', the 'Percussion Musket' or the famous 'Brown Bess Musket'. Civilian guns were confined mainly to sport and fired shot which ranged from dust-shot to buck-shot. Some civilian pistols, however, were used for non-sporting purposes, e.g. dualling. Prior to 1769 lead musket-balls and shot were cast in hand-held pincer-type iron moulds either singly or in multiples. Moulds carved from stone were used in other situations, e.g. aboard ships. Ammunition of this type invariably has a characteristic sprue where excess metal has been clipped off.

Lead musket-balls, antecedent 1769
1087: 0.75 calibre, with sprue - *Cockington*.
1088: 0.5 calibre, with sprue - *Cockington*.
1089: 0.38 calibre, trace of sprue - *Cockington*.

POWDER CHARGER CAPS

As part of their uniform, British infantry musketeers of the period c1660-86 wore a wide bandolier over the right shoulder from which sidearms were hung, e.g. a sword. Similarly draped over their left shoulder was another bandolier from which hung a dozen powder-chargers, six on the front and six on the back (presumably the bandoliers were interchangable according to whether a man was right or left-handed). The musketeer also carried a powder-horn filled with fine priming-powder which was poured direct onto the weapons' priming pan, and a leather pouch for holding lead shot.

Essentially a powder-charger is a flask-shaped (possibly wooden) leather-covered container which held sufficient gunpowder for a single shot. The two free-ends of a looped cord were attached to the top end of the charger, whilst the bight was secured to the bandolier. To prevent gunpowder spilling and to keep it dry, a small, lead, cup-shaped flat-bottomed cap

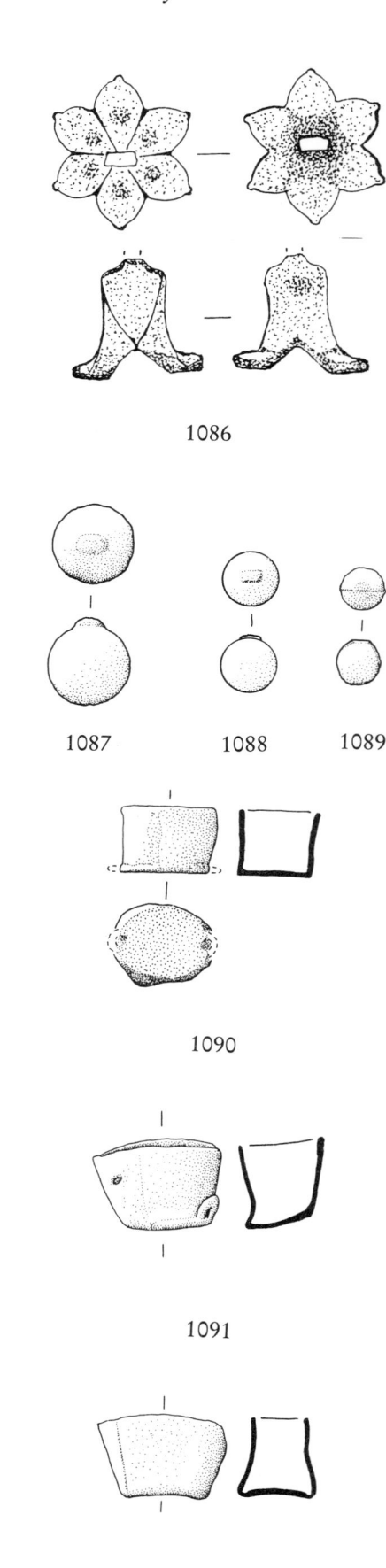

The Stuart Period

(frequently and erroneously described as a 'powder measure') fitted over the powder-charger's open end. The looped cord passed through a pair of integral annulets, one on each side of the cap's closed end, thereby allowing the cap to slide up and down. Powder-chargers and caps vary in size according to the bore of the musket.

Cast lead cup-shaped powder-charger caps, c1660-86
1090: annulets lost, 14mm x 21mm - *Cockington*.
1091: squashed, 18mm x 20mm - *Stokeinteignhead*.
1092: squashed, 18mm x 17mm, annulets lost - *Maidencombe*.

MUSKET RESTS

Very early muskets were extremely heavy and unwieldy due to their length, therefore in order to aim accurately it was necessary to use some form of support. The marksman would utilize any convenient object for this task, however, he did carry a special portable musket-rest for use in circumstances where temporary props were not available. Musket-rests comprise a cast and forged copper-alloy U-shaped fitting which is mounted by means of an integral socket on a long wooden pole. The metalwork section is invariable ornamented with moulding or engraving and frequently has knops which are occasionally zoomorphic. One arm may have a relatively sharp end which probably served as a tool for cleaning the priming hole.

Cast and forged copper-alloy musket-rest head, 17th century
1093: subrectangular cross-section arms, (?) zoomorphic knop on one arm, abraded circular cross-section tapererd end on other arm which is bent, fragmented socket, abraded engraved curlicues on both sides, 87mm x 67.5mm - *Haccombe*.

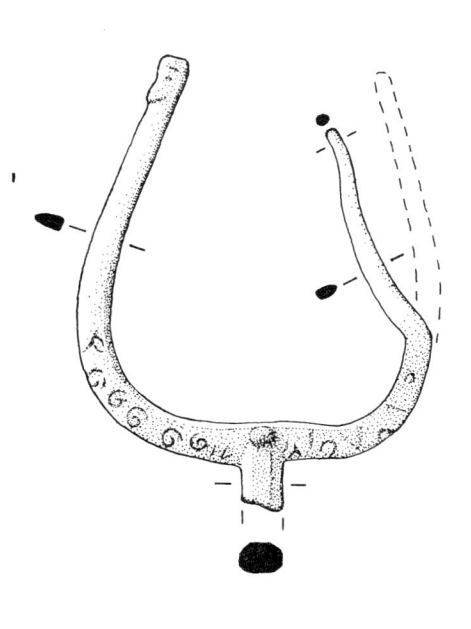

TOYS

Small cast lead/tin-alloy, copper-alloy, or forged iron toy guns have been current since the early 17th century, and imitate handguns and cannons. Invariably, and erroneously, described as a 'petronel', one type of toy handgun which originated around the beginning of the Stuart period, is somewhat similar in appearance to the true petronel pistol used by 16th and 17th-century cavalrymen. However, toy handguns also represent other pistols, e.g. the wheelock. Whatever the type, invariably they are extremely crude, with an overall length of about 75mm - 100mm. Frequently barrels are bored and a touch-hole usually exists. Some have an integral trigger, which therefore is non functional, and a trigger-guard. Although probably it was never the intention, for it was extremely hazardous, these toy pistols could be primed with gunpowder, loaded, and then fired. There is a school of thought that they were produced as gunmakers' samples, however, this is speculation.

Toy pistols were also popular in the late 18th and 19th centuries, but seem to be rarer finds than their antecedents. They are about 900mm long and made of similar metals to earlier types but reflect the style of pistol contemporary with the period. A major difference is a powder-pan and a working trigger which holds a slow match. When the trigger is squeezed the slow-match is lowered to the powder-pan thereby igniting the touchpowder. The barrel is bored, but whether it was intended to fire a lead shot is doubtful.

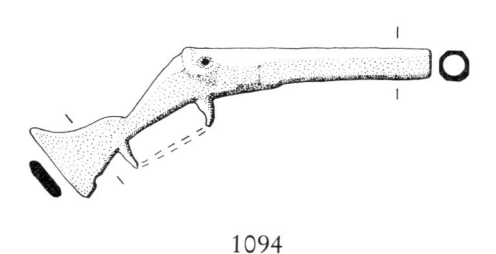

1093

1094

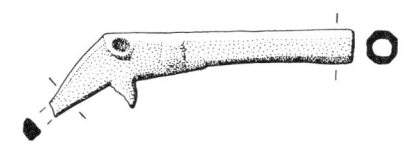

1095

Cast copper-alloy toy handguns, 17th century

1094: fragmented stock, octagonal cross-section barrel, bore c3mm, L. 57mm - *Exeter*.

1095: fragmented trigger-guard, octagonal cross-section barrel, bore 4mm, L. 76mm - *Aish*.

A particularly intriguing three-piece pivoting copper-alloy artefact has defied positive identification. It has been classified as a c17th-century toy or perhaps a crossbow tensioning device of the same period. It has been included with toys for want of a more suitable slot.

Forged copper-alloy possible toy or crossbow tensioner, c17th century

1096: three-piece, laterally cranked body with a hominoid head which pivots on a separate copper-alloy pin that penetrates both sides of a forked third member. The lower section of the forked member appears to be broken. Traces of rust adhering to the lateral body's tail imply it was formerly attached to a fourth member. L. 107mm - *Cockington*.

N.B. An artefact similar to No.1096 was found in Essex by a metal detective.

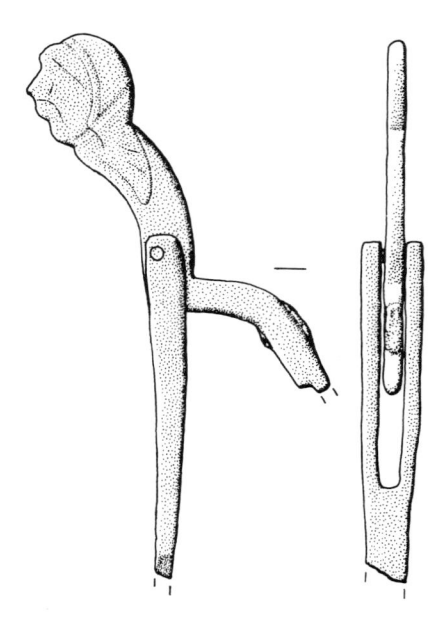

1096

Chapter Eight
The Georgian and Victorian Period

1097

1098

1099

The main seaside towns on Devon's south coast owe their present character to having become fashionable watering-places with the gentry. Exmouth, with its wide and sandy beach, started to attract day trippers from Exeter early in the 18th century; towards the end of the same century it was the county's most popular resort. Sidmouth's transformation from a small fishing and market-town into a genteel holiday-haunt for Exonians was around the 1780s. A few miles down the coast to the west lay Dawlish and Teignmouth, small towns favoured by the residents of Newton Abbot for day trips. Teignmouth started its life as a resort early in the second half of the 18th century, whilst Dawlish began around 1790.

Some further miles to the west again, on the shores of Torbay, lay the small villages of Torquay and Paignton. Torquay drew visitors earlier than Paignton and it is recorded as having taken place about 1790. In the case of Paignton, it remained a small village until c1840, when it also followed its neighbours in the east into the holiday trade. A secondary factor that had a bearing on the development of Torquay as a holiday resort was the Napoleonic Wars. Torbay was used by the Royal Navy as an anchorage for the fleet until Plymouth Breakwater was completed in 1840. Many naval officers sought accommodation in Torquay for their families, a demand that led to a rapid growth of the town. When the navy left for Plymouth, taking their families with them, the vacated properties were soon reoccupied by people suffering from ill health who found the mild climate favourable for convalescing.

Some of the finest examples of these resort's late Georgian and Victorian architecture are extant, e.g. The Beacon at Exmouth, Torquay's Hesketh Crescent, The Terrace and Lisburne Crescent.

The growth of these seaside holiday towns continued well into the 19th century. Many fine Victorian mansions were built in all of them for use as private homes, many of which are extant, some continuing as family residences but most are now converted into hotels, flats or residential homes for the aged or infirm.

Inland towns did not share in this tourism boom and most of them went into decline due to the arrival of the steam railway in 1844. This innovation, coupled with the collapse of the woollen industry in the second half of the 19th century, had the effect of stifling any trade that was related in any way to the coaching service; their workers were forced to seek a livelihood elsewhere. There were a few exceptions, these being towns which had a regular market or fair which helped to sustain their textile-based economy, such as: Newton Abbot, Totnes, Chudleigh, Uffculme and Honiton. This depopulation of the inland towns had the effect of retarding building development to such an extent that it is only in the last forty years or so that some expansion has taken place.

It was during this period that many great country houses were rebuilt, including: Ugbrooke, Haccombe, Cockington, Torre Abbey, Powderham, Bradfield and Nutwell Court. This thirst for change continued well into the 19th century. Apart from the remodelling of existing houses a number of new ones were built in the 18th century, of these Haldon (now largely demolished) and Canonteign were among the finest. Thankfully, a large number of these country residences are extant and are open to the general public. Many of the area's ancient churches were also subjected to what can only be described today as mindless vandalism. What were in many cases beautiful examples of medieval, Tudor and Stuart craftsmanship, were transformed into extremely ugly Victorian monstrosities.

For much of the 18th and 19th centuries farmhouses remained as they had been in the 16th and 17th; no great rebuilding programme took place as in Elizabeth's time which radically altered the architectural appearance of those already standing. Towards the end of the 18th century and for the first decade or so of the 19th, some new building did take place due to a farming boom caused by the country being at war again. This short period of economic prosperity made it possible for farmers to invest in improvements to their properties, but between c1820 and the beginning of the 20th century not a great deal of new building or renovation was carried out.

Southern Devonshire has never been a great manufacturing industry area; the only noteworthy activities, other than farming, fishing, quarrying, tin mining, lacemaking and tourism, have been copper mining, started in the 17th century on a small scale at Ashburton and Brixham, and iron mining, again in a limited capacity from the early 17th century, at Wolborough, Ashburton, Brent and Holne - all of which had faded into oblivion by the last quarter of the 19th century. From c1770 Upton Pynes and Newton St Cyres manganese mines provided the needs of the whole country for very many years. Later, other manganese lodes were discovered at Ashton and Doddiscombeleigh in the Haldon Hills and at Christow on Dartmoor's eastern side. On and off, from the time of Henry VIII, lignite has been mined at Bovey Tracey, and at Bridford limited excavation of barytes was carried out.

Paper manufacturing has existed in the region from the late 17th century, with two mills in the Plymouth area. However, from the 18th century this industry was confined mainly to the valleys of the Creedy and the Culm in the east, where many paper mills were sited. In the early 18th century other paper-mills were built at: Plymouth, Ivybridge, Exeter, Uffculme, probably Colyton, and Halberton. At the mouth of the tiny River Wash, where it flows into Bow Creek at Tuckenhay, near Ashprington, a paper mill operated from the second half of the 18th century up until recent years. Sadly, few of the other mills still produce paper, those that do are in the Culm and Exe valleys.

The famous Axminster woollen carpet factory started in 1755, but unfortunately foundered soon after 1830. Its redundant looms and other machinery formed the basis of Wiltshire's equally famous Wilton carpet factory. However, in 1945 carpet production was started again at Axminster, and it flourishes to this day. Since the early 1950's woollen carpets have also been

The Georgian and Victorian Period

1103

1104

1105

produced at Buckfastleigh.

The 18th and 19th centuries, still with royal patronage, was hand-lacemaking's heyday, and had spread throughout the east of the county to: Ottery St Mary, Beer, Branscombe, Sidbury, Colyton, Seaton, Sidmouth, Exmouth, Uppottery and Luppit. Sadly, by the end of the 19th century mechanisation and changes of fashion had killed off most of the industry, although some is still produced at Honiton and Beer.

Clay is Devon's most important raw material. Pipe and potter's clay was mined at Bovey Tracey and Kingsteignton for many years whilst ball-clay has been continuously mined at Kingsteignton and Chudleigh Knighton since c1730. A smaller deposit of ball-clay was mined at Bishopsteignton from about the same date but has since been worked out. China clay has been mined for many years at Lee Moor on Dartmoor's south-western edge and is still extracted on a grand scale.

COINS

In 1718, during the reign of George I, 'quarter-guineas' were issued for the first time, but proved unpopular as they were too small, therefore they were called in and smelted. George II's reign saw hammered gold coinage withdrawn from circulation in 1733.

Matthew Boulton's new steam-powered press struck copper 'cartwheel' pennies and twopences in 1797 during George III's reign, however, these cumbersome coins were short-lived, for there were no further issues. Guineas, half-guineas and quarter-guineas were not minted between 1797-1813, but 'third-guineas' were issued to alleviate the scarcity of small denominations. Countermarked Spanish silver 'dollars' and 'half-dollars' as emergency coinage circulated concurrently. Between 1804-11 the Bank of England overstruck Spanish dollars and re-issued them as their dollars. The Bank of England had 'three-shillings' and 'one-and-sixpence' silver 'token' coins made in 1811 which circulated generally; these were superseded in 1816 by regal debased silver token coinage. For general circulation a twenty-shilling sovereign replaced the guinea in 1817. Other than a resumption of minting copper farthings and halfpennies in 1821 and 1825 respectively, and the introduction of a gold 'two pounds' in 1823, little of consequence occurred to the coinage during the reign of George IV. After William IVs accession of 1830, in 1834 the half-sovereign was made smaller as it was easily confused with the sixpence, however, in 1835 it reverted to its former size as it was rejected by the general public. The silver groat reappeared in 1836 but wasn't issued after 1837 (other than the 'maundy fourpence'), and silver threehalfpence and threepences were struck for Colonial circulation.

During the reign of the last of the Hanoverian monarchs, Victoria, several changes to the coinage were occasioned. The silver 'florin' made its first appearance in 1849 and the 'double-florin' in 1887, but the latter was not issued after 1890. In 1860 the lighter bronze 'bun' penny replaced the earlier and heavier copper issues of penny.

Foreign 18th and 19th-century coins feature regularly in the area, with Spanish, Portugese and French being the most pervasive, these were mainly copper denominations with a sprinkling of silver.

168   *History Beneath Our Feet*

1106

1107

1108

1109   1110   1111

1112

The Georgian and Victorian Period 169

1113

1115

1114

1116

1117

1118

Gold coins
1097: George I, half-guinea, 1719 - *Upottery*.
1098: Victoria, sovereign, 1872 - *Kingskerswell*.
1099: Victoria, sovereign, 1891 - *Offwell*.
1100: Victoria, sovereign, 1894 - *Newton Poppleford*.

Silver coins
1101: George II, sixpence, 1745 - *Cockington*.
1102: George III, sixpence, 1787 - *Offwell*.
1103: George III, threepence, 1762 - *Kenton*.
1104: George III, Bank of England dollar, 1804 - *Clyst St George*.
1105: George III, halfcrown, 1817 - *Torre Bryan*.
1106: George III, shilling, 1820 - *Newton Abbot*.
1107: George III, sixpence, 1819 - *Cockington*.
1108: Victoria, crown, 1900 - *Newton Abbot*.
1109: Victoria, halfcrown, 1893 - *Exmouth*.
1110: Victoria, shilling, 1872 - *Newton Abbot*.
1111: Victoria, sixpence, 1874 - *Newton Abbot*.

Copper or bronze coins
1112: George I, 'Dump' halfpenny, 1717 - *Newton Abbot*.
1113: George II, farthing, 173[.] - *Newton Abbot*.
1114: George III, halfpenny, 1775 - *Cockington*.
1115: George III, cartwheel twopence, 1797 - *Newton Abbot*.
1116: George III, cartwheel penny, 1797 - *Newton Abbot*.
1117: George III, penny, 1807 - *Cockington*.
1118: George IV, halfpenny, 1827 - *Cockington*.
1119: Victoria, penny, 1875 - *Cockington*.
1120: Victoria, penny, 1886 - *Cockington*.
1121: Victoria, penny, 1899 - *Cockington*.

Continental silver coin
1122: John V, Portugal, 40 reis, pre 1750 - *Whilborough*.

Foreign copper-alloy coins
1123: John V, Portugal, five reis, 1735 - *Haccombe*.
1124: Louis XVI, France, two sou, 1754-93 - *Kingsteignton*.
1125: Japan, late shogunate, tempo tsuho, 1830-53 - *River Teign, Ringmore*.

ADVERTISEMENT TICKETS

Coin-like discs of copper or copper alloy were current in the 19th century as advertising mediums, particularly for trading-establishments. Such tickets, which had no specific value and were not exchangeable, usually had a trader's name and trade and other designs on one or both sides of the flan. Most are the size of a farthing or halfpenny and some are wavy edged.

Copper advertisement-token, 19th century
1126: John Cooke & Sons, sealing wax & wafer manufacturers, stationers & account book makers, London - *River Teign, Shaldon*.

PUB OR ADVERTISEMENT CHECKS

Pub and advertisement checks are similar to tokens and advertising tickets, though lead examples are known as well, but are differentiated by having specified values and could only be exchanged by the issuer or his customers. Combinations of the issuer's name and trading address, e.g. society, pub or club and town, and the value are marked on one or both sides of the flan.

The Georgian and Victorian Period

Copper-alloy pub-checks, 19th century
1127: threehalfpence, J. Murrin, Bradley Hotel, Newton Abbot, maker E. Seage, Exeter - *Newton Abbot.*
1128: threehalfpence, J. Taverner, Bradley Hotel, Newton Abbot, maker C. Vile, Newton Abbot - *Newton Abbot.*

Lead advertisement-check, 19th century
1129: threepence, The George Society, D. 28mm *Uffculme.*

LOVE TOKENS

The custom for a young man to present his sweetheart with a love token fashioned S-shaped from a worn-out copper or silver coin remained current in the 18th and 19th centuries. However, it was also fashionable to use unbent coins, often deliberately abraded on one or both sides to a blank finish on to which was engraved or stamped simple or even elaborate designs incorporating, e.g: hearts, hearts pierced by an arrow, names, dates, initials, other words, lovers' knots, birds, foliate and floriate. Frequently Victorian gentlemen pierced silver love tokens which they suspended from their fob-watch chain.

Silver love tokens, 18th or 19th century
1130: abraded sixpence incuse stamped with a heart on one side and U on the other (probably meaning, love you) - *Newton Abbot.*
1131: George III, sixpence, 1818 - *Bishopsteignton.*

Copper love tokens, probably 19th century
1132: abraded farthing - *Bishopsteignton.*
1133: abraded halfpenny, incuse stamped with P. PLUNKET on one side and LB on the other - *Cockwood.*

FORGERIES

Both regal and token coinage has received the attention of the forger, viz: transforming official copper/copper alloy to silver or silver to gold. This was achieved by coating with silver or gold as necessary (as per example in Tudor chapter). The more expert forger made dies and struck his own coins or cast them from impressions of genuine coins or tokens in clay moulds. Similarly the latter types of forgery were frequently coated in gold or silver accordingly.

Copper-alloy forged token coinage, 19th century
1134: George III, three shilling bank token, 1815 - *Uplyme.*

COMMEMORATIVE MEDALLIONS

The striking of medals or medallions to commemorate historic events or people has been current from at least the Roman period. In the 18th and 19th centuries there was a proliferation issued by the state, the military, the church and schools. Silver examples are not uncommon, though gold are rare; however copper or lead/tin alloy are common.

Cast lead/tin-alloy commemorative medallion, c1740
1135: Admiral Vernon's capture of Portobello from the Spanish. Obv. A VIEW OF FORT CHAGRE, THE BRITISH GLORY REVIVED BY ADMIRAL VERNON. Admiral in uniform with fort behind him. Rev. HE TOOK PORTOBELLO WITH SIX SHIPS ONLY, Nov, 22 1739. View of English fleet. - *Whilborough.*

172   History Beneath Our Feet

1129

1130

1131

1132

1133

1134   1135   1136

The Georgian and Victorian Period

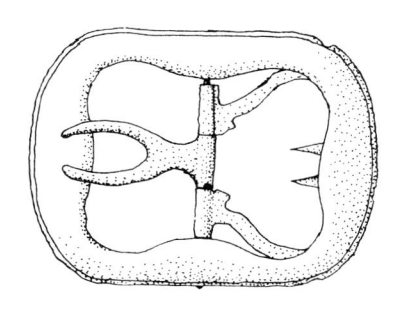

1137

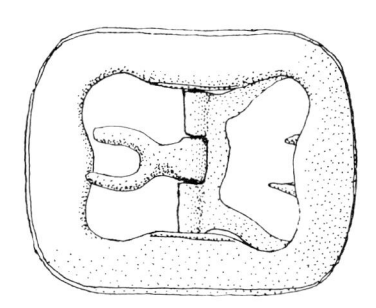

1138

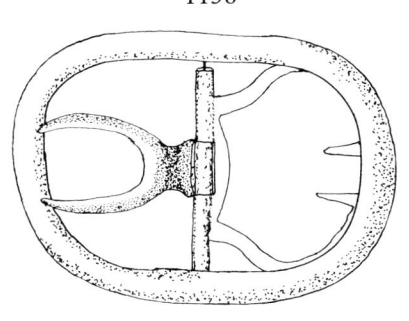

1139

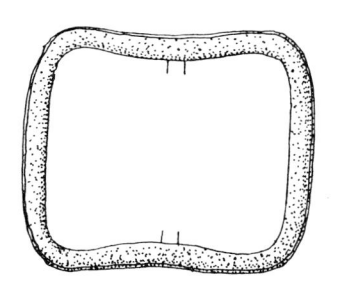

1140

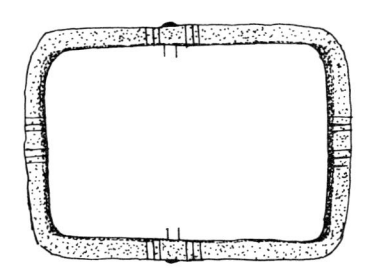

1141

Cast copper-alloy commemorative medallion, 1887
1136: Victoria Diamond Jubilee.
Obv. young head, Rev. old head - *Kingskerswell.*

BUCKLES

Adorning oneself in buckles was a custom that remained current throughout the Georgian period and early Victorian era. Certain types of buckle, especially those worn on footwear, became very large during the last half of the 18th century. Buckles were also worn at the knee, on belts, hats and the nape of the neck as well as being used for many other purposes.

Many styles of metal-buckle were fashionable, frequently very elaborate andoccasionally made of gold or silver, although: steel, iron, tin, copper, copper alloy or lead/tin alloy were the norm. Rich decoration was commonplace: gilding, silvering, Shefield plate, tinning and insets of glass, glass paste or precious or semi-precious gemstones, and with steel buckles, cutwork. Openwork, moulded or engraved decoration is a feature of many buckles, and to a lesser degree, enamelling. Until 1769 buckles were cast but thereafter machine-stamped buckles were concurrent.

With several exceptions, buckle frames which antecede the late 17th century are basically of one-piece construction, however, from c1680 the two-piece buckle became fashionable. This latter term is a misnomer, for two-piece buckles comprise more than two elements, i.e: a drilled frame and a centre-piece of a tongue, chape and spindle - for simplicity the latter three are frequently classed as the chape or centre-piece. Some centre-pieces are steel or iron, therefore few buckles are recovered with these intact, however, when of copper alloy they invariably survive. A popular style of Victorian buckle which continued into the Edwardian era, and indeed is still used today, is clasp-like with two separate sections which hook together.

Cast copper-alloy subrectangular or oval shoe-buckles, c1720-90
1137: engraved linear border, copper-alloy double-spiked loop chape, 50mm x 66mm - *Cockington.*
1138: engraved linear border, copper-alloy double-spiked chape, 52mm x 62mm - *Cockington.*
1139: copper-alloy double-spiked looped chape and double-spiked tongue, 53mm x 72mm - *Cockington.*
1140: concave sides, engraved linear border, 47mm x 55mm *Cockington.*
1141: engraved transverse lines on ends and sides, remains of iron spindle in spindle holes, 45mm x 62mm - *Cockington.*
1142: bifid knops on ends and sides, engraved double linear border, remains of iron spindle and chape, 43mm x 55mm - *Haccombe.*
1143: moulded trefoil knops on ends and sides, 45mm x 54mm *Stokeinteignhead.*
1144: fragmented copper-alloy tongue and chape, 33mm x 46.5mm - *Cockington.*
1145: remains of iron spindle in spindle holes, 36mm x 47mm - *Cockington.*
1146: remains of iron spindle in spindle holes, 31mm x 43mm - *Cockington.*
1147: 27mm x 42mm - *Cockington.*
1148: copper-alloy single-spiked loop chape, 26mm x 36mm

Stokeinteignhead.
1149: fragmented copper-alloy tongue and chape, 30mm x 41mm - *Cockington*.
1150: moulded transverse collars each side of both spindle holes, copper-alloy spindle, fragmented copper-alloy tongue and stud chape, 32mm x 58mm - *Topsham*.
1151: oblique corners, engraved longitudinal lines, engraved linear border, 26mm x 36mm - *Stokeinteignhead*.
1152: serrated ends, concave sides, 27mm x 34mm - *Dawlish Beach*.
1153: slightly concave sides, engraved oblique lines and subrectangles, 29mm x 30mm - *Stokeinteignhead*.
1154: slightly concave sides and ends, moulded transverse and oblique grooves, 33.5mm x 39mm - *Haccombe*.
1155: concave sides, band of engraved dashes around all four sides and similar oblique bands in corners, 46mm x 51mm - *Stokeinteignhead*.
1156: oval knops on ends and sides engraved with concentric ovals and oblique and transverse lines, engraved linear and transverse line border, 49.5mm x 61mm - *Teigngrace*.
1157: intertwined subrectangle and oval with moulded semi-circular border, engraved fleuret on ends and sides, triangular openwork, 31mm x 35mm - *Cockington*.
1158: moulded scrollwork, lozenges and semi-circles; iron spindle, double-spiked tongue and double-spiked loop chape, 35mm x 44mm - *Exeter*.
1159: moulded fleurets and scrollwork, asymmetrical openwork 50mm x 60mm - *Bishopsteignton*.
1160: moulded foliate, engraved transverse lines, asymmetrical openwork, 48mm x 62mm - *Stokeinteignhead*.
1161: engraved sexfoils and fleurets in circles between an inside and outside border of concentric linear and transverse lines, 45mm x 70mm - *Maidencombe*.
1162: engraved fleurets, circles and oblique lines, asymmetrical openwork, 49mm x 67mm - *Maidencombe*.
1163: intertwined figure-eight and ovoid loops, engraved chevrons and concentric lines, asymmetrical openwork, 42mm x 58mm *Alphington*.
1164: moulded scrollwork and circles, 55mm x 74mm - *Haccombe*.

Cast lead/tin-alloy oval or subrectangular shoe-buckles, c1720-90

1165: internal moulded flanges, engraved linear around external edge, moulded linear around internal edge of sides and part of ends, 55mm x 69mm - *Cockington*.
1166: concave sides with internal and external flanges, engraved cross-hatched ends and linear border, 29mm x 34mm - *Stokeinteignhead*.

Forged iron subrectangular shoe-buckle overlaid with lead/tin alloy, c1720-90

1167: engraved fleurets and a border of concentric and transverse lines and curvilinear, 68mm x 91mm - *Haccombe*.

Cast copper-alloy rectangular or square shoe-buckles, c1720-90

1168: engraved foliate and linear border, oblique bands of punched dots, 33mm x 42mm - *Cockington*.
1169: moulded semi-circles border inside and outside, copper-

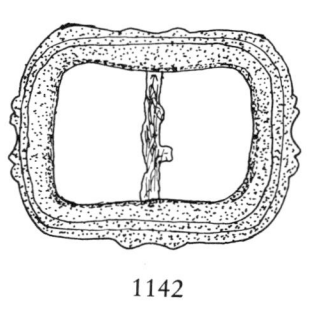

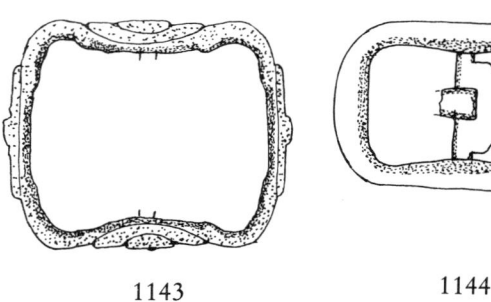

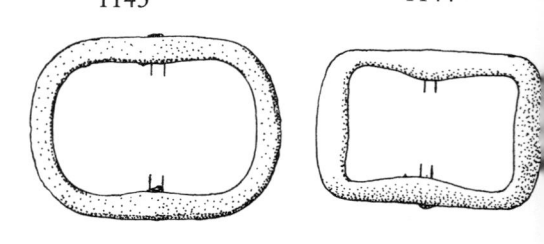

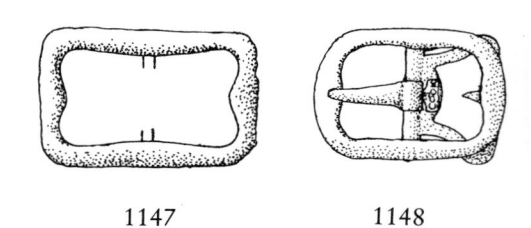

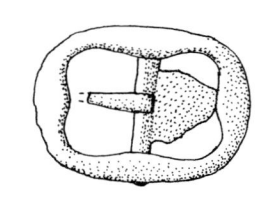

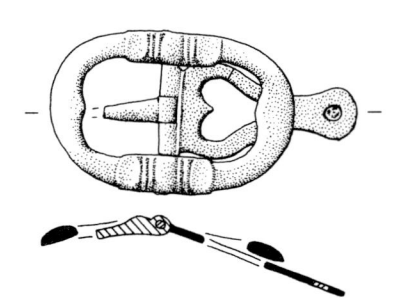

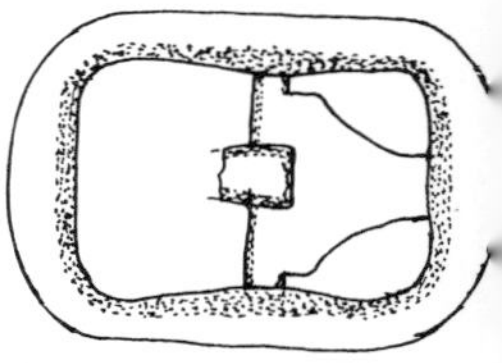

The Georgian and Victorian Period

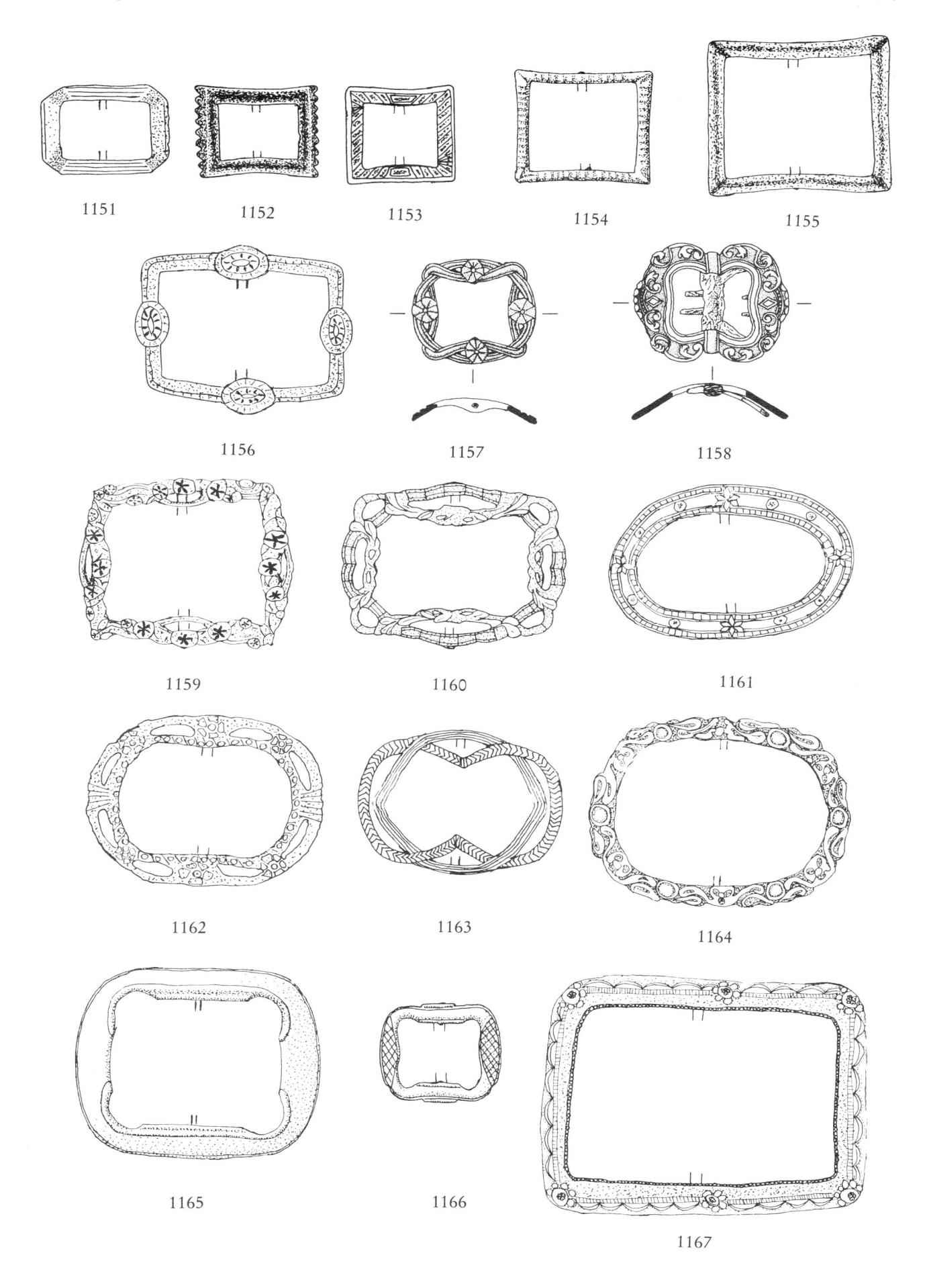

1151

1152

1153

1154

1155

1156

1157

1158

1159

1160

1161

1162

1163

1164

1165

1166

1167

176 History Beneath Our Feet

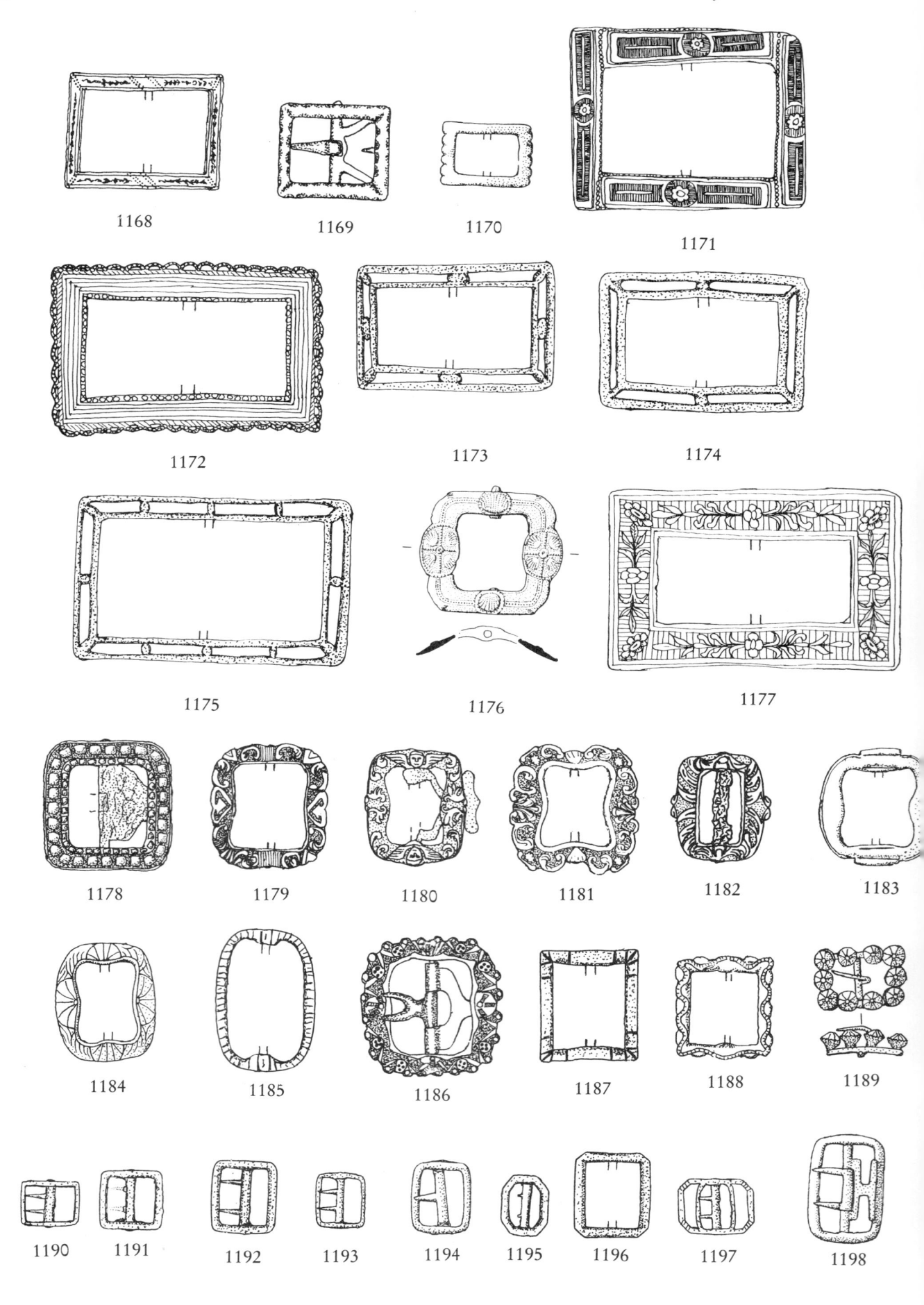

1168 1169 1170 1171

1172 1173 1174

1175 1176 1177

1178 1179 1180 1181 1182 1183

1184 1185 1186 1187 1188 1189

1190 1191 1192 1193 1194 1195 1196 1197 1198

The Georgian and Victorian Period

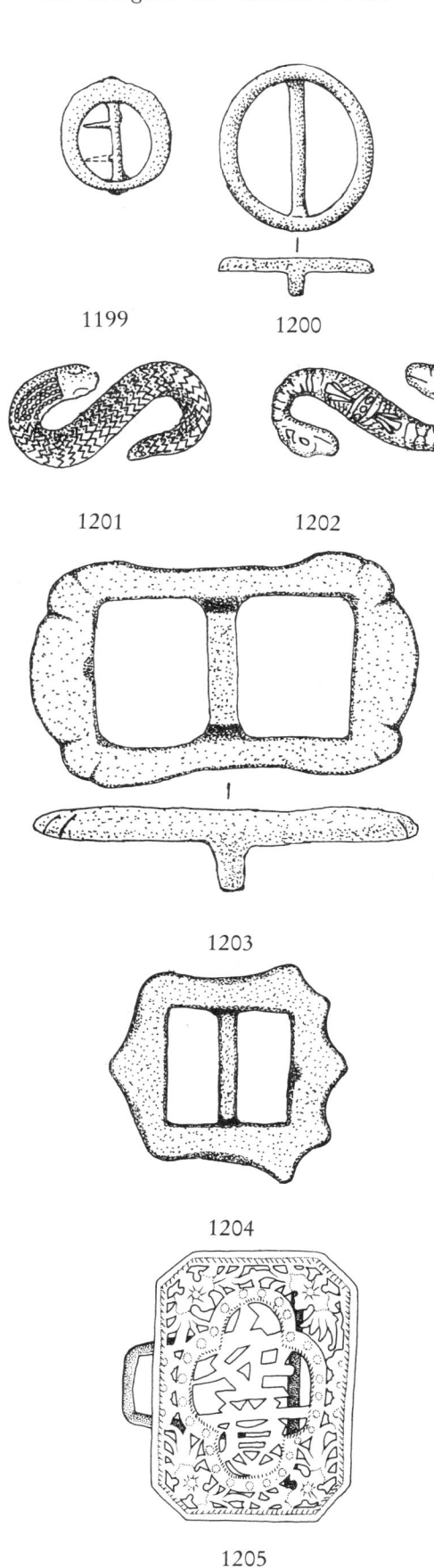

alloy spindle, tongue and single-spiked loop chape, 27mm x 30mm - *Stokeinteignhead*.
1170: serrated ends, 18mm x 24mm - *River Teign, Shaldon*.
1171: engraved fleurets and rectangles formed from transverse lines, 52mm x 63mm - *Newton Abbot*.
1172: wavy outside edges with semi-circular openwork; engraved concentric and oblique lines and inside and outside borders of circles, 49mm x 74mm - *Alphington*.
1173: Artois style, subrectangular openwork, 36mm x 54mm *Alphington*.
1174: Artois style, subrectangular openwork, 40mm x 54mm *Newton Abbot*.
1175: Artois style, rectangular and subrectangular openwork, 47mm x 75mm - *Stokeinteignhead*.
1176: moulded oval on ends each with a beaded cross and escallops in the spandrels, moulded escallops on sides, border of concentric linear bands of punched dots, remains of iron spindle in spindle holes, 35mm x 39mm - *Topsham*.

Cast lead/tin-alloy rectangular shoe-buckle, c1720-90
1177: engraved foliate and fleurets, 51mm x 80mm *River Teign, Coombe Cellars*.

Cast copper-alloy subrectangular stock-, knee- or hat-buckles, c1720-90
1178: two bands of moulded roundels; remains of iron spindle and chape, 37mm x 35mm - *Cockington*.
1179: wavy edged, moulded curlicues and chevrons, engraved transverse lines, 36mm x 32mm - *Kingsteignton*.
1180: moulded angels and foliate, remains of iron spindle and copper- alloy anchor-chape, 33mm x 28mm - *Coffinswell*.
1181: wavy edged; moulded curlicues, escallops and multifoils, 36mm x 35mm - *Cockington*.
1182: bifid knop on each side, moulded curvilinear, remains of iron chape, 31mm x 27mm - *Stokeinteignhead*.
1183: subrectangular knop on each end, engraved linear border, 33mm x 32mm - *Stokeinteignhead*.
1184: engraved inside linear border, semi-circles and curvilinear, 33.5mm x 27.5mm - *Bishopsteignton*.
1185: tinned, engraved transverse grooves, 40mm x 27mm *Haccombe*.

Cast silver subrectangular knee- or hat-buckle, c1720-90
1186: multi lobed-knops with blind holes, moulded trefoils within circles, and oblique wedges, copper-alloy spindle; silver double-spiked tongue and anchor-chape, 39mm x 39mm - *River Exe, Topsham*.

Cast copper-alloy rectangular stock-, knee- or hat-buckles, c1720-90
1187: engraved transverse and oblique lines, 31.5mm x 26.5mm *Cockington*.
1188: multi lobed-knops, moulded wavy border of concentric linear and transverse lines, 29mm x 27mm - *Cockington*.
1189: moulded multi circular-turrets set with clear paste gemstones, copper-alloy spindle and single-spiked chape, 18mm x 24mm - *Cockington*.

Cast copper-alloy rectangular or subrectangular buckles of indeterminate type, probably c1720-90

1190: copper-alloy spindle and double-spiked chape, 13mm x 16mm - *Newton Abbot*.

1191: iron spindle and fragmented copper-alloy double-spiked chape, 16.5mm x 17mm - *Cockington*.

1192: iron spindle and copper-alloy double-spiked chape, 20.5mm x 18mm - *Abbotskerswell*.

1193: iron spindle and copper-alloy double-spiked chape, 15.5mm x 13.5mm - *Haccombe*.

1194: iron spindle and copper-alloy single-spiked chape, 20mm x 16.5mm - *Bishopsteignton*.

1195: oblique corners, iron spindle and fragmented copper-alloy double-spiked chape, 17mm x 13mm - *Cockington*.

1196: oblique corners, 23mm x 21mm - *Cockington*.

1197: oblique corners, integral slightly curved transverse bar either side of spindle hole forming asymmetrical openwork, engraved oblique lines, iron spindle, copper-alloy double-spiked chape, 15.5mm x 20.5mm - *Haccombe*.

1198: copper-alloy spindle, double-spiked tongue and anchor chape, 30.5mm x 20.5mm - *Bishopsteignton*.

Cast copper-alloy oval buckle of indeterminate type, probably c1720-90

1199: iron spindle and fragmented copper-alloy double-spiked chape, 25mm x 23mm - *Haccombe*.

Cast copper-alloy military oval buckle, late 18th early 19th century

1200: recessed central bar, 37mm x 32.5mm - *Newton Abbot*.

Cast copper-alloy possible military S-shaped buckles, 18th-19th centuries

1201: snake, moulded zigzags and circles, 43mm x 24mm - *Cockington*.

1202: double-headed snake, moulded transverse and oblique lines, circles and trefoils, 43mm x 20mm - *Combeinteignhead*.

Cast copper-alloy subrectangular double-loop harness-buckle, late 18th-19th century

1203: recessed centre bar, moulded oblique grooves, 50mm x 62mm - *River Teign, Hackney Marsh*.

Cast copper-alloy asymmetrical double-loop harness-buckle, 19th century

1204: recessed centre bar, 48mm x 50mm - *Ringmore*.

Sheet and wire silver belt-clasp, 19th century

1205: subrectangular, half only, asymmetrical openwork and engraving forming an oriental motif, wire catch soldered to back, 59mm x 43mm - *Chudleigh*.

Cast silver or sheet copper-alloy belt-buckles and clasps, 19th century

1206: all - *South Devon*.

1206

SHOE AND CLOG CLASPS

Between 1790 and 1810 some wooden-soled shoes were fastened with pairs of metal clasps. The same clasps were also worn on clogs from c1850, first in the Lake District, before spreading to Lancashire and Yorkshire - being widely used in mill

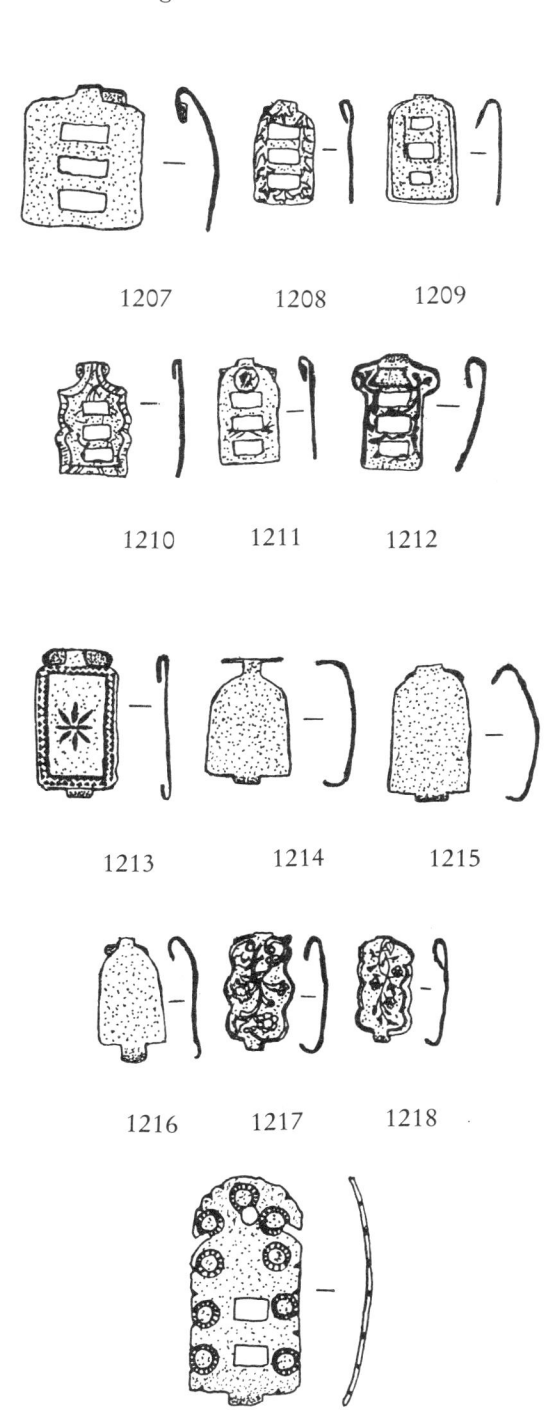

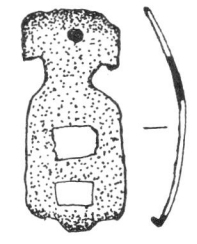

The Georgian and Victorian Period

towns and the countryside. Textile-mill girls normally wore traditional clog-clasps, but they were worn by laundry and bleach-workers as well. They remained current until the 1920s, though it is said they are still worn today in some parts of the north of England.

A pair of clasps comprises one with a downturned anchor-shaped hook on one end and a rectangular hook on the other. The second clasp is similar but with an anchor-shaped hook only. This clasp also has several rectangular lateral slots, usually two or three. Styles and sizes of footwear-clasps vary, some are small, whilst others are quite large, however, most are subrectangular. Although many are plain, frequently they are ornately engraved, embossd or punched. Die-stamped sheet silver, copper alloy or steel were the metals of manufacture, though the latter is rarely found in the ground due to corrosion. A common treatment for steel clasps was coating with a bituminous type paint as a corrosion inhibitor. Silvering or tinning was a common applied-surface treatment for copper-alloy clasps.

Downturned-hook type clasps were affixed to the clog or shoe quarters by passing the anchor-shaped hooks through slits in the leather and then clipping the two clasps together by passing the rectangular hook through the most convenient slot in the other clasp.

Another form of footwear-clasp is very similar to the former, however, in this case the anchor-shaped hooks are not downturned. Instead, each has a rivet hole by which means riveting to the quarter was achieved. Both iron or copper-alloy rivets were current.

Die-stamped copper-alloy subrectangular shoe- or clog-clasps, c1790-1920.

1207: three slots, 28mm x 23mm - *Alphington*.
1208: three slots, engraved foliate, 20.5mm x 11.5mm - *Alphington*.
1209: three slots, engraved linear border and punched dots, 21.5mm x 14mm - *Cockington*.
1210: quatrefoil sides, three slots, engraved linear border and oblique lines, 12mm x 15mm - *Stokeinteignhead*.
1211: three slots, engraved circle, fleuret and oblique lines, 11mm x 12mm - *Cockington*.
1212: lobed knop each side, three slots, engraved foliate, 23mm x 17mm - *Cockington*.
1213: engraved octofoil and border of two rows of punched triangles, 28mm x 15.5mm - *Alphington*.
1214: 24.5mm x 16mm - *Alphington*.
1215: 27mm x 15mm - *Alphington*.
1216: 25mm x 13mm - *Cockington*.
1217: trefoil sides, engraved floriate, 23mm x 13mm - *Coffinswell*.
1218: quatrefoil sides, engraved floriate and linear border, 20.5mm x 11mm - *Alphington*.

Die-stamped copper-alloy subrectangular shoe- or clog-clasps, riveted type, c1790-1920.

1219: two slots, engraved concentric circles and transverse lines, chevron nicks in sides, one rivet hole, 44.5mm x 21mm *Haccombe*.
1220: two slots, one rivet hole, remains of iron rivet, 43.5mm x 19.5mm - *Haccombe*.

The Georgian & Victorian Periods
Distribution of metal detector finds in Southern Devon

1. Abbotskerswell (**MC, MA**)
2. Alphington (**MC, MA**)
3. Axminster (**MC, MA**)
4. Bicton (**MC, MA**)
5. Bigbury Beach (**A**)
6. Bishopsteignton (**MC, MA**)
7. Broadsands Beach, Paignton (**MC, MA**)
8. Chudleigh (**MC, MA**)
9. Clyst Honiton (**MC, MA**)
10. Clyst St George (**MC, MA**)
11. Cockington (**MC, MA**)
12. Cockwood (**MC, MA**)
13. Coffinswell (**MC, MA**)
14. Colaton Raleigh (**MC, MA**)
15. Combeinteignhead (**MC, MA**)
16. Daccombe (**MC, MA**)
17. Dawlish Beach (**MA**)
18. Exeter (**MC, MA**)
19. Exmouth (**MC, MA**)
20. Exminster (**MC, MA**)
21. Fosterville(**MC, MA**)
22. Goodrington Beach, Paignton (**MC, MA**)
23. Haccombe (**MC, MA**)
24. Ide (**MC, MA**)
25. Ipplepen (**MC, MA**)
26. Kenton (**MC**)
27. Kingskerswell (**MC, MA**)
28. Kingsteignton (**MC, MA**)
29. Maidencombe (**MC, MA**)
30. Marldon (**MC, MA**)
31. Musbury (**MC, MA**)
32. Newton Abbot (**MC, MA**)
33. Newton Poppleford (**MC**)
34. Offwell (**MC**)
35. Poltimore (**MC, MA**)
36. Ringmore (**MC, MA**)
37. River Dart, Dittisham (**A**)
38. River Dart, Totnes (**MC, MA**)
39. River Exe, Starcross (**MC, MA**)
40. River Exe, Topsham (**MA**)
41. River Teign, Combe Cellars (**MC, MA**)
42. River Teign, Hackney Marsh (**MC, MA**)
43. River Teign, Ringmore (**MC, MA**)
44. River Teign, Shaldon (**MC, MA**)
45. Shaldon (**MC, MA**)
46. Starcross (**MC, MA**)
47. Stokeinteignhead (**MC, MA**)
48. Teigngrace (**MC, MA**)
49. Teignmouth Beach (**MC, MA**)
50. Topsham (**MC, MA**)
51. Torquay (**MC, MA**)
52. Torre Abbey Sands (**MC, MA**)
53. Torre Bryan (**MC**)
54. Totnes (**MC, MA**)
55. Two Mile Oak (**MC, MA**)
56. Uffculme (**MC, MA**)
57. Ugbrooke (**MC, MA**)
58. Upottery (**MC**)
59. Watcombe (**MC, MA**)
60. Whilborough (**MC, MA**)
61. Wolborough, Newton Abbot (**MC, MA**)
62. Woodbury (**MC, MA**)

Key: **C** = single coin   **MC** = multiple coin
     A = artefact   **MA** = multiple artefact

R. EXE

56

R. CULM

R. CLYST

R. OTTER

58

R. AXE

35

18

9

34

3

24 2

10

31

TEIGN

50
20 40

33
4 14

62

26

46 33
12 19

8
21
57

17

48 28 6
32 42 41 43 49
15 36 45 44
61 23 47
55 1
53 25 27 13 29
16 59
60

DART

11
30 51
52

38
54

22 7

37

N

Scale = 1:316,000 (approx.)

5 miles
8 kilometres

Based upon Ordnance Survey mapping with the permission of the
Controller of Her Majesty's Stationery Office, © Crown copyright.

MOUNTS

Types of horse-furniture current in earlier periods did not remain in fashion in the Georgian and Victorian eras. Nonetheless, cast or die-stamped copper-alloy or cast lead/tin-alloy embellishments were used. It is extremely difficult to differentiate some Georgian and Victorian pieces as styles are very similar. It was still customary to affix mounts to other everyday objects, e.g: personal costume straps, other animal straps, furniture, doors and walls, wheeled vehicles and utensils. It is probable that some of the examples illustrated herein are incorrectly attributed due to lack of evidence.

Draught-horses were not decorated with a great deal of metalwork when engaged on their normal day to day work, however, when entered in a show or competition great quantities were worn. This custom started in the mid 19th century when mass-production made many patterns of horse-brass available. Cast brasses attributed to the 1860s, and mechanically stamped brasses of the late 1870s are known in many shapes, including: square, square with obliquely cut corners, oval, circular, lozenge, shield, crescent or cordate. Frequently they depict the owner's name or initials and more rarely a date. Brasses worn by military horses frequently have engraved initials of their regiment, unit etc. Georgian cordate brasses with engraved lettering exist but are rare; the style of lettering is often the only means of attribution. Harness mounts either have suspension loops, separate or integral rivets, integral pointed or blunt lugs or soldered wire hooks.

Cast copper-alloy bridle-bosses remained popular on mouthpiece ends of bits throughout the two centuries, though cast lead or lead/tin-alloy was increasingly used. Later examples are rivetless and were attached by wire lugs inset into the back with lead. Many bridle-bosses are richly moulded with foliate, floriate or hominoid ornamentation and are invariably gilded, silvered or tinned.

Another type of ornamental brass worn by draught-horses is the fly terret which stood upright from the headband. These may house either a swinging pendant, bell or bells or a plume of feathers.

Cast copper-alloy umbonate bridle-bosses, early 18th century
1221: multifoil, gilded, trefoil knops; moulded beaded circle, fleuret and curvilinear, three rivet holes, three copper-alloy rivets, pierced by (?) small-arms shot, D. 60.3mm - *Ugbrooke*.
1222: multifoil, moulded hominoid face, wavy rim, three rivet holes, three copper-alloy fleuret-headed rivets, D. 50mm - *Abbotskerswell*.
1223: circular, moulded fleuret and border of roundels, two rivet holes, one copper-alloy rivet, D. 47mm - *Chudleigh*.

Cast copper-alloy umbonate bridle-boss, 18th century
1224: multifoil, lobed knops, moulded central fleuret and circle of fleurets, D. 50mm - *Newton Abbot*.

Cast lead bridle-bosses, late 18th-19th century
1225: circular, umbonate centre; moulded central sexfoil with trefoils in the angles, border of fleurets, D. 59mm - *Stokeinteignhead*.

The Georgian and Victorian Period 181

1230

1231

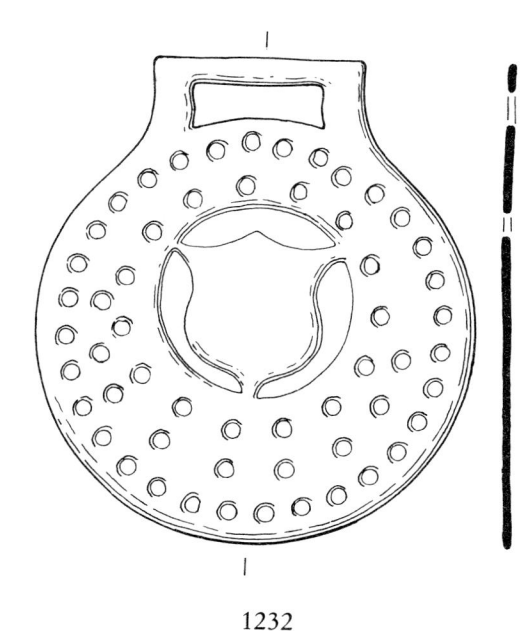

1232

1226: circular, silvered, moulded foliate, fleurets and a beaded circle, D. 50mm - *Combeinteignhead*.
1227: circular, moulded foliate, D. 50mm - *Starcross*.
1228: circular, moulded multifoils and beaded circle, D. 40mm - *Kingskerswell*.
1229: multifoil, moulded foliate and beaded circle, D. 40mm - *Watcombe*.
1230: circular, umbonate, abraded moulded multi-lobed rim, moulded foliate, D. 70mm - *Haccombe*.

Cast or die-stamped copper-alloy suspended or lug-attached horse- harnes mounts, 19th - early 20th century
1231: all - *South Devon*.

Cast copper-alloy suspended horse-harness mounts, 19th - early 20th century
1232: circular, rectangular suspension loop, multi-circular openwork and asymmetrical openwork forming a shield shape, 95mm x 83mm - *Cockington*.
1233: circular, subrectangular suspension loop, multi asymmetrical and circular openwork, 96mm x 83.5mm - *Clyst St George*.

Cast copper-alloy oval horse-harness mounts with integral blunt lugs, 19th - early 20th century
1234: inscribed TYC, possibly Teignmouth Yeomonry Cavalry, three blunt lugs, 22mm x 41mm - *Ringmore*.
1235: inscribed GH, three integral blunt lugs (one lost), 48mm x 37mm - *Cockwood*.

Cast copper-alloy oval horse-harness mounts with separate copper wire hooks, 19th early 20th century
1236: inscribed C, hooks lost, 73mm x 54mm - *Shaldon*.
1237: inscribed EXETER TOWN COUNCIL; remains of one wire hook, three lost; 73mm x 62mm - *Exeter*.
1238: inscribed COUNCIL of EXETER, four wire hooks, 78mm x 63mm - *Exeter*.

Cast copper-alloy rectangular horse-harness mount with separate copper wire hooks, 19th early 20th century
1239: oblique corners, inscribed JLB, wire hook soldered to back, 62mm x 50mm - *Cockwood*.

Cast copper-alloy rectangular horse-harness mount with separatepointed lugs, 19th - early 20th century
1240: oblique corners, inscribed RT, four pointed-lugs soldered to back, 60mm x 49mm - *Kingsteignton*.

Cast copper-alloy asymmetrical horse-harness maker's-plates, 19th - early 20th century
1241: inscribed LIDSTONE MAKER PAIGNTON, remains of four integral lugs, 27mm x 71mm - *Cockington*.
1242: inscribed PASSMORE & COLE MAKERS EXETER, two separate threaded-bolts with remains of iron corrosion around one, 34.5mm x 96mm - *Clyst Honiton*.

Cast and forged copper-alloy fly terret and swinger, 19th - early 20th century
1243: penannular circular cross-section frame with lateral flat-circular pierced projections at top and circular cross-section threaded bolt with moulded collars at bottom,

1233

1234

1235

1236

1237

1238

1239

1240

1241

The Georgian and Victorian Period 183

1242

1243

1244

1245

1246

1247

1248

1249

1250

1251

1252

1253

1254

1255

separate copper-alloy sub-circular swinger with asymmetrical openwork and flat-circular pierced projection at top, copper-alloy pin, 102mm x 57mm - *Kingskerswell.*

Cast copper-alloy asymmetrical terret-swinger, 19th - early 20th century

1244: double-sided, probably Prince Albert, 55mm x 32mm *Exminster.*

1245: circular, double-sided, commemoration of Queen Victoria's golden jubilee, central crown over 1887 with V left and R right, asymmetrical openwork, 55mm x 41mm - *Newton Abbot.*

Cast copper-alloy threaded reign-terret, 19th - early 20th century

1246: fragmented, square and circular cross-section stem with rounded circular collar; moulded head with acorn knop, globular and rounded collars, moulded curvilinear, middle collar has integral hook, L. 82mm - *Cockington.*

Cast copper-alloy symmetrical carriage-mount, c.late 18th - 19th century

1247: lozenge-shaped centre with moulded multifoil, concentric circles and a rounded border interspaced with pellets, moulded acanthus-style ends with asymmetrical openwork, 148mm x 42mm - *Kingskerswell.*

Cast lead/tin-alloy circular probable horse-harness mount, 18th-19th century

1248: fragmented and abraded, sub-triangular knop, border of moulded probable fleurets and central fleuret, asymmetrical openwork, three rivet holes, remains of three iron rivets, 41mm x 34mm - *Kingskerswell.*

Cast copper-alloy asymmetrical convex probable horse-harness mounts with integral lugs, c18th century

1249: moulded curvilinear and transverse bands, three lugs, 74mm x 44mm - *Cockington.*

1250: moulded curvilinear and oblique lines, four lugs, 60.5mm x 37mm - *Cockington.*

1251: moulded oblique grooves, two lugs, 54mm x 26mm - *Cockington.*

1252: moulded transverse bands, two lugs, 41.5mm x 21.5mm *Cockington.*

1253: moulded transverse bands, three lugs, 46.5mm x 18mm *Cockington.*

1254: fragmented, moulded transverse bands, two lugs (one lost), 36mm x 19.5mm - *Cockington.*

1255: moulded circles, two lugs, 35.5mm x 20mm - *Alphington.*

1256: two lugs, 24.5mm x 20mm - *Fosterville.*

1257: moulded lozenge and transverse bands, two lugs (one lost), 34mm x 31.5mm - *Cockington.*

1258: engraved border line and concentric circles, two lugs, 31mm x 15mm - *Daccombe.*

Cast copper-alloy cordate convex horse-harness mount with integral lugs, 18th- 19th century

1259: two lugs, 34mm x 17mm - *Stokeinteignhead.*

Cast copper-alloy shield-shaped convex horse-harness mount with integral, 18th-19th century

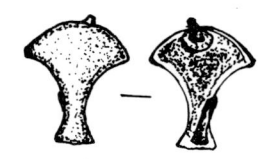

1256

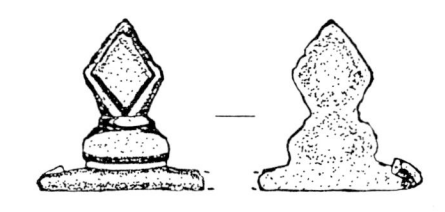

1257

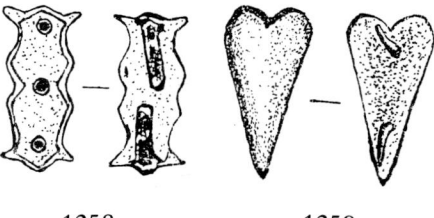

1258   1259

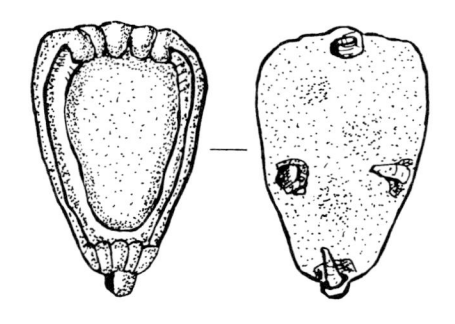

1260

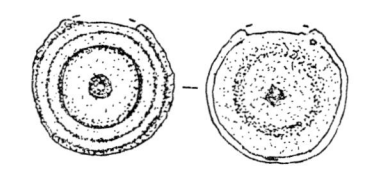

1261

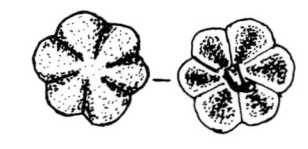

1262

The Georgian and Victorian Period 185

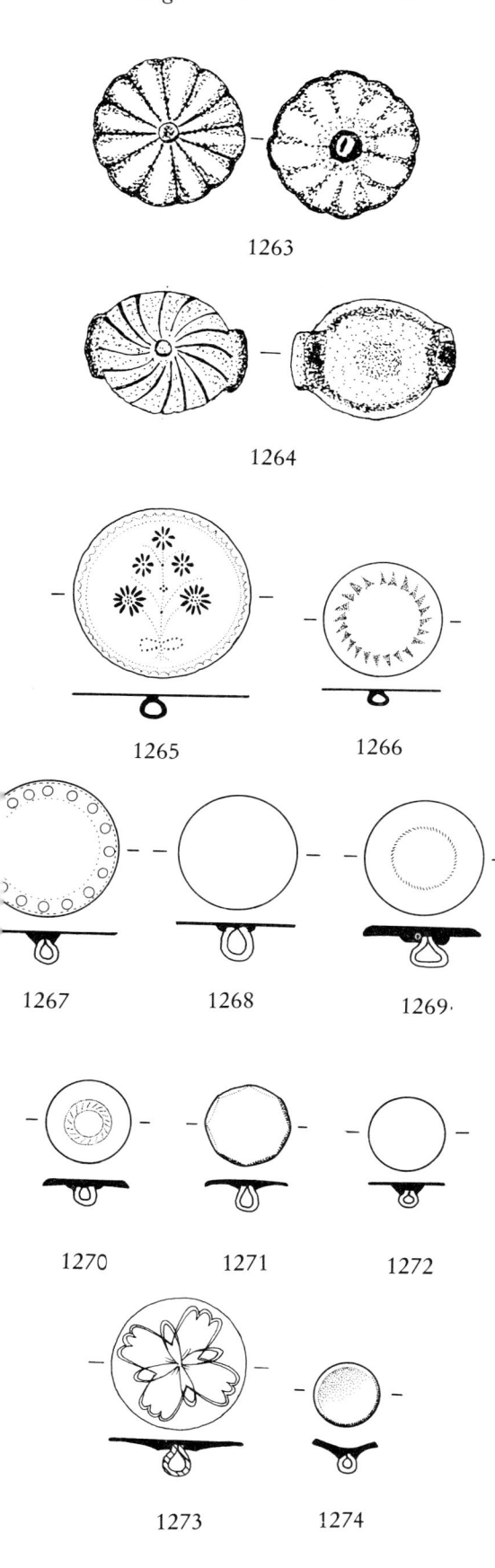

1260: moulded curvilinear, four lugs, 54mm x 32.5mm - *Cockington.*

Cast copper-alloy domed stud-like horse-harness mounts, 18th-19th century

1261: circular, moulded concentric circles, abraded edge, D. 27mm - *Cockington.*
1262: sexfoil, moulded transverse lines, D. 22mm - *Cockington.*
1263: multi-foil, moulded transverse lines and circle, D. 32mm - *Cockington.*

Cast copper-alloy oval domed horse-harness guide with separate rivets, 19th century

1264: moulded curvilinear and circle, two rivet holes, remains of two iron rivets, 27mm x 34mm - *Cockington.*

BUTTONS

Metal buttons attributed to the Georgian and Victorian periods are of either one, two or three-piece construction. Types are classified as: solid die-cut - flat, convex or concave with separate wire shank; shell - flat disc base pierced for separate wire shank, domed shell; solid domed - separate wire shank, or flat - two or more pierced holes for stitching. Copper alloy or lead/tin alloy, frequently tinned, gilded or silvered, were the normal metals for button-making; however, iron, silver or gold were current, although examples of the latter are rare. Predominantly they are circular and to a lesser extent hexagonal or octagonal.

Many Georgian buttons are rather uninteresting plain metal discs, but some are richly ornamented with engine-engraved patterns, particularly the large Dandy-buttons. Livery buttons of the late 18th early 19th century have very attractive moulded crests or other designs, whilst 19th-century sporting buttons depict engine-engraved, embossed or moulded animals, birds or representations of field sports.

Militia, volunteer, regimental or naval buttons with engine-engraved, embossed or moulded motifs were widely used throughout the 19th century and to a lesser degree in the 18th. Many are extremely rare and identification of some is impossible due to lack of primary documentation. As with other items of militaria, finds of such buttons assist greatly with plotting the movements of early military units.

Solid die-cut copper-alloy flat circular two-piece engine-engraved buttons, 18th century

1265: silvered, floriate and border of dots and loopwork, D. 37.5mm - *Cockington.*
1266: silvered, triangles, D. 25mm - *Cockington.*

Solid die-cut lead/tin-alloy flat circular two-piece engine-engraved or plain buttons, 18th century

1267: border of circles and two bands of dashes, D. 30mm - *Cockington.*
1268: D. 25mm - *Stokeinteignhead.*
1269: circle of oblique dashes, D. 25.5mm - *Haccombe.*
1270: concentric circles with oblique dashes, D. 18mm - *Cockington.*
1271: bevelled edge forming an octagen, D. 17.5mm - *Haccombe.*
1272: D. 16mm - *Cockington.*
1273: fleurete, 28.5mm - *Uffculme.*

Solid die-cut lead/tin-alloy concave circular two-piece button, 18th century
1274: D. 14mm - *Haccombe*.

Solid die-cut lead/tin-alloy flat octagonal two-piece engine- engraved button, 18th century
1275: fleuret and border of double row of dots, D. 25mm - *Cockington*.

Solid die-cut silver flat circular two-piece engine-engraved button, 18th century
1276: flat with downturned rim, two cordates surmounted by a crown, D. 15mm - *Cockwood*.

Solid die-cut copper-alloy two-piece flat circular embossed livery buttons, late 18th - 19th century
1277: silvered, bird surmounting WHP, D. 30mm - *Exeter*.
1278: silvered, bird left, D. 25mm - *Haccombe*.
1279: gilt, dragon left between two crowns, D. 25mm - *Cockington*.
1280: gilt, escallop, D. 25mm - *Axminster*.
1281: gilt, rampant lion right on a crown, D. 25mm - *Stokeinteignhead*.
1282: gilt, rampant lion left holding a sprig of foliate, D. 16mm - *Haccombe*.
1283: gilt, rampant bull left, D. 14mm - *Haccombe*.

Solid die-cut copper-alloy two-piece domed circular embossd livery buttons,
1284: gilt, rampant griffin left, D. 24.5mm - *Musbury*.
1285: gilt, crown surmounted by floriate, D. 25mm - *Haccombe*.
1286: gilt, oval quartered-shield of foliate, D. 25mm - *Haccombe*.
1287: gilt, quartered shield surmounted by a helmet and surrounded by scrollwork, D. 25mm - *Cockington*.

Solid die-cut silver two-piece domed circular button, 19th century
1288: silver fleuret on a blue enamelled field, D. 26mm - *Ringmore*.

Shell copper-alloy and paste three-piece flat circular button, 19th century
1289: asymmetrical openwork forming a fleurete and foliate overlaying white paste, shank lost, D. 30mm - *Cockington*.

Sheet copper-alloy embossed flat octofoil button, 19th century
1290: fleuret, D. 14.5mm - *Cockington*.

Shell copper-alloy three-piece circular domed button, 18th century
1291: vent hole in lower half, D. 20mm - *Cockington*.

Shell copper-alloy three-piece domed button, 18th century
1292: D. 14.5mm - *Cockington*.

Shell copper-alloy two-piece domed button, 18th century
1293: D. 16.5mm - *Cockington*.

Solid die-cut copper-alloy two-piece flat circular button, 18th century
1294: D. 13.5mm - *Cockington*.

Shell copper-alloy three-piece embossed domed livery buttons, 19th - early 20th century

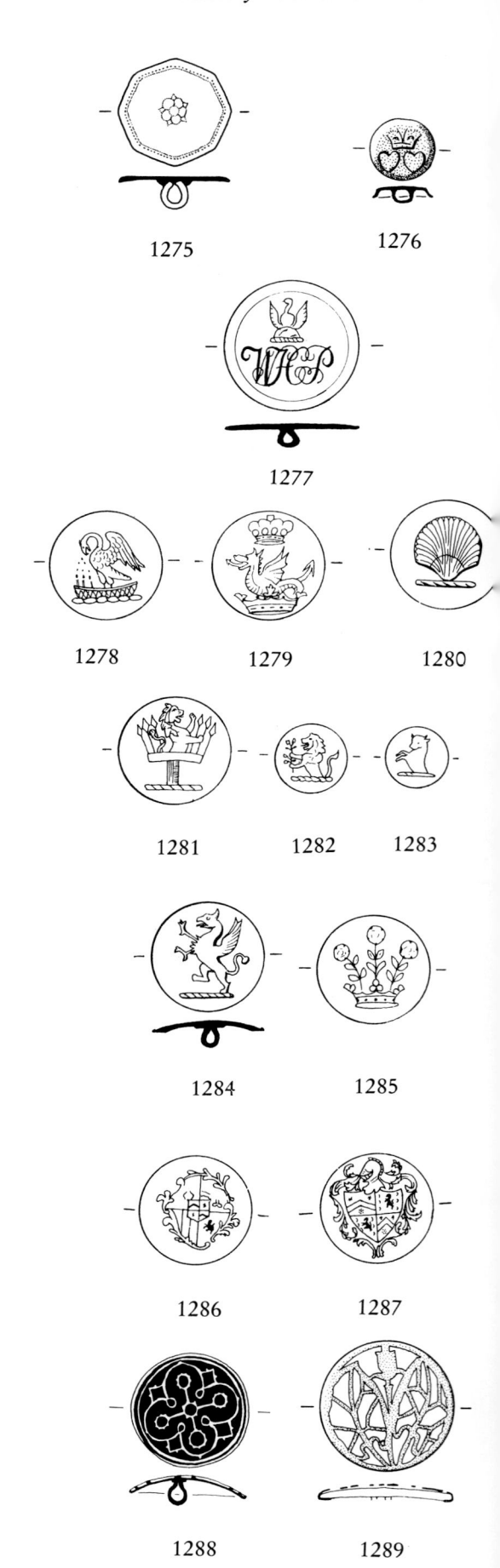

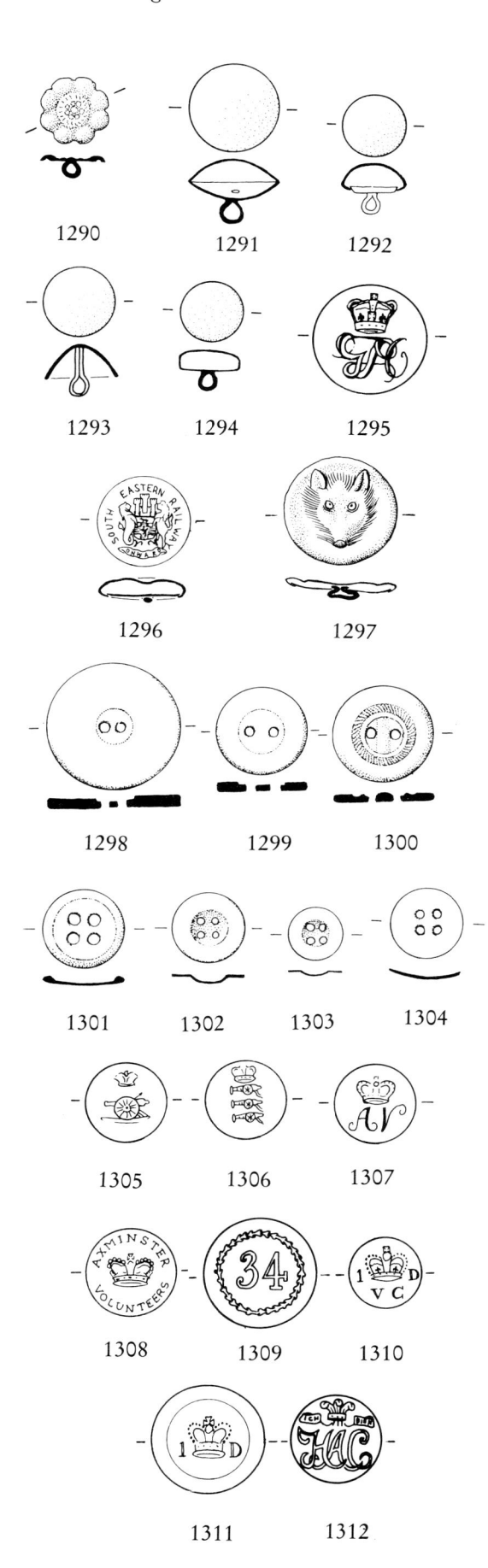

The Georgian and Victorian Period

1295: pre 1902, crowned GR, General Post Office, D. 25mm - *Cockington.*
1296: coat of arms, SOUTH EASTERN RAILWAY, fragment of shank, D. 19mm - *Uffculme.*

Shell copper-alloy three-piece embossed domed sporting button, 19th century

1297: flattened, boar's head, D. 25mm - *Cockwood.*

Solid die-cut lead one-piece flat circular buttons with stitching holes, 19th century

1298: moulded circle, two holes, D. 19.5mm - *Cockington.*
1299: moulded circle, two holes, D. 20mm - *Cockington.*
1300: moulded concentric circles and oblique lines, two holes, D. 22.5mm - *Cockington.*

Solid die-cut copper-alloy concave circular buttons with stitching holes, late 19th early 20th century

1301: moulded circle, four holes, D. 18mm - *Haccombe.*
1302: four holes, D. 16mm - *Cockington.*
1303: four holes, D. 12mm - *Cockington.*
1304: four holes, D. 16mm - *Cockington.*

Solid die-cut copper-alloy two-piece flat circular engine-engraved military buttons

1305: 1790-1831, crowned field-gun, Royal Regiment of Artillery D. 18mm - *Exeter.*
1306: 1794-1802, crowned AV, Axminster Volunteers, D. 18mm - *Axminster.*
1307: 1794-1802, crown with AXMINSTER above and VOLUNTEERS below, Axminster Volunteers, D. 20mm - *Axminster*
1308: c1826-55, silvered, wreathed 34, officer's, 34th (Cumberland) Regiment of Foot, D. 26mm *Cockington.*
1309: 1855-73, crowned three field-guns, Royal Regiment of Artillery, D. 18mm - *Exeter.*
1310: c.early 19th century, crowned VC with 1 left and D right, possibly 1st Devon Volunteer Cavalry, D. 16mm - *Exeter.*
1311: c.early 19th century, crown with 1 left and D right within a linear circle, possibly 1st Devon, D. 25mm - *Exeter.*
1312: 19th century, gilt, Prince of Wales feathers ICH DIEN over HAC almost certainly the Honourable Artillery Company of London, D. 21mm - *Cockington.*

Shell copper-alloy three-piece embossed military buttons

1313: crowned GR IV, 1830-7, William IV, general service, or possibly 1820-30, George IV, royal household, D. 23mm - *Cockington.*
1314: dragon over 3 VETERI FRONDSCIT HONORE, 3rd (East Kent) Regiment of Foot (The Buffs), either an officer's button of c1830 or an officers' mess waiter's button 1855-81, D. 25mm - *Exeter.*
1315: c1855-73 or possibly 1833-8, gilt, crowned three field-guns, Royal Regiment of Artillery, D. 24mm - *Cockington.*
1316: 1855-81, crowned hoop, 1st DEVON MILITIA, castle within, foliate and floriate wreath, SEMPER FIDELIS, 1st or East Devon Militia, D. 25mm - *Exeter.*
1317: 1855-1902, crowned VR within a belt, VOLUNTEER ENGINEERS, D. 24mm - *Cockington.*
1318: pre 1881, wreathed 34, 34th (Cumberland) Regiment of Foot, D. 25mm - *Woodbury.*
1319: pre 1881, crowned 10 within a wreath, 10th (North

Lincoln) Regiment of Foot, D. 25mm - *Woodbury.*
1320: pre 1881, lion and crown above 47, wreath and TARIPA, 47th (TheLancashire) Regiment of Foot, D. 26mm - *Woodbury.*
1321: 1855-81, crowned 37 within a wreath, 37th (North Hampshire) Regiment of Foot, D. 23.5mm - *Exeter.*
1322: c1885, crowned horn, V left R right, E.S.D above, Exeter and South Devon Volunteer Rifles, D. 22mm - *Woodbury.*
1323: probably 19th century, gilt, crowned HRV, (?) Haytor Rifle Volunteers, D. 18mm - *Cockington.*
1324: probably 19th century, unidentified, crowned G, D left Y right, (?) Devon Yeomonry Guard, D. 15mm - *Cockington.*

Hollow-domed die-cut copper-alloy two-piece military buttons

1325: 1873-1902, three field-guns within a shield, Royal Regiment of Artillery, D. 20mm - *Exeter.*
1326: c1856-60, crowned horn, V left R right, E.S.D above, Exeter and South Devon Volunteer Rifles, D. 23mm - *Cockington.*

OTHER JEWELLERY

The types of Georgian or Victorian jewellery are legion and here it is possible only to describe but a few pieces not dealt with elsewhere.

Sheet gold and forged iron solitaire, 19th century
1327: stud only, engine engraved foliate, D. 20mm - *Wolborough, Newton Abbot.*

Cast and wire gold cufflink, 1740-1807
1328: made from two southern India coins, three-figure Pagoda, issued by the Madras Prendency of the East India Company, 29mm x 12mm - *Cockington,*

Sheet and wire silver cufflinks, 18th century
1329: circular, engraved fleurets and a looped border, 16mm x 35mm - *Cockington.*
1330: octagonal, fragmented plate engraved T, the other A, 15.5mm x 36mm - *Cockington.*

Sheet and wire silver oval cufflink, late 18th-19th century
1331: engraved curvilinear, 19mm x 28mm - *Cockington.*

Die-cut and wire silver cufflink, 1862
1332: made from two Victoria two anna coins from India, 16mm x 33mm - *Newton Abbot.*

Sheet and wire silver brooches, 19th century
1333: oval, pin lost; embossed BABY and shield-shapes with pricked dots, border of embossed circles, 7mm x 32mm - *Ringmore.*
1334: oval, embossed BABY, silver pin, 8mm x 33mm - *Cockington.*
1335: three embossd horseshoes, hollow, silver pin, 22mm x 33.5mm - *Cockington.*
1336: embossed cockerel, hollow, silver pin, 36mm x 29.5mm - *Cockington.*

Cast gold and silver wire cravat pin, 19th century
1337: shield-shaped gold head with a moulded cruciform, twisted silver pin, 66mm x 16mm - *Exmouth.*

Sheet and wire silver possible hat-pin, 19th century

The Georgian and Victorian Period 189

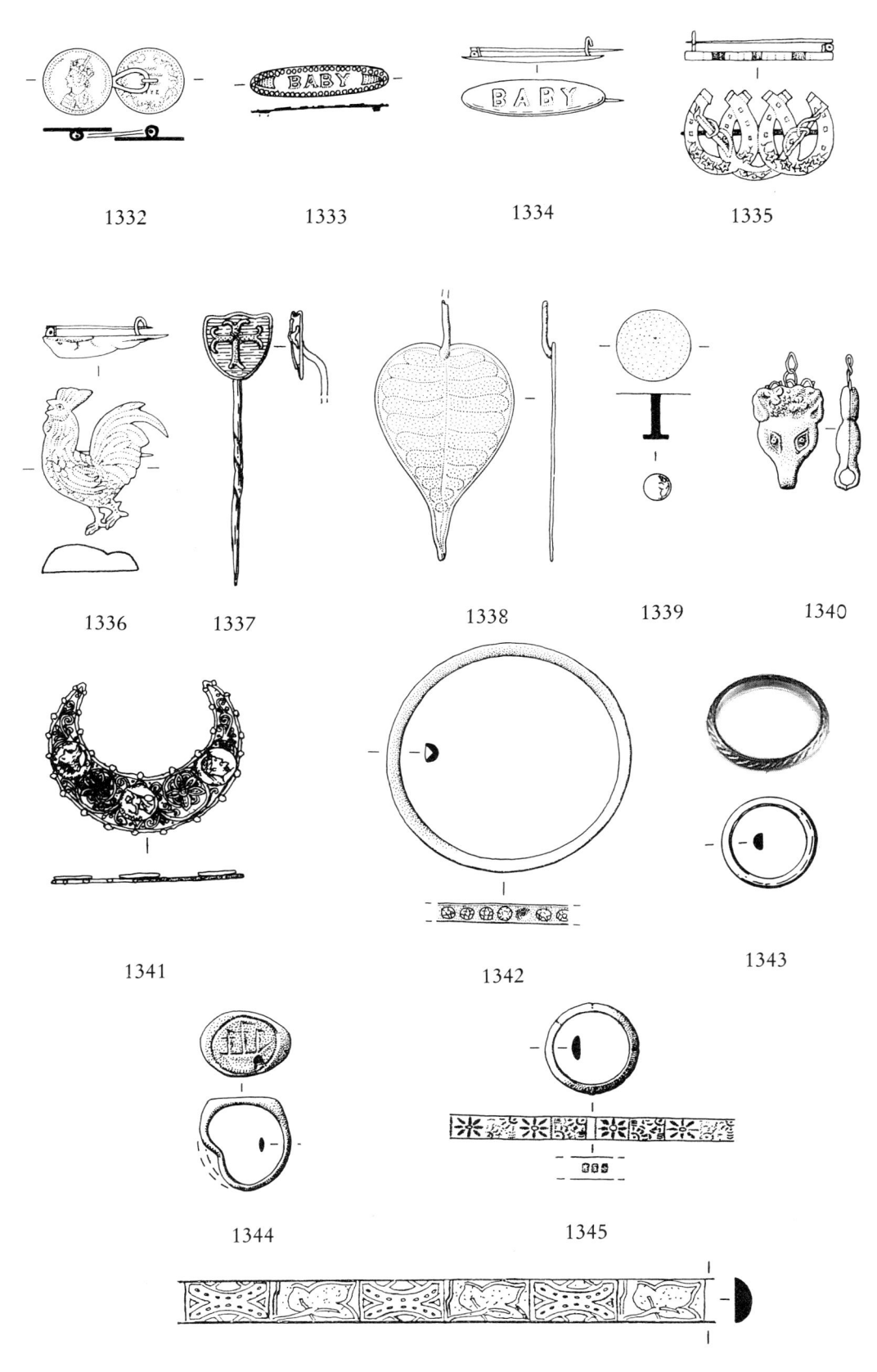

1332

1333

1334

1335

1336

1337

1338

1339

1340

1341

1342

1343

1344

1345

1346

1338: engraved pital leaf, fragmented integral silver (?) pin, 63mm x 32.5mm - *Cockington*.

Sheet and wire silver collar-stud, 19th century
1339: traces of punched dots on small end, 11mm x 17.5mm - *Cockington*.

Sheet and wire copper-alloy pendant, possibly from a chatelaine, 19th century
1340: embossed fox's head with a circular pendant loop beneath and remains of copper-alloy chain-link strap above, 33mm x 16mm - *Newton Abbot*.

Sheet and cast copper-alloy possible brooch, 19th century
1341: crescent-shaped, moulded fleurets and curvilinear, lobed knops around edge, three Roman Ae3/4 coins mounted on front, 37mm x 45mm - *Bishopsteignton*.

Cast copper or copper-alloy bracelet, possibly late 19th century
1342: semi-circular cross-section with the flat face outwards; whole of outside of hoop originally set with 40 facetted red stones (probably glass), 15 of which are lost, external D. 56.5mm, internal D. 50.5mm - *Bigbury Beach*.

FINGER RINGS

The wearing of finger-rings continued in popularity with both sexes throughout the 18th and 19th centuries. As in the 17th, early 18th-century women apparently wore their wedding rings on the thumb. Finger rings with a posie inscription inside the hoop were invariably worn as wedding rings during the 18th century. The so-called 'peasant finger-rings' were current during both periods for ordinary folk. The ubiquitous signet type, in precious or base metals, was greatly revived in the 19th century, although most have directly engraved bezels with merchants or heraldic type devices. However, the more ostentatious intaglios with classical bust devices, so fashionable in earlier times, enjoyed a re-awakening in the 18th century.

Fede finger-rings remained popular until the 19th century, and magical or religious finger-rings well into the same century. Finger rings as commemorative pieces were produced and worn until the time of Queen Victoria's marriage, thereafter the practice seems to have faded. Mourning finger-rings inlaid with a hoop of black enamel field and decorated with a metal design such as a skeleton or foliate and a crystal-covered circular or oval bezel inset with a skull or the deceased's initials in gold thread, were known around 1720. Later 18th-century examples are usually bezel-less and inscribed outside the hoop. It was common practice to have black enamelled mourning finger-rings for those who were married and white enamel for the unmarried.

Special finger-rings, the so-called fancy rings, including clay pipe tobacco stoppers, those with locket bezels (?) for perfume or poison, pugilists' or dial rings remained current until the end of the 18th century. Serjeants' finger-rings ceased to be presented after the **Judicature Law, 1875**.

Gold probable wedding-finger-ring, c18th century
1343: semi-circular cross-section hoop, band of moulded oblique grooves outside, external D. 19mm, internal D. 16mm - *Exeter*.

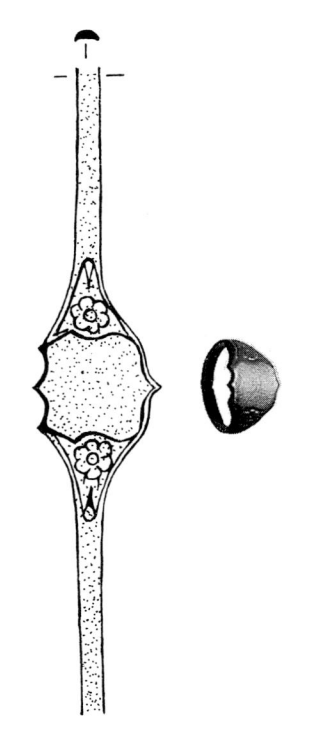

1347

1348

1349

The Georgian and Victorian Period

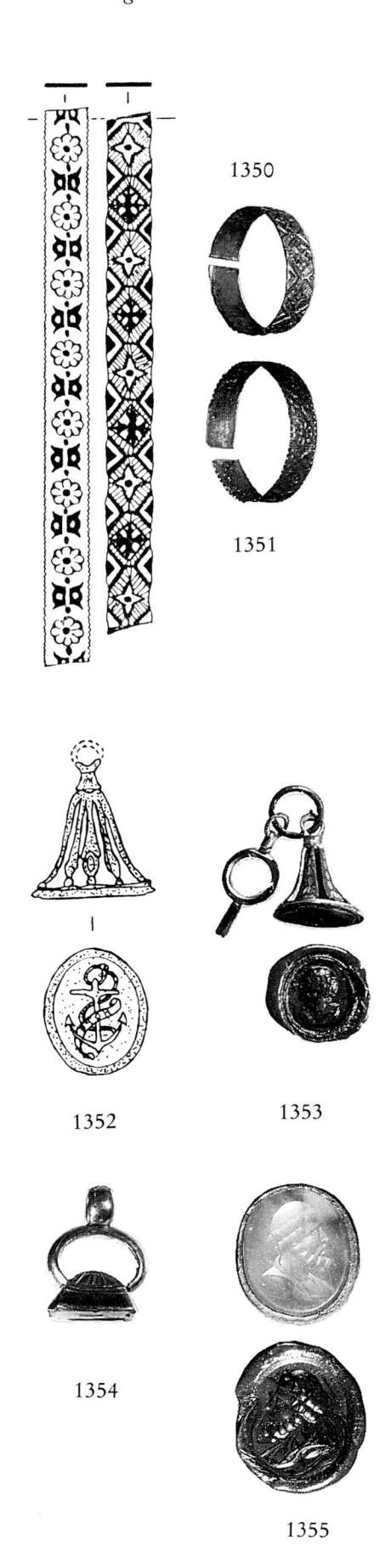

Copper-alloy signet finger-ring, 18th century
1344: crushed hoop, vesica-shaped cross-section hoop, oval bezel, ship device, (? merchants mark), external D. 22mm, internal D. 18mm - *Ipplepen.*

Copper-alloy peasant-finger-rings, 18th century
1345: traces of gilt, semi-circular cross-section hoop, alternate panels of octofoils and curvilinear formed from punched dots, psuedo-hallmark inside, external D. 22mm, internal D. 17.5mm - *Torquay.*

1346: traces of gilt, semi-circular cross-section hoop, alternate panels of moulded foliate and asymmetrical designs, not to scale - *Haccombe.*

1347: traces of gilt, semi-circular cross-section hoop, alternate panels of moulded octofoils and foliate, external D. 19mm, internal D. 16mm - *Newton Abbot.*

1348: traces of gilt, vesica-shaped cross-section hoop, moulded semi- circular band with transverse lines, external D. 20mm, internal D.18mm - *Cockington.*

Gold (22ct) wedding finger-ring, 1848
1349: semi-circular cross-section hoop, Birmingham hallmark, external D. 22mm, internal D. 17.5mm - *Torre Abbey Sands, Torquay.*

Copper-alloy peasant-finger-rings, c19th century
1350: traces of gilt, convex semi-circular cross-section hoop, shield- shaped bezel, engraved fleurets in sub-triangular panels on shoulders, external D. 18mm, internal D. 17mm - *Bishopsteignton.*

1351: duplex type, traces of gilt, penannular flat hoops; outside hoop with serrated edges and alternate embossed fleurets, dots and asymmetrical shapes; inside hoop has embossed chevrons, lozenges, quatrefoils, oblique lines and dots,external D. of outside hoop 19mm, internal D. 18mm; external D. of inside hoop 17.5mm, internal D. 17.4mm - *Cockington*

SEAL MATRICES

Fob-seal matrices which were sometimes purely decorative, remained current for the whole of the Georgian period and well into the Victorian age, whilst seal finger-ring pipe-tampers had disappeared by around the middle of the 18th century. Made from cast gold or copper alloy, usually gilded, fob-seals generally have elaborate openwork bodies terminating in a suspension loop. Directly engraved dies are a characteristic of some, though predominantly they feature semi-precious gemstone intaglios. Rectangular, circular or oval dies are the norm, invariably depicting personal initials, classical busts or abstract devices.

Cast, gilt-copper-alloy fob-seal matrices, late 18th-19th century
1352: oval, cornelian intaglio, anchor & hope device, fragmented circular suspension loop, 32mm x 28mm - *Cockington.*

1353: oval, cornelian intaglio, classical bust device, gilt-copper-alloy suspension ring and watch-key attached, 30mm x 25mm - *Cockington.*

1354: rectangular, cornelian intaglio - *Goodrington Beach, Paignton.*

1355: fragmented, oval, copper-alloy ring set with blue agate intaglio, classical bust device, 24mm x 21mm - *Stokeinteignhead.*

CLOTH SEALS

Marking newly made cloth with leaden seals continued through the 18th century, a practice that finally expired in the 19th.

Cast lead cloth-seal, post 1815
1356: Netherlands, moulded crowned shield with rampant beast, R left A right, REYKNUNG & ACCYNSIN (Customs & Excise), beaded circle - *Abbotskerswell.*

THIMBLES

By the 18th century most copper-alloy thimbles were manufactured in Germany or England. Birmingham had become the centre of the English brass industry, including thimble-making, although John Lofting remained the dominant producer. It was Englishman John Ford's invention (patented in 1769) of a machine for impressing ornamentation on sheet metal which sounded the death-knell for hand-made thimbles, and soon afterwards mass-production of thimbles commenced.

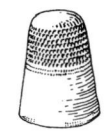

The 18th century saw three shapes for thimbles: until c1750 they were somewhat short and stubby with a flattish crown, from c1790 a slim taller shape with a rounded crown was preferred, and lastly at the very end of the period the beehive shape became fashionable. All three types were made in copper alloy, silver, and occasionally, gold. The taller variety frequently had a steel top. Two-piece construction continued until c1750s (notwithstanding, it was employed on a limited scale into the 19th century) when the deep drawn method commenced. As the century passed the base became wider with a broad border invariably decorated with engraved foliate and fleurets and a pair of lines. On the sides, small circular indentations replaced the waffle-shape of the 17th century; however, the latter was still occasionally employed on the crown. Beehive thimbles are one-piece, therefore post c1750s, and have indentations which start immediately above the base border.

Silver compendium thimbles appeared in the 18th century and wire appliqué thimbles continued to be made, firstly of the stubby type and then much slimmer and taller. Normally such thimbles have an oval or shield-shaped cartouche where the owner's initials were engraved. Enamelled silver, copper alloy or steel thimbles were also produced in the 18th century, although it is rare to find one in good condition. Pinchbeck also found favour for thimble-making at this time, a metal easily mistaken for gold, and even more so when gilded.

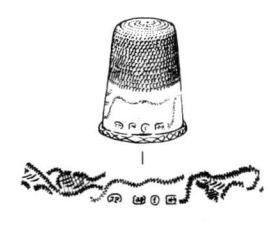

It was the 19th century that saw a transformation in the design and manufacture of thimbles. Other than the several metals used before, a variety of other materials became fashionable for thimble-making. Copper-alloy thimbles were made in one or two-piece form, whilst silver and gold were one-piece. Initially they were beehive-shaped of somewhat squat proportions with a decorative border and a rim around the base. Later, c1830, thimbles became taller, and their height was increased yet again c1850. Silver thimbles of the mid-19th century occasionally have a scalloped edge and an appliqué decorative border as well as engraving. Souvenir and commemorative silver thimbles became extremely popular in the 19th century and are engraved with representations of many great buildings and royal personages. Advertising on thimbles also started in the 19th century, the most

The Georgian and Victorian Period

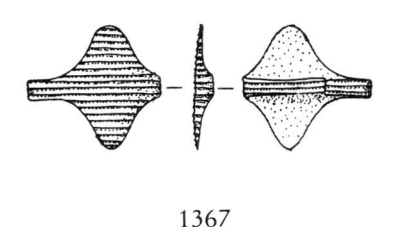

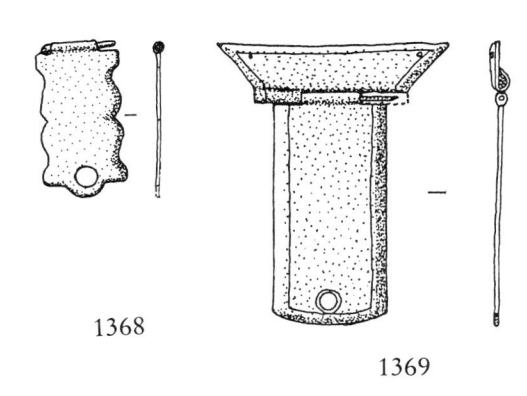

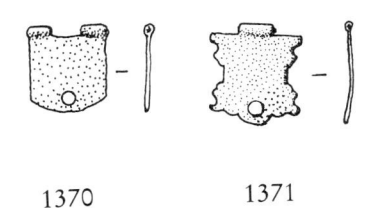

famous of which is the Dorcas, a steel thimble plated both sides with silver. The name Dorcas is stamped around the base.

Victorian gold thimbles are generally 15-carat, whilst those of the later 19th century are usually 9-carat. Invariably gold thimbles have ornate borders and frequently an applied crown of harder material, such as coral. Some gold thimbles are inset with precious or semi-precious gemstones, enamel, glass or porcelain. Both silver and gold thimbles of this period may have a rim or be rimless which can make identification difficult. This problem is compounded if the piece isn't hallmarked.

Very similar to the thimble is the 19th-century finger-guard which is a device with a cut-a-way section at the top for about two thirds of its height and a series of transverse ribs around the sides. Worn on the opposite hand to the thimble, it was for protecting the finger from the needle point, particularly when sewing hems before the advent of the sewing machine. Like thimbles, finger-guards were made from copper alloy or silver. One type is somewhat similar to a finger ring, having an integral, grooved, lozenge-shaped bezel and a penannular, grooved hoop.

Sheet silver two-piece thimble, c1700-50
1357: rounded plain crown, broad border, 20mm x 15mm - *Cockington*.

Sheet copper-alloy one-piece thimbles, 1700-50
1358: flattish crown, broad border, 18mm x 17mm - *Cockington*.
1359: child's, flattish crown, narrow border, 13mm x 14mm - *Haccombe*.
1360: child's, flattish crown, narrow border, 11mm x 12mm - *Cockington*.

Sheet silver one-piece thimbles, 19th century
1361: flattish crown, broad rim engraved with bands of curvilinear, 23mm x 20mm - *Cockington*.
1362: flattish crown, broad rim with band of tooled lozenges; wide border engraved with zigzags, cross-hatching and oblique lines; hallmarked - makers mark JF, lion, 1880, Birmingham, 22mm x 17mm - *Cockington*

Sheet copper-alloy one-piece thimbles, 19th century
1363: rounded crown, narrow rim with chevron nicks, broad border with bands of pricked dots and inscribed REMEMBER ME, 19mm x 15mm - *Cockington*.
1364: flattish crown, narrow rim, broad border with engraved band of vertical lines, 17mm x 15mm - *Cockington*.
1365: child's, flattish crown, narrow rim, broad border engraved band of vertical lines and inscribed I LOVE YOU, 14mm x 13mm - *Cockington*.

Sheet silver one-piece finger-guards, 19th century
1366: transversly ribbed body, rounded crown, broad rim with band of tooled lozenges, broad boarder decorated with engraved bands of zigzags and cross-hatching and pricked dots, 22mm x 18mm - *Cockington*.
1367: finger-ring type, flat cross-section penannular hoop, lozenge-shaped bezel, transverse ribs, 25mm x 25mm - *Newton Abbot*.

BOOK CLASPS

Clasps for securing book-covers in the closed position current during the 18th and 19th centuries are of the hinged variety. Invariably they are copper alloy, although silver examples are known. The former may be gilded or silvered and the latter gilded. Engraved, punched or embossed decoration is usual on many, however, plain specimens are common. Frequently edges are shaped with ornate apertures.

Sheet copper-alloy hinged book-clasps, 18th century
1368: subrectangular, hinged section, quatrefoil sides, lobed knop, circular hole, copper-alloy pin, 31mm x 16.5mm - *Cockington*.

Sheet copper-alloy hinged book-clasps, 19th century
1369: rectangular, hinged section, fragmented subrectangular hasp, circular hole, copper-alloy pin, engraved linear border, 56mm x 44mm - *Cockington*.
1370: subrectangular, circular hole, 17mm x 16mm - *Kingskerswell*.
1371: subrectangular, quatrefoil sides, trefoil end, circular hole, 20mm x 18mm - *Stokeinteignhead*.

SPOONS

Dognose rat-tail spoons remained current throughout the reign of both William III and Anne. However, by 1714 some spoons were being made with a more rounded cross-section stem at the lower end and a rounded upturned terminal. Additionally, the stem between the terminal and the narrow section was made triangular in cross-section which created a central longitudinal spine. This new-look spoon was dubbed Hanoverian. About 1715, after George I's accession, the rat-tail strengthener was displaced by the drop, extended single drop, or double drop, all of which have a rounded end and are much shorter than the former. The bowl underwent a change sometime between 1730-60, for it was made longer, whilst the stem's central spine decreased in length. Conversely, around 1770 the bowl was shortened, whilst the stem became longer. It was customary to engrave initials, crests or coats of arms on terminal backs of Hanoverian spoons. Around 1770 yet another style of spoon became popular - the Old English. On these the central longitudinal spine is absent and the terminal is downturned.

Special spoons were commonplace during the Georgian and Victorian periods. The habit of drinking tea increased in the 18th century with the resulant need of teaspoons. In the rococo period these were moulded with elaborate shells, scrolls and other decoration on both the front and back of bowls and stems. By 1760 picture-back teaspoons were fashionable which depicted moulded motifs on the backs of the bowl. For removing tea dust or leaves from cups a mote skimmer was employed and characteristically had a perforated bowl with either a spiked or rounded stem-terminal. Other strainer-spoons were used in the kitchen as well as on the dining table, some with perforated bowls and others with a separately soldered longitudinal grill. Caddy spoons made their first appearance in the 1760s.

Although generally non-functional, another spoon which comes under the 'special' type, is the love spoon. Many were made by seamen or acquired overseas and given as tokens of love, a custom dating back to the 17th century. Apart from metal they were made from wood, bone, ivory and even coral.

Cast silver Hanoverian teaspoons, c1750-70
1372: fancy back, moulded foliate, top front of stem inscribed

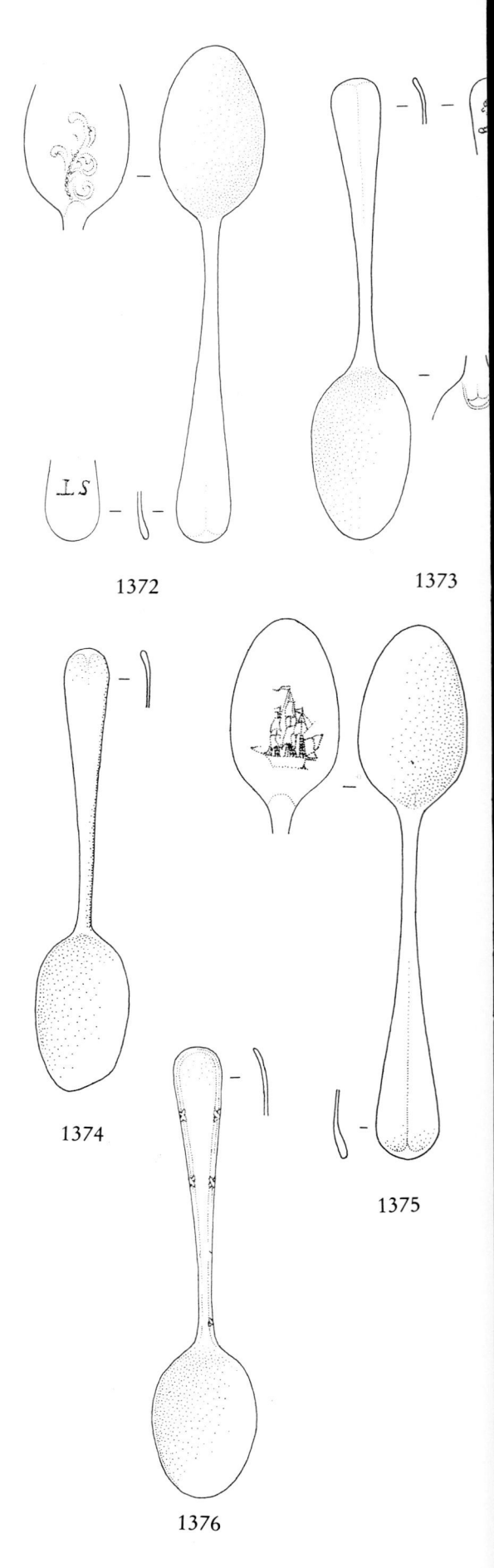

The Georgian and Victorian Period

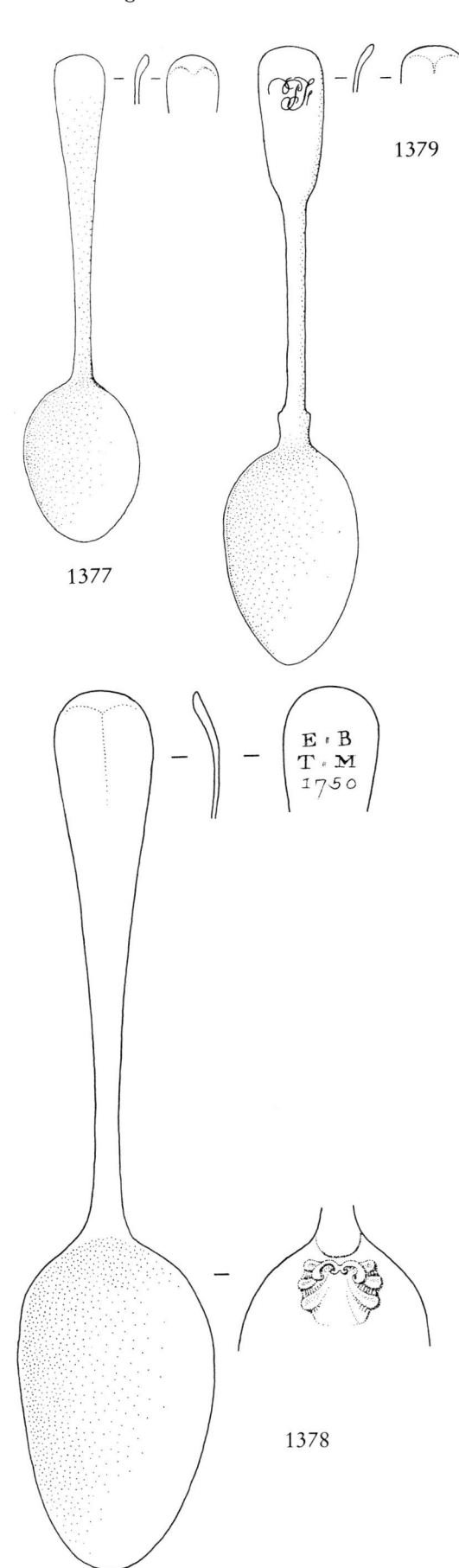

ST, abraded hallmark above the bowl on underside of stem, L. 117.5mm - *Ringmore*.

1373: top front of stem engraved with the family crest of the Mallocks of Cockington, abraded hallmark above the bowl on underside of stem, L. 109mm - *Cockington*.

1374: lower edge of bowl abraded, abraded hallmark above bowl on underside of stem, L. 105mm - *Bishopsteignton*.

Cast silver Hanoverian teaspoon, c1760-70

1375: picture-back, moulded galleon, abraded hallmark above the bowl on underside of stem, 126mm - *Newton Abbot*.

Cast silver Hanoverian teaspoon, c1770

1376: engraved crosses and two bands of punched dots around front of stem, abraded hallmark above bowl on underside of stem, L. 106mm - *Newton Abbot*.

Cast silver Old English teaspoon, c1770-5

1377: L. 111mm - *Ringmore*.

Cast silver Hanoverian table spoon, 1751

1378: rococo shell heel, makers mark R.H. and hallmark above bowl on underside of stem, inscribed 1750 surmounted by E: B T.M on underside top end of stem, L. 199.5mm - *Cockington*.

Cast silver Fiddle pattern dessert spoon, c1800-20

1379: top front of stem inscribed (?) PF, abraded hallmark on top underside of stem, L. 141mm - *Bishopsteignton*.

Cast copper-alloy possible love spoon, probably 19th century

1380: Indian, oval bowl moulded inside with figure under a canopy, fragmented looped-stem moulded with oval segments, L. 77mm - *Marldon*.

KNIVES AND DAGGERS

Types of knife current in the 18th and 19th centuries were restricted to culinary and other domestic or general use, as well as for specialised purposes. Their diversity precludes a detailed study here, other than to say they were made from: iron, steel, silver or copper alloy which frequently was silvered.

Daggers, however, by now were carried mainly by the military, with the quillon type predominant. Nineteenth-century examples, in particular, are frequently very elaborate with partially engraved or moulded blades and ornate hafts and quillons.

Cast and forged copper-alloy quillon, 18th century

1381: fragmented, probable rectangular tang-hole, hemispherical knop on end, maker's mark AU, 57mm x 18mm - *Haccombe*.

Cast and forged copper-alloy quillon-dagger haft, 19th century

1382: fragmented, rectangular tang-hole, moulded mythical creatures (?) mermaid and merman), 39mm x 36mm - *Two Mile Oak*.

RUMBLER BELLS

Globular rumbler bells continued to be cast by bell-founders during the 18th and 19th centuries and in appearance are similar to their antecedents. In the 19th century manufacturers specialising in horse accoutrements also undertook bell-making, and theirs are distinctly different. The bell is still globular but much more symmetrical and of two-piece form, i.e, the bell itself and an iron pea, with cruciform-shaped slits in the bottom half. Suspension loops are rectangular or subrectangular. Similar bells were used on fly terrets, where they were brazed direct to the underside of the transverse arm, making suspension loops unnecessary. Sheet metal rumbler bells were concurrent throughout both periods, although of smaller form, and again are quite distinctive. They are very symmetrically globular and made of four pieces with a pronounced seam between the two hemispheres. Sound holes are as found on earlier examples. Sheet metal suspension loops were the norm.

Sheet copper-alloy rumbler bell, c18th-19th century
1383: four-piece, lateral projecting seam, sheet copper-alloy suspension loop, circular upper and two conjoined circular lower sound-holes, 23mm x 19mm - *Exeter*.

SPURS

Rowel-spurs attributed to the Georgian and Victorian eras were cast and forged from iron or copper-alloy which is frequently tinned or silvered. Sides are usually straight with even-set figure-8 terminals or slightly expanded terminals each with a single hole or a pair of longitudinal more widely spaced holes. Moulded decoration on the sides is not uncommon although many spurs are quite plain. Necks range from fairly long to very short and can be either straight or drooped.

A form of rowel-spur infrequently used from the later Middle Ages until the 18th century, when it became more popular, has one or both sides hinged which allowed greater flexibility when worn with rigid leather boots.

Small multi-point rowels or much larger rowels with five points were both current. Spur-leathers were attached with identical studs as current in the 17th century, although a mushroom-headed rivet stud became popular in the 19th century and continued into the 20th.

Cast and forged copper-alloy rowel-spurs, 18th century
1384: fragmented, short straight neck expanding into the rowel box remains of iron rowel and pin, one straight hinged-side with remains of iron pin, L. 46mm - *Uffculme*.
1385: fragmented, short drooped neck expanding into rowel box, remains of iron pin, straight sides with one even-set figure-8 terminal, one separate hooked-stud with rivet hole and remains of copper- alloy rivet, stud head lost, L. 70mm - *Exeter*.
1386: fragmented, long straight neck with expanded drooped rowel-box, remains of copper-alloy pin, straight sides, silvered or tinned, 131mm - *Cockington*.

Forged iron rowel-spur, late 18th-19th century
1387: fragmented, tinned or silvered, long swan-neck with slightly expanded rowel-box, remains of iron pin, straight sides, L. 115mm - *Cockington*.

Cast and forged copper-alloy rowel-spurs, 19th-20th century
1388: fragmented, gilt, long swan-neck with expanded drooped rowel- box, copper-alloy pin, abraded multi-point copper-alloy rowel, L. 61mm - *Ide*.

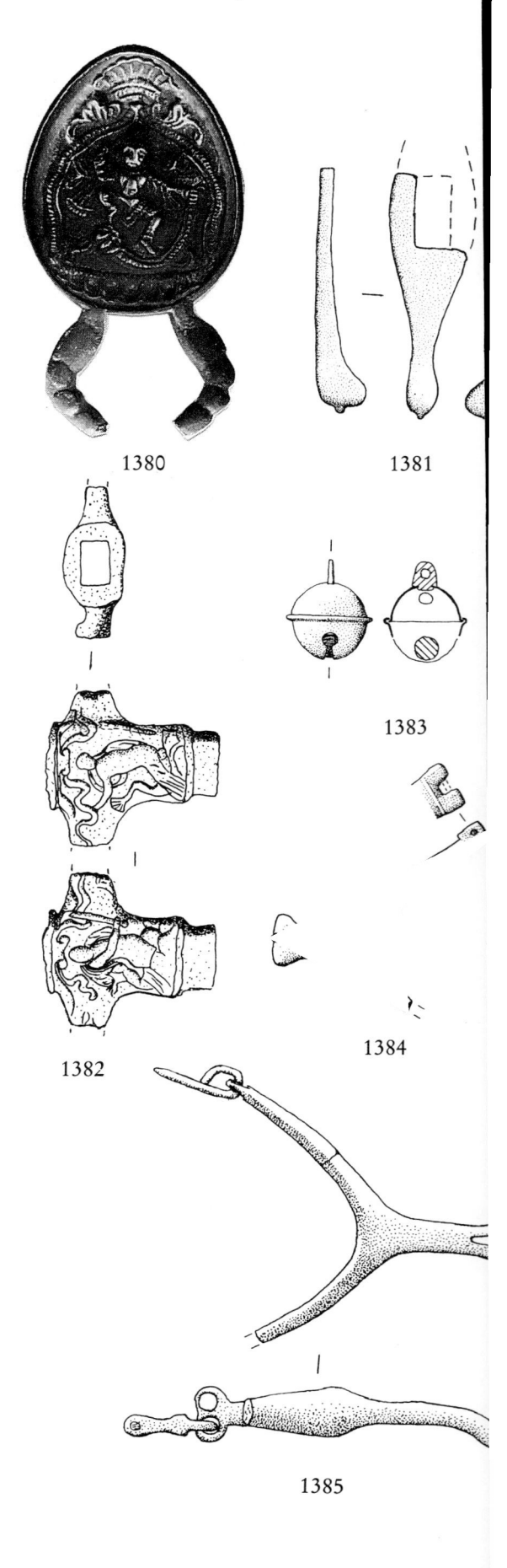

The Georgian and Victorian Period

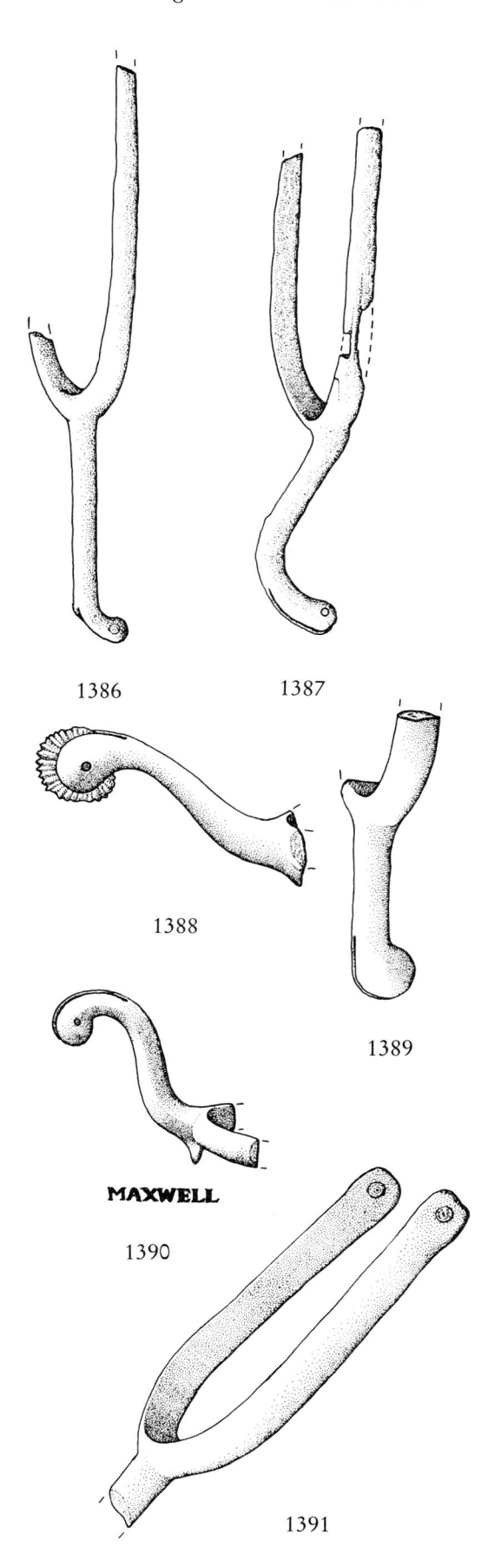

1389: fragmented, straight neck with expanded drooped rowel-box, straight sides, L. 64mm - *Poltimore*.
1390: fragmented, swan-necked rowel-spur with expanded drooped rowel- box, copper-alloy pin, pointed projection at base of neck, incuse makers mark MAXWELL, L. 56.5mm - *Exeter*.

Cast and forged copper-alloy Jack spur, c19th-20th century

1391: fragmented, remains of straight neck, straight sides with slightly expanded terminals each with a stud hole and remains of iron possible mushroom-headed stud, L. 102mm - *Ringmore*.

N.B. Regarding No.1390 - Henry Maxwell, spurrier, established his London business in 1750, practising at several consecutive addresses in the capital until the early 20th century, finally changing to bootmaking. They operate to this day in Savile Row.

RECEPTACLES

Cast iron and cast or sheet copper-alloy receptacles for kitchen use in the Georgian and Victorian periods were much the same as before, although the Victorians increasingly used sheet copper brightware. The production of copper-alloy, silver or gold specialist receptacles grew rapidly throughout both periods. Wares of cast lead/tin-alloy remained current for the 18th century but as the 19th progressed, they slowly succumbed to the advance of the pottery trade. Notwithstanding, many small lead/tin-alloy receptacles with uses unassociated with food or drink continued to be produced.

Cast lead/tin-alloy patten, probably 18th century

1392: underside incuse stamped GXG LOND, D. 100mm - *River Dart, Dittisham*.

Cast lead/tin-alloy tavern pot, c1820-37

1393: incuse stamped IMPERIAL ? PINT IV (?) M DEVON, 93mm x 72mm - *River Exe, Starcross*.

Hollow-cast copper-alloy terminal for a fluted glass vase, 19th century

1394: French, three-dimensional left hand with a lozenge-shaped bezel finger-ring on the first finger, 17th-century style cuff with traces of adhesive inside, integral projection in palm with iron corrosion attached, small circular hole in lower side of cuff with remains of iron bolt, 61mm x 25mm - *Bishopsteignton*.

N.B. Regarding No.1392, LOND may be an abbreviation for LONDON. About 1691-8 the London Pewterers' Company passed a regulation allowing the use of the letter X on extraordinary or hardware as an indication of the higher quantity of tin in the alloy. However, in this instance it may represent an unrecorded London touchmark or the mark of a provincial pewterer who illegally struck his wares with the mark London, a common occurrence in the 18th century. No.1394 was secured by two bolts to a heavy rectangular marble base. The vase had a lateral bend at the bottom which was glued inside the hand. Examples of left and right hand are known which is consistent with vases in pairs.

1392

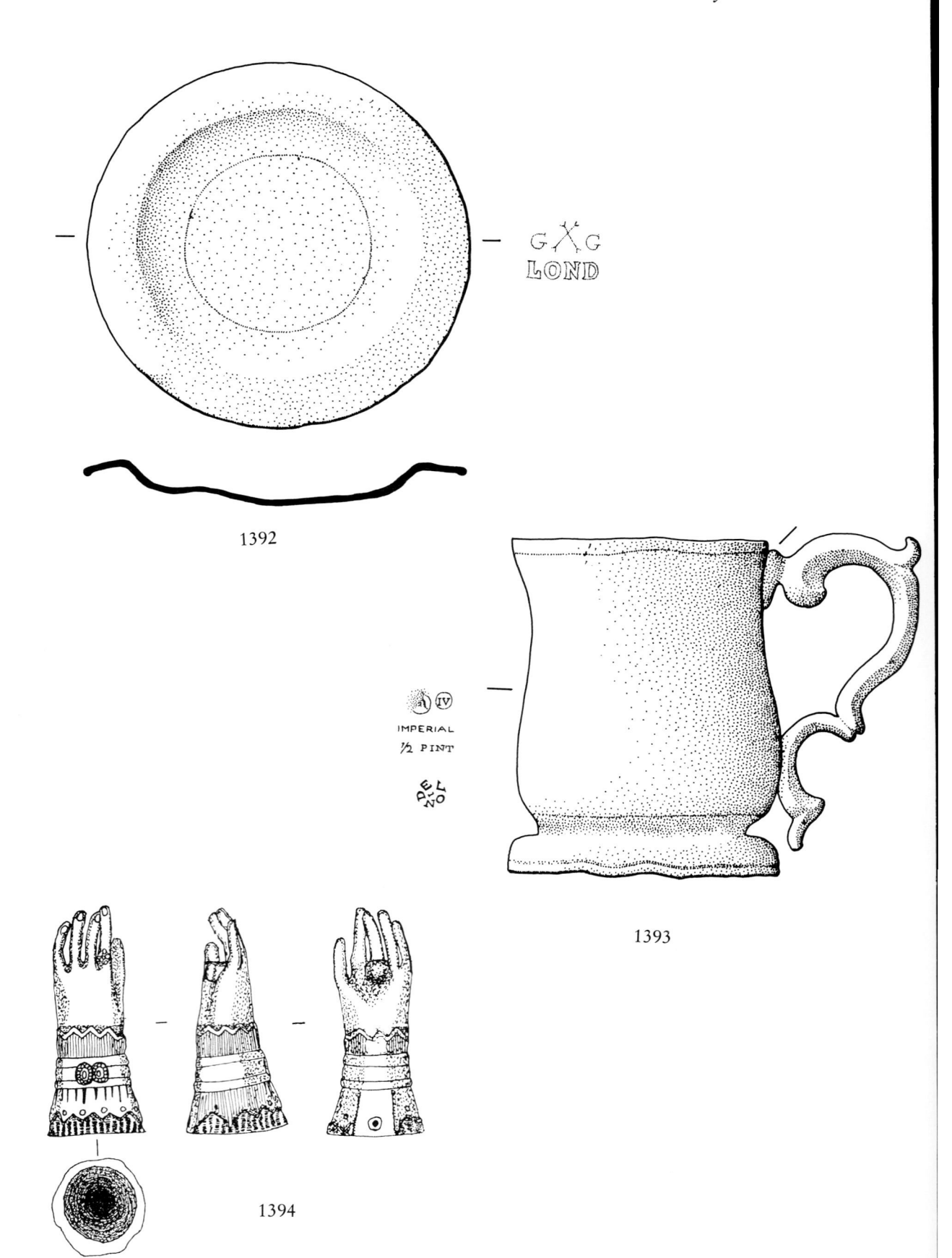

G⚔G
LOND

1393

IMPERIAL
½ PINT

DE L
NO

1394

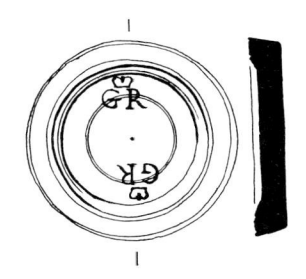

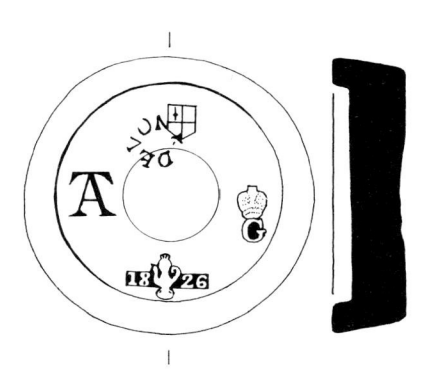

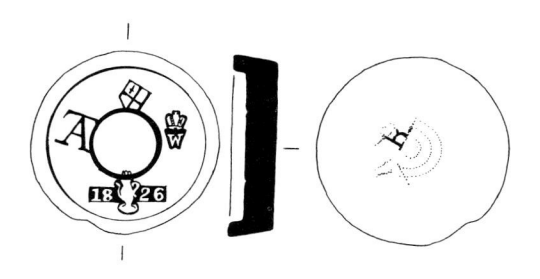

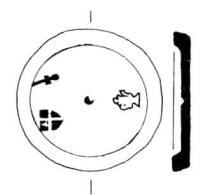

The Georgian and Victorian Period

TRADE WEIGHTS

Authorized lead flat-circular trade-weights of monarchs up to and including Queen Anne, as well as unofficial types, remained current until 1834 when they were banned by law as they were easily tampered with. Nonetheless, they continued in use for some time afterwards, particularly in rural areas. Another class of trade-weight, probably Victorian, comprises a cast copper-alloy flat-circular or truncated-pyramid body filled with lead. Often they were stamped 'cased'. These were just as susceptible to malpractice as lead weights.

Flat-circular trade-weights of copper alloy with London marks were current throughout the kingdom during the Hanoverian period. Indeed, some such London-made weights also have provincial marks which were stamped whilst they were in use outside the capital. All official trade-weights attributable to the four King Georges carry the royal cypher of a G surmounted by a crown, which is confusing. However, trade-weights of George I's reign are marked with the royal cypher, sword and A at 1200 and ewer at 1800; George II's have the sword at 1200, royal cypher at 0900, A at 1500, and ewer at 1800. Furthermore, the top bar of the letter A is plain on trade-weights of these two kings, whilst thereafter it has distinct serifs. For George III and IV the ewer and sword are in the same positions, 1800 and 1200 respectively, the A at 0900, and the royal cypher at 1500.

There is no way of differentiating flat-circular weights of the latter two monarchs until 1826, when that date was included (the figures 18 and 26 respectively were placed either side of the ewer). This again causes confusion, for this mark was current on trade-weights until the end of Queen Victoria's reign. Also from 1826, the sword of St Paul was replaced by the City of London shield which itself has the sword in the upper left-hand quarter. Weights stamped with a crowned GR are provincial and attributed to the late 18th early 19th centuries.

William IV's cypher is a crowned W, and on weights can be differentiated from William III by its position in conjunction with other marks, viz the cypher is at 1500, 1826 and ewer at 1800, City of London shield at 1200, and A at 0900. Marks on London-made Victorian trade-weights vary according to the date of manufacture and denomination. Between 1836-79 the cypher is a crowned V, and thereafter the verification mark 2 is often sandwiched between V R surmounted by a crown with the City of London Shield below. Sometimes the City of London Shield is sandwiched between VR with a crown above and 2 below. Another variant is a crowned V which can be distinguished from the earlier crown by its simplicity. Occasionally the royal cypher is omitted on Victorian trade-weights and is replaced with the City of London Shield surmounting the figure 2.

Even more perplexing is that some provincial Hanoverarian trade-weights are stamped with a letter, or letters, and a number surmounted by a crown which can be mistaken for a royal cypher. Trade weights of this period made or sold within Westminster are stamped with a portcullis which is similar to the Board of Trade's Standards Department portcullis mark found on standard weights from 1866. From c1850 many trade-weights carry the denomination which was stamped by the maker; additionally, from around this date, local verification marks came into use.

George III's reign was the last to issue wool-weights and, as before, all Georgian weights of this type bear the moulded arms of the respective monarch. Bell-shaped weights were current during both periods.

Cast copper-alloy flat-circular trade-weights, late 18th - early 19th century

1395: 2oz, incuse, two crowned GR marks, D. 39mm - *Cockington.*

Cast copper-alloy flat-circular trade-weights, 19th century

1396: George IV, 4oz, moulded crowned G and 18 ewer 26, incuse A, City of London shield and DEVON, D. 55mm - *Cockwood.*

1397: William IV, 2oz, moulded crowned W and 18 ewer 26, incuse A, City of London shield, obscure pattern of punched dots and (?) incuse R on back, D. 35.5mm - *Cockington.*

1398: ?oz, moulded City of London shield and ewer, incuse sword of St Paul, D. 27.5mm - *Uffculme..*

1399: ?oz, moulded, crowned V, City of London shield, ewer, D. 23.5mm - *Stokeinteignhead.*

1400: 1oz, moulded crown, incuse DEVON, D. 27mm - *Stokeinteignhead.*

1401: 1 oz, moulded crowned T and crowned W, possibly Manor of Trowbridge in Wiltshire, incuse conjoined AB (Avoivciupois) and crossed mace and sword, 28.5mm - *Stokeinteignhead.*

1402: 2oz, two moulded transverse ridges on side, two circular projections and three moulded roundels on reverse, moulded horse-furniture depicting the initials C.H.V., D. 35mm - *Totnes.*

N.B. Number 1402 has no recorded parallel. If it is a weight, possibly it formed part of a nest of weights used by a vet for weighing out medicines for horses, the motif being the vet's initials.

COIN WEIGHTS

Coin-weights of Anne and earlier monarchs remained current during the reign of George I. However, after George II's accession new copper-alloy coin-weights for the half-guinea and guinea appeared, each of which is embossed with the crowned value type of reverse with the monarch's bust and title obverse.

As the Portuguese moidore was current in England between the early 1700s and 1770s, along with the official coinage, copper-alloy coin-weights embossed on the obverse with the denomination and maker's initials, and an embossed reverse of a voided cross with other symbols in the spandrels were widely used. Copper or copper-alloy coin-weights were made in London by John Kirk for the guinea, moidore and the new Portuguese Johannes series which began to circulate c1746. The guinea series is embossed with the king's bust and variations of the legend GEORGIUS II on the obverse and the denomination in words on the reverse. Some have an inscription and/or a crowned cartouche. Kirk's moidore series is similar to the earlier one, only the obverse and reverse designs are transposed; additionally the obverse is dated and has a legend IN HOC SIGNO VINCES. The largest of the latter was equivalent to S3.12s. Weights of the Johannes series have his bust and a legend (many varieties) embossed on the obverse, whilst the reverse design is the

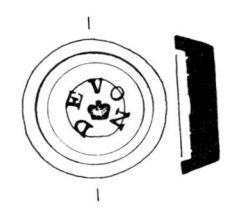

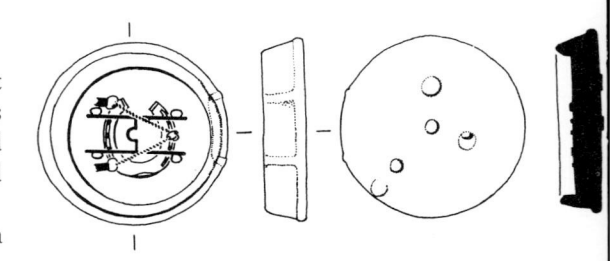

The Georgian and Victorian Period

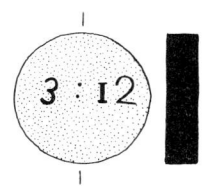

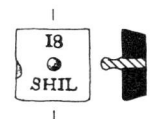

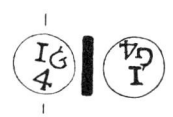

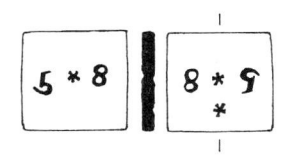

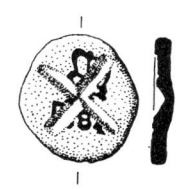

embossed denomination in words, some with a crown and/or a cartouche.

From 1760 numerous sets of coin-weights were produced in Birmingham and occasionally the £3.12s Johannes weight carries the maker's name. It is probable that many sets of coin-weights were manufactured at centres other than Birmingham. Used alongside the former were sets of weights comprising plain copper-alloy discs stamped with the denomination.

- On 15 July 1774 a programme of withdrawing underweight guineas commenced which was completed in several stages by 1776. Sets of copper-alloy coin-weights were made for use with these lightweight coins, the earliest of which are scarce, however, for the double standard and new standard they are plentiful. The obverse of some double standard weights bear the monarch's name and portrait, and the reverse a crowned value within a wreathed border, whilst others have an inscription and date referring to the recoinage on the obverse, and the value on the reverse. Some new standard guinea weights made between 1775-6 carry on the obverse an inscription and date referring to the new standard, and on the reverse the value and an inscription. However, other new standard weights have on the obverse either the monarch's bust and name or the words 'new standard' and a date. Reverse designs are usually a verification mark, which may be a crown, ewer or anchor, and either the value or date and inscription. Frequently such weights carry the unofficial lion-mark of a goldsmith.

For use with the new sovereign coinage of 1817, official copper-alloy coin-weights were issued in 1821, and in 1823 double sovereign weights were released. Both bear on the obverse a crown surmounted by a lion passant, the date and the inscription and ROYAL MINT. Reverses carry the mass and are inscribed with the value and CUR WEIGHT. A further issue of sovereign coin-weights of the same design was issued in 1842 which was followed in 1843 with a new design for both half-sovereign and sovereign coin-weights. These have a moulded bust of Victoria with the date and inscription incuse on the obverse, whilst the reverse has the inscription, denomination and mass incuse. Responsibility for official weights passed to the Board of Trade's Standards Department in 1870 who issued coin-weights into the last decade of the 19th century. From c1842 many unofficial coin-weights were issued, some of which bear a name, e.g. Avery or Ratcliff, and the date and other decoration, whilst others carry only the denomination.

Cast copper-alloy coin-weights, 18th century

1403: Ireland, George I, 9 dwt 5gr, peca or 4 escudos, circular, Obv. harp, [THE S]TANDARD OF IRELAN[D], D left, g right, 9 . 5, beaded circle; Rev. shield, ANNO REG GEORGII QVARTO 1718, beaded circle, D. 21.5mm - *Exeter*.

1404: 1760s, moidore series, 6s: 9d, one side worn or filed, circular, moulded, beaded border, D. 15mm - *Cockington*.

1405: 1760s, Johannes series, S3:   12s, uniface, circular, incuse, 3 : 12, D. 26mm - *Cockwood*.

1406: c1765, Portuguese 2 escudos current for 18 English shillings (from a boxed set of scales and weights), uniface, square, incuse, 18 SHIL, separate copper-alloy knob, 14.5mm x 14mm - *Cockington*.

1407: c1775, circular, quarter-guinea, incuse, Obv. YG, Rev. YG,

D. 11.5mm - *Cockington*.

Cast copper-alloy coin-weights, 19th century

1408: George III, guinea, 5 pennyweight 8 grains, square, incuse, Obv. * 5 * 8, Rev. 5 * 8, 19.5mm x 20mm - *Cockington*.

Cast lead probable coin-weight, c18th century

1409: circular, uniface, incuse, crowned number obliterated by overstamped X, D. 25mm - *Exeter*.

DOOR AND FURNITURE FITTINGS

Metal fittings found on doors and furniture attributed to the 18th and 19th centuries are frequently very elaborate. Characteristic of many is moulded, punched, engraved or openwork decoration. Gilding was commonplace.

Eighteenth-century kehole escutcheons are invariably of sheet copper alloy; two types were current - openwork or engraved. The former frequently have ornate outlines and intricate openwork, whilst the latter are engraved with complex designs of foliate, floriate, circles and crescents. Both kinds have two or more nail holes by which means they were affixed with iron or copper-alloy nails to the door. Sheet copper-alloy handle-escutcheons fitted to doors and drawer fronts of furniture frequently are of the same shape and decoration as keyhole escutchions on the same piece of furniture. Instead of a keyhole-shaped aperture they have a small circular bolt-hole. By the 19th century escutcheons of keyholes were mainly cast, usually shield-shaped or oval with ornate moulded decoration.

Sheet copper-alloy keyhole escutcheons, 18th century

1410: oval, asymmetrical openwork, four nail holes, remains of four iron nails, 62mm x 48mm - *Cockington*.

1411: asymmetrical, asymmetrical openwork, two nail holes, remains of two iron nails, 44mm x 47.5mm - *Cockington*.

1412: asymmetrical, two nail holes, remains of two iron nails, 31.5mm x 28mm - *Cockington*.

1413: asymmetrical, three nail holes, remains of three iron nails; engraved curvilinear, circles and asymmetrical band of small circles, 45mm x 80.5mm - *Cockington*.

1414: asymmetrical, two nail holes, remains of two iron nails; engraved curvilinear, concentric circles and circles, 42mm x 79mm *Cockington*.

1415: oval, four semi-circular protrusions with a nail hole in each, engraved foliate, fleurets and small circles, 58mm x 46mm - *Cockington*.

1416: asymmetrical, three nail holes, remains of three iron nails, engraved circles, fleurets, curvilinear and oblique lines, 62mm x 56mm - *Cockington*.

1417: asymmetrical, fragmented, two nail holes, remains of two iron nails; engraved circles, fleurets curvilinear and oblique lines, 42mm x 57mm - *Cockington*.

Cast copper-alloy keyhole escutcheon, 18th century

1418: asymmetrical, fragmented, two nail holes, remains of two iron nails, moulded foliate and small circles, 31mm x 56.5mm - *Cockington*.

Cast copper-alloy oval keyhole-escutcheon, 19th century

1419: elaborate edge, three nail holes; moulded foliate, scrollwork and a face (?) a cat, oval openwork each side, 64mm x 50mm - *Stokeinteignhead*.

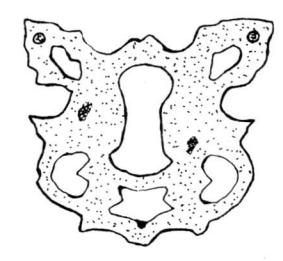

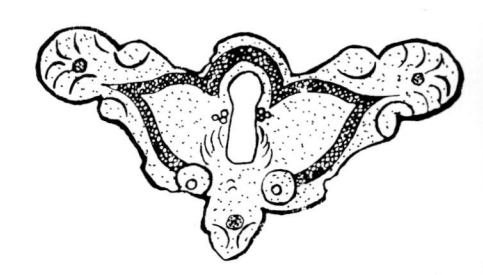

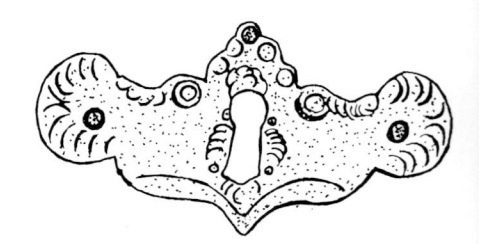

The Georgian and Victorian Period 203

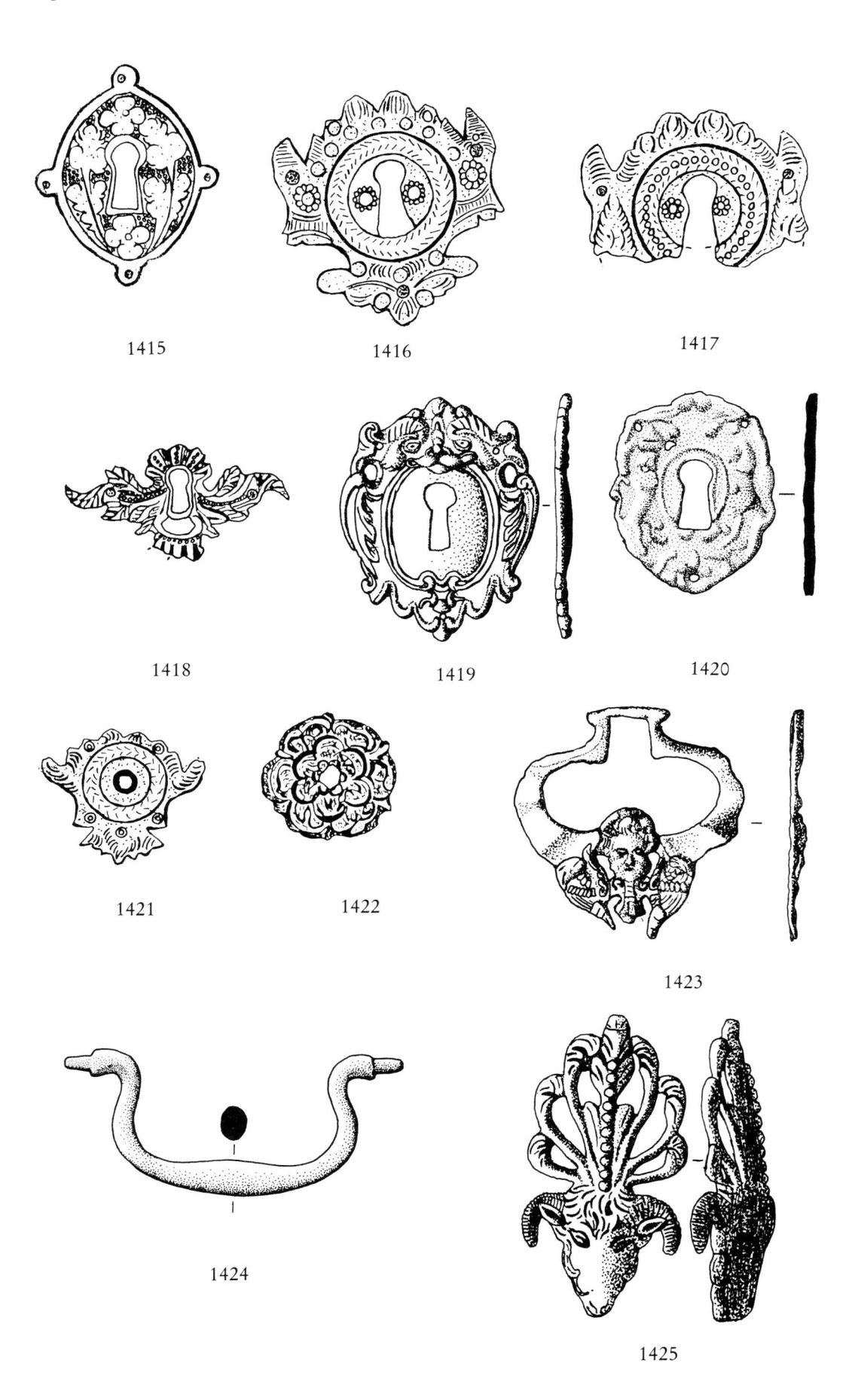

1415

1416

1417

1418

1419

1420

1421

1422

1423

1424

1425

1420: moulded rampant lions and scrollwork, three nail holes, 53mm x 41.5mm - *Exeter.*

Sheet copper-alloy drawer escutcheon, 18th century

1421: asymmetrical; engraved concentric circles, circles, curvilinear and oblique lines, central circular bolt-hole, 35mm x 41.5mm - *Cockington.*

1422: sexfoil, moulded fleuret, central irregular-shaped bolt-hole, D. 33mm - *Cockington.*

Cast copper-alloy drawer-handle, 18th century

1423: asymmetrical, annular, asymmetrical openwork, moulded cherub's face, 60.5mm x 58mm - *Kingskerswell.*

1424: arched, oval and circular cross-section, L. 85mm - *Bishopsteignton.*

Cast copper-alloy furniture-mounts, 18th century

1425: asymmetrical, convex, moulded ram's head surmounted by acanthus ornament, asymmetrical openwork, integral circular cross-section projection on back, 78.5mm x 40mm - *River Dart, Totnes.*

1426: asymmetrical, moulded cinquefoil interspaced with trefoils, sub-triangular openwork, circular nail-hole, 38.5mm x 44mm - *Cockington.*

Cast copper-alloy furniture-mount, 19th century

1427: asymmetrical, convex, moulded stag's head, circular cross-section projection on back with female thread, 45mm x 37mm - *Kingskerswell.*

Sheet copper-alloy furniture-mounts, 19th century

1428: vesica-shaped, symmetrical band of engraved oblique lines and rectangles, engraved vesica-shapes of oblique lines, twoscrew/nail holes, 26.5mm x 49mm - *Stokeinteignhead.*

1429: oval, silvered, engraved border of oblique lines, engraved curlicues, two screw/nail holes, 19.5mm x 41mm, *Stokeinteignhead.*

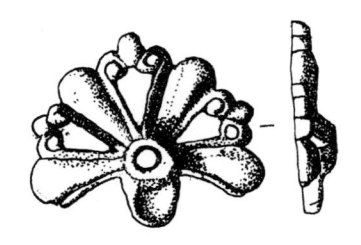

PIPE TAMPERS OR STOPPERS

Clay pipe tobacco smoking was probably introduced into England from the New World c1558 by Elizabethan adventurers who had learned of it from the American Indians. The first clay pipes undoubtedly also came from America, however, locally-made metal-pipes soon appeared which proved unpopular as conducted heat made the stem hot which in turn burned the smoker's lips: thereafter clay pipes were manufactured in this country

In the early days of clay pipe smoking, pipe bowls were tiny, due to the scarcity and prohibitive cost of tobacco. Nowadays this type of pipe is known by several names, viz: 'fairy pipe', 'celtic pipe' or 'elfin pipe'. Initially a pipe stem's diameter was only marginally less than the bowl and was about 150mm long, but before the passing of the 17th century they were lengthened considerably. The mid-18th century saw some pipe stems as much as 900mm in length which were reserved for indoor use. Similarly pipe bowls increased in size as time progressed; 19th-century examples are known that hold 2oz of tobacco! Many 18th and 19th-century clay pipe bowls, and less so, stems, have delightful moulded ornamentation. Stems of this period often incorporate engraved sheet silver ferrules.

In order to lengthen the burning time, it was necessary to compress the tobacco in the pipe bowl. Early pipe-smokers probably utilized any suitable similar sized object to the interior

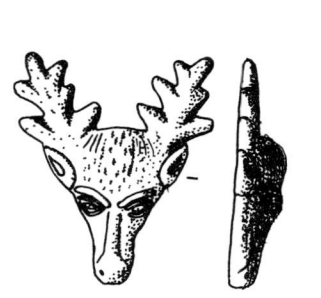

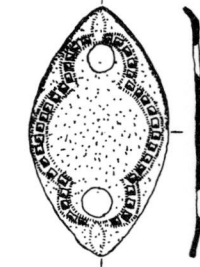

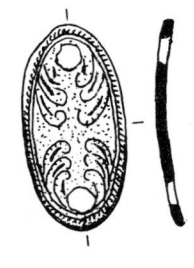

The Georgian and Victorian Period

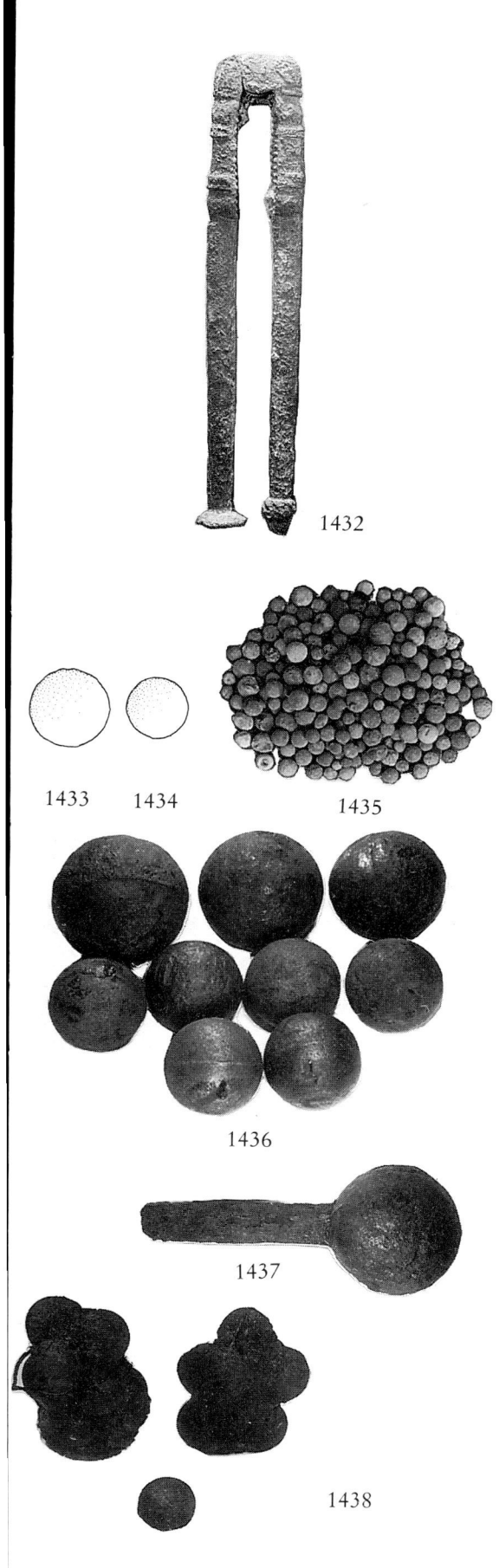

of the bowl, such as a twig, to press the tobacco down. Purpose-made carved wood tampers (from the beginning of the 19th century called stoppers) with metal base-ferrules appeared in the last quarter of the 16th century. At this time materials other than wood eg bone were used for this type of tamper It is possible that cast copper-alloy pipe-tampers were used prior to 1600, however, it was in the 17th century that their use became widespread.

One 17th-century type has a flat oval or circular handle with the king's bust or Commonwealth arms moulded on both sides. Three-dimensional forms were current right through into the 19th century, and include: hominoid busts, limbs or digits; animal legs, and animals or birds. Compendium pipe-tampers are known in several types, perhaps the most common is the nut-cracker with one or both terminals forming a tamper. The signet finger-ring tamper, usually directly engraved with the owners initials, was current from the mid-17th century until the early 18th.

Cast copper-alloy pipe-tampers, probably 18th century
1430: abraded, three-dimensional standing male figure in Elizabethan style costume holding unidentified object in right hand, fragmented left arm, 57mm x 8mm - *Uffculme.*
1431: three-dimensional standing male figure in Elizabethan style costume, 67mm x 12mm - *Whilborough.*
1432: nutcracker type, one terminal as a tamper, the other an acorn knop, L. 108.5mm - *Coffinswell*

LEAD MUSKET-BALLS AND SHOT

After 1769 musket balls and shot were made in a shot tower, whereby molten lead was poured over a sieve located at the top of the tower. Droplets of lead formed into globules as they fell and were quickly quenched in a tank of water in the tower's base. Different calibres were made by changing the sieve. Characteristic of this type of lead-shot is the lack of a sprue mark, however, caution is advised when using this absent feature for dating, for it is also missing from pre-1769 hand-finished precision shot used with dualling pistols.

Lead musket-balls and shot, post 1769
1433: 0.75 calibre - *Cockington.*
1434: 0.5 calibre - *Cockington.*
1435: a selection of musket balls and shot, antecedant and post 1769, all - *South Devon*

CANNON BALLS

Ammunition for cannons was made from iron as lead required too great a charge of powder (stone cannon-balls are known, although in this country their use antecedes the 15th century). Cannons first appeared in the mid-14th century and have been manufactured up to 825mm bore. In Britain the largest cannon balls found are naval types, however, those discovered inland are normally leftover from the Civil War (notwithstanding, enemy ships did bombard some parts of the coastline).

Apart from the conventional globular cannon ball, a host of other devices have been used over the centuries, e.g: grape shot - a number of small shot placed in a hessian bag and secured by cord; chain shot - half cannon-balls linked by a chain; bar shot - two cannon-balls joined by an iron bar; grapnel shot - a cannon ball with projecting blades for cutting rigging; expanding shot - half cannon-balls or other shapes linked by chains or bars - anti-personnel or for severing rigging or bringing down masts; expanding blade shot - cannon balls with slotted blades which flew open in flight - anti-personnel; incendiary shot - devices with spikes which stuck into woodwork and flanges which held self-igniting combustibles; carcass shot - metal-framed self-igniting incendiary device; other incendiary devices which ignited on firing; explosive cannon balls or heated cannon-balls.

Cast-iron cannon-balls, 18th century
1436: 8lb, 7lb, & 2lb - *Broadsands & Goodrington Beaches, Paignton.*
1437: bar shot, one ball lost, 8lb - *Broadsands Beach, Paignton.*
1438: grapeshot, 9x4oz = 2lb 4oz - *Broadsands Beach, Paignton*

TOYS

Toys attributed to the Georgian and Victorian periods are made of fabric, pottery, metal, wood, or several of these materials. It is the intention here, to deal with just a few of the smaller metal types.

Probably one of the most frequently found are toy cannons which are known in a range of types and sizes. These miniature replicas, complete with touch-hole and bored barrel, are made from cast-iron, copper alloy or lead. Originally, some were mounted on copper-alloy or iron-wheeled wooden carriages, whilst others were conveyed on wheeled carriages made of the same metal as the barrel. Barrels of both kinds are separate from their carriage and detachable. Despite the evidence of found examples with burst barrels, there has been disagreement as to whether or not toy cannons were actually fired. A snippet dated December 26th 1808 in the diary of Rev William Holland, a Somerset parson, suggests that the copper alloy type certainly were, 'William asked one of the young Hartwells to dine here and they have been firing little brass cannons all morning'. The aforementioned danger associated with firing toy handguns also applied to toy cannons.

Especially popular in the 18th-19th century period, although antecedent by some centuries, were cast copper-alloy, lead or lead/tin-alloy toy clocks or watches. These usually have two sides, both convex, one with a moulded clock-face and the other decorated with a moulded design, often foliate and floriate.

Cast copper-alloy toy cannons, 18th-19th century
1439: bore 4mm, L. 53mm - *Ringmore.*
1440: bore 2mm, L. 49mm - *Bishopsteignton.*
1441: bore 2.5mm, L. 46mm - *Newton Abbot.*
1442: bore 4mm, L. 37.5mm - *Cockwood.*

Cast lead/tin-alloy circular toy clock, 18th century
1443: back plate, convex; moulded crown wreathed with foliate, roses and thistles, concentric circles and fleurets, D. 52mm - *River Exe, Starcross.*

FIREARMS

A wide variety of firearms were current in the Georgian and Victorian eras and is far too specialist a subject to deal with here. Although parts of such weapons do turn up occasionally, it is rare to hear of a complete gun of this period being recovered by a metal detector. When one is found, invariably it is from an inland waterway or maritime location.

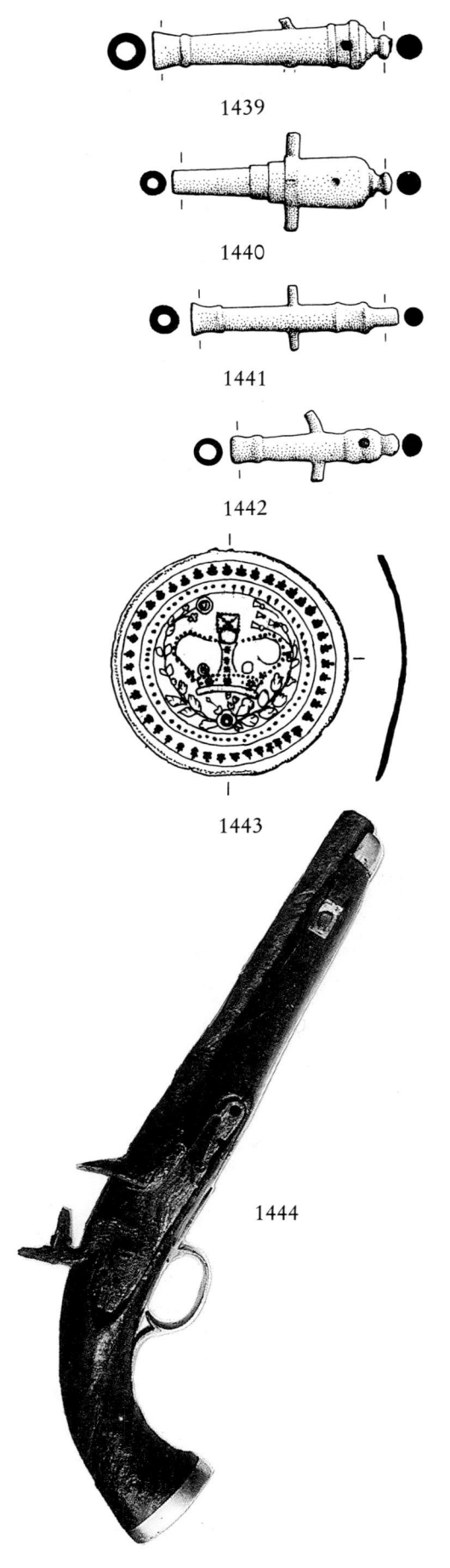

The Georgian and Victorian Period 207

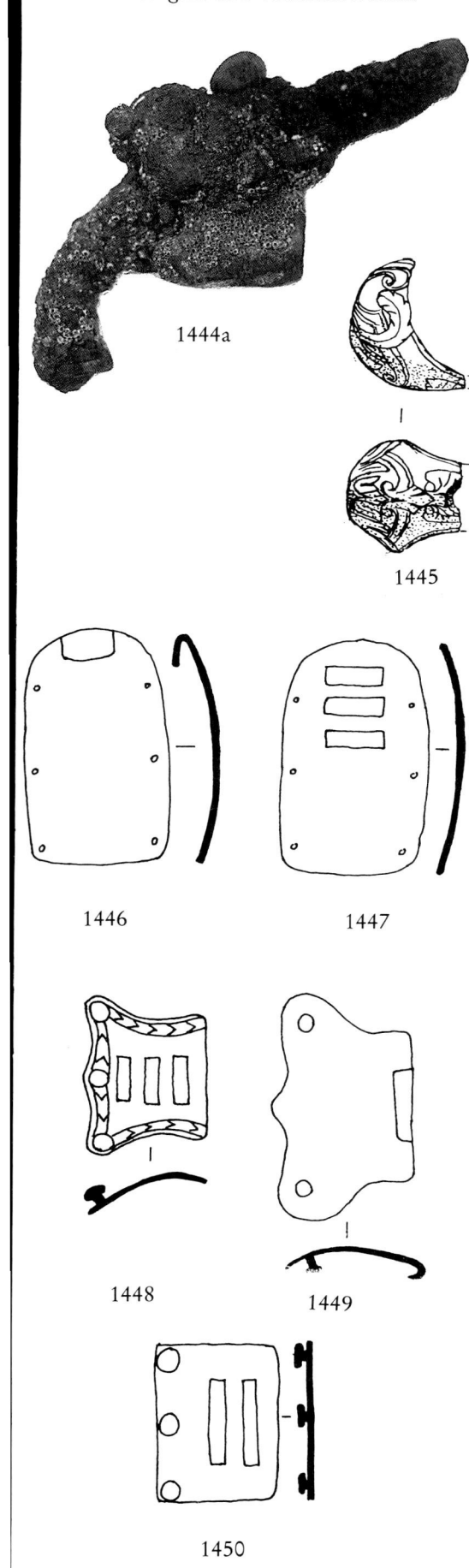

Flintlock pistol, not to scale, c.late 18th century
1444: military-type, iron barrel, brass furniture, probably Belgian - *Teignmouth Beach*.
1444a: the same pistol before restoration.

Cast copper-alloy pistol butt, 18th century
1445: engraved foliate and scrollwork, 26mm x 20.5mm - *Abbotskerswell*.

N.B. No.1444 is similar to the 'Javelin Men' pistols designed to protect the Mayor of Exeter, Captain John Cook, 1770-90.

OTHER MILITARIA

A type of clasp frequently confused with the clog or shoe-clasp is the military leather neck-stock sheet copper-alloy or silver clasp. Although documented evidence is rather scant, apparently neck-stocks were worn between 1786-1862 as replacements for cravats. A pair of clasps were sewn inside the stock thereby allowing the stock to be closed in precisely the same manner as footwear. Both sections are subrectangular, one of which has several rectangular or subrectangular transverse slots, usually three, whilst the other has a small downturned hook. The clasps of the lower ranks are undecorated, whilst those worn by officers may have an engraved regimental motif or other design.

Sheet copper-alloy or silver clasps, similar to military stock-clasps, of varying size and shape, which have from one to four separate copper-alloy rivets, are an enigma. However, as they frequently turn up on known 18th-19th-century military sites it implies such an application. Invariably clasps of this type are similarly engraved with a military motif or other design. It has been suggested that they were attached to leather pouches. Both types of clasp are frequently very crude and die-stamped

Die-stamped military neck-stock clasps, c1786-1862
1446: subrectangular, downturned hook, six sewing-holes, 54mm x 32mm - *Cockington*.
1447: subrectangular, three rectangular slots, six sewing-holes, 54mm x 32mm - *Cockington*.

Probable military clasps, 18th-19th century
1448: asymmetrical, three rectangular slots, three rivet holes, three separate copper-alloy rivets, band of engraved chevrons between two lines, 36.5mm x 27.5mm - *Haccombe*.
1449: asymmetrical, downturned hook, two rivet holes, two separate copper-alloy rivets, 52mm x 31mm - *Cockington*.
1450: rectangular, two rectangular slots, three rivet holes, three separate copper-alloy rivets, 36mm x 27.5mm - *Stokeinteignhead*.

The 18th-19th-century soldier's uniform was adorned with little by way of badges, however, between c1777 - c1816 an oval copper-alloy plate was worn on the chest where the cross-belts overlapped. Cross-belt plates are cast, and are inscribed with the regimental name and number or name of regiment only. A separate copper-alloy stud and separate copper-alloy hook project from the back, by which means the plate was affixed

Cast copper-alloy oval cross-belt plates, 18th-19th century
1451: 1758-1853, N DEVON M (North Devon Militia), circular

hole for hook, hook lost, separate copper-alloy stud, 68.5mm x 51.5mm - *Colaton Raleigh.*
1452: 1798-1802, 1803-, ARMED ASSOCIATION 1798, separate copper-alloy hook and stud, 70mm x 52mm - *Colaton Raleigh.*
1453: late 1700s - very early 1800s, crowned Gr, EXMINSTER HUNDRED REG. VOL (Exminster Hundred Volunteer Regiment), inscribed GR surmounted by a crown, inscribed CURTIS EXON on the rear (maker), separate copper-alloy stud and remains of separate copper-alloy hook, 77mm x 59mm - *Wolborough, Newton Abbot.*

N.B. Under the Militia Act, 1757 all Protestant men aged between 18 and 45 were liable to be chosen by lot to serve for three years in the militia unless they could raise £10.00 for a substitute. In 1802 Catholics were eligible to join. Volunteers were accepted in place of chosen men and many militia regiments comprised volunteer companies. In 1798 a separate volunteer force of men aged between 15 and 60, called the Armed Association, was formed after an attempted invasion by the French at Bantry Bay. These were raised under the Lord Lieutenant of each county, and were armed and trained for the defence of the realm. These were the Home Guard of its day. In 1802 the Armed Association was disbanded, however, they were reformed in 1803, although most men were enrolled in the volunteer corps or became special constables to aid the civil authorities.

A return of 1796 chronicles that 813 men were liable for service in the militia for the Hundred of Exminster. Yet another return, dated 1806, states that the Exminster Infantry Volunteers had a strength of 404 men, commanded by Lieutenant-Colonel Viscount Courtenay, and they wore a uniform of white breeches and scarlet tunic with yellow facings. Local volunteer units were disbanded c1808.

The 19th century saw an increase in the types of militaria, the most well known of which besides buttons were copper-alloy or white metal badges. These were worn on: headgear, the arm, collar, shoulder, waist belt, ammunition pouch and back pack. Officers badges were occasionally made from silver. As indicated earlier, forms of badges were also attached to military horse harness and vehicles.

Sheet copper-alloy leather ammunition-pouch badge, 1875
1454: horn with 24 between rope, BICTON RIFLE VOLUNTEERS, 24th Bicton Rifle Volunteers, threaded fastenings (one lost) on back, 33mm x 12mm - *Bicton.*

Sheet copper-alloy Universal Plate Badge for a shako helmet, 1800-12
1455: crowned GR, HONI . SOIT . QUI . MAL . Y . PENSE ., lion below, flags either side, eight sewing-holes, 154.5mm x 103mm - *Poltimore.*

Cast copper-alloy possible military badge, c19th century
1456: shield with stag, fish and seal within; two creels, crossed fishing rods and crown above, NEWFOUNDLAND below, two muskets left, oar and boat-hook right, traces of red, green, light and dark blue enamel, 54mm x 42mm -

The Georgian and Victorian Period

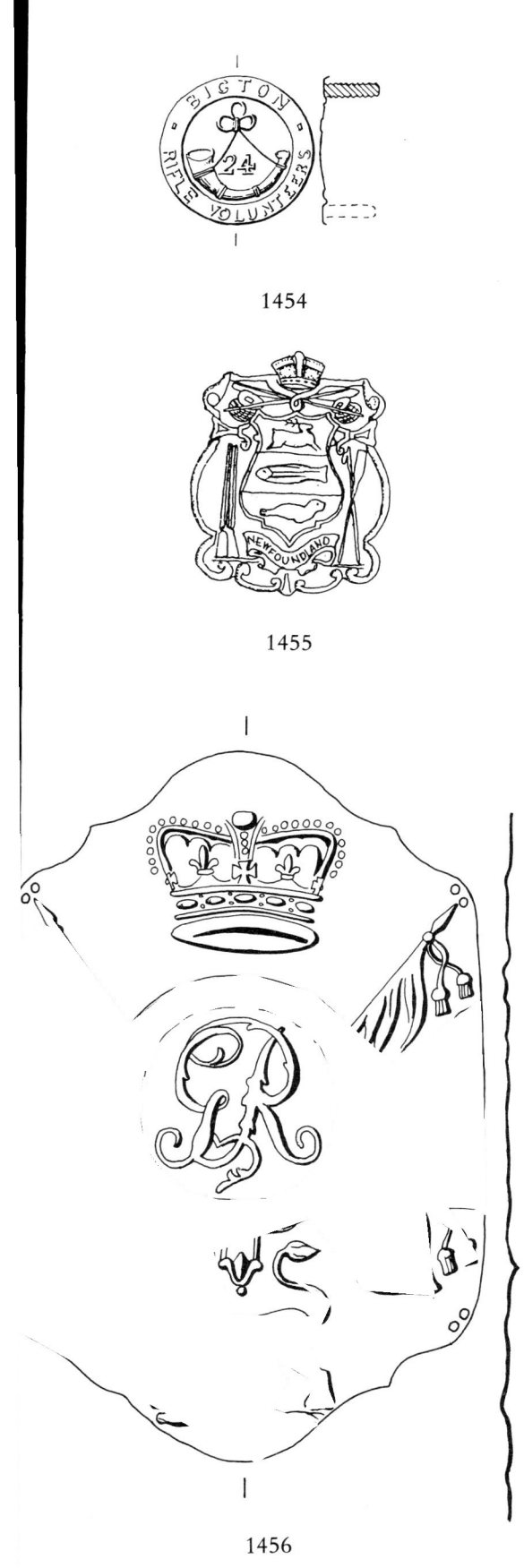

1454

1455

1456

Cockington.

Sheet copper-alloy shoulder-epaulet, c1800-50
1457: officers, probably general service, upper section lost, 100mm x 73mm - *Wolborough.*

N.B. Despite extensive enquiries at home and Canada No.1456 remains unidentified. The author would welcome any information.

JEWS HARPS

The Jews harp is a small mouth-held lyre-shaped musical instrument which was held by holding the frame between the teeth and striking an iron tongue with the fingers. They were current from the Middle Ages right up until the 18th century. However, medieval examples, the frames of which are either forged iron or copper alloy, are uncommon. Frequently Jew's harps attributed to the Middle Ages are decorated with punchwork or engraving, and some have barleytwist loops. It is probable that medieval types remained current during the Tudor period

The 17th and 18th centuries saw a change to somewhat smaller sizes of Jew's harp which invariably were forged from copper alloy and undecorated. The main difference between pieces attributed to these two centuries seems to be that those of the 17th have a flattened top. It is extremely rare to recover a Jew's harp with the tongue intact; usually all that remains is a trace of rust adhereing to the top of the loop.

Forged copper-alloy Jew's harps, 18th century
1458: lozenge-shaped cross-section, remains of corroded iron tongue, 59m x 26mm - *Cockington.*
1459: lozenge-shaped cross-section, 50.5mm x 24mm - *Stokeinteignhead.*

DOG COLLARS

Collars have adorned the necks of pet or hunting-dogs and other animals for centuries and, shamefully, were even used on slaves. A chain could be attached to a collar thereby allowing an animal, or a slave, to be tethered or led; however, collars were frequently purely decorative. A variety of materials has been used for making them, including: leather, fabric or cast or sheet metal. The wealthy preferred gold or silver collars, some of which were set with gemstones, or in the later Middle Ages, hung with pendants similar to those used on horse harness. Other forms of decoration current throughout time have been: moulding, engraving, punchwork, openwork, appliqués, gilding, silvering or tinning.

Several methods of constructing collars are known, viz: a simple leather or fabric strap, separate sections of leather or fabric and metal riveted together, a continuous band of metal, separate sections of metal hinged together, separate chain-like links or a combination of the latter two. All of these various kinds are adjustable and have some form of buckle or even a lockable clasp that often has a nameplate inbuilt. Both Georgian and Victorian dog-collars were manufactured in the aforementioned styles.

Copper-alloy dog-collar, not to scale, 19th century
1460: silvered or tinned, chain-link, rectangular serrated-edge

nameplate inscribed *H.A.STREET*, lockable clasp with four adjustment holes - *Whilborough*.

SKIRT LIFTERS

Skirt lifters are tong-like devices used by late 18th and 19th-century ladies to raise their dress hems, thereby preventing them trailing in the quagmire that formed the normal surface of most roads. They were cast and forged from copper alloy or iron and invariably gilded, silvered or tinned. Riveted to each of the jaws was a separate padded-metal disc which clamped the hem. A locking catch was provided between the pair of handles which was usually covered by a separate decorative metal plate. A loop on the catch allowed the skirt lifter to be suspended from the girdle by means of a chain.

Cast and forged copper-alloy skirt-lifter, c18th century
1461: moulded winged face with suspension loop and separate annular ring, L. 155mm - *Kingskerswell*.

DENTURE-LIKE OBJECTS

It is known that the history of false teeth goes back until at least the time of the ancient Greeks who tied artificial ones to adjacent sound teeth with ligatures. The Etruscans are credited with making the first bridge-work dentures c700 BC; these could actually be used for mastication rather than just for improving the appearance of the wearer. In Britain and on the Continent from the Roman period onwards many attempts were made at producing false dentures using a range of different materials, including: bone, ivory, agate, silver, copper alloy or human teeth extracted from corpses. All of these proved useless for masticating and were purely cosmetic.

Frenchman Pierre Fauchard, around 1728, developed the first upper dentures which were held in place by metal springs fixed to the lower jaw. Some recipiants are said to have been successful in masticating with these, however, it remained normal practice for dentures to be removed at mealtimes. It was also in France, in the 1730s, that the first attempt was made at using wax for making an impression of gums and sound teeth, although this technique was further developed later in the century by Philip Pfaff, Frederick the Great of Prussia's dentist.

Sheet gold or silver plates inset with carved ivory teeth were used during the first half of the 19th century. Similar to these plates are gold or silver over-dentures which were current from the late 19th century until around 1930. As the name implies, such a teeth-like plate is thought to have fitted over natural teeth as a splint when the lower jaw was cracked. Such injuries were even occasioned during tooth extraction. Denture plates of both of these types were beaten into shape on a copper-alloy swaging block. Presumably a wax impression of the patient's teeth and gums was made first from which a mould was formed for casting the swaging block.

Sheet silver over-denture, c1890-1930
1462: 54mm x 26mm - *Alphington*.

Cast copper-alloy swaging block, c1890-1930
1463: 33mm x 46mm - *Exeter*.

WHISTLES

Whistles have been used for centuries for sounding a warning,

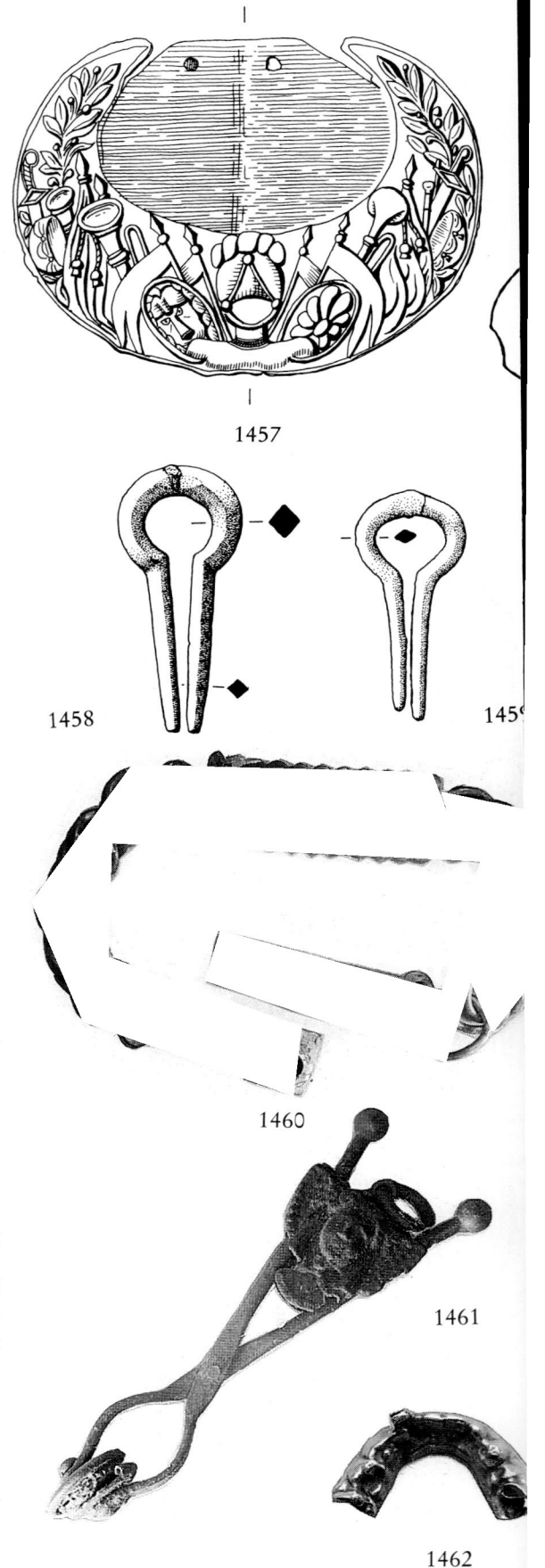

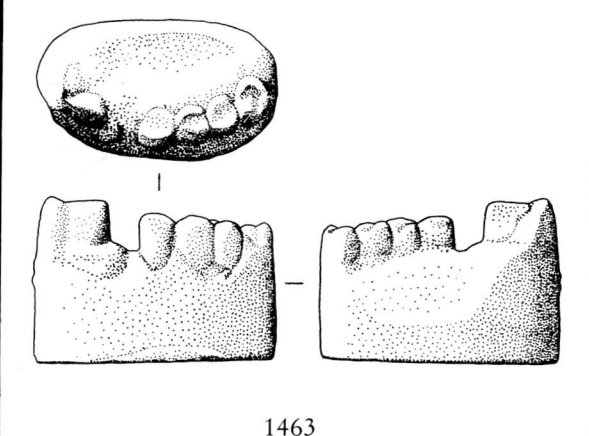

The Georgian and Victorian Period   211

attracting attention or signalling - especially in hawking. Copper alloy, silver or lead-tin alloy have been the chief metals of manufacture, though other material, such as wood, has been used. As random discoveries Victorian cast lead/tin-alloy whistles are noted for their ubiquity. Sizes vary. Invariably a suspension loop is provided on an elaborate terminal and moulded decoration is not uncommon.

Cast lead/tin-alloy whistles, 19th century
1464: slightly corroded, moulded transverse bands, asymmetrical sound-hole, L. 69mm - *Ringmore*.
1465: moulded transverse bands and foliate, asymmetrical sound-hole, L. 87.5mm - *Newton Abbot*.

PENCIL SHARPENERS

The word pencil originally related to the smaller hair-brushes used by artists, hence 'pencil-brush'. Pencils as writing instruments were invented around 1843 and, as now, were made from two sections of grooved wood glued together to make a cylinder. The central groove was filled with plumbago mined in Cumberland or the Malvern Hills. Initially pencils were hand-made but by 1851 the established machine-made manufactory centre was Cumberland's Keswick.

The purpose-built pencil sharpener was probably invented somtime between 1843-51 These were cast lead/tin alloy in the form of a tapering cylinder with a pair of wing-like projections on top as a handle. One edge of a longitudinal slot in the body housed a steel cutting-edge. Invariably much of the body and handle was covered in elaborate moulded decoration and frequently there was a cartouche with a set of initials which was probably a makers mark.

Cast lead/tin-alloy pencil sharpener, 19th century
1466: moulded scrollwork and cartouche with SO, traces of corroded steel cutting-edge, L. 36mm - *Cockington*.

WATCH KEYS

Watch keys attributed to the 18th and 19th centuries occasionally are exquisite works of art and usually made of gilded copper alloy. Silver or gold examples are known but the latter is uncommon. Normally watch-keys hung from the fob chain.

Mid-18th-century cranked watch-keys comprise a vertical winding-shaft with a square aperture for winding the main spring. An integral transverse bar terminates in a similar square aperture which winds the striking mechanism. A vertical pivot at the other end of the bar houses a trefoil-shaped handle which invariably has a small hole which serves as a suspension loop, and may have openwork or moulded or engraved decoration on both sides.

Styles of 19th-century watch key are numerous and come in: circular, oval, rectangular, subrectangular, asymmetrical or three-dimensional form. A vertical solid or hollow square winding-shaft, which may be separately made of iron, projects from the bottom, whilst many have an integral suspension loop to which is attached a separate split-ring. Openwork, moulded, engraved or semi-precious gemstone ornamentation is characteristic of many, and some feature the watchmaker's name or a numeral denoting the size of the winding shaft.

Cast and forged copper-alloy watch-keys, 18th and 19th centuries
1467: a selection from South Devon.

1463

1464   1465   1466

1467